T0237030

Lecture Notes in Computer Science   11900

More information about this series at http://www.springer.com/series/7412

Marcus Magnor · Alexander Sorkine-Hornung (Eds.)

Real VR – Immersive Digital Reality

How to Import the Real World into Head-Mounted Immersive Displays

 Springer

Editors
Marcus Magnor 🆔
TU Braunschweig
Braunschweig, Germany

Alexander Sorkine-Hornung
Facebook Zurich
Zurich, Switzerland

ISSN 0302-9743   ISSN 1611-3349 (electronic)
Lecture Notes in Computer Science
ISBN 978-3-030-41815-1   ISBN 978-3-030-41816-8 (eBook)
https://doi.org/10.1007/978-3-030-41816-8

LNCS Sublibrary: SL6 – Image Processing, Computer Vision, Pattern Recognition, and Graphics

This Springer imprint is published by the registered company Springer Nature Switzerland AG
The registered company address is: Gewerbestrasse 11, 6330 Cham, Switzerland

Preface

Since the times of the Lumière brothers, the way we watch movies has not fundamentally changed: whether in movie theaters, on mobile devices, or on TV at home, we still experience movies as outside observers, watching the action through a "peephole" whose size is defined by the angular extent of the display. As soon as we look away from the screen or turn around, we are immediately reminded that we are only "voyeurs". With the full field-of-view, head-mounted, and tracked displays that have recently become available on the consumer market, this outside-observer paradigm of visual entertainment is quickly giving way to a truly immersive experience. Now, the action fully encompasses the viewer, drawing us in and making us part of the action much more than was possible before.

Currently, immersive visual entertainment is almost completely geared towards 3D graphics-generated content (Virtual Reality), limiting commercial application scenarios today mainly to video games. The reason is simple: in order to provide for stereo vision and ego-motion parallax (both of which are essential for perceiving genuine immersion), the scene must be rendered in real-time from arbitrary vantage points. For 3D graphics, this is easily accomplished using off-the-shelf graphics hardware and standard rendering algorithms. To do the same from video footage acquired of real-world events, on the other hand, constitutes an intricate, interdisciplinary challenge.

Still, the prospect of being able to experience real-world recordings in true visual immersion is highly compelling. It has the potential to revolutionize the way we watch and enjoy movies, series, sports broadcasts, etc. For this reason some of the largest computer, internet, and social media companies of the world are heavily investing in immersive technology. Obviously, immense rewards can be expected.

December 2019

Marcus Magnor
Alexander Sorkine-Hornung

Organization

Editors

Marcus Magnor   TU Braunschweig, Germany
Alexander Sorkine-Hornung   Facebook Zurich, Switzerland

Authors

Thiemo Alldieck   TU Braunschweig, Germany
Ugur Akpinar   Tampere University, Finland
Tobias Bertel   University of Bath, UK
Robert Bregovic   Tampere University, Finland
Susana Castillo   TU Braunschweig, Germany
Darren Cosker   University of Bath, UK
Amir Dini   Graz University of Technology, Austria
Peter Eisert   Fraunhofer-Institut Berlin, Germany
Atanas Gotchev   Tampere University, Finland
Jean-Yves Guillemaut   University of Surrey, UK
Steve Grogorick   TU Braunschweig, Germany
Peter Hedman   University College London, UK
Anna Hilsmann   Fraunhofer-Institut Berlin, Germany
Adrian Hilton   University of Surrey, UK
Philip J. B. Jackson   University of Surrey, UK
Alexander Kainz   Graz University of Technology, Austria
Moritz Kappel   TU Braunschweig, Germany
Hansung Kim   University of Surrey, UK
Johannes Kopf   Graz University of Technology, Austria
Isabel Lesjak   Graz University of Technology, Austria
Marcus Magnor   TU Braunschweig, Germany
Jani Mäkinen   Tampere University, Finland
Yuta Miyanishi   Tampere University, Finland
Moritz Mühlhausen   TU Braunschweig, Germany
Armin Mustafa   University of Surrey, UK
Anjul Patney   Facebook Redmond, USA
Johanna Pirker   Graz University of Technology, Austria
Luca Remaggi   University of Surrey, UK
Christian Richardt   University of Bath, UK
Erdem Sahin   Tampere University, Finland
Frank Steinicke   University of Hamburg, Germany
Qi Sun   Adobe Inc. San José, USA
Catherine Taylor   University of Bath, UK
James Tompkin   Brown University, USA

Suren Vagharshakyan   Tampere University, Finland
Marco Volino   University of Surrey, UK
Gordon Wetzstein   Stanford University, USA
Feng Xu   Tsinghua University Beijing, China

Acknowledgments

This book is the result of collaborative work by 38 internationally renowned scientists, engineers, and practitioners, from academia and industry. It is these experts and the time and effort they devoted that has made this book possible, and we thank all contributing authors. The idea for this book emerged in summer 2019 at the Dagstuhl seminar on "Real VR" where many of the authors had met to discuss the challenges of how to experience the real world in immersive displays. We are grateful to the Dagstuhl scientific board for supporting our seminar, and we thank the staff at Dagstuhl castle for their great hospitality and outstanding service.

This book presents mainly fundamental research results that everyone can read about, re-implement, and use free of charge. This is possible only because of publicly funded research. We gratefully acknowledge the support from all funding agencies who invested in the research presented here. In particular, Marcus Magnor gratefully acknowledges support from the Reinhart Koselleck grant "Immersive Digital Reality" by the German Science Foundation (DFG MA2555/15-1).

While all of the above were necessary ingredients to make this book happen, there is one person without whom the book would not be what it is: Susana Castillo was the good soul of the project who reminded authors of deadlines, collected copyright permission forms, made sure all chapter files compile, copy-edited the text, and so much more. Thank you, Susana, for your help, commitment, and perseverance!

Contents

Capture

Capture, Reconstruction, and Representation of the Visual Real World
for Virtual Reality.   3
    Christian Richardt, James Tompkin, and Gordon Wetzstein

Light Field Video for Immersive Content Production. 33
    Marco Volino, Armin Mustafa, Jean-Yves Guillemaut, and Adrian Hilton

Reconstruction and Representation

Densely-Sampled Light Field Reconstruction 67
    Suren Vagharshakyan, Robert Bregovic, and Atanas Gotchev

Multiview Panorama Alignment and Optical Flow Refinement 96
    Moritz Mühlhausen and Marcus Magnor

Image-Based Scene Representations for Head-Motion Parallax
in 360° Panoramas 109
    Tobias Bertel, Feng Xu, and Christian Richardt

Viewpoint-Free Photography for Virtual Reality 132
    Peter Hedman

Hybrid Human Modeling: Making Volumetric Video Animatable 167
    Peter Eisert and Anna Hilsmann

Reconstructing 3D Human Avatars from Monocular Images. 188
    Thiemo Alldieck, Moritz Kappel, Susana Castillo, and Marcus Magnor

Display and Perception

State of the Art in Perceptual VR Displays. 221
    Gordon Wetzstein, Anjul Patney, and Qi Sun

Design and Characterization of Light Field and Holographic
Near-Eye Displays 244
    Erdem Sahin, Jani Mäkinen, Ugur Akpinar, Yuta Miyanishi,
    and Atanas Gotchev

Subtle Visual Attention Guidance in VR 272
    Steve Grogorick and Marcus Magnor

Redirected Walking in VR   285
   Qi Sun, Anjul Patney, and Frank Steinicke

Immersive Virtual Reality Audio Rendering Adapted to the Listener
and the Room   293
   Hansung Kim, Luca Remaggi, Philip J. B. Jackson, and Adrian Hilton

Applications

Immersive Learning in Real VR   321
   *Johanna Pirker, Isabel Lesjak, Johannes Kopf, Alexander Kainz,
   and Amir Dini*

Interacting with Real Objects in Virtual Worlds   337
   Catherine Taylor and Darren Cosker

Author Index   355

Capture

Capture, Reconstruction, and Representation of the Visual Real World for Virtual Reality

Christian Richardt[1]([✉]) [iD], James Tompkin[2] [iD], and Gordon Wetzstein[3] [iD]

[1] University of Bath, Bath, UK
christian@richardt.name
[2] Brown University, Providence, USA
james_tompkin@brown.edu
[3] Stanford University, Stanford, USA
gordon.wetzstein@stanford.edu
https://richardt.name/,
http://jamestompkin.com/,
http://www.computationalimaging.org/

Abstract. We provide an overview of the concerns, current practice, and limitations for capturing, reconstructing, and representing the real world visually within virtual reality. Given that our goals are to capture, transmit, and depict complex real-world phenomena to humans, these challenges cover the opto-electro-mechanical, computational, informational, and perceptual fields. Practically producing a system for real-world VR capture requires navigating a complex design space and pushing the state of the art in each of these areas. As such, we outline several promising directions for future work to improve the quality and flexibility of real-world VR capture systems.

Keywords: Cameras · Reconstruction · Representation · Virtual reality · Image-based rendering · Novel-view synthesis

1 Introduction

One of the high-level goals of virtual reality is to reproduce how the real world *looks* in a way which is indistinguishable from reality. Achieving this arguably-quixotic goal requires us to solve significant problems across capture, reconstruction, and representation, and raises many questions: "Which camera system should we use to sample enough of the environment for our application?"; "How should we model the world and which algorithm should we use to recover these models?"; "How should we store the data for easy compression and transmission?", and "How can we achieve simple and high-quality rendering for human viewing?". Solving any one of these problems is a challenge, and this challenge is exacerbated by the interplay between the questions. This provides us with a complex design space to navigate if we wish to build practical and high-quality systems for real-world VR reproduction.

M. Magnor and A. Sorkine-Hornung (Eds.): Real VR, LNCS 11900, pp. 3–32, 2020.
https://doi.org/10.1007/978-3-030-41816-8_1

Yet, significant progress has been made over the past 5 years in our ability to capture and display the visual properties of the real world, driven by the need to provide content for low-cost VR headsets. Many compelling applications are now within reach: the broad area of telepresence, e.g., for VR communications; for remote operation, e.g., medical robotics; for cultural heritage and virtual tourism; and for storytelling via documentaries, movies, and games. We wish the tools for these applications to be simple in all stages of authorship, and for the applications to be comfortable and easy to use, requiring only novice intuition (the "can my grandparents use this?" test).

So, broadly, what issues concern us when we wish to capture the world in a way that is visually indistinguishable to humans?

Objects, Scenes, and Subjects. Typically *what* we wish to capture helps determine *how* we should capture it for later analysis or virtual reality presentation. Capturing a single *object* in a studio has long been accomplished with so-called *outside-in* multi-camera systems: cameras are placed to encircle or ensphere an object and allow its multi-view capture. Generally, the more cameras we have, the higher the quality of reproduction. Further, such controlled environment conditions allow higher-quality capture than unconstrained settings, e.g., outdoors.

To capture *scenes*, we use an *inside-out* camera system in which multiple cameras face the world. These may be arranged into a circle or sphere to capture 360° for immersive VR, though planar configurations to densely capture narrower fields of view are also common (often called *light field cameras*). The distance between the cameras – or baseline – determines for how near and how far away we can reconstruct the geometry of the scene. Further, VR capture typically predicates that the camera and its paraphernalia are not visible in the scene, which informs the capture scenario design.

One special class of object exists for which much work has been directed: human beings. As social creatures, we wish to represent ourselves realistically, especially as many applications are driven by social interaction. Often, these methods use databases of human shape and appearance to create efficient and high-quality representations.

Photons, Rays, and Waves. Given an intended capture scenario, we next wish to maximize our capture fidelity. Our lens systems play a significant part in overall quality, and typically the camera configuration and lens systems are co-designed. At the camera sensor, output fidelity spans three major axes: spatial resolution, temporal resolution, and spectral resolution (i.e., color). Each of these must be tempered by our ability to store, process, and eventually transmit these data. Given that our output is to a human observer, then there is an eventual limit beyond which no additional captured information is perceived (which, arguably, we are fast approaching [78]).

Geometry and Appearance. The raw output from a multi-camera system must be reconstructed into a representation which is comfortable and easy to view. For video, existing real-world capture for VR is typically monoscopic and 360°,

3DoF: rotation only   6DoF: rotation + translation

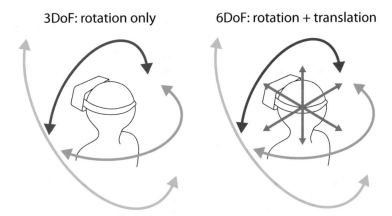

Fig. 1. VR systems provide either three or six degrees of freedom (DoF) for head motion. **Left:** '3DoF' lets a user look around the virtual world from a fixed point. **Right:** '6DoF' lets the user move in the virtual world like in the real world.

which requires stitching multiple camera images via a spherical proxy geometry. Current state-of-the-art systems produce stereoscopic 360° images, which have complex disparity challenges. Both of these are so-called '3DoF' or three-degrees-of-freedom representations describing the three rotation angles available within a VR headset. This is insufficient to represent human motion within the headset as humans can also translate along three axes (Fig. 1).

As such, one near-term goal of VR production is '6DoF', which allows realistic response to human head and body motions and solves the disparity challenges of the stereo 360° format by allowing stereo rendering in any viewing direction. The range of 6DoF movement available is a key concern: the larger the 'headbox' required, the larger the camera baseline must be to accommodate the eventual range of user motion. Sparser sampling of the scene requires us to reconstruct more sophisticated scene models to 'fill in the gaps' during rendering. Thus, depth and geometry reconstruction become critical pieces of the processing, transmission, and render systems. Likewise, complex scene object which display view-dependent appearance effects, such as shiny or translucent objects, make this reconstruction and depiction problem harder.

Many representations exist, including simple proxy geometry, depth, layered images, voxels, point clouds, signed distance fields, and textured 3D geometry. Each has a complementary rendering system, e.g., image-based rendering or ray casting. Each also has different compression and storage methods for efficient transmission. Further, state-of-the-art 'neural rendering' learned representations now also exist, with a 'neural' version of each classic representation.

Humans as Creators. Producing VR content requires the ability to *edit* the captured material. These operations could be color matching between cameras, editing scene content to remove unwanted artifacts, editing the perceptual result such as adjusting disparity for comfort, or even adding new elements to a scene.

As such, any reconstructed representation must be malleable to the editing tasks. More sophisticated productions may wish to edit content by integrating captured and purely virtual content, which requires a more sophisticated reconstruction such as to represent real-world occlusions and integrate object lighting with illumination capture.

Humans as Consumers, Visual Expectation, and Avoiding the Visual Gap. Human perception has limitations which may be exploited. Many compelling applications – and even many *users* – may not need flawless reproduction, and the positive impact of, say, stronger personal connection through immersive telecommunications is likely to outweigh any failures in subtle appearance reproduction. Further, 'indistinguishable from reality' is different from 'photorealistic': we typically know when we are looking at camera-captured media, yet, this is sufficient for much of our storytelling. Likewise, 'perceptually realistic' is different from 'indistinguishable from reality' as it lightens the burden on scrutiny. Some 'non-photorealistic' depictions may help us *avoid entirely* complex challenges of fidelity and representation.

That said, VR is still a new and hopeful technology, and current limitations which are easy to overlook at this nascent stage – especially to technologists developing these techniques – may be more significant barriers to adoption. VR sickness is one such issue; here, 6DoF reconstruction and rendering holds promise to significantly reduce its effects and make VR more accessible.

2   Current Practice

Capturing the real world for rendering in virtual reality [59,85] is fundamentally about creating novel views of a scene given only a sparsely sampled set of images [7,13,21,30,55,92]. These techniques are closely related to 3D reconstruction [16] and image-based rendering (IBR) [20,93], and have many important applications in VR, including telepresence and digitizing avatars; capturing faces, hands, or whole body performances; and capturing cinematic experiences with dedicated VR camera rigs. Novel-view synthesis and image-based rendering are active and long-running fields of research that have produced a large variety of techniques and systems working towards the goal of capturing the real world in all its visual fidelity. Many of the proposed systems share a similar high-level structure, which is embodied by the **VR Capture Pipeline**:

Capture → Reconstruction → Representation → Compression → Rendering

In this section, we will look at each stage of this pipeline and provide an overview of the range of VR capture techniques and their trade-offs. For any particular approach or system, the most important design choice is the data representation to be used, as this constrains many of the other pipeline stages. In particular, the choice constrains reconstruction, compression, and rendering.

2.1   Capture

Most virtual reality capture approaches rely on one or more color cameras to capture the visual appearance and dynamics of a scene (see examples in Fig. 2). Sometimes, special cameras are used, such as RGBD cameras which capture depth maps in addition to color footage, or special attachments like mirrors.

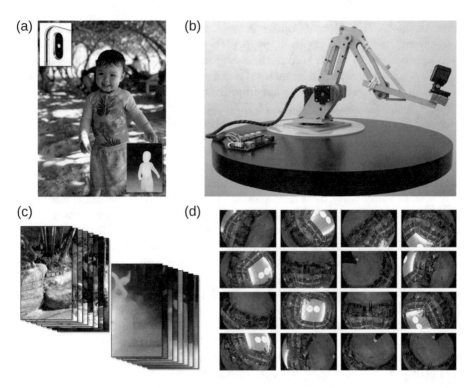

Fig. 2. Visual overview of capture approaches: (a) one static (RGBD) camera, (b) one moving camera, (c) one moving RGBD camera, and (d) a multi-camera capture with 16 cameras. Figures reproduced from: (a) Kopf *et al.* [49], (b) Luo *et al.* [58], (c) Hedman *et al.* [33], and (d) Parra Pozo *et al.* [78].

One Static Camera can capture a partial view of a static scene, typically with perspective lenses. This content can still be compelling, as demonstrated by Facebook's 3D photos [49], which are captured by dual-lens cameras on commodity mobile phones to provide depth in addition to color. Wider views require wider camera optics, such as fisheye lenses (>90°) or catadioptic systems [1] for omnidirectional video.

One Moving Camera can capture more of a static scene by sweeping over it across time. Panorama stitching approaches [6, 101] assume a camera that rotates around its optical center, so that it captures all light rays converging at a single point in space – the center of the panorama. By translating the camera in space, even more light rays can be captured, e.g., free-hand motion can help to capture omnidirectional stereo [5,79,86], layered depth panoramas [123], or 3D photography [32]. More elaborate setups have a camera moving along the surface of a plane or sphere to capture different portions of a static light field [58,75], with adaptations to unstructured light fields too [18,63].

One Moving RGBD Camera makes it easier to reconstruct the geometry of the scene from the captured depth maps. A pioneer in this category is the KinectFusion approach [69], which reconstructs a global truncated signed distance field (TSDF) representation of a scene from registered input depth maps alone. There are many more recent variants that improve on the scale and robustness of this kind of scene reconstruction [17,71,114]. Alternatively, Instant 3D Photography [33] aligns multiple RGBD images captured with a dual-lens camera into a consistent textured 3D panoramic surface.

Multi-camera Rigs are required for video capture and to capture multiple viewing directions simultaneously. Consumer 360° cameras are now commercially available as commodity devices that stitch two or more video streams into a single 360° video [53,81,111]. Stereo cameras capture two viewpoints side by side, and their baseline can be magnified in post production [124]. Multiple viewpoints can also be interpolated and manipulated in a post-process after video capture [56]. A ring of video cameras captures sufficient information for compelling omnidirectional stereo video [3,9,87], while a rotating camera rig can even capture live omnidirectional stereo video [48]. The Facebook Manifold camera [78] has 16 cinema cameras in a large sphere configuration to evenly capture views in all directions. Light fields [25,30,55] are based on a dense sampling of viewpoints, which requires many co-located cameras. A different camera setup distributes cameras on a dome or around a capture volume, for example to capture objects and people in a light stage [19] or as volumetric video [15].

2.2 Reconstruction

Reconstruction interprets and combines the information contained in the captured imagery to create a unified model. The first step is often camera calibration and structure from motion, i.e., characterizing the imaging devices used, including their lens distortion, and determining which views of a scene they captured. Multiple structure-from-motion implementations are publicly available, including Bundler [96], VisualSfM [117], AliceVision [41,65], MVE [27], Theia [99] and COLMAP [88], with the latter currently enjoying the widest use. However, general-purpose structure-from-motion tools do not perform well for the kind of inside-out capture commonly used for environment capture [5,32]. This has led to the development of specifically tailored structure-from-motion solutions that assume camera motion on a spherical surface [100,109], which is a good match for handheld [5,32,86] or spherical [58,75] capture approaches. One of the outputs of structure from motion is also a sparse 3D point cloud of feature points in the scene, which can be useful for image alignment [53] or view warping [36].

Once the viewpoints are reconstructed, the next step is generally to combine all the captured information into a single model of the scene. In classical panorama stitching, this is achieved by aligning and blending the individual input views on a spherical or cylindrical image surface [6, 101]. While still panoramas can hide alignment artifact to some degree using clever stitching or blending approaches [32, 121, 122], this becomes much harder for panoramic videos, as the visual content, and hence any artifacts, keep changing over time. To address this, the stitching needs to vary over time in accordance with the scene [53, 81, 111]. To achieve more complex projections, such as the multi-perspective omnidirectional stereo (ODS) projection [39, 79], requires dense correspondence between input views so that intermediate views can be synthesized [3, 9, 86, 87]. Most approaches use optical flow for this purpose, as it provides useful flexibility in case of calibration errors or scene motion.

The reconstruction of 3D geometry goes beyond the purely image-based approaches discussed before by recovering the 3D structure of a scene or object. Most approaches start by estimating per-view depth maps using multi-view stereo (MVS) techniques [28, 37, 89, 90] or deep learning [33, 72, 91], unless depth maps are directly available from RGBD cameras. In theory, these per-view depth maps can be integrated into a global geometry model of the scene [12, 32, 91] if the camera poses and depth maps are estimated sufficiently accurately. Approaches such as KinectFusion [69] and BundleFusion [17] integrate noisy depth maps over time to improve the accuracy of the surface reconstruction. Having a large number of views also leads to a cleaner geometry reconstruction [15]. Hedman *et al.* [33] introduce a locally varying depth map alignment step to integrate differently normalized depth maps from mobile phones or neural networks into a globally consistent depth map. However, because of calibration and depth estimation errors, better view synthesis results can often be obtained with per-view geometry [11, 35, 75] that is smoothly blended across the synthesized novel view.

2.3 Representation

Many approaches have been proposed to represent captured scenes or objects. View synthesis techniques can be classified by how heavily they rely on the input image data vs. proxy geometry in their representation. For example, light field rendering [55] represents one extreme that does not use any geometry at all, but that requires densely sampled input views, whereas conventional 3D rendering with polygon meshes and textures is the other extreme in requiring detailed geometry but few input images (i.e., the textures) for the rendering. Geometric representations of a scene can be either modeled or estimated from the input images, for example using classical 3D computer vision pipelines [31, 102]. To provide an overview, Shum *et al.* [92, 93] organized representations along a continuum according to how much geometry they use:

- *No geometry:* Primarily image-based approaches, such as panoramas or 360° video.

– *Implicit geometry:* Approaches using posed images and/or relying on 2D image correspondences, such as optical flow.
– *Explicit geometry:* Textured meshes or point clouds with actual 3D geometry.

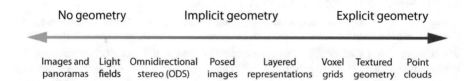

Fig. 3. Updated continuum of image-based rendering representations, inspired by Shum *et al.* [92, 93]. Please see the discussion in Sect. 2.3 for details.

Figure 3 contains an updated version of Shum *et al.*'s continuum of representations and Fig. 4 illustrates examples from across this continuum.

There is no universally best representation – all have their advantages and disadvantages and provide different trade-offs. There is also often no hard boundary between representations, so there is some overlap; hybrids that combine multiple representations are also possible. In the limit, i.e., with infinite resolution, the representations are theoretically interchangeable. However, any conversion always requires resampling, which is usually a lossy process that reduces overall fidelity. There are usually also practical limits: for example, the physical size of cameras which limits the maximum camera density that is achievable in practice.

Images and Panoramas provide the most basic snapshot of what a scene or object looked like. They represent a photographic likeness that captures visual appearance of a scene or object from a single point of view with a fixed field of view. Panoramas [6, 101] and 360° videos [53, 81] capture a wide or even complete field of view. Images and panoramas enjoy great popularity as they are easy to capture with modern mobile phones and consumer cameras, and have become straightforward to share. However, their main limitation is that they only provide information for a single point of view (i.e., only 3DoF) and do not provide a sense of depth perception or motion parallax, and thus do not support any translational change of viewpoint.

Light Fields are represented by a dense spatio-angular sampling of a scene [55], generally using a regular 2D grid of camera viewpoints or a microlens array camera. More general camera configurations are supported by the Lumigraph [30], a closely-related variant of light fields. As the comprehensive coverage of an object in a scene is challenging to obtain in practice, Davis *et al.* [18] proposed a guidance approach that helps users in capturing missing viewpoints. We can also consider videos captured with a moving camera to be a densely-sampled light field along the camera path, which can be exploited for accurate scene reconstruction [45, 120].

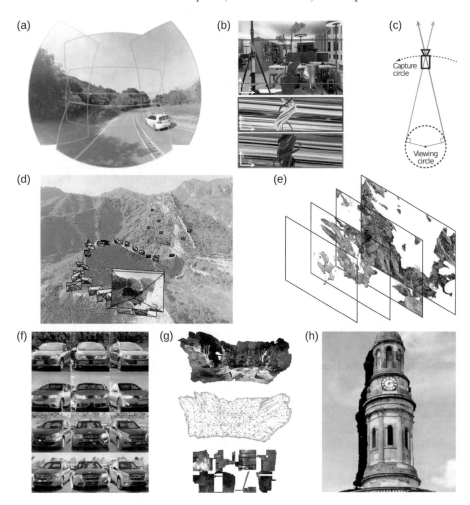

Fig. 4. Visual examples that illustrate the range of image-based rendering representations: (a) panoramas [81], (b) light fields [120], (c) omnidirectional stereo, (d) posed images [96], (e) layered representations such as multiplane images [63], (f) voxel grids with deep features [70], (g) textured geometry [33], and (h) point clouds [72].

Omnidirectional Stereo (ODS) is a multi-perspective circular projection [39,79] that has become a popular medium for stereoscopic and 360° VR photos and videos [3,9,86,87]. ODS encodes two panoramic views: one for the left eye and one for the right eye. This has the advantage that there is binocular disparity – and hence the perception of depth – in all viewing directions along the equator, though distortion exists away from the equator (Fig. 5). The format is an excellent fit for existing video processing, compression, and transmission pipelines, as it can be packed into a single frame, e.g., via side-by-side, top-bottom, or double cubemap formats.

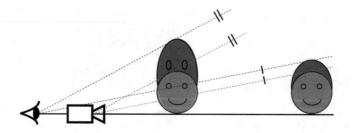

Fig. 5. Omnidirectional stereo introduces vertical distortion as cameras lie on a larger circle than the viewing circle. The red faces, as seen by the camera, appear vertically stretched (blue faces) when rendered using parallel rays for a viewpoint behind the camera. Figure adapted from Anderson *et al.* [3].

Posed Images have known camera geometry (camera position and orientation) in addition to the image data. This enables scene reconstruction in the form of point clouds using multi-view stereo. Even sparse point clouds are sufficient for providing a compelling overview of community photo collections as demonstrated by Snavely *et al.*'s PhotoTourism work [96]. Novel views can be interpolated from existing ones by establishing correspondences between adjacent viewpoints. In practice, optical flow is often used for flow-based blending [3,5,58,86,87], which significantly reduces blurry ghosting artifacts and produces results with high visual fidelity.

Layered Representations consist of multiple semi-transparent layers that encapsulate the appearance of a scene or object without any explicit geometry. The underlying idea goes back to Disney's multiplane camera (1937), in which multiple transparent cel sheets are positioned at different depths from the camera. This allows each cel sheet to be moved independently and creates the effect of motion parallax over time. Early approaches computed layered representations using custom-tailored optimization frameworks [112,113]. Recently, advances in deep learning have revived and accelerated progress in the reconstruction of so-called multiplane images (MPIs) [25,63,98,124].

Voxel Grids can represent regularly sampled occupancy ('filled or empty'), color, opacity, or distance (e.g., truncated signed distance fields [69]) to enable novel-view synthesis. Managing memory as a resource with voxel grids is critical given their n^3 nature but often sparse occupancy, and octree-based voxel grids help here. New voxel grids storing deep features [57,70,94,107] aim to enable novel-view synthesis at a higher quality but with a lower memory use, by passing the job of detail representation to a CNN. We discuss this emerging work on neural scene representations in more detail in Sect. 3.

Textured Geometry makes it easy to render novel views in real time with existing 3D graphics pipelines, with good support on mobile devices. Mesh geometry can model hard occlusion boundaries, but it needs to be reconstructed accurately from usually-noisy depth maps. For the highest quality depth maps, many observations from different viewpoints must be combined, for example, for volumetric video [15] or light fields [75]. One consumer-facing example are Facebook's 3D Photos [49], which use an image and lower-resolution depth map from an off-the-shelf mobile phone. The final 3D photo can be looked at from different directions by tilting the phone. Several approaches separate foreground and background objects in a scene into multiple textured layers [32,33,91,123], to preserve clean occlusion boundaries. This generally requires some kind of inpainting to fill the areas behind foreground objects. In the real world, the appearance of objects also often depends on the viewing direction, e.g., when objects are shiny. This effect can be modeled using surface light fields [115] or view-dependent blending [34]. In general, modeling and editing favors geometric approaches, as there are better software tools available for textured meshes than other representations.

Point Clouds represent a scene as an unordered collection of points, which may or may not have colors and/or surface normals. They are readily obtained from structure-from-motion and multi-view stereo tools, RGBD images [72], or Lidar scans of a scene. However, they are inherently sparse, tend to be noisy and non-uniformly distributed in reconstruction space (rather than camera space), and contain gaps that make them impractical for rendering high-quality novel views (although this is slowly changing thanks to neural re-rendering [62]). Nevertheless, they are often a useful intermediate representation or debugging tool.

2.4   Compression

Raw scene representations can become very large (hundreds of gigabytes). This can make them difficult to store given limited space on disk or in memory, to transmit over networks in a reasonable time, or even to render them in real time. Thus, compression and decompression are indispensable for practical scene capture and rendering systems.

The light fields introduced by Levoy and Hanrahan [55] in 1996 were up to 1.6 GB in size. This would easily fill a large hard drive at the time, and would never fit in memory. However, light fields are highly redundant within images and between images, so they are highly compressible. Levoy and Hanrahan designed a custom light-field compression scheme that combines vector quantization of 2D or 4D tiles (24:1 compression) with gzip entropy encoding (another 5:1 compression) for a total compression of 120:1. This scheme allowed fast random-access decompression entirely in software, so that real-time rendering became feasible.

Recently, image compression techniques such as JPEG have become computationally affordable, even in real-time applications. Existing video codecs, such as h.264 and h.265, can also often be used directly for compressing video-based representations, such as 360° video [53,81] or omnidirectional stereo videos [3,87].

Collet *et al.* [15] encode their volumetric free-viewpoint videos in a standard MPEG-DASH file. Thanks to mesh tracking, their geometry has a temporally consistent parameterization. Therefore, the resulting texture atlases are unwrapped consistently and can be compressed effectively using the standard h.264 video codec. The mesh geometry is encoded as a custom unit inside the video stream and compressed using linear motion prediction, 16-bit quantization of vertex positions and UV coordinates, and Golomb coding.

Google's panoramic light fields require 4–6 GB of image data each [75] and so also need compression. As for the original light fields paper [55], fast random access is required for rendering novel views of the light field. Overbeck *et al.* [75] build on the open-source VP9 codec and encode most light field images relative to a sparse set of reference views, which are like key frames in standard videos. In practice, they decode all reference images when loading the light field from disk and keep them in memory. They also contribute an extension to VP9 that enables random access to individual image tiles. This allows their system to decode any tile from any other image immediately. Most light fields can hence be compressed at high quality by $40\times$–$200\times$.

2.5 Rendering

The final step of the VR capture pipeline is to render the novel views corresponding to the user's location, so that they see the correct views of the captured scene as they move. Most rendering approaches adopt the standard graphics pipeline, which has the benefit of efficient hardware implementations across a large range of devices, from mobile to desktop setups. This efficient rendering hardware enables rendering in real time, and even hitting the high frame rates of 80–144 Hz required to feed state-of-the-art VR head-mounted displays [50].

Panoramas and omnidirectional stereo content only require a change to perspective projection to be viewed by users. This does not require any explicit geometry and can be implemented in 2D or, equivalently, by using textured spheres viewed from virtual perspective cameras. Many other approaches also use textured geometry directly [17,32,33,69,91]. Even multiplane images [25,63,98,124] can be rendered using textured geometry, by texturing the semi-transparent layers on parallel planes that are appropriately spaced, and using alpha compositing in the z-buffer during rendering.

Modern graphics pipelines are also programmable using shaders, which provides an opportunity to influence the rendering more locally depending on the viewing direction, for example. Flow-based blending has been used to interpolate novel views on the fly [58] and per pixel or light ray [86], also in a view-dependent fashion [5]. When many input views are combined to synthesize novel views, they also require spatial blending to ensure smooth transitions [75]. Ultimately, the decision of how to blend multiple observations of a single surface point can even be optimized using a deep neural network [34]. However, evaluating the neural network per frame at run time noticeably impacts frame rate, which does not yet reach real-time rates.

3   Neural Scene Representations and Rendering

Over the last few years, a new class of algorithms has emerged that has great potential for capturing, representing, and rendering real scenes in virtual environments – neural scene representations and rendering. The idea behind these algorithms is similar to classical approaches: given a set of input views, distill these into an intermediate representation, and then render the scene from novel viewpoints using the intermediate representation. However, a neural representation differs from a classical scene representation, such as a polygon mesh, a 3D point cloud, an implicit function, or a voxel grid, in being differentiable with respect to its parameters. In combination with a differentiable renderer that takes the neural scene representation as well as a camera position and orientation, i.e., a pose, as input and computes a 2D image from the camera's perspective, neural scene representations allow for end-to-end optimization of the representation supervised only on the images.

For example, Sitzmann et al. [94] recently proposed a voxel representation where each voxel is located in a Cartesian grid and stores a feature vector. A differentiable renderer with occlusion reasoning then projects these 3D features into 2D images and a 2D image-to-image translation rendering network then converts the projected features into the RGB values of the final images. During training, the weights of the voxel features are optimized given only a set of posed RGB images of the scene. Once optimized, the neural voxels can be rendered into 2D RGB images given an arbitrary camera pose. Due to the fact that the intermediate voxel representation is inherently defined in a three-dimensional space, all projected views will be approximately consistent across different camera perspectives. This can be interpreted as choosing a neural network architecture that is aware of the 3D structure of the scene, simply by choosing an adequate scene representation. Several different classes of neural scene representations have been proposed over the last few years, which we briefly outline in the following.

Image-Based Rendering with Deep Flow Prediction and Learned Image Blending. Recently, deep learning has been used to aid image-based rendering via learning subtasks, such as the prediction of occlusion-aware optical flow between views [42,43,76,125] and/or the computation of the blending weights [26,34]. While this approach can achieve photorealism, it requires a dense set of high-resolution photographs to be available at render time and an error-prone reconstruction step to obtain a geometric proxy.

Unstructured or Weakly Structured Latent Representations. Other approaches aim at distilling an intermediate representation, or *embedding*, from the images. The benefit of such an approach is that the input views may not be necessary during inference anymore, after the embedding is learned. This is beneficial for multiple reasons: the used computational resources (such as memory) can be optimized; embeddings have the potential to disentangle different effects, such as lighting, shading, geometry, etc., which can make them more interpretable or potentially even editable [51,61,118]; embeddings can sometimes also be interpolated or new examples within this latent space could even be generated. Therefore, learning structured embeddings is a topic of great interest.

Several approaches have been proposed that rely on embedding views into a latent space, but without enforcing any geometrical constraints [22,24,104]. Weakly structured embeddings [14,84,116], such as learning rotation-equivariant features by explicitly rotating the latent space feature vectors, have also been proposed. However, all of these approaches have in common that there are little to no guarantees that the synthesized views create consistent perspective projections because the underlying network structures do not enforce or capture the 3D structure of the scene explicitly. In other words, the choice of embedding captures the structure of the data weakly or not at all.

Using Proxy Geometries and Neural Textures. In many applications, such as reconstructing faces [126], hands, or whole body performances, we have detailed prior knowledge of the types of objects in the scene. For example, the image or 3D model of a face can be well described by a blendshape – a low-dimensional geometric basis function representation that only requires a few coefficients to model the face. Nonlinear optimization can be used to fit a blendshape representation to an image or video or a face. Similarly, parametric representations of hands or bodies exist and can be used to fit a 3D proxy geometry to 2D images or videos. Although such proxy geometries represent a good first-order approximation of the underlying shape, many subtle details of the appearance, like the interior of the mouth, facial hair, or other perceptually important details, are typically not modeled in a convincing manner. However, such proxy geometries have great potential for neural scene representations because they can be rendered using existing computer graphics pipelines from arbitrary perspectives. To adequately model the appearance using a neural scene representation, a clever idea is to use the proxy geometry and texture it with a 2D texture containing learnable features. These features can then be optimized in a training stage for a given example image or video and later re-rendered. This approach uses little memory, because we do not have to learn a 3D model but only a texture and the neural renderer is a simple 2D (convolutional) neural network that computes an image-to-image translation from 2D features to RGB pixel values. This idea has so far been applied to deep video portraits [46] and it has been explored as a more general concept of neural textures [105].

One of the limitations of parametric representations is that they exist only for specific types of objects, such as faces, hands, and bodies. However, the idea of proxy geometry can also be applied to more general 3D computer vision pipelines. In this case, the reconstructed geometry is often coarse, it can have holes or it may be missing other parts. Yet, such an incomplete or noisy point cloud or mesh can still be easily rendered into arbitrary camera poses and an image-to-image translation network could then learn how to map from the incomplete projection of the point cloud to a photorealistic image. This idea was recently explored by Martin-Brualla *et al.* [60] and represents another example of combining proxy geometry with a differentiable (part of a) renderer.

Multiplane Image Representations. Many recent proposals on neural scene representations are based on the idea of decomposing a set of input views, or a light field, into a layered representation that can be re-projected into the input views but also into novel views. This is another example of using proxy geometry along with learnable parts, but the proxy geometry is a simple set of planes that can easily be projected into different cameras using homographies. Wetzstein *et al.* [52,112,113] optimized such representations for display application from densely sampled input light fields via computed tomography or non-negative matrix and tensor factorizations. More recently, deep learning based approaches have been proposed to optimize such representations using the input of small baseline stereo cameras [98,124], from single-input image [106], or from four input images [25] with learned gradient descent. The primary challenge in these deep learning based approaches is to work with a set of sparsely sampled input views and ensure that the views synthesized in between these given images look perceptually realistic. Another related approach recently proposed guided camera placement for such irregularly sampled light fields [63]. Most of these layered view synthesis approaches optimize RGBA color values at each position of the layers. The additional alpha channel allows for transparency-aware "soft" reconstructions by blending the layers for perspectives from different camera perspectives [80]. Figure 6 shows a visual comparison of classic and learned multiplane view synthesis approaches.

One benefit for multiplane image representations is that they are simple and, once optimized, enable real-time rendering of the layered representation. A downside is that novel views can only be synthesized over a limited baseline, i.e., we cannot synthesize novel views that look at the layers from the side.

Deep Voxel Representations. Another specific type of proxy geometry is a voxel grid, which overcomes the limited-baseline issue of sparse layered representations. For example, Sitzmann *et al.* [94] proposed an occlusion-aware volume renderer in combination with a grid of features that is trained only on posed 2D RGB images of a scene. Nguyen-Phuoc *et al.*'s HoloGAN [70] shows that deep voxel representations can also be learned from natural images in an unsupervised manner. The implicit deep 3D features enable disentangling of 3D pose and object identity, which can further be decomposed into shape and appearance. A different variant of this idea was recently shown to be able to generate real-time 3D reconstructions of human faces and actors [57,110]. One of the downsides of voxel representations is the relatively high memory footprint required to store all the voxels. Representing RGBA values or feature vectors on a Cartesian grid has the benefits of allowing convolutions and other intuitive operations to be performed on the grid [74], for example using a convolutional neural network, but this requires values to be stored at all locations of the grid even if no object is present.

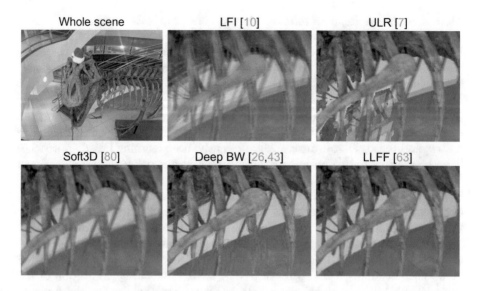

Fig. 6. Visual comparison of view synthesis results on the challenging T-Rex scene between traditional and neural rendering approaches. Light field interpolation [10] fails to align objects at different depths. Unstructured lumigraph rendering [7] suffers from poorly reconstructed geometry due to the thin ribs. Soft 3D reconstruction [80] shows blurry views caused by depth uncertainty. Deep backwards warping [26,43] exhibits visual artifacts near occlusion boundaries like the thin ribs. Local light-field fusion [63] smoothly blends neighboring local light fields to render novel views to minimize visual artifacts. Figure adapted from Mildenhall *et al.* [63].

Deep Point Cloud Representations. Differentiable point clouds have the potential to overcome some of the memory limitations of layered or voxel-based representations by adaptively changing the positions of the points [119]. This relates to the approach of Martin-Brualla *et al.* [60] who used a fixed (i.e., non-optimizable) proxy geometry. Neural re-rendering of point clouds is a promising postprocessing step that not only fills in gaps in rasterized point cloud renderings [2], but also provides control over scene appearance [62]. A challenge of working with differentiable point clouds is to update the locations of the 3D points by back-propagating through a differentiable renderer, such as a splatting algorithm.

Continuous Neural Representations. Finally, differentiable continuous scene representations have also been explored. For example, Park *et al.* [77] recently proposed to model a signed distance function as a neural network and train it to learn an object's shape supervised on a 3D model of that object. Sitzmann *et al.* [95] introduced a differentiable renderer for such continuous scene representations to be able to train it in an end-to-end manner supervised only by posed 2D RGB images. Moreover, their approach allows for the scene representation to be generalized across object classes, enabling interpolation of the representations (see Fig. 7), generating entirely new objects of a specific class, or fitting a 3D representation to a single 2D RGB image.

Fig. 7. Interpolating latent code vectors of cars and chairs in the ShapeNet dataset while rotating the camera around the model. Features smoothly transition from one model to another. Figure reproduced from Sitzmann *et al.* [95].

In summary, different variants of neural scene representation are emerging and show great potential to applications in capturing, representing, and rendering real environments in VR and beyond.

4   Limitations of Current Practice and Future Research Directions

Thus far, we have described current practice; next, we will discuss limitations of current practice and potential future research directions to overcome them. One useful framing device to help conceptualize these limitations is by what type of artifacts they introduce and by how much it affects the overall experience (Fig. 8). Model-based approaches tend to introduce world inconsistencies which make them look fake, e.g., incorrect geometry, missing translucency or specular reflections, or suffering from Uncanny Valley effects in the case of humans. Image-based approaches introduce a different axis of artifacts relating to resolution and sampling, interpolation and warping, and tell-tale image compression errors. Navigating the design space between pure model-based (e.g., classic computer graphics) and pure image-based techniques (e.g., dense light fields) exposes our world reproduction to many artifacts; throughout these operations, our goal is to remain within some human-perception tolerable region which minimizes both world fakeness and image artifacts.

Saturating the Senses (Vision): Current technologies for capture fall short of convincing real-world depiction purely from a raw pixel perspective, but are perhaps closer than you might anticipate. While perception varies from person to person, for spatial resolution, Facebook's Manifold camera [78] with 8K RED sensors over 180° ($\approx$0.0225° resolution) is approaching the needed spatial resolution to match 20/20 visual acuity (0.0167° resolution). Temporal sampling of 60 Hz (16.6 ms per frame) is also approaching experimental rates for the task of individual image recognition (at least 14 ms [44]), though flickering artifacts can be seen at higher framerates. Static human eye dynamic range is relatively low (100:1, or 6.5 stops) vs. the approximately 15 stops available on the sensor [23], though eye dynamic contrast is extremely large (10^{14}, or 46 stops) and sensitive to very low luminance levels (10^{-6} cd/m^2). While signal-to-noise ratios are improving at high ISO levels, the sensor would still struggle to produce a non-noisy image at this light level. This high sensitivity and low noise improves color reproduction. Binocular stereo provides depth cues from eye vergence, which is reproduced through multi-view renderings of the multi-camera reconstructions of the world geometry.

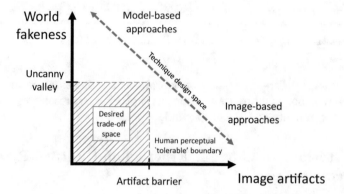

Fig. 8. One way to conceptualize our design-space trade-off is as one between model- and image-based methods. Model-based techniques tend to suffer 'uncanny valley' effects where the world appears only *almost* real, which is off-putting for human reproduction. On the other hand, image-based techniques exhibit characteristic artifacts which reduce quality and are easy to identify as 'unreal', such as sampling and compression artifacts. Our goal is to find a representation which minimizes both effects. Reproduced from whiteboard discussions with Brian Cabral and colleagues at the Dagstuhl RealVR seminar (July 2019).

For display, current technologies also fall sort but may be closer than anticipated. The current best-in-class headset (Valve Index, September 2019 [108]) has a display panel resolution of 1440 × 1600 pixels per eye, and an LCD panel with dense subpixels to reduce the 'screen door' effect. Over a field of view of ≈130°, this provides 0.09° resolution. Temporal resolution is up to 144 Hz. One limitation with headsets is eye accommodation to allow focusing. This can be accomplished with very dense sensors for near-eye light field displays [52], or to use eye tracking and variable-depth displays [50].

These limits highlight the general quality issue with reconstructing imagery into VR-rendered representations: that the fidelity of the representation must match the fidelity of the display. Capture pixel resolution currently outstrips display resolution, but our true problem is one of reconstructing a representation which, when rendered, still saturates the display. This is easier for image-based rather than model-based reconstruction methods as they are 'closer to the camera', but image-based methods can limit another of our key senses: motion.

Saturating the Senses (Motion): Vision combines with the vestibular and proprioception senses to provide human beings with an awareness of motion. This must be keenly attended to in VR, with reproduction of motion parallax and occlusion required to achieve 6DoF video. However, the 'headbox' of allowable motion is limited by the baseline of the capturing camera system. Most 6DoF camera systems have baselines smaller than one meter; practically building and using a larger camera system is challenging. Beyond this, content must be hallucinated (or inpainted) in a plausible way [124], for which we can only expect 'good at best' quality and which becomes harder and harder as we move farther outside the baseline.

Motion also requires fast display pose estimation; head-motion rotation velocity in daily life can achieve 9 rad/s [8]. Current outside-in tracking systems (Valve Index) and inside-out (Oculus Quest [73]) provide millimeter-level tracking at sufficient framerates to meet their display framerates, though precise details are unspecified. Future work in this area will aim to track more of the human body beyond the head (hands, full-body pose) for greater interaction with our reconstructed VR worlds [50].

Capturing Everything Easily: Casual capture is another area of persistent need. Professional cameras and workflows are expensive and require expertise, and few systems exist to allow novice users to capture a scene with cheap hardware. For static scenes, casual capture can exploit the space/time swap: that space can be traded for time by moving the camera [5]. This lets the user 'sweep over' the scene from different poses, say with a smartphone, to complete the capture [69].

However, much interesting content is of dynamic scenes, which requires algorithms and representations to be temporally consistency. This is a much stricter requirement on accuracy as human sensitivity to perceptual effects over time is strong, e.g., any flickering at the edges of objects within a geometry reconstruction is particularly noticeable. Representations which explicitly accommodate time can also help; one example is spatiotemporal atlases for time-varying texture and geometry [82], but future work is needed for other representations along the image-to-model-based spectrum.

Complex material acquisition is another limitation and area of significant future work. Beyond simple Lambertian diffuse texture, we need to represent materials with shiny or glossy reflectances via 4D BRDFs, and to be able to capture transparent materials like glass. Without these effects, the world can look fake as objects do not visually respond realistically to human motion. Some methods exist for spatially-varying BRDF capture of objects from smartphones [68], but scaling these to scenes requires sampling many directions and is typically not possible for dynamic scenes. This suggests further work in data-driven methods to fit known material models to sparse scene samples.

Similarly, we also wish to capture complex illumination, typically for editing applications like object insertion or relighting [61]. 360° imagery can act as environment reflection maps for lighting objects [103], but illumination estimation from perspective views is an ill-posed problem and requires learning-based methods [29,54]. Future work into plausible illumination reconstruction using data-driven methods and inverse or differentiable rendering techniques holds promise.

Finally, to go beyond visual reproduction and into complex editing and interaction, capture must extend beyond representations of geometry and appearance and into object and scene semantics [47], context via hierarchical scene and relationship graphs [83], and even the capture of other physical properties such as material properties like mass and elasticity and how they relate to aural properties, and functional properties like mechanical actuation and articulation for improved simulation and interaction.

Big Data Problems: Cameras which saturate our senses will produce terabytes of data for video sequences of just a few minutes in length. This question of compression is one that may initially seem tantalizingly simple because of the high level of redundancy in the data, e.g., for light field or 6DoF imagery, where each view is 'just a little bit different'. However, the minor differences in these samples are often what makes the viewing effect convincing, and so they are important to reproduce.

Some representations focus on compression, storage, and transmission factors, such as formats that fit within a classic 2D video pipeline, like side-by-side omnidirectional stereo or RGB+D 360° representations [91]. Here, changes in time are well-handled. However, compressing in screen space in 2D can significantly limit flexibility and ultimately quality, making correct occlusion and motion parallax difficult. Scene-space reconstruction and parameterization allows these effects; however, for geometry-based reconstructions, these changes require more work to maintain temporal handling for easy compression. Work in 4D geometry from video addresses some of these challenges for human avatars [66,67], but representing larger dynamic scenes is still complex.

Our discussion in this chapter has also implicitly considered pre-recorded and post-processed data, but one significant area of future work is in producing high-quality representations and systems for live or streamed experiences. Future work is needed to produce real-time reconstruction approaches which exploit any and every natural redundancy in the data to reduce computation time and network transmission.

Perceptual Realism: We can capture to saturate human senses, and we can capture precise geometry, illumination, and materials for physically-based and model-based representations, but this still leaves many other challenges relating to perceptual effects. One classic effect discussed above is the uncanny valley [64], which hypothesizes perceptual effects to robot appearance and now has a casual understanding relating to digital human avatars. This effect is poorly understood and hard to quantify, particularly for geometry. Approaches to hide the problem with stylization can be successful. However, principled progress requires future work in better computational models of human perception, especially models which are differentiable and so can be used to optimize a (neural) reconstruction function. These would allow faster exploration of a complex design space for capture, reconstruction, representation, and ultimately display by narrowing to only those effects we will see (and see comfortably).

Neural Rendering: Neural rendering techniques are plentiful and promising, with the space of possible techniques currently being explored. Neural scene representations exist to aid capture, stylization, hallucination, and view synthesis. That said, there are caveats with scene generality, representation size, real-time rendering, and editability.

The scene generality limitation is that many current techniques learn a neural representation which is specific to just one object or scene. This approach allows high-quality rendering, but new scenes require retraining the networks from new training data [34,94]. Future work to increase generalizability should look at how to resolve the trade-off between network capacity and quality. This problem is also related to the size of the neural representation and the ability to render quickly. Each network has millions of parameters and requires a large GPU to process, which limits their applicability via memory, rendering, and distribution costs. Future work should investigate efficient and compressible representations for neural scene rendering.

Finally, one benefit of physically-based scene models is that they can be edited easily. This is not the case for most neural representations, which have obtuse 'black box' representations which are difficult to inspect let alone edit. Current works attempt to build interfaces to help understand the generation process for 2D image synthesis [4] and steer it towards exposing more useful controls [40]; these must be extended for neural scene rendering to be useful for VR. Going forward, effort should be placed in constraining the learned representations to be implicitly editable in predictable ways.

Tools and Workflow: The question of editable representations – both classic and neural – highlights the critical role of tools and workflow in the capture and reconstruction pipeline. This area is often overlooked by academia but is vitally important; it requires partnerships between industry and academia to make reliable progress in creating useful tools that are actually adopted.

One question is the ease of use: hardware and software tools are currently catered towards experts, and casual capture is important, but both sets of users would benefit from representations which allow easier processing and manipulation of data. The problem is that different representations are better or worse for different tasks, and so the choice of production capture and representation often depends upon the scene content. For example, distant content can be better as an image-based representation to maximize image quality (suggesting 360° video), but up-close content can be better as depth- or model-based reconstruction to maximize realistic motion effects (suggesting depth or multi-view camera capture). The 'chicken and egg' problem of not knowing which systems to use until the content is captured lacks flexibility, and this has knock-on effects for the post-production workflow that also depends on the representation.

If the best representation for the job is task specific, then the underlying question could be one of how to allow easy *conversion* between representations. Most conversion operations require resampling, which is often lossy. This conversion must also happen quickly and be memory efficient to allow engineers and artists to flexibly pick the best representation for the task at hand.

Editing tools themselves for multi-view content are also nascent, with limitations both in low-level reconstruction for matting and depth/layer decomposition, for interactive user operations like selection, geometry and appearance editing, and for imagery integration operations like compositing and CG insertion. Each of these tasks must be completed in spatio-temporally consistent ways, which requires high-accuracy reconstruction and typically some form of additional explicit consistency constraint.

While the craft has made significant progress over the past five years, we also lack higher-level tools and understanding for storytelling in VR, especially to allow novice users to express their ideas and experiences. VR can be a powerful method of 'experiential storytelling' – to put the viewer in the shoes of another. Efforts to reduce the cost and increase the ease of use and accessibility of our creative tools will democratize the capture, reconstruction, and editing pipeline and help more people tell effective stories.

Trust and Privacy: One new area of research is to build reconstructions and representations which respect privacy. This topic is often seen as more pressing for augmented reality systems (above VR systems), for which real-world capture, reconstruction, and representation techniques are equally as important. Scene capture can often include other humans who have not given permission for their representation, and these people may need to be anonymized in a realistic way [38]. Recent work has also looked at ways to prevent information leakage via *unwanted* scene reconstructions of people's homes derived from AR/VR headset tracking structure-from-motion systems [97]. Future work is needed on the security of information contained within neural representations.

5   Conclusion

If VR is to become more than just a technology for synthetic scenes – to use its powerful telepresence capability to impact domains across industry, commerce, healthcare, and the arts – then we must be able to capture and reproduce the dynamic visual world with high fidelity. We have discussed a range of existing and state-of-the-art solutions to capturing, reconstructing, representing, transmitting, and rendering the world for VR applications. Challenges remain: finding the sweet spots in the complex design space is difficult, and fundamental trade-offs about capture sampling and reproduction quality still remain. However, new neural representations which combine geometry proxies and learned appearance representation functions offer one potential approach to overcoming these trade-offs with domain-specific data-driven representations. Even with these challenges, the field of VR has made significant progress in the past five years, and capturing and distributing the real world is now easier than ever. We await the coming progress over the next five years with bated breath, particularly for VR's potential to improve the quality of telecommunications and ultimately reduce our carbon footprint by reducing the need for travel.

References

1. Aggarwal, R., Vohra, A., Namboodiri, A.M.: Panoramic stereo videos with a single camera. In: Proceedings of the International Conference on Computer Vision and Pattern Recognition (CVPR), pp. 3755–3763, June 2016. https://doi.org/10.1109/CVPR.2016.408

2. Aliev, K.A., Ulyanov, D., Lempitsky, V.: Neural point-based graphics (2019). arXiv:1906.08240

3. Anderson, R., et al.: Jump: virtual reality video. ACM Trans. Graph. (Proc. SIGGRAPH Asia) **35**(6), 198:1–198:13 (2016). https://doi.org/10.1145/2980179.2980257

4. Bau, D., et al.: Seeing what a GAN cannot generate. In: Proceedings of the International Conference on Computer Vision (ICCV) (2019)

5. Bertel, T., Campbell, N.D.F., Richardt, C.: MegaParallax: casual 360° panoramas with motion parallax. IEEE Trans. Visual Comput. Graphics **25**(5), 1828–1835 (2019). https://doi.org/10.1109/TVCG.2019.2898799

6. Brown, M., Lowe, D.G.: Automatic panoramic image stitching using invariant features. Int. J. Comput. Vis. **74**(1) (2007). https://doi.org/10.1007/s11263-006-0002-3

7. Buehler, C., Bosse, M., McMillan, L., Gortler, S., Cohen, M.: Unstructured lumigraph rendering. In: Proceedings of the Annual Conference on Computer Graphics and Interactive Techniques (SIGGRAPH), pp. 425–432 (2001). https://doi.org/10.1145/383259.383309

8. Bussone, W.: Linear and angular head accelerations in daily life. Ph.D. thesis, Virginia Tech (2005)

9. Cabral, B.: VR capture: designing and building an open source 3D-360 video camera. In: SIGGRAPH Asia Keynote, December 2016

10. Chai, J.X., Tong, X., Chan, S.C., Shum, H.Y.: Plenoptic sampling. In: Proceedings of the Annual Conference on Computer Graphics and Interactive Techniques (SIGGRAPH), pp. 307–318 (2000). https://doi.org/10.1145/344779.344932

11. Chaurasia, G., Duchêne, S., Sorkine-Hornung, O., Drettakis, G.: Depth synthesis and local warps for plausible image-based navigation. ACM Trans. Graph. **32**(3), 30:1–30:12 (2013). https://doi.org/10.1145/2487228.2487238

12. Chaurasia, G., Sorkine-Hornung, O., Drettakis, G.: Silhouette-aware warping for image-based rendering. Comput. Graph. Forum (Proc. Eurographics Symp. Rendering) **30**(4), 1223–1232 (2011). https://doi.org/10.1111/j.1467-8659.2011.01981.x

13. Chen, S.E., Williams, L.: View interpolation for image synthesis. In: Proceedings of the Annual Conference on Computer Graphics and Interactive Techniques (SIGGRAPH), pp. 279–288 (1993). https://doi.org/10.1145/166117.166153

14. Cohen, T.S., Welling, M.: Transformation properties of learned visual representations. In: Proceedings of the International Conference on Learning Representations (ICLR) (2015)

15. Collet, A., et al.: High-quality streamable free-viewpoint video. ACM Trans. Graph. (Proc. SIGGRAPH) **34**(4), 69:1–69:13 (2015). https://doi.org/10.1145/2766945

16. Curless, B., Seitz, S., Bouguet, J.Y., Debevec, P., Levoy, M., Nayar, S.K.: 3D photography. In: SIGGRAPH Courses (2000). http://www.cs.cmu.edu/~seitz/course/3DPhoto.html

17. Dai, A., Nießner, M., Zollhöfer, M., Izadi, S., Theobalt, C.: BundleFusion: real-time globally consistent 3D reconstruction using on-the-fly surface reintegration. ACM Trans. Graph. **36**(3), 24:1–24:18 (2017). https://doi.org/10.1145/3054739

18. Davis, A., Levoy, M., Durand, F.: Unstructured light fields. Comput. Graph. Forum (Proc. Eurographics) **31**(2), 305–314 (2012). https://doi.org/10.1111/j.1467-8659.2012.03009.x

19. Debevec, P.: The light stages and their applications to photoreal digital actors. In: SIGGRAPH Asia Technical Briefs (2012)

20. Debevec, P., Bregler, C., Cohen, M.F., McMillan, L., Sillion, F., Szeliski, R.: Image-based modeling, rendering, and lighting. In: SIGGRAPH Courses (2000). https://www.pauldebevec.com/IBMR99/

21. Debevec, P.E., Taylor, C.J., Malik, J.: Modeling and rendering architecture from photographs: a hybrid geometry- and image-based approach. In: Proceedings of the Annual Conference on Computer Graphics and Interactive Techniques (SIGGRAPH), pp. 11–20, August 1996. https://doi.org/10.1145/237170.237191

22. Dosovitskiy, A., Springenberg, J.T., Tatarchenko, M., Brox, T.: Learning to generate chairs, tables and cars with convolutional networks. IEEE Trans. Pattern Anal. Mach. Intell. **39**(4), 692–705 (2017). https://doi.org/10.1109/TPAMI.2016.2567384

23. DXOMARK: RED Helium 8K DxOMark sensor score: 108—a new all-time-high score! https://www.dxomark.com/red-helium-8k-dxomark-sensor-score-108-a-new-all-time-high-score2/. Accessed 30 Oct 2019

24. Eslami, S.M.A., et al.: Neural scene representation and rendering. Science **360**(6394), 1204–1210 (2018). https://doi.org/10.1126/science.aar6170

25. Flynn, J., et al.: DeepView: view synthesis with learned gradient descent. In: Proceedings of the International Conference on Computer Vision and Pattern Recognition (CVPR), pp. 2367–2376, June 2019

26. Flynn, J., Neulander, I., Philbin, J., Snavely, N.: DeepStereo: learning to predict new views from the world's imagery. In: Proceedings of the International Conference on Computer Vision and Pattern Recognition (CVPR), pp. 5515–5524, June 2016. https://doi.org/10.1109/CVPR.2016.595

27. Fuhrmann, S., Langguth, F., Goesele, M.: MVE: a multi-view reconstruction environment. In: Proceedings of the Eurographics Workshop on Graphics and Cultural Heritage, pp. 11–18 (2014). https://doi.org/10.2312/gch.20141299

28. Galliani, S., Lasinger, K., Schindler, K.: Massively parallel multiview stereopsis by surface normal diffusion. In: Proceedings of the International Conference on Computer Vision (ICCV), pp. 873–881, December 2015. https://doi.org/10.1109/ICCV.2015.106

29. Garon, M., Sunkavalli, K., Hadap, S., Carr, N., Lalonde, J.F.: Fast spatially-varying indoor lighting estimation. In: Proceedings of the International Conference on Computer Vision and Pattern Recognition (CVPR) (2019)

30. Gortler, S.J., Grzeszczuk, R., Szeliski, R., Cohen, M.F.: The lumigraph. In: Proceedings of the Annual Conference on Computer Graphics and Interactive Techniques (SIGGRAPH), pp. 43–54, August 1996. https://doi.org/10.1145/237170.237200

31. Hartley, R., Zisserman, A.: Multiple View Geometry in Computer Vision. Cambridge University Press (2004). https://doi.org/10.1017/CBO9780511811685

32. Hedman, P., Alsisan, S., Szeliski, R., Kopf, J.: Casual 3D photography. ACM Trans. Graph. (Proc. SIGGRAPH Asia) **36**(6), 234:1–234:15 (2017). https://doi.org/10.1145/3130800.3130828

33. Hedman, P., Kopf, J.: Instant 3D photography. ACM Trans. Graph. (Proc. SIG-GRAPH) **37**(4), 101:1–101:12 (2018). https://doi.org/10.1145/3197517.3201384

34. Hedman, P., Philip, J., Price, T., Frahm, J.M., Drettakis, G.: Deep blending for free-viewpoint image-based rendering. ACM Trans. Graph. (Proc. SIGGRAPH Asia) **37**(6), 257:1–257:15 (2018). https://doi.org/10.1145/3272127.3275084

35. Hedman, P., Ritschel, T., Drettakis, G., Brostow, G.: Scalable inside-out image-based rendering. ACM Trans. Graph. (Proc. SIGGRAPH Asia) **35**(6), 231:1–231:11 (2016). https://doi.org/10.1145/2980179.2982420

36. Huang, J., Chen, Z., Ceylan, D., Jin, H.: 6-DOF VR videos with a single 360-camera. In: Proceedings of IEEE Virtual Reality (VR), pp. 37–44, March 2017. https://doi.org/10.1109/VR.2017.7892229

37. Huang, P.H., Matzen, K., Kopf, J., Ahuja, N., Huang, J.B.: DeepMVS: learning multi-view stereopsis. In: Proceedings of the International Conference on Computer Vision and Pattern Recognition (CVPR) (2018)

38. Hukkelås, H., Mester, R., Lindseth, F.: DeepPrivacy: a generative adversarial network for face anonymization. In: Bebis, G., et al. (eds.) ISVC 2019. LNCS, vol. 11844, pp. 565–578. Springer, Cham (2019). https://doi.org/10.1007/978-3-030-33720-9_44

39. Ishiguro, H., Yamamoto, M., Tsuji, S.: Omni-directional stereo. IEEE Trans. Pattern Anal. Mach. Intell. **14**(2), 257–262 (1992). https://doi.org/10.1109/34.121792

40. Jahanian, A., Chai, L., Isola, P.: On the "steerability" of generative adversarial networks (2019). arXiv:1907.07171

41. Jancosek, M., Pajdla, T.: Multi-view reconstruction preserving weakly-supported surfaces. In: Proceedings of the International Conference on Computer Vision and Pattern Recognition (CVPR), pp. 3121–3128, June 2011. https://doi.org/10.1109/CVPR.2011.5995693

42. Ji, D., Kwon, J., McFarland, M., Savarese, S.: Deep view morphing. In: Proceedings of the International Conference on Computer Vision and Pattern Recognition (CVPR), pp. 7092–7100, July 2017. https://doi.org/10.1109/CVPR.2017.750

43. Kalantari, N.K., Wang, T.C., Ramamoorthi, R.: Learning-based view synthesis for light field cameras. ACM Trans. Graph. (Proc. SIGGRAPH Asia) **35**(6), 193:1–193:10 (2016). https://doi.org/10.1145/2980179.2980251

44. Keysers, C., Xiao, D.K., Földiák, P., Perrett, D.I.: The speed of sight. J. Cogn. Neurosci. **13**(1), 90–101 (2001). https://doi.org/10.1162/089892901564199

45. Kim, C., Zimmer, H., Pritch, Y., Sorkine-Hornung, A., Gross, M.: Scene reconstruction from high spatio-angular resolution light fields. ACM Trans. Graph. (Proc. SIGGRAPH) **32**(4), 73:1–73:12 (2013). https://doi.org/10.1145/2461912.2461926

46. Kim, H., et al.: Deep video portraits. ACM Trans. Graph. (Proc. SIGGRAPH) **37**(4), 163:1–163:14 (2018). https://doi.org/10.1145/3197517.3201283

47. Kirillov, A., He, K., Girshick, R., Rother, C., Dollár, P.: Panoptic segmentation. In: Proceedings of the International Conference on Computer Vision and Pattern Recognition (CVPR) (2019)

48. Konrad, R., Dansereau, D.G., Masood, A., Wetzstein, G.: SpinVR: towards live-streaming 3D virtual reality video. ACM Trans. Graph. (Proc. SIGGRAPH Asia) **36**(6), 209:1–209:12 (2017). https://doi.org/10.1145/3130800.3130836

49. Kopf, J., et al.: Practical 3D photography. In: Proceedings of CVPR Workshops (2019)

50. Koulieris, G.A., Akşit, K., Stengel, M., Mantiuk, R.K., Mania, K., Richardt, C.: Near-eye display and tracking technologies for virtual and augmented reality. Comput. Graph. Forum **38**(2), 493–519 (2019). https://doi.org/10.1111/cgf.13654

51. Kulkarni, T.D., Whitney, W., Kohli, P., Tenenbaum, J.B.: Deep convolutional inverse graphics network. In: Advances in Neural Information Processing Systems (NIPS) (2015)

52. Lanman, D., Wetzstein, G., Hirsch, M., Heidrich, W., Raskar, R.: Polarization fields: dynamic light field display using multi-layer LCDs. ACM Trans. Graph. (Proc. SIGGRAPH Asia) **30**(6), 186:1–186:10 (2011). https://doi.org/10.1145/2070781.2024220

53. Lee, J., Kim, B., Kim, K., Kim, Y., Noh, J.: Rich360: optimized spherical representation from structured panoramic camera arrays. ACM Trans. Graph. (Proc. SIGGRAPH) **35**(4), 63:1–63:11 (2016). https://doi.org/10.1145/2897824.2925983

54. LeGendre, C., et al.: DeepLight: learning illumination for unconstrained mobile mixed reality. In: Proceedings of the International Conference on Computer Vision and Pattern Recognition (CVPR) (2019)

55. Levoy, M., Hanrahan, P.: Light field rendering. In: Proceedings of the Annual Conference on Computer Graphics and Interactive Techniques (SIGGRAPH), pp. 31–42, August 1996. https://doi.org/10.1145/237170.237199

56. Lipski, C., Linz, C., Berger, K., Sellent, A., Magnor, M.: Virtual video camera: image-based viewpoint navigation through space and time. Comput. Graph. Forum **29**(8), 2555–2568 (2010). https://doi.org/10.1111/j.1467-8659.2010.01824.x

57. Lombardi, S., Simon, T., Saragih, J., Schwartz, G., Lehrmann, A., Sheikh, Y.: Neural volumes: learning dynamic renderable volumes from images. ACM Trans. Graph. (Proc. SIGGRAPH) **38**(4), 65:1–65:14 (2019). https://doi.org/10.1145/3306346.3323020

58. Luo, B., Xu, F., Richardt, C., Yong, J.H.: Parallax360: stereoscopic 360° scene representation for head-motion parallax. IEEE Trans. Vis. Comput. Graph. **24**(4), 1545–1553 (2018). https://doi.org/10.1109/TVCG.2018.2794071

59. Magnor, M., Grau, O., Sorkine-Hornung, O., Theobalt, C. (eds.): Digital Representations of the Real World: How to Capture, Model, and Render Visual Reality. A K Peters/CRC Press, New York (2015)

60. Martin-Brualla, R., et al.: LookinGood: enhancing performance capture with real-time neural re-rendering. ACM Trans. Graph. (Proc. SIGGRAPH Asia) **37**(6), 255:1–255:14 (2018). https://doi.org/10.1145/3272127.3275099

61. Meka, A., et al.: Deep reflectance fields: high-quality facial reflectance field inference from color gradient illumination. ACM Trans. Graph. (Proc. SIGGRAPH) **38**(4), 77:1–77:12 (2019). https://doi.org/10.1145/3306346.3323027

62. Meshry, M., et al.: Neural rerendering in the wild. In: Proceedings of the International Conference on Computer Vision and Pattern Recognition (CVPR) (2019)

63. Mildenhall, B., et al.: Local light field fusion: practical view synthesis with prescriptive sampling guidelines. ACM Trans. Graph. (Proc. SIGGRAPH) **38**(4), 29:1–29:14 (2019). https://doi.org/10.1145/3306346.3322980

64. Mori, M.: The uncanny valley. Energy **7**(4), 33–35 (1970). (in Japanese)

65. Moulon, P., Monasse, P., Marlet, R.: Adaptive structure from motion with a *Contrario* model estimation. In: Lee, K.M., Matsushita, Y., Rehg, J.M., Hu, Z. (eds.) ACCV 2012. LNCS, vol. 7727, pp. 257–270. Springer, Heidelberg (2013). https://doi.org/10.1007/978-3-642-37447-0_20

66. Mustafa, A., Volino, M., Guillemaut, J.Y., Hilton, A.: 4D temporally coherent light-field video. In: Proceedings of International Conference on 3D Vision (3DV) (2017)

67. Mustafa, A., Volino, M., Kim, H., Guillemaut, J.Y., Hilton, A.: Temporally coherent general dynamic scene reconstruction (2019). arXiv:1907.08195

68. Nam, G., Lee, J.H., Gutierrez, D., Kim, M.H.: Practical SVBRDF acquisition of 3D objects with unstructured flash photography. ACM Trans. Graph. (Proc. SIGGRAPH Asia) **37**(6), 267:1–267:12 (2018). https://doi.org/10.1145/3272127.3275017

69. Newcombe, R.A., et al.: KinectFusion: real-time dense surface mapping and tracking. In: Proceedings of the International Symposium on Mixed and Augmented Reality (ISMAR), pp. 127–136, October 2011. https://doi.org/10.1109/ISMAR.2011.6092378

70. Nguyen-Phuoc, T., Li, C., Theis, L., Richardt, C., Yang, Y.L.: HoloGAN: unsupervised learning of 3D representations from natural images. In: Proceedings of the International Conference on Computer Vision (ICCV) (2019)

71. Nießner, M., Zollhöfer, M., Izadi, S., Stamminger, M.: Real-time 3D reconstruction at scale using voxel hashing. ACM Trans. Graph. (Proc. SIGGRAPH Asia) **32**(6), 169:1–169:11 (2013). https://doi.org/10.1145/2508363.2508374

72. Niklaus, S., Mai, L., Yang, J., Liu, F.: 3D Ken Burns effect from a single image. ACM Trans. Graph. (Proc. SIGGRAPH Asia) **38**(6), 184:1–184:15 (2019). https://doi.org/10.1145/3355089.3356528

73. Oculus: From the lab to the living room: the story behind Facebook's Oculus Insight technology and a new era of consumer VR. https://tech.fb.com/the-story-behind-oculus-insight-technology/. Accessed 30 Oct 2019

74. Olszewski, K., Tulyakov, S., Woodford, O., Li, H., Luo, L.: Transformable bottleneck networks. In: Proceedings of the International Conference on Computer Vision (ICCV) (2019)

75. Overbeck, R.S., Erickson, D., Evangelakos, D., Pharr, M., Debevec, P.: A system for acquiring, compressing, and rendering panoramic light field stills for virtual reality. ACM Trans. Graph. (Proc. SIGGRAPH Asia) **37**(6), 197:1–197:15 (2018). https://doi.org/10.1145/3272127.3275031

76. Park, E., Yang, J., Yumer, E., Ceylan, D., Berg, A.C.: Transformation-grounded image generation network for novel 3D view synthesis. In: Proceedings of the International Conference on Computer Vision and Pattern Recognition (CVPR), pp. 702–711, July 2017. https://doi.org/10.1109/CVPR.2017.82

77. Park, J.J., Florence, P., Straub, J., Newcombe, R., Lovegrove, S.: DeepSDF: learning continuous signed distance functions for shape representation. In: Proceedings of the International Conference on Computer Vision and Pattern Recognition (CVPR) (2019)

78. Parra Pozo, A., et al.: An integrated 6DoF video camera and system design. ACM Trans. Graph. (Proc. SIGGRAPH Asia) **38**(6), 216:1–216:16 (2019). https://doi.org/10.1145/3355089.3356555. https://github.com/facebook/facebook360dep

79. Peleg, S., Ben-Ezra, M., Pritch, Y.: Omnistereo: panoramic stereo imaging. IEEE Trans. Pattern Anal. Mach. Intell. **23**(3), 279–290 (2001). https://doi.org/10.1109/34.910880

80. Penner, E., Zhang, L.: Soft 3D reconstruction for view synthesis. ACM Trans. Graph. (Proc. SIGGRAPH Asia) **36**(6), 235:1–235:11 (2017). https://doi.org/10.1145/3130800.3130855

81. Perazzi, F., et al.: Panoramic video from unstructured camera arrays. Comput. Graph. Forum (Proc. Eurographics) **34**(2), 57–68 (2015). https://doi.org/10.1111/cgf.12541

82. Prada, F., Kazhdan, M., Chuang, M., Collet, A., Hoppe, H.: Spatiotemporal atlas parameterization for evolving meshes. ACM Trans. Graph. (Proc. SIGGRAPH) **36**(4), 58:1–58:12 (2017). https://doi.org/10.1145/3072959.3073679

83. Qi, M., Li, W., Yang, Z., Wang, Y., Luo, J.: Attentive relational networks for mapping images to scene graphs. In: Proceedings of the International Conference on Computer Vision and Pattern Recognition (CVPR) (2019)

84. Rhodin, H., Salzmann, M., Fua, P.: Unsupervised geometry-aware representation for 3D human pose estimation. In: Ferrari, V., Hebert, M., Sminchisescu, C., Weiss, Y. (eds.) ECCV 2018. LNCS, vol. 11214, pp. 765–782. Springer, Cham (2018). https://doi.org/10.1007/978-3-030-01249-6_46

85. Richardt, C., Hedman, P., Overbeck, R.S., Cabral, B., Konrad, R., Sullivan, S.: Capture4VR: from VR photography to VR video. In: SIGGRAPH Courses (2019). https://doi.org/10.1145/3305366.3328028

86. Richardt, C., Pritch, Y., Zimmer, H., Sorkine-Hornung, A.: Megastereo: constructing high-resolution stereo panoramas. In: Proceedings of the International Conference on Computer Vision and Pattern Recognition (CVPR), pp. 1256–1263, June 2013. https://doi.org/10.1109/CVPR.2013.166

87. Schroers, C., Bazin, J.C., Sorkine-Hornung, A.: An omnistereoscopic video pipeline for capture and display of real-world VR. ACM Trans. Graph. **37**(3), 37:1–37:13 (2018). https://doi.org/10.1145/3225150

88. Schönberger, J.L., Frahm, J.M.: Structure-from-motion revisited. In: Proceedings of the International Conference on Computer Vision and Pattern Recognition (CVPR), pp. 4104–4113 (2016). https://doi.org/10.1109/CVPR.2016.445

89. Schönberger, J.L., Zheng, E., Frahm, J.-M., Pollefeys, M.: Pixelwise view selection for unstructured multi-view stereo. In: Leibe, B., Matas, J., Sebe, N., Welling, M. (eds.) ECCV 2016. LNCS, vol. 9907, pp. 501–518. Springer, Cham (2016). https://doi.org/10.1007/978-3-319-46487-9_31

90. Seitz, S.M., Curless, B., Diebel, J., Scharstein, D., Szeliski, R.: A comparison and evaluation of multi-view stereo reconstruction algorithms. In: Proceedings of the International Conference on Computer Vision and Pattern Recognition (CVPR), vol. 1, pp. 519–528 (2006). https://doi.org/10.1109/CVPR.2006.19

91. Serrano, A., et al.: Motion parallax for 360° RGBD video. IEEE Trans. Vis. Comput. Graph. **25**(5), 1817–1827 (2019). https://doi.org/10.1109/TVCG.2019.2898757

92. Shum, H., Kang, S.B.: Review of image-based rendering techniques. In: Proceedings of the SPIE Visual Communications and Image Processing, vol. 4067 (2000). https://doi.org/10.1117/12.386541

93. Shum, H.Y., Chan, S.C., Kang, S.B.: Image-Based Rendering. Springer, Boston (2007). https://doi.org/10.1007/978-0-387-32668-9

94. Sitzmann, V., Thies, J., Heide, F., Nießner, M., Wetzstein, G., Zollhöfer, M.: DeepVoxels: learning persistent 3D feature embeddings. In: Proceedings of the International Conference on Computer Vision and Pattern Recognition (CVPR), pp. 2437–2446 (2019)

95. Sitzmann, V., Zollhöfer, M., Wetzstein, G.: Scene representation networks: continuous 3D-structure-aware neural scene representations. In: Advances in Neural Information Processing Systems (NeurIPS) (2019)

96. Snavely, N., Seitz, S.M., Szeliski, R.: Photo tourism: exploring photo collections in 3D. ACM Trans. Graph. (Proc. SIGGRAPH) **25**(3), 835–846 (2006). https://doi.org/10.1145/1141911.1141964

97. Speciale, P., Schönberger, J.L., Kang, S.B., Sinha, S.N., Pollefeys, M.: Privacy preserving image-based localization. In: Proceedings of the International Conference on Computer Vision and Pattern Recognition (CVPR) (2019)

98. Srinivasan, P.P., Tucker, R., Barron, J.T., Ramamoorthi, R., Ng, R., Snavely, N.: Pushing the boundaries of view extrapolation with multiplane images. In: Proceedings of the International Conference on Computer Vision and Pattern Recognition (CVPR) (2019)

99. Sweeney, C.: Theia multiview geometry library (2016). http://theia-sfm.org

100. Sweeney, C., Holynski, A., Curless, B., Seitz, S.M.: Structure from motion for panorama-style videos (2019). arXiv:1906.03539

101. Szeliski, R.: Image alignment and stitching: a tutorial. Found. Trends Comput. Graph. Vis. **2**(1), 1–104 (2006). https://doi.org/10.1561/0600000009

102. Szeliski, R.: Computer Vision: Algorithms and Applications. Springer, London (2010). https://doi.org/10.1007/978-1-84882-935-0. http://szeliski.org/Book/

103. Tarko, J., Tompkin, J., Richardt, C.: Real-time virtual object insertion for moving 360° videos. In: Proceedings of the International Conference on Virtual-Reality Continuum and its Applications in Industry (VRCAI) (2019)

104. Tatarchenko, M., Dosovitskiy, A., Brox, T.: Multi-view 3D models from single images with a convolutional network. In: Leibe, B., Matas, J., Sebe, N., Welling, M. (eds.) ECCV 2016. LNCS, vol. 9911, pp. 322–337. Springer, Cham (2016). https://doi.org/10.1007/978-3-319-46478-7_20

105. Thies, J., Zollhöfer, M., Nießner, M.: Deferred neural rendering: image synthesis using neural textures. ACM Trans. Graph. (Proc. SIGGRAPH) **38**(4), 66:1–66:12 (2019). https://doi.org/10.1145/3306346.3323035

106. Tulsiani, S., Tucker, R., Snavely, N.: Layer-structured 3D scene inference via view synthesis. In: Ferrari, V., Hebert, M., Sminchisescu, C., Weiss, Y. (eds.) ECCV 2018. LNCS, vol. 11211, pp. 311–327. Springer, Cham (2018). https://doi.org/10.1007/978-3-030-01234-2_19

107. Tung, H.Y.F., Cheng, R., Fragkiadaki, K.: Learning spatial common sense with geometry-aware recurrent networks. In: Proceedings of the International Conference on Computer Vision and Pattern Recognition (CVPR), pp. 2595–2603 (2019)

108. Valve: Index headset. www.valvesoftware.com/en/index/headset. Accessed 30 Oct 2019

109. Ventura, J.: Structure from motion on a sphere. In: Leibe, B., Matas, J., Sebe, N., Welling, M. (eds.) ECCV 2016. LNCS, vol. 9907, pp. 53–68. Springer, Cham (2016). https://doi.org/10.1007/978-3-319-46487-9_4

110. Wei, S.E., et al.: VR facial animation via multiview image translation. ACM Trans. Graph. (Proc. SIGGRAPH) **38**(4), 67:1–67:16 (2019). https://doi.org/10.1145/3306346.3323030

111. Weissig, C., Schreer, O., Eisert, P., Kauff, P.: The ultimate immersive experience: panoramic 3D video acquisition. In: Schoeffmann, K., Merialdo, B., Hauptmann, A.G., Ngo, C.-W., Andreopoulos, Y., Breiteneder, C. (eds.) MMM 2012. LNCS, vol. 7131, pp. 671–681. Springer, Heidelberg (2012). https://doi.org/10.1007/978-3-642-27355-1_72

112. Wetzstein, G., Lanman, D., Heidrich, W., Raskar, R.: Layered 3D: tomographic image synthesis for attenuation-based light field and high dynamic range displays. ACM Trans. Graph. (Proc. SIGGRAPH) **30**(4), 95:1–95:12 (2011). https://doi.org/10.1145/2010324.1964990

113. Wetzstein, G., Lanman, D., Hirsch, M., Raskar, R.: Tensor displays: compressive light field synthesis using multilayer displays with directional backlighting. ACM Trans. Graph. (Proc. SIGGRAPH) **31**(4), 80:1–80:11 (2012). https://doi.org/10.1145/2185520.2185576

114. Whelan, T., Salas-Moreno, R.F., Glocker, B., Davison, A.J., Leutenegger, S.: ElasticFusion: real-time dense SLAM and light source estimation. Int. J. Robot. Res. **35**(14), 1697–1716 (2016). https://doi.org/10.1177/0278364916669237

115. Wood, D.N., et al.: Surface light fields for 3D photography. In: Proceedings of the Annual Conference on Computer Graphics and Interactive Techniques (SIGGRAPH), pp. 287–296 (2000). https://doi.org/10.1145/344779.344925

116. Worrall, D.E., Garbin, S.J., Turmukhambetov, D., Brostow, G.J.: Interpretable transformations with encoder-decoder networks. In: Proceedings of the International Conference on Computer Vision (ICCV), pp. 5737–5746 (2017). https://doi.org/10.1109/ICCV.2017.611

117. Wu, C.: VisualSFM: a visual structure from motion system (2011). http://ccwu.me/vsfm/

118. Yang, J., Reed, S.E., Yang, M.H., Lee, H.: Weakly-supervised disentangling with recurrent transformations for 3D view synthesis. In: Advances in Neural Information Processing Systems (NIPS), pp. 1099–1107 (2015)

119. Yifan, W., Serena, F., Wu, S., Öztireli, C., Sorkine-Hornung, O.: Differentiable surface splatting for point-based geometry processing. ACM Trans. Graph. (Proc. SIGGRAPH Asia) **38**(6) (2019). https://doi.org/10.1145/3355089.3356513

120. Yücer, K., Sorkine-Hornung, A., Wang, O., Sorkine-Hornung, O.: Efficient 3D object segmentation from densely sampled light fields with applications to 3D reconstruction. ACM Trans. Graph. **35**(3), 22:1–22:15 (2016). https://doi.org/10.1145/2876504

121. Zaragoza, J., Chin, T.J., Tran, Q.H., Brown, M.S., Suter, D.: As-projective-as-possible image stitching with moving DLT. IEEE Trans. Pattern Anal. Mach. Intell. **36**(7), 1285–1298 (2014). https://doi.org/10.1109/TPAMI.2013.247

122. Zhang, F., Liu, F.: Parallax-tolerant image stitching. In: Proceedings of the International Conference on Computer Vision and Pattern Recognition (CVPR), pp. 3262–3269, June 2014. https://doi.org/10.1109/CVPR.2014.423

123. Zheng, K.C., Kang, S.B., Cohen, M.F., Szeliski, R.: Layered depth panoramas. In: Proceedings of the International Conference on Computer Vision and Pattern Recognition (CVPR) (2007). https://doi.org/10.1109/CVPR.2007.383295

124. Zhou, T., Tucker, R., Flynn, J., Fyffe, G., Snavely, N.: Stereo magnification: learning view synthesis using multiplane images. ACM Trans. Graph. (Proc. SIGGRAPH) **37**(4), 65:1–65:12 (2018). https://doi.org/10.1145/3197517.3201323

125. Zhou, T., Tulsiani, S., Sun, W., Malik, J., Efros, A.A.: View synthesis by appearance flow. In: Leibe, B., Matas, J., Sebe, N., Welling, M. (eds.) ECCV 2016. LNCS, vol. 9908, pp. 286–301. Springer, Cham (2016). https://doi.org/10.1007/978-3-319-46493-0_18

126. Zollhöfer, M., et al.: State of the art on monocular 3D face reconstruction, tracking, and applications. Comput. Graph. Forum **37**(2), 523–550 (2018). https://doi.org/10.1111/cgf.13382

Light Field Video for Immersive Content Production

Marco Volino$^{(\boxtimes)}$ ⓘ, Armin Mustafa ⓘ, Jean-Yves Guillemaut ⓘ,
and Adrian Hilton ⓘ

Centre for Vision, Speech and Signal Processing,
University of Surrey, Guildford, UK
{m.volino,a.mustafa,j.guillemaut,a.hilton}@surrey.ac.uk
https://www.surrey.ac.uk/centre-vision-speech-signal-processing

Abstract. Light field video for content production is gaining both research and commercial interest as it has the potential to push the level of immersion for augmented and virtual reality to a close-to-reality experience. Light fields densely sample the viewing space of an object or scene using hundreds or even thousands of images with small displacements in between. However, a lack of standardised formats for compression, storage and transmission, along with the lack of tools to enable editing of light field data currently make it impractical for use in real-world content production. In this chapter we address two fundamental problems with light field data, namely representation and compression. Firstly we propose a method to obtain a 4D temporally coherent representation from the input light field video. This is an essential problem to solve that will enable efficient compression editing. Secondly, we present a method for compression of light field data based on the eigen texture method that provides a compact representation and enables efficient view-dependent rendering at interactive frame rates. These approaches achieve an order of magnitude compression and temporally consistent representation that are important steps towards practical toolsets for light field video content production.

Keywords: Light fields · 4D reconstruction · Representation · Compression

1 Introduction

The rise in popularity of virtual and augmented reality (VR/AR) has fueled an increasing demand for high-quality digital characters and environments to enable immersive storytelling. Currently immersive content is produced using either artist-driven computer generated imagery or 360 video capture. The use of computer generated imagery and game engines allow interactivity, such as head movement, but do not achieve photo-realism in a practical or cost effective

M. Volino, A. Mustafa—Equal author contribution.

M. Magnor and A. Sorkine-Hornung (Eds.): Real VR, LNCS 11900, pp. 33–64, 2020.
https://doi.org/10.1007/978-3-030-41816-8_2

manner. Alternatively 360 video and stereo 360 video achieve photo-realism from a fixed location but do not allow head movement, also known as 6 degrees-of-freedom (6DoF), or realistic parallax. Light field technology has emerged as a solution for capturing objects and scenes with photo-realism whilst allowing realistic changes in viewpoint with correct parallax [14, 19]. However, a number of open problems must be addressed before light field technology can be practically deployed for real-world productions.

For a given scene, a light field describes the light intensity passing through every point in space and in every direction. In order to capture a light field it is necessary to densely sample a scene using hundreds [34] or even thousands [30, 47] of images. To date, light fields have primarily been used for capture of static scenes due to the requirement for a large number of viewpoints. Recently, motivated by applications in immersive AR/VR content production, arrays of video cameras have be employed to acquire light fields of dynamic scenes [21, 44]. However, image and video based techniques for compression and editing cannot be directly applied to light field data as they fail to exploit the spatial and temporal redundancy present in the light field. Hence there is a need for an efficient light field video representation that is capable of exploiting the spatio-temporal redundancy inherent within light field data to enable compression and facilitate editing.

In this chapter we address two main issues that limit the use of light field video for immersive content production: Representation and Compression. We perform reliable temporal alignment of partial surfaces for complex dynamic scenes exploiting properties of the light field to obtain robust 4D temporal representation of the scene. Sparse temporal correspondence tracks are obtained for each view for the dynamic sequence using feature matching. These sparse temporal correspondence tracks are used to initialize a dense flow estimation. A novel sparse-to-dense flow is proposed exploiting Epipolar Plane Images (EPI) using oriented light field windows to obtain a temporally coherent dense 4D representation of the scene.

For compression, we introduce a compact light field representation that enables up to a 95% decrease in data size and offers efficient rendering at interactive frame rates on commodity graphics hardware whilst maintaining the visual quality of the captured light field. To summarize, the contributions of this chapter are:

- Temporally coherent 4D reconstruction of dynamic light field video for efficient editing.
- EPI retrieval from sparse light field video for spatio-temporal correspondence.
- Sparse-to-dense scene flow exploiting EPI image information.
- A novel Eigen texture representation for light fields which is compact and preserves the view-dependent photo-realism of the captured light field.
- Efficient light field rendering and synthesis of novel views by interpolation in Eigen space to achieve photo realistic rendering with real-time interactive performance on commodity graphics hardware.

The work presented in this chapter is based on the following published papers: '4D Temporally Coherent Dynamic Light Field Video' [27] and 'Light Field Compression using Eigen Textures' [39]. The remainder of the chapter is structured as follows: Sect. 2 provides a background on light field capture, compression and 4D scene reconstruction; Sect. 3 presents the proposed methods for establishing 4D temporal correspondence for light field video sequences and representation and compression of light field data using eigen textures; Sect. 4 presents quantitative and qualitative evaluation of the proposed methods for 4D correspondence and light field representation and compression; finally Sect. 5 concludes the chapter and proposes how these strands of work can be extended and combined to create a robust and compressible 4D representation for light field video.

2   Related Work

2.1   Light Fields

The origins of the light field can be traced back to the notes of Leonardo Da Vinci in which he postulated that the view of the world from any point in space is formed by the intersection of an infinite number of *radiant pyramids* from all directions [18]. This idea was later formalized by Adelson and Bergen [1] and became known as the plenoptic function, a seven dimensional function of 3D position, 2D viewing direction, observed wavelength, and time. The pioneering works of Levoy and Hanrahan [19] and Gortler *et al.* [14] showed that the plenoptic function could be reduced to four dimensions under the assumption that an object is observed from outside its convex hull and the object remained static. This allowed light fields to be represented by the intersection of light rays travelling between two planes. These assumptions reduced the dimensionality and inspired the design of light field acquisition hardware.

The general principle of light field photography was pioneered in 1908 by Gabriel Lippmann under the name of integral photography. However, practical methods for light field acquisition have only started to emerge in recent years using digital camera technology. Early approaches to capture light fields performed a dense sampling of the 3D space by moving a camera around the scene. These approaches used either a camera mounted on a gantry [19] or more recently a hand-held camera [9]. In these approaches, each frame effectively captures a 2D slice of the 4D light field. Due to the need to physically move the camera around the scene, these approaches are limited to static scenes. Alternatively, a micro lens array can be placed in front of a conventional image sensor [28] (e.g. Lytro Illum and Raytrix cameras). Micro lens arrays trade off spatial resolution of the image sensor to angular resolution of the lens array. These approaches use image-based rendering techniques to synthesise new views by interpolating the information from the captured views. As they do not explicitly capture the scene geometry, a large number of camera views (typically about 100) are required in order to densely sample the light field.

2.2   4D Scene Reconstruction

For conventional single view depth sequences and multiple view reconstruction of dynamic scenes techniques have been introduced to align sequences using correspondence information between frames. Methods have been proposed to obtain sparse [16,25,35,49] and dense [4,23,48] correspondence between consecutive frames for entire sequences. Existing sparse correspondence methods work independently on a frame-by-frame basis for a single view [35] or multiple views [16] and require a strong prior initialization [49]. Existing feature matching techniques either work in 2D [35] or 3D [23] or for sparse [16,49] or dense [48] points. Other methods are limited to RGBD data [48] or stereo pairs [23] for dynamic scenes. Dense matching techniques include scene flow methods. Scene flow techniques [4,42] typically estimate the pairwise surface or volume correspondence between reconstructions at successive frames but do not extend to 4D alignment or correspondence across complete sequences due to drift and failure for rapid and complex motion. In this paper we propose sparse-to-dense temporal alignment exploiting the high spatio-temporal redundancy in light fields to robustly align light field video captured with sparse camera arrays.

2.3   Light Field Compression

Light field images obtained from multiple camera views inherently contain a large amount of redundancy. As such light field coding and compression has been well studied, see Viola *et al.* [38] for an overview of a number of techniques. Numerical methods that have been commonly employed to compress light field data include vector quantization [19,45], wavelet transforms [8], non-negative matrix factorization [7] and principal component analysis (PCA) [7,45]. In this section we focus on light field compression schemes that utilize scene geometry to aid compression [7,30,45].

Surface light fields are an alternative approach to parameterize a 4D light field that defines the radiance with respect to every point on a surface in all directions [7,24,45]. Wood *et al.* [45] extract and compress *lumispheres*, which store the directional radiance for every surface point mapped onto the surface of a sphere, using both vector quantization and PCA. Light field mapping [7] partitions the surface light field based on the elementary shape primitives of the 3D surface. Appearance variation is resampled on a per primitive basis, compressed using PCA and stored in surface and view map images giving further reduction through standard image compression.

Other light field image compression techniques have been inspired by video coding and compression [6,22,30]. These works treat a subset of the sampled light field images as reference frames, or *i-frames*. Images within the local neighbourhood of each *i-frame* image of the light field array are compressed via predicted frames or *p-frames*. These methods are capable of achieving high compression ratios and capitalize on work in video compression.

One method of appearance representation and compression that has not yet been explored for use with light fields is Eigen textures. Using PCA, a linear subspace can be computed from a set of images, enabling compression through dimensionality reduction. Appearance modelling through PCA was used as a method for face recognition [37]. Later, Nishino *et al.* [29] proposed the Eigen texture method that allowed compression and synthesis of novel views from a sparse set of viewpoints. More recently, Boukhayma *et al.* [5] extended this idea to handle dynamic objects by projecting the object's dynamic appearance onto a dynamic structured geometric proxy at each time instance. This approach considers dynamic appearance but does not preserve view-dependent surface appearance in the representation that is captured with light fields.

3   Method

3.1   Overview

An overview of the framework to obtain compressed light field video for immersive content production is shown in Fig. 1. A 4D temporally coherent representation is created from the input light field video, explained in Sect. 3.3. This is followed by compression of light field video using eigen textures explained in Sect. 3.4. This gives a compressed 4D light field at each time instance that can be used for immersive content production with efficient storage and could facilitate editing operations.

Fig. 1. Light field video for immersive content production.

3.2   Light Field Capture

In order to capture light field video, an array consisting of 20 FLIR Grasshooper3 machine vision cameras [12] was constructed. The cameras were uniformly spaced in a 5 × 4 grid configuration over an area of 50 cm × 50 cm. Synchronised video streams were captured with 5MP resolution at 30 frames per second. The overall dimensions of the camera rig were designed to capture video over a range of viewpoints that a person could comfortably achieve from a seated position.

The intended use case of this work is to produce content for seated VR experiences. The camera array was used to capture human actors performing short theatrical scenes against a chroma key background. This simplified object isolation for reconstruction purposes and also for the final composition into virtual environments. Throughout this chapter the sparse 5 × 4 camera array is used to capture light field video of human actors, as shown in Fig. 2.

Fig. 2. Sparse light field video array used to capture an actor as part of Kinch & the Double World production tests - Photo credit: Figment Productions.

3.3   4D Temporal Alignment of Light Field Video

The high spatial and temporal redundancy in light field video makes it challenging to use in content production for AR/VR. The aim of the work presented in this section is to obtain a 4D temporally coherent representation of dynamic light field video exploiting spatio-temporal redundancy. This provides an efficient structured representation for light field compression, editing and use in immersive VR content production.

Overview

Given an independent per-frame surface or depth reconstruction from the light field video captured with a sparse camera array the problem is to simultaneously estimate the temporal correspondence of the input light field across all views for the entire sequence. This is achieved efficiently by estimating the temporal alignment of the reconstructed surface between each time frame and propagating this across all light field camera views. A coarse-to-fine approach is introduced that initially estimates temporal correspondence based on sparse features and then estimates dense scene flow initialised from the sparse features. To ensure robust tracking, key-frames are identified as a reference to minimise drift in long-term tracking. An overview of the 4D temporally coherent reconstruction of light field video is presented in Fig. 3.

Mesh Reconstruction: Light field video of the dynamic scene is captured using a camera array. Multiple-view stereo is performed to obtain a per frame surface mesh reconstruction [32].

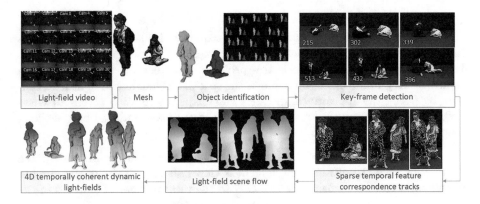

Fig. 3. 4D light field video framework.

Object Identification: The reconstructed point cloud is clustered in 3D [31] with each cluster representing a unique foreground object, shown in Fig. 4.

Key-Frame Detection: Key-frames are detected for light field video exploiting redundant spatial information across views to identify a set of unique reference frames for stable long-term tracking. Surface tracking is performed between key-frames to reduce the accumulation of errors in sequential tracking due to large non-rigid motion for long sequences ($\approx$700 frames).

Sparse Temporal Feature Correspondence Tracks: Reconstructed 3D points projected at all frames are matched frame-to-frame across the sequence to estimate sparse temporal feature tracks for each dynamic object for each light field camera view. These sparse temporal correspondence tracks are used to initialize light field scene flow to handle occlusions and improve robustness.

Light Field Scene Flow: We propose to estimate dense scene flow between images by exploiting EPI information from light field video based on oriented light field windows [33] initialised by the sparse feature correspondence per light field view at each time instant. This exploits the spatio-temporal redundancy in light fields to give 2D dense correspondences which are back-projected to the 3D mesh to obtain a 4D spatio-temporally coherent dynamic light field video representation.

Fig. 4. Object identification example on light field frame.

Key-Frame Detection

Aligning per-frame reconstruction for long sequences leads to drift due to accumulation of errors in alignment between frames and failure is observed due to large non-rigid motion. To tackle this problem we detect key-frames across the sequence. Key-frame detection exploits the spatial redundancy in light field capture by fusing the appearance, distance and shape information across all views (N_v) in the sparse camera array. Temporal coherence is introduced between key-frames as explained in Sect. 3.3.

Appearance Metric ($M_{i,j}^c$): This measures appearance similarity between frame i and j for each object region in light field view c. It is the ratio of the number of temporal feature correspondences $Q_{i,j}^c$ to the total number of features in the object region at frame i, R_i^c and j, R_j^c: $M_{i,j}^c = \frac{2Q_{i,j}^c}{R_i^c + R_j^c}$

Distance Metric ($L_{i,j}^c$): This metric measures the distance between frame i and j for each object in each view c, it is defined as: $L_{i,j}^c = \frac{j-i}{D_{max}^c}$ where $j > i$ and D_{max}^c is the maximum number of frames between key-frames for view c. This term ensures that the distance between two key-frames does not exceed D_{max}^c. This is set to 100.

Shape Metric ($I_{i,j}^c$): Gives the shape overlap between pairs of frames for each object in the light field video. It is defined as the ratio of the intersection of the aligned segmentation [10] $h_{i,j}^c$ to the union of the area $A_{i,j}^c$: $I_{i,j}^c = \frac{h_{i,j}^c}{A_{i,j}^c}$

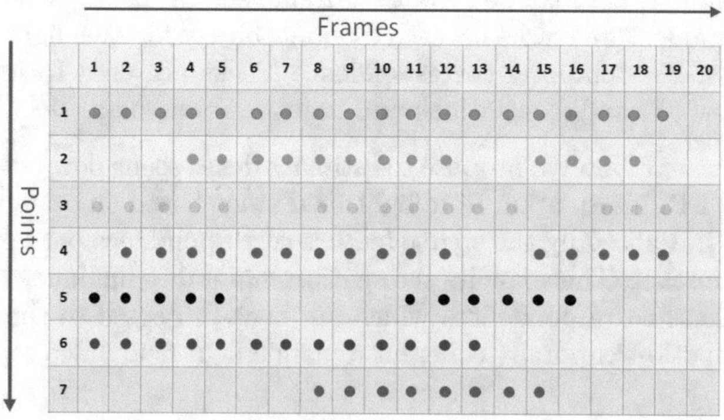

Fig. 5. Example of sparse feature correspondence tracks.

Key-Frame Similarity Metric: The metrics defined above are used to calculate the similarity between frames as follows: $D_{i,j} = 1 - \frac{1}{3N_v} \sum_{c=1}^{N_v} (M_{i,j}^c + I_{i,j}^c + L_{i,j}^c)$. All frames with similarity >0.75 are selected as key-frames defined as $K_i = \{k^{i+1}, k^{i+2}, \ldots, k^{N_f^i}\}$ where $i = 1$ to N_k (number of key-frames in light field video) and N_f^i is the number of frames between K_i and K_{i+1}.

Sparse Temporal Feature Correspondence

Numerous approaches have been proposed to temporally align moving objects in 2D using either feature matching or optical flow. However these methods may fail in the case of occlusion, movement parallel to the view direction, large motions, and visual ambiguity. To overcome these limitations we match sparse feature points from all light field camera views at each time instant for each object. This is used to estimate the similarity between the object surface observed at different frames of the light field video for key-frame detection and subsequently to initialize dense light field scene flow between frames.

3D points corresponding to each dynamic object are projected at each frame to ensure spatial light field coherence. The features for each light field camera view are defined as: $F_i^c = \{f_1^c, f_2^c, ..., f_{R_i^c}^c\}$, where $c = 1$ to N_v and $N_v = 20$ in our case. R_i^c are the 3D points visible at each frame i. Nearest neighbour matching is used to establish matches between features. The ratio of the first to second nearest neighbour descriptor matching score is used to eliminate ambiguous matches ($ratio < 0.85$). This is followed by a symmetry test which employs the principle of forward and backward match consistency to remove erroneous inconsistent correspondences. To further refine the sparse matching and eliminate outliers we enforce local spatial coherence in the matching. For matches in an $m \times m$ ($m = 11$) neighbourhood of each feature we find the average Euclidean distance and constrain the match to be within a threshold ($\pm \eta < 2 \times$ Average Euclidean distance).

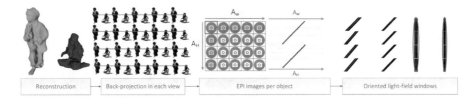

Fig. 6. An example of EPI representation of sparse light field (blue ellipse represents Gaussian weighted window).

Sparse temporal correspondence tracks are obtained by performing exhaustive matching between all frames N_f^i for each key-frame for the entire sequence. Feature matching is performed between frames such that features at view c frame i, F_i^c are matched to features at view c to frames $j = \{i + 1, \ldots, N_f^i\}$. This gives us correspondences for all the frames N_f^i with key-frame K_i. Point tracks are constructed from this correspondence information for key-frame K_i. The same process is repeated for key-points which are not part of point tracks at the corresponding key-frame for all frames $j = \{i + 1, \ldots, N_f^i\}$. Any new point-tracks are added to the list of point tracks for key-frame K_i. The exhaustive matching between frames per key-frame handles reappearance and disappearance of points due to occlusion or object movement. An example of sparse feature correspondence tracks in shown in Fig. 5. Frame 1 is a key-frame and each point track is represented by a unique colour with missing points showing partial feature correspondence tracks. Sparse correspondences are also obtained between all key-frames to initialise dense light field flow.

Light Field Scene Flow

Dense temporal correspondence is estimated using a novel light field scene flow method using pairwise dense correspondence which is estimated using the light field oriented window matching. This combines information across all light field views to achieve robust temporal correspondence. The sparse feature correspondences provides a robust initialisation of the proposed dense flow for large non-rigid shape deformation in the light field video.

The high-level of inherent redundancy in the light field images is used to improve the robustness and reliability of dense scene flow by using oriented light field windows on the EPI for matching. This has been shown to improve the temporal correspondences for scene flow [33]. In this paper we propose a novel method to obtain EPIs from sparse light field data to improve the quality of dense scene flow. Our approach uses oriented light field windows [33] to represent surface appearance information for matching as illustrated in Fig. 6.

Epipolar Plane Image (EPI). Traditional light field data is captured with a plenoptic camera or a dense camera array typically capturing 200–300 views [34]. An example dataset is illustrated in Fig. 7(a) captured with 289 images. Given a dense set of views the EPI provides a representation for estimating correspondence across views from the regular structure of the image i.e. slant lines correspond to the same surface point. The 2D slice of such representation has the same width as the captured image and height is given by the number of views in a camera array row (17 in Fig. 7(a)). With dense sampling the disparity between adjacent views is typically sub-pixel giving slant lines in the EPI. Approaches have been proposed to estimate depth and segmentation from this dense EPI representation [41,47]. However for sparse camera sampling the disparity between views may be several pixels making it difficult to directly establish surface correspondence from the EPI, Fig. 7(b). In our case of sparse views with just 20 cameras, the height of this EPI reduces to 5 pixels which makes it challenging to utilize the regularity of the information from EPI obtained from light fields.

In this paper we aim to use the EPIs to introduce spatio-temporal coherence in dynamic light field video. We propose a novel method to create an EPI parametrized representation from sparse light field capture. We assume that the calibration is known. All the images at each time instant are undistorted and rectified with respect to the reference camera. The depth information at each time instant is used to resample the light field to create an EPI representation of sparse light field data. The algorithm to obtain EPI from image, calibration and depth information is illustrated in Fig. 6; the stages are as follows:

- The dense point-cloud P of each dynamic object is projected on the undistorted and rectified images. $B_{l,k}^c$ is the set of points in view c. For each row k of the projected points on the dynamic object a 2D EPI is obtained.
- The size of 2D EPI is set to $W \times H$, where W is the width of input images and $H = N_w \times \mu$ is estimated corresponding to the number of cameras in

each row (N_w). μ is a constant introduced to increase the distance between views due to sparse camera sampling. It is set to 50 in our case to maximize performance. For each row of the camera array, H_o 2D EPIs are obtained for each dynamic object, where H_o is the height of the object. The corresponding projected points $B_{l,k}^c$ for each point $P_{l,k}$ are plotted on the 2D EPI with x coordinates the same as that of input images and y coordinates are estimated using the translation information from the calibration, defined as:

$\frac{H \times \text{Distance between consecutive cameras}}{\text{Maximum distance between pair of cameras}}$

– Given the set of image samples corresponding to a given surface point we fit a line in the EPI due to imperfect camera array. A scene point is represented by a line in the 2D EPI. A similar process is repeated for the entire pointcloud P to obtain multiple 2D EPIs. Given a 2 dimensional camera array there are 2 sets of EPIs obtained by re-sampling along epipolar lines in the vertical and horizontal directions.

The EPIs obtained from sparse camera arrays are used to constrain dense light field flow using oriented light field windows.

Oriented Light Field Windows. Oriented light field windows exploit the regularity information in the EPI to enable more robust and accurate pixel comparisons [33] over spatial windows that suffer from defocus blur and loss of precision. In this section we propose to use these oriented light field windows on the EPIs obtained from the sparse light field data to estimate the light field scene flow temporal correspondence.

Each scene point can be represented by an oriented window in the light field ray space. The shear of the ray is related to the depth of the 3D point and the size of the window is defined by spatial and angular Gaussian weights. However the ray moves with object motion, hence there is a need to account for shear and translation. The oriented light field window corresponding to a scene point for a light field, L is computed as follows:

$$O_{d,x0,y0}(x, y, u, v) = (W * S_d * T_{x0,y0})\,[L] \qquad (1)$$

where, x_0, y_0 is the centre of the window, x, y represents the image plane and u, v represents the camera plane. S_d is the shear operation for depth d, defined as $S_d\,[L] = L_d(x, y, u, v) = L(x + u\left(1 - \frac{1}{d}\right), y + v\left(1 - \frac{1}{d}\right), u, v)$, $T_{x0,y0}$ is the translation operator defined as, $T_{x0,y0}\,[L] = L_{x0,y0}(x, y, u, v) = L(x + x0, y + y0, u, v)$ and W is the Gaussian weighted windows defined as: $W\,[L] = L(x, y, u, v)N(x, y; \sigma_{xy}^2)A(u, v)$. $N()$ is the 2D Gaussian distribution windows and $A(u, v)$ is the corresponding row and column of the camera array (shown as green cameras in Fig. 6, 3rd step) of the reference light field view $((u_c, v_c)$ shown in red box), defined as:

$$A(u, v) = \begin{cases} 1, & \text{if } v = v_c \text{ or } u = u_c \\ 0, & otherwise \end{cases}$$

This formulation could be easily extended to dense camera array. We propose to use this oriented light field window to robustly estimate the dense scene flow for light field video.

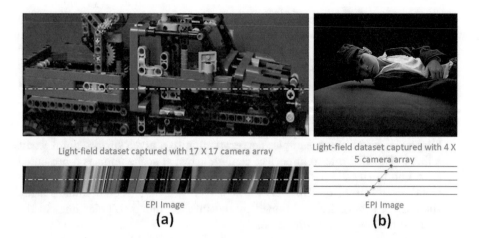

Fig. 7. Illustration of EPI from (a) dense Stanford dataset [34] (EPI from [41]) and (b) sparse light field capture.

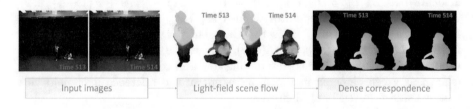

Fig. 8. Illustration of dense correspondence between frames and key-frames for full sequence 4D alignment: arrows indicate sparse correspondence tracks and dense correspondence.

Dense Light Field Scene Flow. Oriented light field windows are used to estimate flow between consecutive frames and between key-frames, Fig. 8, using the sparse temporal feature correspondence as initialization for each view. Flow is estimated on the object region for each light field view, as illustrated in Fig. 9, to obtain dense temporal correspondence.

Fig. 9. Light field scene flow for two consecutive frames.

The flow is formulated as a translation of each pixel location $p = (x_p, y_p)$ in image I by $m_p = (\delta x_p, \delta y_p)$ in time. We formulate the computation of flow $\boldsymbol{M}$ per view for each dynamic object by minimization of the cost function:

$$E(\boldsymbol{M}) = \sum_{p \in I} \lambda_L E_L(p, m_p) + \lambda_C E_C(p, m_p) + \lambda_R E_R(p, m_p) \tag{2}$$

The cost consists of three terms: the light field consistency E_L for the oriented light field window alignment; the appearance term E_C for brightness coherency; and the regularization term E_R to avoid sudden peaks in flow and maintain the consistency. Colour and regularization terms are common to optical flow problems [36] and the light field consistency is introduced for the first time to improve dense flow for sparse light field video.

Light Field Consistency: The 2D EPIs obtained from the sparse light field views are used to define oriented light field windows for each scene point. These windows encapsulate the observed multi-view light field appearance of the corresponding surface point and can be matched over time to estimate the temporal correspondence, defined as:

$$E_L(p, m_p) = \left\| O_{d_t, p}(p, u, v, t) - O_{d_{t+1}, p+m_p}(p, u, v, t+1) \right\|^2$$

where $O_{d_t, m}()$ is the oriented light field window at time t with depth d_t as defined in Eq. 1.

Appearance Consistency: This adds the brightness consistency assumption to the cost function generalized for all N_v light field cameras for both time steps. This term is obtained by integrating the sum of three penalizers over the reference image domain. $e_C^T()$ penalizes deviation from the brightness constancy assumption in time for same views; $e_C^V()$ penalizes deviation from the brightness constancy assumption between the reference view and each of the other views at time $t + 1$. $e_C^S()$ forces the flow to be close to nearby sparse temporal correspondences.

$$E_C(p, m_p) = e_C^T(p, m_p) + e_C^V(p, m_p) + e_C^S(p, m_p)$$

$$e_C^T(p, m_p) = \sum_{i=1}^{N_v} \left\| (I_i(p, t) - I_i(p + m_p, t + 1)) \right\|^2$$

$$e_C^V(p, m_p) = \sum_{i=2}^{N_v} \left\| (I_1(p, t) - I_i(p + m_p, t + 1)) \right\|^2$$

$$e_C^S(p, m_p) = \sum_{i=1}^{N_v} e_C^S = \begin{cases} 0 & \text{if } p \in N \\ \infty & \text{otherwise} \end{cases}$$

where $I_i(p, t)$ is the intensity at point p and time t in camera i. This term denotes that the flow vector m is located within a window from a sparse constraint at p and it forces the flow to approximate the sparse 2D temporal correspondence tracks.

Regularization: This penalizes the absolute difference of the flow field to enforce motion smoothness and handle occlusions and areas with low confidence.

$$E_R(p, m_p) = \sum_{p,q \in N_p} \|\Delta m\|^2 \left(\lambda_R^L e_R^L(p, q, m_p, m_q) + \right.$$

$$\left. \lambda_R^C e_R^C(p, q, m_p, m_q)\right)$$

$$e_R^L(p, q, m_p, m_q) = \operatorname*{mean}_{q \in N_p} E_L(q, m_q) - \operatorname*{min}_{q \in N_p} E_L(q, m_q)$$

$$e_R^C(p, q, m_p, m_q) = \operatorname*{mean}_{q \in N_p} E_C(q, m_q) - \operatorname*{min}_{q \in N_p} E_C(q, m_q)$$

where $\Delta m = m_p - m_q$ and we compute e_R^L and e_R^C as the minimum subtracted from the mean data energy within the search window N_p for each pixel p.

Occlusions: To detect occlusions, we compare the forward flow from t to $t+1$, and the backward flow from $t+1$ to t. Occluded pixels are robustly indicated by large differences in the forward/backward motion and excluded as outliers.

Optimization: For each pixel p, the energy is estimated as defined in Eq. 2 on a window N_p, as in the SimpleFlow algorithm [36] to estimate the flow vector m. The optical flow is optimized over a multi-scale pyramid with warping between pyramid levels, resulting in a coarse-to-fine strategy that allows the estimation of large displacements by minimizing the equation defined as: $F(\boldsymbol{M}) = \arg\min E(\boldsymbol{M})$

4D Temporally Coherent Light Field Video. The estimated dense flow for each view is back projected to the 3D visible surface to establish dense 4D correspondence between frames (N_f^i) and between key-frames K_i as seen in Fig. 8 to obtain 4D temporally coherent light field video. Dense 4D correspondence is first obtained for the light field view with maximum visibility of 3D points. To increase surface coverage correspondences are added in order of visibility of 3D points for different sparse light field views. Dense temporal correspondence is propagated to new surface regions as they appear using the sparse feature correspondence tracks and respective dense light field scene flow. Dense scene flow is estimated between key-frames for robust long-term surface tracking.

3.4   Eigen Texture Representation of Light Field Images

In this section we describe how the Eigen texture representation is extracted from a time instance in a multiple camera light field dataset. An overview of the pipeline is shown in Fig. 10. Given the input light field images, a geometric proxy is reconstructed and UV coordinates are generated. Camera calibration parameters and the 3D reconstruction are used to generate a UV map for each camera used to capture the light field. Camera UV maps are processed to ensure there are a consistent number of pixels by filling in any holes caused by occlusion or viewpoint changes. The filled camera UV maps are used in a PCA based framework to generate the Eigen texture representation for light fields. Each of the stages are described in further detail throughout this section along with the view-dependent rendering pipeline.

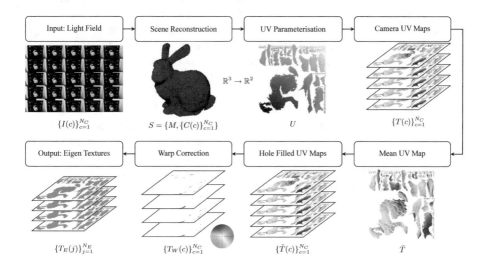

Fig. 10. Eigen texture representation of light fields.

Input Data and Pre-processing. The input to our approach is a collection of images $\{I(c)\}_{c=1}^{N_C}$ captured from N_C cameras arranged in a rectangular array, as is common in light field video capture [34,44]. Scene geometry is modelled through explicit chart-based camera calibration, dense multiple view stereo and Poisson surface reconstruction. If calibration is not available, photogrammetry is employed to estimate camera calibration and model scene geometry [3,13,46]. Scene geometry, $S = \{M, \{C(c)\}_{c=1}^{N_C}\}$, consists of a triangular mesh model M and cameras $\{C(c)\}_{c=1}^{N_C}$. $C(c)$ represents the cth camera of N_C cameras consisting of a 3×4 projection matrix that maps 3D world coordinates to 2D image coordinates. The triangular mesh model is defined as $M = \{V, Y, U\}$, where V is the 3D mesh vertices, Y is the mesh connectivity and U defines a $\mathbb{R}^3 \to \mathbb{R}^2$ mapping from mesh vertices to UV coordinates. U are generated automatically using least-squares conformal maps [20].

Camera UV Map Processing. Using the reconstructed scene model M and camera parameters $\{C(c)\}_{c=1}^{N_C}$, we resample the observed surface appearance for each camera into a set of UV maps $\{T(c)\}_{c=1}^{N_C}$ based on the UV coordinates U of M. To achieve this, a 3D mesh vertex is projected into the image domain of camera c using the camera projection matrix and the colour of the pixel copied to the UV coordinate location associated with the vertex. To handle occlusions in the scene, depth testing is performed using a depth map rendered using the scene geometry and camera parameters. A binary value is stored in the alpha channel (α) of the UV map which indicates if a vertex is visible from the camera's viewpoint. This encodes surface appearance and visibility into the cth camera UV map $T(c)$, an example of which shown in Fig. 11(b). This is performed in a custom graphics shader that interpolates vertex and UV coordinate values to give appearance and visibility across the complete mesh surface in each camera UV map, see Fig. 11 for an example. This process results in N_C UV maps in which observations of a point on the 3D surface are mapped into the same pixel location in the 2D texture domain across all UV maps.

As each camera has variations in surface visibility, each UV map has a different number of visible pixels. To construct the Eigen texture representation, described in Sect. 3.4, it is required that all UV maps have an equal number of visible pixels. To this end, we first construct an average UV map $\bar{T}$ which is then used to fill holes in $T(c)$. An average UV map $\bar{T}$ is generated as shown in Eq. 3. This is computed on a per-pixel basis and results in a UV map in which the pixel values have been averaged over all visible pixels, resulting in an appearance value for all surface points in all UV maps $T(c)$.

$$\bar{T}(l) = \frac{1}{\sum_{c=1}^{N_C} v(c,l)} \sum_{c=1}^{N_C} v(c,l)T(c,l) \tag{3}$$

where $\bar{T}$ is the average over all N_C camera UV maps, $\bar{T}(l)$ is the average value for the lth pixel, $v(c,l)$ is a binary value determined by the visibility encoded in the alpha channel of the camera UV map. Hole filling of the $T(c)$ takes place according to the conditions in Eq. 4.

$$\hat{T}(c,l) = \begin{cases} T(c,l), & \text{if } v(c,l) = 1 \\ \bar{T}(l), & \text{otherwise} \end{cases} \tag{4}$$

where $T(c,l)$ and $\hat{T}(c,l)$ are values of the lth pixel of camera c for the camera UV map and hole filled UV map, respectively. $\bar{T}(i)$ is the lth pixel in the mean texture map and $v(c,l)$ returns the value in the alpha channel that determines the surface visibility.

To account for small errors in camera parameters and geometry estimation we employ optical flow image warping [11]. We compute the optical flow field between a given camera UV map $\hat{T}(c)$ and a defined reference camera UV map $\hat{T}(c_{ref})$, typically a camera located in the centre of the camera array, resulting in an optical flow field per camera $\{T_W(c)\}_{c=1}^{N_C}$. The flow fields are then applied to each $\hat{T}(c)$ to correct for small errors and bring all $\{\hat{T}(c)\}_{c=1}^{N_C}$ into alignment with $\hat{T}(c_{ref})$.

Eigen Texture Construction. In this section, we describe the construction of the Eigen texture representation for light field data. We define the function $\hat{T}(c,l,\lambda)$ which returns a scalar value for the lth pixel of wavelength λ in the hole filled UV map $\hat{T}(c)$ for camera c. As the input of the proposed method is RGB images, λ refers to the red, green and blue image channels. However, the approach is independent of colour representation and could also be used to compress other attributes. A pixel in a UV map $\hat{T}(c)$ is represented in row-vector form, as shown in Eq. 5.

$$\mathbf{x}(c,l) = \left[\hat{T}(c,l,\lambda_r) - \bar{T}(l,\lambda_r), \hat{T}(c,l,\lambda_g) - \bar{T}(l,\lambda_g), \right.$$
$$\left. \hat{T}(c,l,\lambda_b) - \bar{T}(l,\lambda_b) \right] \tag{5}$$

where $\mathbf{x}(c,l)$ returns intensity values for the red (λ_r), green (λ_g) and blue (λ_b) image channels for the lth pixel of the cth camera in row-vector form. A complete image can then be represented in row-vector form, as shown in Eq. 6.

$$\mathbf{x}(c) = [\mathbf{x}(c,1), \mathbf{x}(c,2)..., \mathbf{x}(c,N_P)] \tag{6}$$

where $\mathbf{x}(c)$ returns a row-vector consisting of the RGB pixel intensities for all N_P visible pixels (i.e. $v(c,k) = 1$) in the hole filled UV map $\hat{T}(c)$. Subsequently, N_C UV maps can be compiled into matrix $\mathbf{X}$ where rows represent all valid pixels in a UV map and columns represent all samples of a point on the model's surface captured by N_C cameras, as shown in Eq. 7.

$$\mathbf{X} = \begin{bmatrix} \mathbf{x}(1) \\ \mathbf{x}(2) \\ \vdots \\ \mathbf{x}(N_C) \end{bmatrix} \tag{7}$$

where $\mathbf{X}$ is a matrix of the RGB pixel intensities with dimensions N_C rows by $3N_p$ columns. Prior to vectorization of $\hat{T}(c)$, the mean texture $\bar{T}$ is subtracted allowing PCA to be performed. In this form, a UV map can be thought of as a point in a $3N_P$ dimensional space. To compute the Eigen texture representation, singular value decomposition (SVD) is performed on the matrix $\mathbf{X}^\top \mathbf{X}$ to find the Eigen vectors and Eigen values, as shown in Eq. 8. As the number of UV maps is less than the number of pixels, $N_C < 3N_P$, there are $N_C - 1$ rather than $3N_P$ non-zero values [37].

$$\mathbf{X}^\top \mathbf{X} = \mathbf{W} \Sigma \mathbf{W}^\top \tag{8}$$

where $\mathbf{W}$ is the orthogonal Eigen vectors and $\Sigma = diag(\sigma)_{1 \le i \le N_C}$ are the Eigen values. The rows of $\mathbf{W}$ are sorted in order of the magnitude of the Eigen values. The high amount of redundancy in the light field images allows the number of Eigen textures N_E to represent the view-dependent variation with $N_E \ll N_C$. Back projecting the vectorised input filled camera UV maps into the Eigen space results in weighting coefficients $\{\{\omega(c,n)\}_{c=1}^{N_C}\}_{n=1}^{N_E}$ required to reconstruct the input. The weights are computed for each camera and stored for use at render-time. Eigen textures $\{T_E(n)\}_{n=1}^{N_E}$ are stored as image files along with the weighting coefficients to reconstruct the UV map from each camera.

Eigen Texture Rendering. Here we discuss the Eigen texture rendering pipeline, an overview is shown in Fig. 12. The Eigen textures $\{T_E(n)\}_{n=1}^{N_E}$ and per

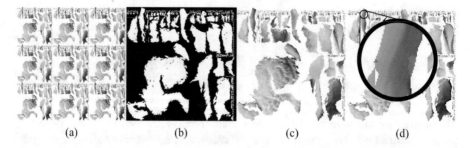

Fig. 11. Examples of (a) Camera UV maps $\{T(c)\}_{c=1}^{N_C}$, (b) binary visibility map (stored in the alpha channel of the camera UV maps), (c) mean UV map $\bar{T}$ and (d) filled camera UV map $\hat{T}(c,i)$, with pixel that require filling highlighted in red.

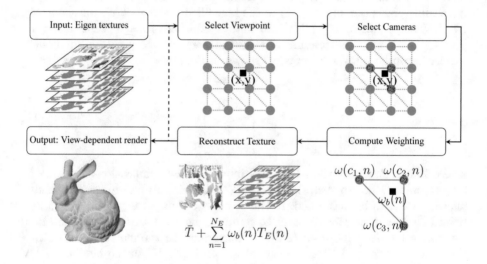

Fig. 12. Light field Eigen texture rendering.

camera reconstruction weights $\{\{\omega(c,n)\}_{c=1}^{N_C}\}_{n=1}^{N_E}$ are first loaded into memory. A viewing position (x,y), constrained to lie on an estimated plane and within the bounds of the camera array, is selected by the user. The three closest cameras to the viewing position measured by Euclidean distance are selected for rendering, denoted as c_1, c_2 and c_3. Given the viewing position and positions of the selected rendering cameras, a weighting based on barycentric coordinates is computed. These barycentric weights are then combined with the Eigen texture reconstruction weight for the selected cameras to give the interpolated reconstruction weights, as shown in Eq. 9.

$$\omega_b(n) = b_1\omega(c_1,n) + b_2\omega(c_2,n) + b_3\omega(c_3,n) \tag{9}$$

Fig. 13. Dense 2D and 4D correspondence for Walking sequence across key-frames.

where $b_{\{1,2,3\}}$ are the barycentric weights, $\omega(c_{\{1,2,3\}}, n)$ are the Eigen texture reconstruction parameters for cameras $c_{\{1,2,3\}}$ and $\omega_b(n)$ is the barycentric weighted reconstruction parameters. The use of a barycentric weighting scheme ensures a smooth transition between camera reconstruction weights in both the horizontal and vertical directions. An alternative weighting scheme could be used, e.g. bi-linear. However, in the current implementation it would be subject to $\sum_{i=1}^{3} b_i = 1$. The final view-dependent texture T_V for viewpoint v is computed by the linear combination of the mean texture, Eigen textures and Eigen texture reconstruction weights, shown in Eq. 10.

$$T_v = \bar{T} + \sum_{n=1}^{N_E} \omega_b(n) T_E(n) \tag{10}$$

where $\bar{T}$ is the mean texture, $T_E(n)$ are the computed Eigen textures, $\omega_b(n)$ are the barycentric weighted reconstruction weights corresponding to the nth Eigen texture, and T_v is the resulting view-dependent texture. This enables efficient view-dependent rendering directly from the Eigen texture representation.

4   Results and Evaluation

In this section we present a quantitative and qualitative evaluations of both the temporal alignment and eigen-texture representation of light field video. The Eigen texture representation is evaluated in terms of storage reduction, rendering quality and rendering performance. All presented results were generated using a desktop PC with an Intel i7 CPU, 64 GB of RAM and a Nvidia Geforce GTX 1080 GPU.

4.1   4D Light Field Video

The proposed approach is tested on various light field captures. The properties of the evaluation datasets are presented in Table 1. Algorithm parameters set empirically are constant for all results. Sparse and dense correspondence are obtained on the sparse light field dynamic data and the colour coded results are shown in Fig. 13 for Walking dataset and in Fig. 14 for Sitting and Waking up dataset using the method explained in Sect. 3.3. To illustrate the 2D dense alignment the silhouette of the dense mesh on key-frames is colour coded and

Fig. 14. Sparse temporal correspondences and dense flow results on 2 light field sequences: Sitting and Waking up.

the colours are propagated between frames using dense scene flow explained in Sect. 3.3. Results of the proposed 4D temporal alignment, illustrated in Fig. 15 shows that the colour of the points remains consistent between frames. The proposed approach is qualitatively shown to propagate the correspondences reliably over the entire light field video for complex dynamic scenes with large non-rigid motion.

Qualitative Evaluation: For comparative evaluation we use: (a) state-of-the-art dense flow algorithm Deepflow [43]; (b) dense flow without light field consistency (DFwLF) in Eq. 2; (c) a recent algorithm for alignment of partial surfaces (4DMatch) [26]; and (d) Simple flow [36]. Qualitative results against DFwLF, 4DMatch, Deepflow, and Simpleflow shown in Fig. 16 indicate that the propagated colour map does not remain consistent across the sequence for large motion as compared to the proposed method (red regions indicate correspondence failure).

Table 1. Properties of all datasets: Length is the length of the sequence, KF gives the number of key-frames detected for the dynamic sequence and Avg. sparse tracks gives the number of sparse temporal correspondence tracks averaged over the entire sequence for each object.

Datasets	Length	Views	Shot level	Resolution	KF	Avg. sparse tracks
Walking	667	20	Far	2448 × 2048	15	1934
Sitting	694	20	Mid-level	2448 × 2048	13	1046
Wakingup	270	20	Close-up	2448 × 2048	7	2083
Running	140	20	Far	2448 × 2048	5	1278
Magician	353	20	Close-up	2448 × 2048	6	1312

Table 2. Silhouette overlap error for all the datasets. Prop. represents proposed approach, 4DM is 4DMatch, DF is Deepflow and SF is Simpleflow.

Datasets	Prop.	DFwLF	4DM	DF	SF
Walking	**0.45**	0.59	0.58	0.81	1.05
Sitting	**0.51**	0.73	0.71	1.13	1.83
Waking up	**0.39**	0.56	0.53	0.89	1.17
Running	**0.65**	0.87	0.92	1.23	1.95
Magician	**0.59**	0.82	0.83	1.05	1.67

Table 3. Temporal coherence evaluation for Walking dataset against existing methods: S.D. is the standard deviation.

Methods	Frame-to-frame		Keyframe-to-frame	
	Mean	S.D.	Mean	S.D.
Proposed	**3.78**	1.45	**4.34**	1.74
DFwLF	5.93	2.60	7.41	3.73
4DM	5.30	2.12	6.95	3.12
DF	6.28	3.77	15.79	6.36
SF	7.82	4.31	21.92	8.45

Quantitative Evaluation: For quantitative evaluation we compare the silhouette overlap error (SOE). Dense correspondence over time is used to create propagated mask for each image. The propagated mask is overlapped with the silhouette of the projected surface reconstruction at each frame to evaluate the accuracy of the dense propagation. The error is defined as: $SOE = \frac{1}{N_v \times N_F} \sum_{i=1}^{N_v} \sum_{c=1}^{N_F} \frac{\text{Area of intersection}}{\text{Area of back-projected mask}}$. Evaluation against the different techniques is shown in Table 2 for all datasets. As observed the silhouette overlap error is lowest for the proposed approach showing relatively high accuracy.

We evaluate the temporal coherence across Walking sequence, by evaluating the variation in appearance for each scene point between frames and between key-frames and frames for state-of-the-art methods, defined as: $\sqrt{\frac{\Delta r^2 + \Delta g^2 + \Delta b^2}{3}}$, where Δ is the difference operator. Evaluation shown in Table 3 against state-of-the-art methods demonstrates the stability of long term temporal tracking for proposed method. Evaluation of the proposed method against dense flow without light field consistency (DFwLF) demonstrates the usefulness of information from the EPIs in the dense flow in Sect. 3.3.

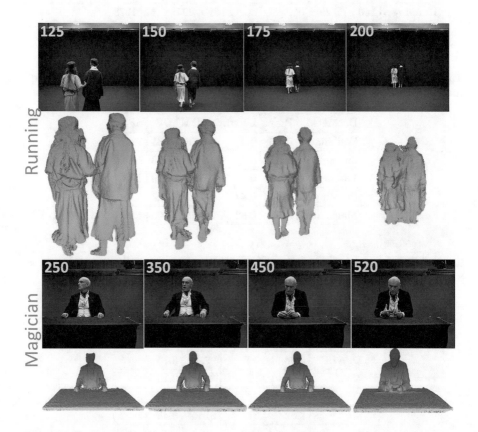

Fig. 15. 4D temporal alignment between frames for Walking and Magician dataset.

Light Field Camera Array Configuration: We evaluate the performance of the proposed 4D temporal alignment with different light field camera configurations shown in Fig. 17. The completeness of the 3D points at each time instant for all camera configurations as observed in Table 4 is defined as:

$$\frac{100}{MN} \sum_{i=1}^{N} \sum_{c=1}^{M} \frac{\text{Number of 3D points propagated in each configuration}}{\text{Number of 3D points propagated with full camera array}}$$

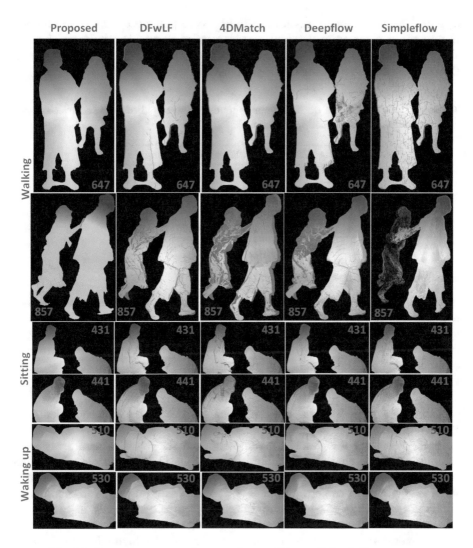

Fig. 16. Dense flow comparison results on different light field sequences.

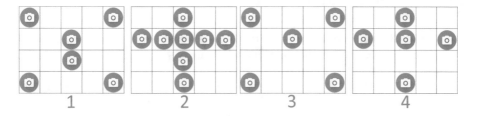

Fig. 17. Different light field camera array configurations.

The evaluation demonstrates a drop in 3D correspondence with the reduction in number of cameras in different camera configurations, specially for close-up shots (Wakeup and Magician). However configuration 1 and 3 with cameras in the corners provide a better coverage compared to 2 and 4.

Table 4. Completeness of dense 3D correspondence averaged over the entire sequence in % for different camera configurations.

Config	Walk	Sit	Wake	Run	Magician
1	95.15	92.58	89.64	91.03	90.82
2	91.33	86.73	86.98	88.78	89.90
3	90.76	85.15	86.05	87.21	86.21
4	87.82	82.40	85.16	86.56	80.91

4.2 Eigen Texture Representation

In this section, we present a quantitative evaluation of the Eigen texture representation. We compare UV maps reconstructed from the Eigen texture representation to the camera UV maps extracted from the scene model and camera images. The storage requirements of the Eigen texture representation are also compared against the camera UV maps. The evaluation is performed on individual frames from the light field video boy and girl datasets. To test the limits of the algorithm, we also use scenes from the Stanford light field archive [34] captured by a single camera on a robotic gantry resulting in the equivalent of a 17×17 camera array.

Scene geometry and camera parameters from the 5×4 camera array were computed using a chart-based calibration pipeline [2,15], multiple view stereo [32], and Poisson surface reconstruction [17]. For the Stanford datasets [34], scene geometry and camera parameters were estimated using photogrammetry [3]. Scenes were chosen to give a mixture of objects and materials, e.g. Bunny is a Lambertian surface with few specular highlights whereas Amethyst and Chest contain metal and glass structures with strong specular highlights. In the case of the Tarot dataset, the scene was reconstructed with photogrammetry and the glass ball was manually modelled with a sphere as it is not currently possible to geometrically reconstruct such a complex object.

UV Map Reconstruction Quality. The UV map reconstruction quality is performed by comparing the hole filled UV maps $\{\hat{T}(c)\}_{c=1}^{N_C}$ to the UV maps reconstructed using the Eigen texture representation with the per camera reconstruction parameters. This is a direct comparison of the reconstructed output T_V to expected output $\{\hat{T}(c)\}_{c=1}^{N_C}$. The UV maps are compared using the structural similarity index measure (SSIM) [40] which is considered across all visible foreground surface points. SSIM values range from ± 1 with $+1$ achieved only when comparing identical images.

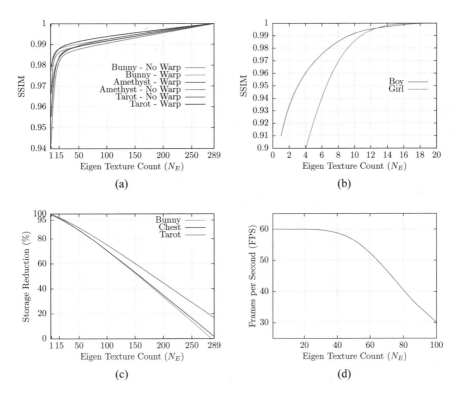

Fig. 18. Quantitative evaluation of the proposed approach: (a) Rendering quality against the number of Eigen textures with and without optical flow correction using scenes from the Stanford light field gallery [34]; (b) Rendering quality against the number of Eigen textures for 5 × 4 light field dataset; (c) Storage reduction for Stanford light field dataset; (d) Rendering performance against number of Eigen textures.

Figure 18(a) and (b) show SSIM values versus the number of Eigen textures used for rendering N_E for the evaluation of the datasets. We see that as N_E is increased, the difference between the reconstructed UV map T_V and the camera UV map decreases. In the Amethyst, Bunny, and Chest datasets, there is an increase in quality, up to an SSIM 0.98, until $N_E = 15$ after which it is a linear increase. This represents a 20:1 reduction in the number of textures required. The same relationship is also observed in the Boy and Girl datasets, but in a less dramatic fashion requiring 7 and 9 Eigen textures for an SSIM of 0.98 for the Boy and Girl datasets, respectively. The reason for this is that the Amethyst, Bunny, and Chest light field datasets consist of 289 images compared to the relatively sparse light field with 20 images in the Boy and Girl datasets. This results in increased redundancy that is exploited by the Eigen texture representation and results in less Eigen textures to represent the variation in the captured images. Rendering results from the evaluation datasets can be found in Fig. 19.

Warping. An inaccurate geometric proxy and errors in camera parameters result in misalignment in the texture domain. These errors affect compression as they lead to a requirement for more Eigen textures to represent the surface variation. Figure 18(a) demonstrates this by comparing the eigen texture representation using the evaluation datasets with and without optical flow correction applied. It can be seen that performing the optical flow based warping allows a higher UV map reconstruction quality with fewer Eigen textures. This is due to the appearance being in alignment minimizing the surface variation.

Storage. Table 5 shows the storage requirements for the evaluation datasets and Fig. 18(c) shows storage reduction against N_E. A comparison is made between the storage requirements of the camera UV maps $\{\bar{T}(c)\}_{c=1}^{N_C}$ and the Eigen texture representation consisting of a mean texture $\bar{T}$ and Eigen textures $\{T_E(j)\}_{j=1}^{N_E}$. This ensures we are comparing the data input and output to the Eigen texture representation. It can be seen that as N_E is increased the storage reduction decreases. Taking the values of N_E that result in a SSIM of 0.98, $N_E = 15$ for Amethyst, Bunny, Chest, and Tarot datasets results in a storage reduction of >96% and for the Boy and Girl datasets by approximately 60%.

Table 5. Storage requirements of light field datasets in represented as images, per camera texture maps and eigen textures. [†]For Amethyst, Bunny, Chest, and Tarot datasets $N_E = 15$, for Boy and Girl datasets $N_E = 7$.

Dataset	N_C	Storage (MB)		
		$\{I(c)\}_{c=1}^{N_C}$	$\{\hat{T}(c)\}_{c=1}^{N_C}$	$\{T_E(j)\}_{j=1}^{N_E}$ [†]
Amethyst	289	769.4	359.6.2	13.4 (96%)
Bunny	289	770.3	276.5	9.5 (97%)
Chest	289	756.4	387.7	14.8 (96%)
Tarot	289	1100	425.5	12.0 (97%)
Boy	20	97.7	16.4	5.7 (65%)
Girl	20	105	21.7	7.2 (67%)

Rendering Performance. A trade off must be considered between rendering quality and rendering complexity. As more components are added to the Eigen texture representation, the more computationally complex the rendering pipeline becomes. An evaluation of the rendering efficiency was performed by monitoring the rendering frame rate against N_E. Figure 18(d) shows the Eigen texture representation is able to achieve and maintain interactive frame rates (60 fps) for $N_E \leq 40$ At $N_E \geq 40$ the frame rate begins to fall in an almost linear fashion to 30 fps at $N_E = 100$.

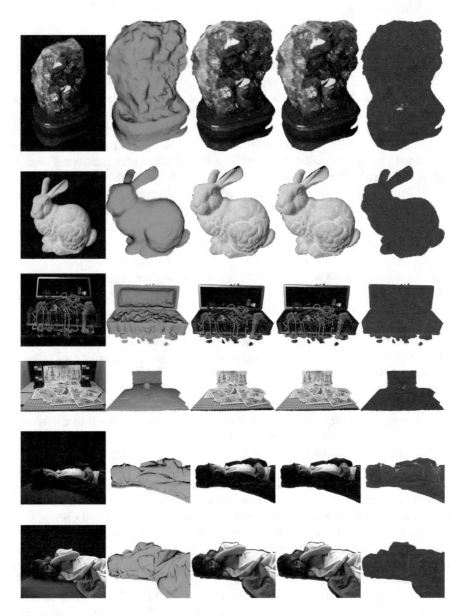

Fig. 19. Results: Rows (top to bottom) show Amethyst, Bunny, Chest, Tarot, Boy, and Girl datasets, respectively. From left to right, selected image from dataset, scene reconstruction model, render using camera UV map, Eigen texture render using $N_E = 15$ for Amethyst, Bunny, and Chest, and $N_E = 7$ for Boy and Girl datasets. Heat maps show the normalized error in RGB pixel values, for illustrative purposes this error has been scaled 5 times.

4.3   Limitations

The proposed method for 4D light field video fails for fast spinning objects; scenes with uniform appearance and highly crowded dynamic environments. This is due to the failure of sparse and dense correspondence due to high ambiguity.

The proposed Eigen texture representation will be unable to effectively compress the appearance in the presence of gross geometric errors. In practice, it is not possible to get accurate geometry as the light field scenes used in the evaluation contain complex specular objects and transparent surfaces that exhibit refraction, e.g. Amethyst, Chest, and Tarot. Despite the approximate geometric reconstruction, the proposed approach is able to achieve high quality renderings with a >95% reduction in data size for dense light fields. This can be observed in the Tarot dataset where the compressed Eigen texture representation is able to reproduce the complex refraction within the glass ball.

5   Conclusions and Future Work

Light fields have the potential to revolutionise the way we create immersive content. However they also introduce a new set of challenges. Firstly, the light field representation is significantly larger than conventional image/video representations due to the increased dimensionality. This poses challenges in terms of data storage and transmission. An important aspect to ensure acceptance of the technology will therefore be standardisation as well as the development of efficient compression techniques tailored to light field data. Another challenging aspect relates to the development of creative tools dedicated to light field editing. There is currently a lack of software tools for light field post production. Finally, giving the user the ability to freely explore and move in a scene introduces new challenges in terms of storytelling and narratives for VR content production.

This chapter has introduced the first algorithm to obtain a 4D temporally coherent representation of dynamic light field video. A novel method to obtain EPIs from sparse light field video for spatio-temporal correspondence is proposed. Sparse-to-dense light field scene flow is introduced exploiting information from the EPIs. Dense correspondence is fused spatially for 4D temporally coherent light field video. The proposed approach is evaluated on various light field sequences of complex dynamic scenes with large non-rigid deformations to obtain a temporally consistent 4D representation and demonstrating accuracy of the resulting 4D alignment. 4D light field video provides a spatio-temporally coherent representation to support subsequent light field video compression or editing to replicate the functionality of conventional video editing allowing the propagation of edits both spatially across views and temporally across frames.

We have also proposed and demonstrated that the Eigen texture method can be used effectively to represent and render light fields. We have described how to construct an Eigen texture representation from a light field camera array and how this Eigen texture basis can be used to perform view-dependent rendering. A quantitative evaluation was performed in which it was shown that a storage saving of >95% could be obtained for dense light fields using the Eigen texture representation with a minimal loss in quality. It was also shown that in datasets that used large numbers of cameras, a higher storage reduction was achieved as the representation was able to exploit the increased redundancy.

Future work in representation will investigate creating a deformable mesh for each object for the dynamic sequence in between key-frames. This would create a more complete and efficient 4D representation for immersive content production. Extending this method to more complex crowded scenes will also be investigated by exploiting human pose information. Future work in compression will investigate extending this approach to dynamic scenes in a way that exploits the large redundancy both spatially and temporally while preserving both dynamic and view-dependent surface appearance.

Acknowledgements. This work was supported by 'Live action light fields for immersive virtual reality experiences' (InnovateUK 102686), EPSRC Audio-Visual Media Research Platform Grant (EP/P022529/1), Royal Academy of Engineering Research Fellowship (RF-201718-17177) and 'Polymersive: Immersive Video Production Tools for Studio and Live Events' (InnovateUK 105168). The authors would also like to thank project partners from Figment Productions and Foundry for the creative direction of the data capture used in this work.

References

1. Adelson, E.H., Bergen, J.R.: The plenoptic function and the elements of early vision. In: Landy, M., Movshon, J.A. (eds.) Computational Models of Visual Processing, pp. 3–20. MIT Press, Cambridge (1991)
2. Agarwal, S., Mierle, K., et al.: Ceres solver. http://ceres-solver.org
3. Agisoft: Agisoft Photoscan v1.3.2 (2017). http://www.agisoft.com/
4. Basha, T., Moses, Y., Kiryati, N.: Multi-view scene flow estimation: a view centered variational approach. In: CVPR, pp. 1506–1513 (2010)
5. Boukhayma, A., Tsiminaki, V., Franco, J.-S., Boyer, E.: Eigen appearance maps of dynamic shapes. In: Leibe, B., Matas, J., Sebe, N., Welling, M. (eds.) ECCV 2016. LNCS, vol. 9905, pp. 230–245. Springer, Cham (2016). https://doi.org/10.1007/978-3-319-46448-0_14. http://link.springer.com/10.1007/978-3-319-46448-014
6. Zhang, C., Li, J.: Compression of lumigraph with multiple reference frame (MRF) prediction and just-in-time rendering. In: Proceedings of the Data Compression Conference (DCC 2000) (2000). https://doi.org/10.1109/DCC.2000.838165
7. Chen, W.C., Bouguet, J.Y., Chu, M.H., Grzeszczuk, R.: Light field mapping: efficient representation and hardware rendering of surface light fields. In: Proceedings of the 29th Annual Conference on Computer Graphics and Interactive Techniques (SIGGRAPH 2002). ACM (2002). https://doi.org/10.1145/566570.566601. http://doi.acm.org/10.1145/566570.566601
8. Chang, C.L., Zhu, X., Ramanathan, P., Girod, B.: Light field compression using disparity-compensated lifting and shape adaptation. IEEE Trans. Image Process. **15**(4), 793–806 (2006). https://doi.org/10.1109/TIP.2005.863954
9. Davis, A., Levoy, M., Durand, F.: Unstructured light fields. Comput. Graph. Forum **31**(2pt1), 305–314 (2012). https://doi.org/10.1111/j.1467-8659.2012.03009.x. http://dx.doi.org/10.1111/j.1467-8659.2012.03009.x

10. Evangelidis, G.D., Psarakis, E.Z.: Parametric image alignment using enhanced correlation coefficient maximization. IEEE Trans. Pattern Anal. Mach. Intell. **30**, 1858–1865 (2008)
11. Farnebäck, G.: Two-frame motion estimation based on polynomial expansion. In: Bigun, J., Gustavsson, T. (eds.) SCIA 2003. LNCS, vol. 2749, pp. 363–370. Springer, Heidelberg (2003). https://doi.org/10.1007/3-540-45103-X_50
12. FLIR: Grasshopper3.   https://www.flir.co.uk/products/grasshopper3-usb3/?model=GS3-U3-51S5C-C
13. Fuhrmann, S., Langguth, F., Goesele, M.: MVE-a multi-view reconstruction environment. In: Eurographics Workshops on Graphics and Cultural Heritage, pp. 11–18 (2014). https://doi.org/10.2312/gch.20141299. http://diglib.eg.org/handle/10.2312/gch.20141299.011-018
14. Gortler, S.J., Grzeszczuk, R., Szeliski, R., Cohen, M.F.: The lumigraph. In: Proceedings of the 23rd Annual Conference on Computer Graphics and Interactive Techniques (SIGGRAPH 1996), pp. 43–54. ACM, New York (1996). https://doi.org/10.1145/237170.237200. http://doi.acm.org/10.1145/237170.237200
15. Itseez: Open source computer vision library v2.4. http://opencv.org/ (2017)
16. Joo, H., et al.: Panoptic studio: a massively multiview system for social motion capture. In: ICCV (2015)
17. Kazhdan, M., Bolitho, M., Hoppe, H.: Poisson surface reconstruction. In: Proceedings of the Fourth Eurographics Symposium on Geometry Processing (SGP 2006), pp. 61–70. Eurographics Association (2006). http://dl.acm.org/citation.cfm?id=1281957.1281965
18. Kemp, M.: Leonardo on Painting: Anthology of Writings by Leonardo da Vinci, with a Selection of Documents Relating to His Career as an Artist. Yale Nota Bene, New Haven (2001). https://search.library.wisc.edu/catalog/999923957902121
19. Levoy, M., Hanrahan, P.: Light field rendering. In: Proceedings of the 23rd Annual Conference on Computer Graphics and Interactive Techniques (SIGGRAPH 1996), pp. 31–42. ACM, New York (1996). https://doi.org/10.1145/237170.237199. http://doi.acm.org/10.1145/237170.237199
20. Lévy, B., Petitjean, S., Ray, N., Maillot, J.: Least squares conformal maps for automatic texture atlas generation. ACM Trans. Graph. **21**(3), 362–371 (2002). https://doi.org/10.1145/566654.566590. http://dl.acm.org/citation.cfm?id=566590
21. Lytro: Lytro immerge. https://www.lytro.com/immerge
22. Magnor, M., Girod, B.: Data compression for light-field rendering. IEEE Trans. Circ. Syst. Video Technol. **10**(3), 338–343 (2000). https://doi.org/10.1109/76.836278
23. Menze, M., Geiger, A.: Object scene flow for autonomous vehicles. In: CVPR (2015)
24. Miller, G., Rubin, S., Ponceleon, D.: Lazy decompression of surface light fields for precomputed global illumination. In: Drettakis, G., Max, N. (eds.) Rendering Techniques '98. EUROGRAPHICS, pp. 281–292. Springer, Vienna (1998). https://doi.org/10.1007/978-3-7091-6453-2_26
25. Mustafa, A., Hilton, A.: Semantically coherent co-segmentation and reconstruction of dynamic scenes. In: CVPR (2017)
26. Mustafa, A., Kim, H., Hilton, A.: 4D match trees for non-rigid surface alignment. In: Leibe, B., Matas, J., Sebe, N., Welling, M. (eds.) ECCV 2016. LNCS, vol. 9905, pp. 213–229. Springer, Cham (2016). https://doi.org/10.1007/978-3-319-46448-0_13
27. Mustafa, A., Volino, M., Guillemaut, J., Hilton, A.: 4D temporally coherent light-field video. In: 2017 International Conference on 3D Vision (3DV), pp. 29–37 (2017). https://doi.org/10.1109/3DV.2017.00014

28. Ng, R., Levoy, M., Duval, G., Horowitz, M., Hanrahan, P.: Light field photography with a hand-held plenoptic camera. Computer Science Technical Report CSTR (2005)
29. Nishino, K., Sato, Y., Ikeuchi, K.: Eigen-texture method: appearance compression and synthesis based on a 3D model. IEEE Trans. Pattern Anal. Mach. Intell. **23**(11), 1257–1265 (2001). https://doi.org/10.1109/34.969116
30. Overbeck, R.S., Erickson, D., Evangelakos, D., Pharr, M., Debevec, P.: A system for acquiring, processing, and rendering panoramic light field stills for virtual reality. ACM Trans. Graph. **37**(6), 197:1–197:15 (2018). https://doi.org/10.1145/3272127. 3275031. http://doi.acm.org/10.1145/3272127.3275031
31. Rusu, R.B.: Semantic 3D object maps for everyday manipulation in human living environments. Ph.D. thesis, Computer Science department, Technische Universitaet Muenchen, Germany (2009)
32. Seitz, S., Curless, B., Diebel, J., Scharstein, D., Szeliski, R.: A comparison and evaluation of multi-view stereo reconstruction algorithms. In: CVPR, pp. 519–528 (2006)
33. Srinivasan, P., Tao, M., Ng, R., Ramamoorthi, R.: Oriented light-field windows for scene flow. In: ICCV, December 2015
34. Stanford Graphics Laboratory: The (New) Stanford Light Field Archive (2008). http://lightfield.stanford.edu/
35. Sundaram, N., Brox, T., Keutzer, K.: Dense point trajectories by GPU-accelerated large displacement optical flow. In: Daniilidis, K., Maragos, P., Paragios, N. (eds.) ECCV 2010. LNCS, vol. 6311, pp. 438–451. Springer, Heidelberg (2010). https:// doi.org/10.1007/978-3-642-15549-9_32
36. Tao, M.W., Bai, J., Kohli, P., Paris, S.: SimpleFlow: a non-iterative, sublinear optical flow algorithm. In: Computer Graphics Forum (Eurographics 2012), vol. 31, no. 2, May 2012. http://graphics.berkeley.edu/papers/Tao-SAN-2012-05/
37. Turk, M., Pentland, A.: Eigenfaces for recognition. J. Cogn. Neurosci. **3**(1), 71–86 (1991). https://doi.org/10.1162/jocn.1991.3.1.71. http://dx.doi.org/10.1162/jocn. 1991.3.1.71
38. Viola, I., Řeřábek, M., Ebrahimi, T.: Comparison and evaluation of light field image coding approaches. IEEE J. Sel. Top. Sign. Process. **11**(7), 1092–1106 (2017). https://doi.org/10.1109/JSTSP.2017.2740167
39. Volino, M., Mustafa, A., Guillemaut, J.Y., Hilton, A.: Light field compression using eigen textures. In: International Conference on 3D Vision (3DV) (2019)
40. Wang, Z., Bovik, A., Sheikh, H., Simoncelli, E.: Image quality assessment: from error visibility to structural similarity. IEEE Trans. Image Process. **13**(4), 600–612 (2004). https://doi.org/10.1109/TIP.2003.819861. http://www.ncbi.nlm.nih. gov/pubmed/15376593. http://ieeexplore.ieee.org/document/1284395/
41. Wanner, S., Goldluecke, B.: Globally consistent depth labeling of 4D light fields. In: CVPR, pp. 41–48, June 2012
42. Wedel, A., Brox, T., Vaudrey, T., Rabe, C., Franke, U., Cremers, D.: Stereoscopic scene flow computation for 3D motion understanding. IJCV **95**, 29–51 (2011)
43. Weinzaepfel, P., Revaud, J., Harchaoui, Z., Schmid, C.: DeepFlow: large displacement optical flow with deep matching. In: ICCV, pp. 1385–1392 (2013)

44. Wilburn, B., et al.: High performance imaging using large camera arrays. ACM Trans. Graph. **24**(3), 765–776 (2005). https://doi.org/10.1145/1073204.1073259. http://doi.acm.org/10.1145/1073204.1073259

45. Wood, D.N., et al.: Surface light fields for 3D photography. In: Proceedings of the 27th Annual Conference on Computer Graphics and Interactive Techniques, pp. 287–296 (2000). https://doi.org/10.1145/344779.344925. http://doi.acm.org/10.1145/344779.344925

46. Wu, C.: Towards linear-time incremental structure from motion. In: Proceedings - 2013 International Conference on 3D Vision (3DV 2013), pp. 127–134 (2013). https://doi.org/10.1109/3DV.2013.25

47. Yücer, K., Sorkine-Hornung, A., Wang, O., Sorkine-Hornung, O.: Efficient 3D object segmentation from densely sampled light fields with applications to 3D reconstruction. ACM Trans. Graph. **35**(3), 22:1–22:15 (2016). https://doi.org/10.1145/2876504. http://doi.acm.org/10.1145/2876504

48. Zanfir, A., Sminchisescu, C.: Large displacement 3D scene flow with occlusion reasoning. In: ICCV (2015)

49. Zheng, E., Ji, D., Dunn, E., Frahm, J.M.: Sparse dynamic 3D reconstruction from unsynchronized videos. In: ICCV (2015)

Reconstruction and Representation

Densely-Sampled Light Field Reconstruction

Suren Vagharshakyan⬤, Robert Bregovic⬤, and Atanas Gotchev$^{(\boxtimes)}$⬤

Tampere University, Tampere, Finland
{suren.vagharshakyan,robert.bregovic,atanas.gotchev}@tuni.fi

Abstract. In this chapter, we motivate the use of densely-sampled light fields as the representation which can bring the required density of light rays for the correct recreation of 3D visual cues such as focus and continuous parallax and can serve as an intermediary between light field sensing and light field display. We consider the problem of reconstructing such a representation from few camera views and approach it in a sparsification framework. More specifically, we demonstrate that the light field is well structured in the set of so-called epipolar images and can be sparsely represented by a dictionary of directional and multi-scale atoms called shearlets. We present the corresponding regularization method, along with its main algorithm and speed-accelerating modifications. Finally, we illustrate its applicability for the cases of holographic stereograms and light field compression.

Keywords: Light field · Sparsification · Shearlet transform

1 Introduction

Human observers interact with the visual world through light. It is light what is sensed by photoreceptors and converted into neural impulses to be further processed by the brain. A number of visual cues, such as stereopsis, focus, motion, and head parallax help the human to perceive, understand, and navigate through the three-dimensional world. These cues all depend on the way how light is presented and sensed. And it is light what contemporary displays emit in their attempt to recreate the visual world. The aim in designing 3D displays, such as multi-view, light field, holographic, or head-mounted has been to generate visual cues as realistically as possible. Generally speaking, this is achievable by generating and controlling a high amount of directional light rays to meet the visual acuity of the human visual system. This brings the question how to formalize and represent light in such a way so to effectively drive 3D displays and how to sense visual scenes in order to generate that display-driven representation.

In this book chapter, we advocate the use of densely-sampled light field: an over-complete, yet discrete representation of light in terms of ray optics. The densely-sampled light field can play the role of intermediary between the light as captured by (multiple) cameras and light as recreated by 3D displays. It comes

© Springer Nature Switzerland AG 2020
M. Magnor and A. Sorkine-Hornung (Eds.): Real VR, LNCS 11900, pp. 67–95, 2020.
https://doi.org/10.1007/978-3-030-41816-8_3

within the framework of the plenoptic function, and as a result of a particular effective light field parameterization. Therefore, in Sect. 2, we overview the mathematical formalization of the plenoptic function, and its various aspects of parameterization, approximation and sampling. By discussing the spectral support of 4D light field in different cases, we come up with the corresponding sampling conditions. We overview also recent methods for spatial and angular light field reconstruction which employ various approaches: from depth estimation, through machine learning to sparsity.

Section 3 presents our take on the problem of densely-sampled light field reconstruction. We motivate a sparsification-based approach and discuss the corresponding transform and regularization method. At the end, we present a few applications to illustrate the applicability and performance of the proposed method.

The presented chapter originates from a doctoral thesis with the same title [56].

2   Basics of Light Field Processing

2.1   Light Field Modeling and Parameterization

Plenoptic function, as a concept to describe the space of all possible light rays, was first presented by Adelson and Bergen in [1]. The idea arose from observation that information about the scene can be modeled as a dense array of light rays of various intensities. Plenoptic function was introduced as tool for efficient mathematical parameterization of light. In such setup, all light rays are parameterized by their location (V_x, V_y, V_z) and direction (θ, ϕ). By adding wavelength λ and time instance t, the $7D$ plenoptic function describing light intensity in a given space is defined in the form

$$P = P(V_x, V_y, V_z, \theta, \phi, \lambda, t).$$

This function can be simplified, as shown by McMillan and Bishop in [45], by considering still light field (fixing time) and replacing the continuous intensity (wavelength) by one of the primary colors (RGB representation). Moreover, in practice we tend to discretize positions and angles, which in turn, results in a discrete 5D light field function.

Two Plane Parameterization. Levoy and Hanrahan remarked in [41], that the aforementioned 5D light field function can be further reduced to only 4 dimensions assuming that the medium through which light rays propagate is completely transparent. In this case the ray intensity is constant and a ray can be simply parameterized using corresponding intersection points with two planes – see Fig. 1(a) for illustration. This is referred to as *two-plane parameterization* $L(s, t, u, v)$ with the (s, t) and the (u, v) plane being also referred to as the camera and the image plane, respectively.

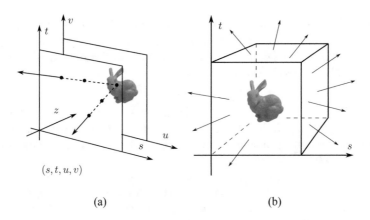

(a)   (b)

Fig. 1. (a) Two-plane parametrization, where an arbitrary ray is parameterized using intersection points with two parallel planes. (b) Light radiance information described by considering radiance over the rays intersecting the sides of a cube.

A special case of the two-plane parameterization is the so called Lumigraph presented by Gortler *et al.* in [24]. Lumigraph enables a convenient description for scene or object that is placed inside a virtual cube. Each of the six cube faces is parameterized using a two-plane parameterization with the planes themselves being the sides of the cube as illustrated in Fig. 1(b). Therefore, having 4D Lumigraph description of a scene, an arbitrary view can be formed by selecting required samples directly from the Lumigraph thereby avoiding complex calculations.

The two-plane parameterization is a simple and efficient tool especially useful in the problems of analysis and synthesis of arbitrary views (continuous light field) from a given discrete light field. This is achieved by first considering discrete subdivision in each of the s, t, u, v dimensions and, second, associating each discrete sample (i, j, p, q) to coefficient $x_{i,j,p,q}$ with reconstruction kernel $B_{i,j,p,q}(s, t, u, v)$. Consequently, the reconstructed continuous light field $\tilde{L}$ is obtained as follows

$$\tilde{L}(s, t, u, v) = \sum_i \sum_j \sum_p \sum_q x_{i,j,p,q} B_{i,j,p,q}(s, t, u, v).$$

A comparison of the reconstruction quality for different basis functions B has been performed in [24]. It has been shown that the use of a quadralinear kernel is beneficial in terms of computational efficiency vs. quality due to the lack of band-limited property of light field functions.

The two-plane parameterization is a convenient way to efficiently represent a light field acquired with an array of cameras. Examples of such an acquisition system are presented in [60], where a single camera moves on a plane using gantry and in [61], where instead of a gantry an array of cameras is used. Recently, a light field camera (plenoptic camera) capturing system has been introduced in [21,46].

The main difference of the light field camera with respect to the conventional camera is the additional layer of microlens array in front of the sensor. Obtained data from a light field camera can be interpreted as uniformly sampled two-plane parameterized light field over a small baseline.

Epipolar Plane Images. Epipolar constraint term originates from the analysis of stereo images [27]. It has been shown, that the two dimensional search of matching features in an image stereo pair can be reduced to one dimension, if camera locations are available.

In [6] epipolar constraint is generalized for the case of a light field captured by a dense set of cameras that are strictly over a straight-line (t constant). Such special case of the light field is also referred to as a horizontal parallax only light field. Stacking those images into a cube (s, u, v) and slicing the cube along u, the obtained 2D image (s, v) is a so-called epipolar-plane image (EPI). Independent analysis/processing performed on each EPI can be combined into a three-dimensional representation of the whole scene. More details covering the definition and morphological properties of EPI are presented in Sect. 3.

Alternative Parametrizations. The considered specific visual acquisition system usually motivates the introduction of new parameterizations of the light field function. Beside the two-plane parameterization, two notable examples are the spherical and cylindrical parameterizations that are introduced for efficient parameterization of multiple captured images from the same location.

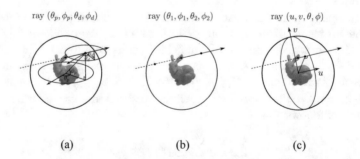

ray $(\theta_p, \phi_p, \theta_d, \phi_d)$ ray $(\theta_1, \phi_1, \theta_2, \phi_2)$ ray (u, v, θ, ϕ)

(a)   (b)   (c)

Fig. 2. Identical ray in different spherical light field parameterizations.

In the concentric mosaic (cylindrical parameterization), introduced by He and Shum in [52], each ray is described by only three parameters: radius, rotation angle, and vertical elevation, thereby reducing the plenoptic function to three dimensions. The acquisition system consists of a camera moving over planar concentric circles. Similar to view synthesis in case of panoramic images, novel views are rendered by combining the appropriate captured rays. Novel view synthesis works only when the corresponding viewpoint is located inside the planar circular region with the reconstruction quality increasing with the number of concentric circles.

Similar to the Lumigraph, spherical parameterizations assume a finite size scene, such that a unit sphere encapsulates the whole scene. As shown by Ihm *et al.* in [31], in a spherical parameterization the position of the light ray emanated from a scene is parameterized using an intersection point on the positional sphere (θ_p, ϕ_p) used as a convex hull of the scene and the direction of the ray is identified by the intersection point with the directional sphere (θ_d, ϕ_d). This is illustrated in Fig. 2(a). Thus, the two-sphere or spherical 4D light field parameterization is defined as $L^{\mathrm{sphere}}(\theta_p, \phi_p, \theta_d, \phi_d)$ function.

Alternative sphere-sphere parameterization (2SP) and sphere-plane parameterization (SPP) are presented in [10]. In 2SP parameterization each light ray is parameterized by its two intersection points with the same sphere, as illustrated in Fig. 2(b). In SPP parameterization, light ray is parameterized by its angle and 2D coordinate of the intersection point of the ray and orthogonal plane, as illustrated in Fig. 2(c).

The spherical LF parameterizations are easily applicable to synthetic data, though, they can also be used when recording real scenes, one example of a sensing setup being the Stanford spherical gantry [41]. More recently Overbeck *et al.* in [47] also presented a spherical LF capturing system. In the proposed new capturing system, two cameras are rotated over the sphere surface in the space, which allows capturing spherical LF of the outside environment. Captured LF data provides information required to generate novel views located within the recorded spherical volume.

2.2 Light Field Sampling and Reconstruction

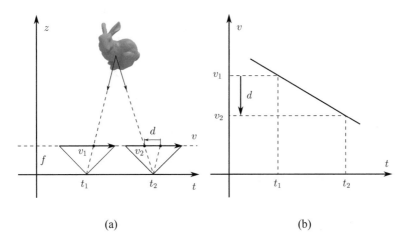

(a)   (b)

Fig. 3. (a) Two plane parameterization of a light field for fixed values of s and u axis. (b) Radiance of a 3D point observed from different position of camera.

The two-plane parameterization is instrumental when defining light field sampling. Consider the camera plane (s, t) and the image plane (u, v), as illustrated in Fig. 3(a). For the purpose of sampling, it is suitable to define the (u, v) plane relatively to (s, t) coordinates [16]. A discrete uniform grid is considered on the camera plane (s, t), where each point on the grid represents a pin-hole camera location. Pixels corresponding to the camera form a uniform grid on the image plane (u, v). Each pixel value is formed by the weighted sum of the light radiance arriving at a certain angle to the camera plane. Thus, an arbitrary ray intersecting both planes uniquely determines the quadruple $q = (u, v, s, t)$.

A simplified spectral analysis of the 4D LF function can be carried out if assuming occlusion-free scenes with Lambertian reflectance. The former assumption implies that the same 3D point can be observed from any location of the camera plane and the latter implies that the radiance of a point is constant in all directions. Then, the observed 4D LF function has a distinct form, which can be easily explained using the EPI notion. Recall that EPI is formed by fixing the parameters s, u and varying parameters t, v for the LF function, such as $E_{(s,u)}(t, v) = L(u, v, s, t)$ is conventionally called horizontal EPI. Identically, vertical EPI is defined as $E_{(v,u)}(t, v) = L(u, v, s, t)$. Formation of an epipolar line on EPI slice is exemplified in Fig. 3. In EPI, any scene point is represented by a corresponding line with an intensity proportional to the light radiance from the point in different directions. For Lambertian scenes, this line has constant intensity. The disparity d between two images located at (s, t_1) and (s, t_2) of the same observed 3D point is

$$d = v_2 - v_1 = (t_1 - t_2)f/z,$$

where $z = z(q)$ represents the scene depth, i.e. the distance of the surface point corresponding to the ray q from the camera plane.

Assuming $t_1 = 0$ to be the origin of the axis t,

$$L(q) = L\left(u + \frac{f}{z(q)}s, v + \frac{f}{z(q)}t, 0, 0\right).$$

For a simplified case of constant-depth plane $z(q) = z_0$, it can be shown that:

$$\hat{L}(\Omega_u, \Omega_v, \Omega_s, \Omega_t) = 4\pi^2 \hat{L}'(\Omega_u, \Omega_v)\delta(\Omega_s - f\Omega_u/z_0)\delta(\Omega_t - f\Omega_v/z_0), \quad (1)$$

where $\hat{L}'(\Omega_u, \Omega_v)$ is the Fourier transform of $L'(u, v) = L(u, v, 0, 0)$ and δ is the Dirac delta function. Thus, for the constant-depth plane scene, the support of the 4D function $\hat{L}$ on the 2D plane (Ω_v, Ω_t) is bounded by the line $\Omega_t = \Omega_v f/z_0$, as shown in Fig. 4(a). The same is true for (Ω_u, Ω_s) plane and the corresponding line $\Omega_s = \Omega_u f/z_0$.

Assume an uniform 4D lattice $\Delta q = (\Delta u, \Delta v, \Delta s, \Delta t)$, and a sampling function $p(q) = \text{III}_{\Delta q}(q)$, where $\text{III}_T(t)$ is the Dirac comb function, [44], and $L_s(q) = L(q)p(q)$.

The Fourier transform of the sampled LF L_s at angular frequency $\Omega_q = (\Omega_u, \Omega_v, \Omega_s, \Omega_t)$ is

$$\hat{L}_s(\Omega_q) = \hat{L}(\Omega_q) * \text{III}_{2\pi/\Delta q}(\Omega_q).$$

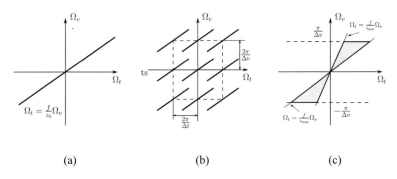

(a)   (b)   (c)

Fig. 4. The Fourier transform support on (Ω_t, Ω_v) plane, (a) continuous light field with a constant depth, (b) sampled light field with a constant depth, (c) depth varies between $z_{\min}$ and $z_{\max}$.

The convolution with the Dirac comb function implies that $\hat{L}_s$ consists of periodical replicas of L at a 4D uniform lattice defined as

$$\left\{ \frac{2\pi}{\Delta u}m_1, \frac{2\pi}{\Delta v}m_2, \frac{2\pi}{\Delta s}l_1, \frac{2\pi}{\Delta t}l_2 \right\}_{m_1,m_2,l_1,l_2 \in \mathbb{Z}}$$

as illustrated in Fig. 4(b) for the case of constant depth.

For the case of multiple depth planes, instead of single line, there will be multiple lines on the Fourier plane. It has been proved that all of them are confined between the lines $\Omega_t = f\Omega_v/z_{\max}$, $\Omega_t = f\Omega_v/z_{\min}$ corresponding to the minimum and maximum depth $[z_{\min}, z_{\max}]$, c.f. Fig. 4(c) [16]. This bow-tie support shape forms the baseband of the light field. Its periodical replicas would be generated during sampling and have to be filtered out during reconstruction. To avoid aliasing, the sampling intervals have to be chosen with respect to the min and max depth of the scene. This is specifically important for the distances between cameras on the camera plane, i.e. along the t and s axes. It has be shown that

$$\Delta t_{\max} = \frac{1}{K_{f_v} f \left(z_{\min}^{-1} - z_{\max}^{-1} \right)},$$

where $K_{f_v} = \min \left(B_v^s, 1/(2\Delta v), 1/(2\delta v) \right)$ is the maximum frequency in axis Ω_v. K_{f_v} depends on the complexity of texture information represented with the highest scene texture frequency B_v^s and on the rendering camera resolution δv. If textural complexity is ignored and full resolution images are rendered then the maximal frequency is $K_{f_v} = 1/(2\Delta v)$ [16].

Figure 5 illustrates cases of different reconstruction filters [16]. Figure 5(a) presents direct interpolation when the constant-depth plane is at the infinity. Figure 5(b) depicts an optimal filter support of a constant-depth plane rendering at z_{opt}, where $z_{opt}^{-1} = (z_{min}^{-1} + z_{max}^{-1})/2$. For the case of the optimal filter, camera spacing can be increased such that replicas are placed compactly as shown in Fig. 5(c).

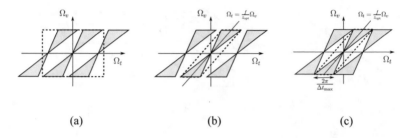

(a)   (b)   (c)

Fig. 5. (a) Direct reconstruction filter with implicit assumption of infinite depth. (b) Filtering using z_{opt}. (c) Optimal packing in frequency domain is achieved in case of critical camera spacing distance Δt_{max}.

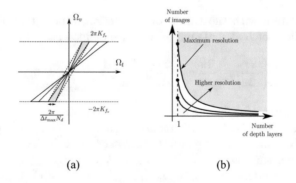

(a)   (b)

Fig. 6. (a) Uniform multi-layer depth decomposition represented in the frequency domain. (b) Minimum sampling curve for different rendering resolutions. Any point in the highlighted region represents redundancy for rendering in joint image and geometric space.

Further optimization of the sampling rate and corresponding reconstruction filters can be achieved by considering depth layering. Narrower bands corresponding to dominant depth layers can be specified and then each depth layer can be processed by the corresponding optimal filter, as illustrated in Fig. 6(a). Thus, for N_d number of layers, the minimum sampling rate is decreased and corresponding maximum distance of camera spacing is increased $\Delta t_{max,N_d} = \Delta t_{max} N_d$.

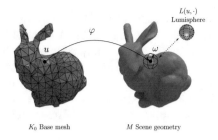

$L(u, \cdot)$
Lumisphere

φ

u

ω

K_0 Base mesh M Scene geometry

Fig. 7. Surface light field as presented in [62].

The fundamental relation between the number of depth layers N_d and the number of camera images N_i has been derived in [16] in the form $N_d\sqrt{N_i} = K_{f_v}$, resulting in the so-called *optimal sampling curve*, c.f. Fig. 6(b). The curve particularly suggests that the number of required images in classical plenoptic sampling is still high and more advanced methods are required for achieving similar reconstruction quality with smaller number of images.

More recent works have addressed the problem of the high number of images needed for LF sampling and reconstruction. Alternatively to depth layering, the concept of surface light field has been proposed in [62]. The approach makes a connection between surface geometric modeling and the corresponding radiated light field. A scene surface is modeled by a simplified base mesh K_0, which is projected onto the more complex geometric surface M (Fig. 7). The latter gives rise to a surface light field $L(u, \omega)$, which represents the radiance of a light ray in direction ω at a point u on K_0. $L(u, \omega)$ is considered piecewise-linear and composed of LF primitives, called *lumispheres*, parameterized by the ray direction ω. Lumispheres are recovered from given images by least-squares approximation. The model is applicable to non-Lambertian scenes with complex radiance functions, however the reconstruction quality heavily depends on the accuracy of the approximated scene geometry.

The relation between the two-plane parameterized light field and surface light field along with the corresponding spectral analysis has been developed in [15]. In summary, the work has aimed at approximating the non-bandlimited Fourier transform of the surface light field and at modeling occlusions in the spectral domain. Further, more accurate LF bandwidth estimations have been developed for the cases of essential bandwidth [18], finite field of view [23] and finite scene width [22].

2.3   General Methods for Light Field Reconstruction

In this section, we present an overview of recent approaches and methods which deal with light field reconstruction. The majority of methods uses depth in one or another form and therefore the accurate depth estimation from light field is also discussed. More recent methods employ also modern machine learning approaches. Continuous light field reconstruction through sparsification is discussed as well.

Depth Based Methods. Wanner *et al.* [58] have proposed a method for disparity estimation directly from the light field. A structure tensor is applied on epipolar plane images for fast local disparity estimation. Then, globally consistent disparity maps with sub-pixel precision are obtained from local estimates through convex regularization. They are used in a variational inverse problem aimed at spatial and angular super-resolution. The method has been developed for processing data from plenoptic cameras, therefore relatively small disparity range has been considered.

Conventional disparity estimation methods employ a three-step framework comprising cost volume construction based on hypotheses, cost volume filtering (i.e. regularization using aggregation in the spatial domain), and label selection (i.e. selection of most probable hypothesis, typically winner-takes-all) [30]. A similar framework has been used in [32] for an accurate disparity estimation from light fields acquired by plenoptic cameras (i.e. relatively small disparity range between sub-aperture images). To handle such data, an accurate sub-pixel displacement algorithm using 2D Fourier transform for the cost volume construction. Suitable depth hypothesis layers are formed and used to find per-pixel disparities. The latter are enhanced through a discrete multi-label optimization based on graph cuts and iterative quadratic fitting. The final disparity map is with sub-pixel precision and can be used for LF angular or spatial super-resolution.

Alternative methods for disparity estimation from plenoptic data have been presented in [53, 65].

The case of wide field of view horizontal parallax LF capture has been addressed in [34]. Conventional disparity estimation methods are inefficient for the high amount of data in such imagery. Therefore, the proposed technique utilizes a fine-to-coarse refinement technique with the aim to obtain accurate disparity maps from sufficiently densely sampled light fields and avoid explicit global regularization. A novel sparse representation for a set of adjacent EPIs has been presented, comprising a set of distinct lines, obtained by considering densely sampled LF. This representation is obtained at edges on the high-resolution image first and then further proceeded to successive coarse EPI resolutions to obtain disparity estimation on smooth spatial areas, where edges are not well-defined. The proposed technique implies EPI constraints between images and is especially efficient for processing high spatio-angular LF datasets.

Machine Learning Methods. The machine learning instrumentation has proven quite effective for solving the problem of light field reconstruction. Kalantari *et al.* [33] have proposed a learning-based approach aimed at synthesizing intermediate views from sub-sampled plenoptic images, e.g. such captured by the Lytro Illum camera. The work utilizes two neural networks: one for disparity estimation and another for view synthesis using the estimated disparity. Both networks have been trained simultaneously by minimizing the error between synthesized and ground truth views. The disparity-estimating CNN, which consists of four convolution layers with decreasing kernel sizes followed by a rectified linear unit, has generated high quality disparity maps. Even though, a subsequent color prediction CNN is required to model the complex relationship between the final image and warped images around occlusions. The method has demonstrated superior results when compared with [32,58], especially around occlusion boundaries.

In [64], the LF angular super-resolution has been formulated as a problem of EPI high-frequency details reconstruction. The given low resolution EPI is considered as a subsampled version of the densely sampled EPI. The former undergoes a convolution with a smoothing kernel (e.g. Gaussian kernel) with the aim to extract low-frequency features. The result is processed by a CNN, which acts as a high-frequency reconstruction operator. It is designed as a residual neural network with three convolution layers with decreasing kernel sizes together with a rectified linear unit. This network is used only to predict angular domain detail information from blurred and upsampled EPI. Further, the spatial detail of the EPI is recovered through a non-blind deblur operation based on the method from [35]. The whole densely sampled light field is reconstructed by applying the proposed "blur - restoration - deblur" framework for every EPI in both horizontal and vertical directions.

The so-proposed method has demonstrated good reconstruction results for up to 5 pixels disparity between adjacent views. For higher disparities, the deblurring kernel has proven inefficient. This limitation has been addressed in [63] by proposing a depth-assisted rendering technique for multiview imagery with large disparity range [57]. The method uses a roughly discretized disparity map, obtained using the method in [30]. For each discrete disparity region, appropriate shearing is applied on corresponding EPI region, to get a disparity range small enough to be processed by the original "blur - restoration - deblur" method. The final result is formed by blending together multiple super-resolved EPIs regions.

A two-step method for disparity estimation by EPI analysis has been presented in [25]. For a given 4D LF, hyperplane orientations are predicted for the central image using a CNN applied on horizontal and vertical EPIs. The predicted orientations (i.e. disparities) are then refined by a generalized total variation regularization procedure based on the method in [7]. The approach has been improved in [26] by designing a neural network working on 3D subsets of the 4D LF (using 2D spatial and one angular dimension). This allows to effectively suppress artifacts in spatial domain.

An end-to-end neural network architecture for disparity estimation from 4D light field has been proposed in [51]. The input data consists of views containing horizontal, vertical, and two diagonal images in stacks, always containing the central view. The designed network has a multi-stream structure, such that every 1D image stack subset is processed through three convolution layers in order to get sets of features describing the corresponding image stack. The feature sets are concatenated together and processed together by additional convolution layers followed by a rectified linear unit. The work discusses also the optimal number of input views. The proposed method has demonstrated high-quality results for the HCI 4D Light Field Benchmark [29].

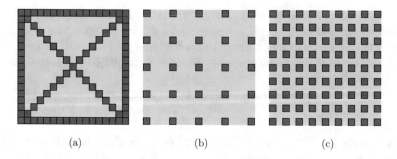

(a)   (b)   (c)

Fig. 8. Sampling pattern where every rectangle represents one view from a LF consisting of 17×17 views. (a) box and two diagonals pattern consisting of 93 views used for method [50]. (b), (c) uniformly decimated setup consisting of 5×5 and 9×9 views respectively.

Extraction of non-Lambertian scene properties from LF has been attempted in [4]. The authors have proposed an encoder-decoder network aimed at decomposing the LF data into disparity, diffuse and specular components. The encoder part reduced the multidimensional structure of the light field. Further, multiple decoders extract the targeted intrinsic components. The encoder is applied on each epipolar-plane independently. It contains 18 residual blocks, which are gradually decreasing the input epipolar volume to in spatial domain and increasing its feature domain. The encoder features are further processed by the multiple decoder pathways. The auto-encoder path reconstructs the original input data, while the three other decoders generate disparity, diffuse, and specular components, respectively. All decoders are constructed of residual blocks with transpose convolution layers. A dichromatic reflection model is considered, such that the final radiance is formed by the sum of the diffusion and specular information.

Light Field Reconstruction by Sparsification in Fourier Domain. Shi *et al.* [50] have proposed to cast the LF reconstruction as a problem of sparsification in a transform domain. The authors have motivated the choice to seek LF sparsity in continuous Fourier domain rather than in discrete Fourier domain.

A signal of length N is k-sparse in the continuous Fourier domain, if it can be represented as a combination of $k < N$ frequencies, not necessarily located at integer coordinates (hence, continuous). Therefore, the signal reconstruction requires estimating both the frequencies and the corresponding transform coefficients. Consider the reconstruction of a two dimensional signal $\{x[u, v], \forall u, v = 0, \ldots, N - 1\}$ from a set of measurements $x_S = \{x[u, v], \forall (u, v) \in S\}$. The sparsifying solution is obtained by solving the following minimization problem

$$\underset{a_l, \omega_{u_l}, \omega_{v_l}}{\arg \min} \sum_{(u,v) \in S} \left\| x(u, v) - \frac{1}{N} \sum_{l=0}^{k} a_l \exp\left(2\pi i \frac{u\omega_{u_l} + v\omega_{v_l}}{N} \right) \right\|_2^2$$

which can be represented more compactly in matrix form

$$\arg\min_{a,\omega} \|x_S - A_\omega a\|_2^2,$$

where $a = \{a_l\}_{l=0}^k, \omega = \{(\omega_{u_l}, \omega_{v_l})\}_{l=0}^k$.

The problem is solved by alternating minimization: for fixed k frequency locations ω, the corresponding optimal coefficients a are estimated as $a = A_\omega^\dagger x_S$, while the optimal frequency locations ω are found by

$$\omega^* = \arg\min_\omega \|x_s - A_\omega A_\omega^\dagger x_S\|_2^2.$$

The functional is minimized by gradient descent, where the gradient is approximated by evaluating the error function over 8 directions around every frequency position and updating it in most descending direction.

In [50], the sampling set S is composed from a set of 1D discrete sampling lines. These lines are used in a voting scheme based on the Fourier slice theorem aimed at obtaining reliable initial estimates for the frequency positions.

Using the proposed sparsification method, the 4D light field $L(x, y, u, v)$ is reconstructed at all angular locations (u, v) from the given sampling set S, illustrated by the red squares in Fig. 8, by independently reconstructing each $\hat{L}_{\omega_x, \omega_y}(u, v)$ 2D slice for fixed spatial frequencies.

The proposed method has shown prominent reconstruction quality especially for light fields representing non-Lambertian scenes.

3   Light Field Reconstruction Trough Sparse Modelling

3.1   Problem Formulation

Densely sampled light field (DSLF) refers to a regular light field representation consisting of parallax camera views, where the maximum disparity between adjacent views is one pixel at most. This is an attractive representation since it allows generating arbitrary rays by simple (quad-)linear interpolation [43].

Direct capture of a DSLF over a large baseline at full parallax requires a high number of densely positioned cameras. Such setting is inefficient and in many cases unfeasible. In reality, light fields have been captured by an array of cameras, either unstructured or uniformly located on a line or 2D grid. The lack of proper physical setting for DSLF capture sets the fundamental problem of reconstructing, computationally, the densely sampled LF from multiperspective images, considered as LF samples on coarser grids. For the sake of simplicity, these grids are usually assumed regular, which reflects the case of horizontally and vertically aligned (rectified) cameras. As discussed in the previous section, rectified views when put together, form LF slices referred to as EPIs, which implicitly represent the scene geometry.

Hereafter, we set the DSLF reconstruction problem as problem of reconstructing densely sampled EPI (DSEPI) from decimated (in angular dimension or in camera plane) LF samples. The concept of densely sampled EPI is inspired by [43], where the limit of necessary sampling in angular dimension is formulated in terms of depth.

For the sake of simplicity, in most derivations, we consider the horizontal parallax case, where EPIs are formed after stacking all images together and taking 2D slices along the horizontal and camera motion dimensions for a fixed vertical coordinate. Rows in a particular EPI represent horizontal lines from different perspective views. While put in the context of DSEPI, these rows are separated by blank areas of the missing intermediate views. An illustration of this sampling is presented in Fig. 10(a), (c). Reconstructing DSEPIs for all vertical coordinates gives the fully-reconstructed DSLF.

We formulate the problem of DSEPI reconstruction in terms of signal reconstruction with sparsity constrains. More specifically, we consider the reconstruction in some suitable transform domain, where the LF is sparse. Based on the structural properties of DSEPI, we adopt shearlet frames as the sparsification transform employing their directional sensitivity properties and present the main reconstruction method and its accelerations. While it is initially formulated to handle coarse sampling in angular domain, the approach is flexible enough to address also the problem of LF super-resolution in spatial domain.

3.2   Sparse Representation

Various image processing problems, such as denoising, deblurring, inpainting, and super-resolution can be formalized by a system of linear equations

$$y = Ax + \epsilon, \tag{2}$$

where A is the process, modeled in some metric space, which acts on the input (unknown) image x resulting in the available (distorted, undersampled, blurred) image y, additionally contaminated by noise ϵ. The latter is usually modeled as an independent and identically distributed Gaussian with zero mean and standard deviation σ, i.e. $(\epsilon \sim \mathcal{N}(0, \sigma^2 I))$.

The corresponding inverse problem of finding x can be formulated in least squares (LS) sense

$$\bar{x} = \arg\min_x \|y - Ax\|_2^2 .$$

Typical image processing problems result in an undetermined system of linear equations, which implies an infinite set of solutions for x satisfying $\|y - Ax\|_2^2 = 0$. Such cases are considered ill-posed and require additional regularization to determine the desirable solution. In the general case, a minimization of a cost function, composed of a fidelity term f and a penalty (regularization) term s is attempted:

$$\arg\min_x f(x) + \lambda s(x). \tag{3}$$

The fidelity term $f(x)$ ensures the consistency between the solution and the measurements. The penalty term or regularizer $s(x)$ guarantees the prior model of the signal. In line with the least squares formulation, the fidelity term can be defined as $f(x) = \frac{1}{2\sigma^2}\|y - Ax\|_2^2$. In order to solve Eq. 3 given the model Eq. 2, state of the art approaches have been employing the Alternating Direction Method of Multipliers (ADMM) [59]. A more recent version, referred to as Plug-and-Play (P&P ADMM) has proposed to avoid explicitly presenting s by introducing a regularization procedure in the form of denoising thresholding [17].

Consider a dictionary given by a matrix D, the sparse representation of a signal x refers to the coefficients α, such that

$$\arg\min \|\alpha\|_0, \text{ subject to } x = D\alpha, \tag{4}$$

where $\|\alpha\|_0 = \#(\alpha_k \neq 0)$ denotes the pseudo-norm l_0 which equals the number of non-zero coefficients. The entries of the matrix D can be the analysis functions of a fixed transform $D = \{\phi_n\}_{n \in \Gamma}$, such that $(Dx)[n] = \langle \phi_n, x \rangle$. Finding the sparse representation is an NP-Hard problem. A sufficiently sparse α can be found by replacing the l_0 pseudo-norm with the l_1 norm, leading to what is known as Basis Pursuit (BP) algorithm [11]

$$\min_\alpha \|\alpha\|_1, \text{ subject to } x = D\alpha. \tag{5}$$

It has been proved that the problems 4 and 5 are equivalent in the case of *sufficient sparsity* quantified as

$$\|x\|_0 < \frac{1}{2}\left(1 + \frac{1}{\mu(D)}\right),$$

where $\mu(D) = \max_{k \neq l} \frac{\langle \phi_k \phi_l \rangle}{\|\phi_k\|_2 \|\phi_l\|_2}$ represents the *mutual coherence* of the dictionary [12].

The design of the sparsifying dictionary depends on the set of considered signals and the application at hand. For signals representing natural images formed by conventional digital cameras, various dictionaries have been proposed ranging from the widely-used discrete cosine and wavelet transforms to more dedicated, usually directional transforms such as curvelets, ridgelets, bandlets, etc. [44]. Dictionaries can be also learned through approaches such as K-SVD algorithm [2] and sparse coding [38].

Consider a transform in the form of a tight frame, which is a generalization of a basis. The frame is defined by its analysis $\alpha = \Phi x$ and synthesis $x = \Psi\alpha$ transforms, such that in the general case $\Psi\Phi = I$ and $\Phi\Psi \neq I$. The regularization term in the minimizer in Eq. 3 can be formulated in terms of sparse transform coefficients $s(\alpha) = \|\alpha\|_p$, where $p = 0, 1$. The regularization is implemented in the form of a thresholding operator $\mathcal{T}_t(\cdot)$, acting on the transform coefficients and yielding a denoised version of the signal $\mathcal{D}(x, \sigma) = \Psi\mathcal{T}_{t(\sigma)}(\Phi x)$ [44].

Following the approach proposed in [8], the solution can be found by iterations

$$x_{k+1} = \Psi\mathcal{T}_\lambda\Phi(x_k + A(y - x_k)). \tag{6}$$

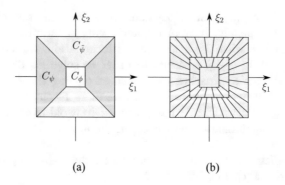

Fig. 9. (a) Outlined regions are corresponding to frequency plane separation for shearlet transform design. Two cone-adapted regions are corresponding to $C_\psi, C_{\tilde{\psi}}$ set of filters and central rectangle region corresponds to C_ϕ low pass filter. (b) Frequency plane tilling obtained by whole shearlet transform using two scales of decomposition $J = 2$.

It has been shown that the convergence of Eq. 6 is equivalent to solving the minimization problem

$$\arg\min_\alpha \frac{1}{2} \|A\Psi\alpha - y\|_2^2 + \frac{\varkappa}{2} \|(I - \Phi\Psi)\alpha\|_2^2 + \lambda \|\alpha\|_1, \tag{7}$$

with $\varkappa = 1$, referred to as balanced approach [8,49]. Its solution has been eventually derived in the following iterative form [9]

$$
\begin{aligned}
a) &\quad x_k = \Psi\alpha_k \\
b) &\quad \eta_k = \Phi\left(x_k + \frac{1}{\varkappa}(y - Ax_k)\right) \\
c) &\quad \omega_{k+1} = \mathcal{T}_{\gamma\lambda}\left(\alpha_k + \gamma\varkappa(\eta_k - \alpha_k)\right)
\end{aligned}
\tag{8}
$$

3.3   Shearlet Frame

Suitable sparsifying dictionaries (transforms) have been studied predominantly for the case of natural images. For such images, dictionaries have been required to optimally approximate curvilinear singularities of the underlying 2D functions. The optimal approximation, in this case, is defined using the decay rate of l_2 error of the best N-term approximation. More specifically, the development of such systems has been specified for *cartoon-like functions* consisting of C^2 functions being compactly supported on the unit square, except for a closed C^2 discontinuity curve. Examples of developed systems include *curvelets* [14], and *contourlets* [19]. What is common for such systems is their ability to handle directional properties in images.

The construction of discrete shearlet frame has followed a similar approach by controlling the orientation of the system's atoms trough a shear operator [36].

It is precisely this property, which makes the shearlet frame particularly interesting for EPI representation, since EPI structure is formed by shearing rather
than rotation or other curve motion. The compactly-supported shearlet system
is of special interest since it contains atoms which are compactly supported in
both spatial and Fourier domains [37]. Though it is not a Parseval frame, it is
still applicable for approximating (sparsifying) *cartoon-like functions*. The theoretical framework of the universal shearlet system has been developed in [20]. It
includes a parameterized systems family, which, for varying parameter value, can
describe the wavelet system, the parabolic shearlet system and the ridgelet system [13]. Departing from the non-separable shearlet transform described in [42],
hereafter we present a modified version, which has been purposefully designed for
efficient representation of functions having singularities along straight lines, in
contract to the image-inspired case of parabolic curves approximated by ridges.

The cone-adapted discrete shearlet system SH is defined as a set of 2D
functions formed by shearing S, translation and parabolic scaling A transforms applied on generator functions: a scaling function ϕ and two shearlets
$\psi, \widetilde{\psi} \in L^2(\mathbb{R}^2)$. For $c = (c_1, c_2) \in \mathbb{R}_+^2$, the system is defined as

$$\text{SH}(\phi, \psi, \widetilde{\psi}; c) = \Phi(\phi; c_1) \cup \Psi(\psi; c) \cup \widetilde{\Psi}(\widetilde{\psi}; c). \tag{9}$$

With reference to Fig. 9(a), the subset $\Psi(\psi; c)$ corresponds to the cone-shaped
region C_ψ, the subset $\widetilde{\Psi}(\widetilde{\psi}; c)$ corresponds to the region $C_{\widetilde{\psi}}$ and $\Phi(\phi; c_1)$ – to
the central part C_ϕ. This division of the frequency plane is achieved using the
following definitions

$$\Phi(\phi; c_1) = \{\phi_m = \phi(\cdot - c_1 m) : m \in \mathbb{Z}^2\}$$

$$\Psi(\psi; c) = \{\psi_{j,k,m} = 2^{3/4j} \psi(S_k A_{2^j} \cdot - M_c m) : j \geq 0, |k| \leq \lceil 2^{j/2} \rceil, m \in \mathbb{Z}^2\}$$

$$\widetilde{\Psi}(\widetilde{\psi}; c) = \{\widetilde{\psi}_{j,k,m} = 2^{3/4j} \widetilde{\psi}(S_k^\mathsf{T} \widetilde{A}_{2^j} \cdot - \widetilde{M}_c m) : j \geq 0, |k| \leq \lceil 2^{j/2} \rceil, m \in \mathbb{Z}^2\}$$

where A and $\widetilde{A}$ are scaling matrices, S_k is a shearing matrix, $M_c = \text{diag}(c_1, c_2)$
and $\widetilde{M}_c = \text{diag}(c_2, c_1)$ are (translation) sampling matrices, as follows

$$A = \begin{pmatrix} 2^j & 0 \\ 0 & 2^{j/2} \end{pmatrix}, \widetilde{A} = \begin{pmatrix} 2^{j/2} & 0 \\ 0 & 2^j \end{pmatrix}, S_k = \begin{pmatrix} 1 & k \\ 0 & 1 \end{pmatrix}.$$

This construction is suitable for images with parabolic singularities. By modifying the scaling matrix to become $A = \text{diag}(2^j, 2^{-1})$, the shearlet system can
be tuned to handle images with line singularities, where the new scaling matrix
would guide the required number of shears in each scale of the frequency plane
tilling.

The above proposed transform is continuous; however, it has to handle discrete signals. A natural assumption to start with is to consider a sufficiently
large $J > 0$, for which a continuous 2D signal function f is represented by the
discrete signal f^d and the scaling function ϕ

$$f(x_1, x_2) = \sum_{(k_1, k_2) \in \mathbb{Z}^2} 2^J f^d[k_1, k_2] \phi(2^J x_1 - k_1, 2^J x_2 - k_2).$$

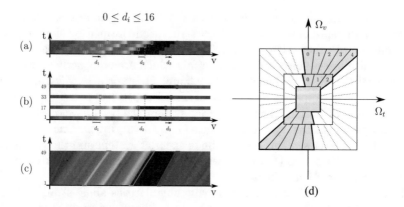

Fig. 10. (a) Subsampled densely sampled epipolar-plane image, assuming that disparities between consecutive rows are no higher than 16 px. (b) Subsampled data can be interpreted as every 16-th row of desirable densely sampled light field. (c) Corresponding densely sampled light field with disparities do not exceeding 1 px. (d) Highlighted shearlet transform atoms used in EPI reconstruction algorithm. Selected atoms correspond to EPI structure. Each disparity layer ($k = 0, 1, ...4$) represented by one transform atom in each scale ($j = 0, 1$).

In a further assumption, $\phi(x_1, x_2) = \phi^1(x_1)\phi^1(x_2)$. Then, the 1D scaling and wavelet functions $\psi^1(x)$, $\phi^1(x)$ are represented by two-scale equations

$$\phi^1(x) = \sum_{k \in \mathbb{Z}} h_k \sqrt{2}\phi^1(2x - k) \quad \text{and} \quad \psi^1(x) = \sum_{k \in \mathbb{Z}} g_k \sqrt{2}\phi^1(2x - k).$$

The coefficients g_k and h_k are Fourier coefficients of the trigonometric polynomial H_j and G_j

$$H_0 \equiv 1, \quad H_j(\xi) = \prod_{i=0}^{j-1} H(2^i \xi), \quad G_j(\xi) = G(2^{j-1}\xi)H_{j-1}(\xi), \quad j = 0, \ldots, J. \quad (10)$$

For better performance, it has been suggested to select a 2D non-separable wavelet function $\psi(x_1, x_2)$ corresponding to the scaling function $\phi(x_1, x_2)$ such as

$$\hat{\psi}(\xi_1, \xi_2) = P(\xi_1/2, \xi_2)\hat{\psi}^1(\xi_1)\hat{\phi}^1(\xi_2),$$

where $P(\xi_1, \xi_2)$ is trigonometric polynomial representing 2D fan filter with wedge-shaped essential support [42]. By appropriate selection of the sampling grid M_c, the coefficients of the shearlet transform corresponding to the system elements $\{\psi_{j,0,m}\}_{m \in \mathbb{Z}^2}$ can be calculated by applying a digital filter $p_j * (g_{J-j} \otimes h_{J-j/2})$ on the discrete signal f^d, where p_j are the Fourier coefficients of a scaled 2D fan filter $P(2^{J-j-1}\xi_1, 2^{J-j/2}\xi_2)$.

A proper discretization of the whole system [42,55] eventually leads to the following digital implementation:

$$\Psi_{j,k}^d = S_{k2-(j+1)}^d \left(p_j * (g_{J-j} \otimes h_{J+1})\right), j = 0, \dots, J-1, |k| \leq 2^j + 1.$$

This set of transform filters corresponds to the cone-shaped region C_ψ of the frequency plane highlighted in Fig. 9(a). The region $C_{\tilde{\psi}}$ is covered by the filters $\hat{\tilde{\psi}}_{j,k}^d(\xi_1, \xi_2) = \hat{\psi}_{j,k}^d(\xi_2, \xi_1)$. The central region C_Φ is dealt with a single filter $\phi^d = h_J \otimes h_J$.

The constructed discrete shearlet system is not orthogonal, therefore dual frame elements are required for the synthesis transform. Using auxiliary notation

$$\hat{\Psi}^d = |\hat{\phi}^d|^2 + \sum_{j=0}^{J-1} \sum_{|k|\leq 2^j+1} \left(|\hat{\psi}_{j,k}^d|^2 + |\hat{\tilde{\psi}}_{j,k}^d|^2 \right)$$

the dual elements are defined as follows

$$\hat{\varphi}^d = \frac{\hat{\phi}^d}{\hat{\Psi}^d}, \quad \hat{\gamma}_{j,k}^d = \frac{\hat{\psi}_{j,k}^d}{\hat{\Psi}^d}, \quad \hat{\tilde{\gamma}}_{j,k}^d = \frac{\hat{\tilde{\psi}}_{j,k}^d}{\hat{\Psi}^d}.$$

Finally, the analysis operator corresponding to the construction shearlet frame is given by

$$S(f_J^d) = \left\{ s_{j,k} = f_J^d * \bar{\psi}_{j,k}^d, \tilde{s}_{j,k} = f_J^d * \bar{\tilde{\psi}}_{j,k}^d, s_0 = f_J^d * \bar{\phi}^d \right\}$$

and the synthesis operator uses the dual elements

$$S^* \left(\{s_{j,k}, s_0\}\right) = \sum_{j=0}^{J-1} \sum_{|k|\leq 2^j+1} \left(s_{j,k} * \gamma_{j,k}^d + \tilde{s}_{j,k} * \tilde{\gamma}_{j,k}^d \right) + s_0 * \phi^d.$$

3.4   Epipolar-Plane Image Reconstruction

Main Method. The epipolar-plane image reconstruction can be formulated as a sparse regularization problem utilizing the shearlet frame [55]. The input signal is a subsampled EPI y with respect to the desired DSEPI x: $y = Mx$, where M is the masking or subsampling matrix. The input EPI has disparities between adjacent views in the range $[d_{\min}, d_{\max}]$ pixels. A pre-shearing operation is applied to guarantee positive disparities $[0, d_{\text{range}}]$, with $d_{\text{range}} = d_{\max} - d_{\min}$. The subsampled EPI is organized to get the size of the target DSEPI, i.e. the k-th row (view) takes kd_{range}-th row of the densely sampled epipolar-plane image. This organization enforces the densely sampled condition, where the disparities are in the range $[0, 1]$ px. An example of desirable densely sampled EPI is given in Fig. 10(c) where every 16-th row corresponds to the properly-relocated rows in the input EPI at Fig. 10(a).

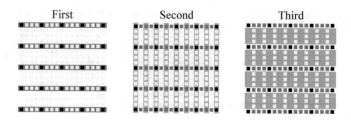

Fig. 11. Proposed fast processing order illustrated for 17×17 array of images. Reconstruction is divided into three steps (blue, orange, green) to decrease the disparity range in the successive steps.

The sparsifying shearlet transform is implemented at $J = \lceil \log_2(d_{\text{range}}) \rceil$ scales. This number guarantees an alias-free central low-pass region. The participating shearlet atoms are selected according to the desired disparity range $[0, 1]$ pixels, c.f. Fig. 10(b) and (d).

The proposed algorithm is a version of the algorithm in Eq. 8 and employs an iterative scheme involving the analysis transform S and its synthesis (dual) counterpart S^*[55]

$$x_{k+1} = S^* \left(\mathcal{T}_{\lambda_k} \left(S(x_k + \alpha_k(y - Mx_k)) \right) \right), \tag{11}$$

where $(\mathcal{T}_\lambda x)(k) = \begin{cases} x(k), & |x(k)| \geq \lambda \\ 0, & |x(k)| < \lambda \end{cases}$ is a hard thresholding operator taking linearly decaying thresholding values λ_n in the range $[\lambda_{\max}, \lambda_{\min}]$. A large value of the parameter α_k provides additional convergence acceleration. This result is partially related to the sparsity of the measurements matrix M. Typically, the number of available samples is significantly smaller than the number of reconstructed samples. Therefore, significant amplification is required to increase the influence of available samples at every thresholding iteration. Nevertheless, an unlimited increase of the parameter α_k diverges the series x_k. The factor can be also made adaptive [5,55].

Full Parallax Processing. The presented reconstruction algorithm assumes EPI formed by an 1D parallax. Full parallax light field data can be processed in consequent manner, i.e. reconstructing the vertical DSEPIs after obtaining all horizontal DSEPIs. This direct approach assumes the same disparity range in both directions. However, the number of shearlet scales, and hence the computational cost, is directly determined by the disparity range. This motivates processing full-parallax EPIs in a hierarchical reconstruction (HR) order [55]. Consider the example in Fig. 11: there is a 5×5 array of input images and the targeted DSLF contains an 17×17 array of images. The reconstruction is performed in three steps by alternating the reconstruction directions, thus making use of the already twice-decreased maximal disparity. For large disparity range, the number of alternating steps can be increased in the same fashion, building a hierarchy where disparities of the subsequent step are reduced twice by the current step.

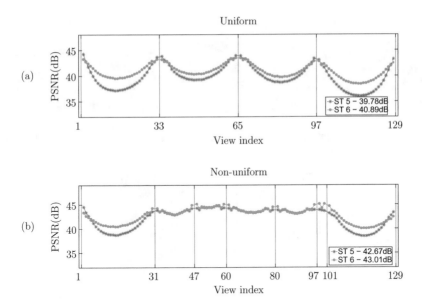

Fig. 12. Comparison of the DSLF reconstruction performance between uniform (a) and non-uniform (b) sampling. Used *ST 5* and *ST 6* methods correspond to the used $J = 5$ and $J = 6$ number of scales in the shearlet transform.

Performance. This method has demonstrated a superior performance against the state-of-the-art and specifically against view interpolation methods relying on depth and hence requiring multi-view depth estimation [55].

While the main method has been developed to handle uniformly-sampled LFs (i.e. rectified views from equidistantly spaced cameras), non-uniform sampling can be handled equally successfully [55]. It is worth mentioning that the required input parameter d_{range} has no direct interpretation in the case of non-uniform sampling and the number of shearlet scales has to be determined by the maximum disparity between adjacent views in order to increase the performance, c.f. Fig. 12(b).

The shearlet atoms are directly related to properties of LF imagery and the imposed sparsity allows avoiding any depth estimation, which might be required for view interpolation otherwise. The LF views are reconstructed as a weighted combination of atoms which can handle cases corresponding to non-Lambertian scenes, which are challenging for depth estimation. Figure 13 illustrates the performance of the proposed method for a semi-transparent scene and against a well-known disparity estimation algorithm, referred to as semi-global block matching (SGBM) [28].

Ground truth   Shearlet   SGBM

Fig. 13. Semi-transparent DSEPI reconstruction using the proposed method and SGBM [28].

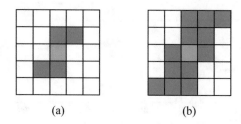

(a)   (b)

Fig. 14. (a) Proposed w window (green) for modelling guidance map. (b) Neighbourhood (green) for forming matting Laplacian matrix entry with respect to reference pixel (orange).

3.5   Acceleration Methods

The basic reconstruction algorithm in Eq. 11 is applied per EPI of a given LF. However, there are correlations between neighboring EPIs as well as between different color components in the same EPI, which can be further explored to achieve an accelerated processing [54].

Colorization. Colorization uses a grayscale image, which guides the reconstruction of another image where the color information is available in isolated regions only [39,40]. The missing color information is recovered and propagated using the local structure of the guiding image [39]. Colorization is attractive and computationally efficient approach for DSEPI reconstruction, considering the luminance channel as the appropriate guidance map for the two chrominance channels [54].

Let E denotes the given luminance channel of DSEPI, which is fully reconstructed. The unknown color image x is modelled as a linear function of the known guidance map at every pixel within a small spatial window w,

$$x[i] \approx aE[i] + b, \forall i \in w.$$

Finding the unknowns is performed through a cost function minimization

$$\min_{x,a,b} J(x,a,b) = \sum_j \left(\sum_{i \in w_j} (x[i] - a_j E[i] - b_j)^2 + \varepsilon a_j^2 \right),$$

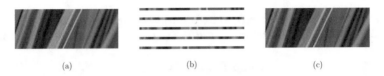

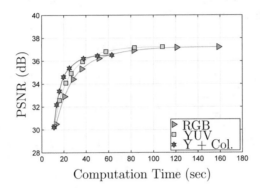

Fig. 15. (a) Luminance (grayscale) DSEPI obtained by shearlet-based sparsification, to be further used as guide for colorization. (b) Color information of the DSEPI is available only from input coarse set of views. (c) Colorization result obtained by solving the problem with Eq. 12.

Fig. 16. Performance of colorization technique averaged over multiple datasets (Y+Col.) and compared to reference reconstruction method applied on RGB channels independently (RGB), and to reconstruction in YUV color space (YUV).

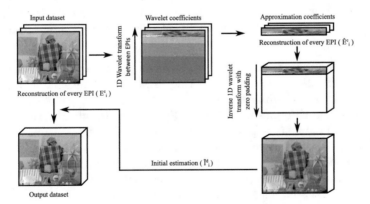

Fig. 17. Reconstruction flowchart using wavelet transform approximation (lowpass) coefficients as an initial estimation for original set reconstruction.

where a regularization coefficient ε ensures the numerical stability. The minimization problem can be reformulated in terms of *matting Laplacian* Λ matrix such as

$$\min_{a,b} J(x,a,b) = x^{\mathsf{T}} \Lambda x,$$

where the symmetric matrix Λ depends on E and w only [39]. The proper choice of the local window w plays a crucial role for the algorithm performance. Figure 14(a) illustrates possible windowing for DSEPI reconstruction, where the window shape has been motivated in [54]. With structure and local windowing information represented in Λ, the colorization problem can be formulated as constrained quadratic minimization,

$$\min_{x} x^{\mathsf{T}} \Lambda x, \ \ \text{subject to } Mx = y, \tag{12}$$

where M is the diagonal measuring matrix and y contains the available color information identical to the one in Eq. 11. The problem can be solved by e.g. the conjugate gradient method $(\Lambda + \lambda M)x = \lambda My$ with sufficiently high λ. Figure 15 illustrates the approach in terms of input guidance map and color and output reconstructed (colorized) DSEPI. The quality of the colorization is mainly dependent on the accuracy of the guidance map. Therefore in order to provide an overall high quality accelerated reconstruction it is required to efficiently distribute the processing resources between reconstructing the luminance channel Y and colorizing the RGB color channels. As seen in Fig. 16, same or better quality of reconstruction can be achieved for less time. Alternatively, the three decorrelated channels YUV can be reconstructed independently using the shearlet-based sparsification, with higher priority assigned to the Y channel reconstruction. As a rule of thumb, it should be processed with twice more iterations than the U and V channels to get decent reconstruction results.

Decorrelation Transform. Another acceleration can be considered by exploiting spatial correlation between neighboring EPIs of the same light field. The winning idea is to use one-dimensional wavelet transform along the vertical direction (i.e. between EPIs), as illustrated in Fig. 17 [54]. In this way, the imagery is decomposed in coarse (low-pass) component and detail components. The coarse DSEPI approximation is reconstructed first: per-EPI and then by inverse 1D wavelet transform to get a global low-pass approximation which serves as an initial estimate for the sparsity-based reconstruction. This approach strongly depends on the spatial image structure. For scenes containing objects with vertically uniform color, the wavelet based processing allows to significantly decrease the computation time while for scenes with more complex structures in vertical direction, the method shows no significant acceleration [54].

4   Applications

Densely sampled light field has a number of applications, where a dense set of views or rays is required. Here, we present a few applications, to illustrate its use.

4.1   Holographic Stereograms

Holographic stereograms are printed digital holograms, where small holographic elements (so-called *hogels*) act as multi-view pixels when illuminated with proper light [48]. In holographic stereograms, each ray of the LF is considered source of a windowed plane wave with the corresponding amplitude and the entire LF is formed as a superposition of plane waves. For convenience, the two planes of the LF parameterization are located at the camera plane and the hologram plane. Thus, all rays intersecting a point on the hologram plane form a hogel. A fringe pattern corresponding to a hogel on the holographic stereogram is calculated using the superposition of the plane waves generated by the rays in the hogel. The resolution of each hogel is directly related to the angular resolution of the given LF and high angular resolution is needed for an accurate calculation of the fringe pattern corresponding to each hogel. All fringe patterns together form the entire holographic stereogram.

The method described in Sect. 3 has been used to generate synthetic holographic stereograms and to compare with depth-based view synthesis methods [48]. The presented results have demonstrated the importance of using DSLF for the holographic stereogram calculation and the efficiency of the proposed shearlet based algorithm for obtaining DSLF, which performed better compared to the depth-based approaches [48].

4.2   Light Field Compression

Typically, the LF compression problem is interpreted as compression of the corresponding sub-aperture views. By using an enhanced inter-view prediction scheme, significant improvement in compression can be achieved. DSLF reconstruction can be used for predicting views [3]. In this approach, the given LF is uniformly decimated in the angular domain first to form a set of key views. This is aimed at decreasing the number of images which go to the compression engine. The key views are converted further into a pseudo video sequence and compressed using high-efficiency video coding (HEVC) encoder. At the decoding side, the full LF is obtained by decoding the key views and then using them for DSLF reconstruction. Apparently, the interplay between view decimation and encoding parameters is the key performance factor [3]. As an anchor method, the direct encoding of the full set of the image from LF as a pseudo video sequence has been considered. The obtained results have demonstrated the efficiency of the proposed compression scheme especially in low bit-rates compared to the anchor method. Since the reconstruction method based on the shearlet transform relies only on keys views, in a low bit-rate scenario, the bit budget allows to achieve high quality for the key views and, as a consequence, high quality for the reconstructed DSLF. On the other hand, the anchor achieves effective compression in high bit-rates due to its various prediction modes for highly correlated views and handling residual information in an effective manner.

References

1. Adelson, E.H., Bergen, J.R.: The plenoptic function and the elements of early vision. In: Computational Models of Visual Processing, pp. 3–20 (1991)
2. Aharon, M., Elad, M., Bruckstein, A.: K-SVD: an algorithm for designing overcomplete dictionaries for sparse representation. IEEE Trans. Signal Process. **54**(11), 4311–4322 (2006)
3. Ahmad, W., Vagharshakyan, S., Sjöström, M., Gotchev, A., Bregovic, R., Olsson, R.: Shearlet transform based prediction scheme for light field compression. In: 2018 Data Compression Conference, pp. 396–396, March 2018
4. Alperovich, A., Johannsen, O., Strecke, M., Goldluecke, B.: Light field intrinsics with a deep encoder-decoder network. In: IEEE Conference on Computer Vision and Pattern Recognition (CVPR), June 2018
5. Blumensath, T., Davies, M.E.: Normalized iterative hard thresholding: guaranteed stability and performance. IEEE J. Sel. Top. Signal Process. **4**(2), 298–309 (2010)
6. Bolles, R.C., Baker, H.H., Marimont, D.H.: Epipolar-plane image analysis: an approach to determining structure from motion. Int. J. Comput. Vis. **1**(1), 7–55 (1987)
7. Bredies, K., Kunisch, K., Pock, T.: Total generalized variation. SIAM J. Imaging Sci. **3**(3), 492–526 (2010)
8. Cai, J.F., Chan, R.H., Shen, Z.: A framelet-based image inpainting algorithm. Appl. Comput. Harmonic Anal. **24**(2), 131–149 (2008)
9. Cai, J.F., Shen, Z.: Framelet based deconvolution. J. Comput. Math. **28**(3), 289–308 (2010)
10. Camahort, E., Lerios, A., Fussell, D.: Uniformly sampled light fields. In: Drettakis, G., Max, N. (eds.) Rendering Techniques 1998, Eurographics, pp. 117–130. Springer, Vienna (1998). https://doi.org/10.1007/978-3-7091-6453-2_11
11. Candès, E.J., Romberg, J., Tao, T.: Robust uncertainty principles: exact signal reconstruction from highly incomplete frequency information. IEEE Trans. Inf. Theory **52**(2), 489–509 (2006)
12. Candes, E.J., Tao, T.: Decoding by linear programming. IEEE Trans. Inf. Theory **51**(12), 4203–4215 (2005)
13. Candès, E.J., Donoho, D.L.: Ridgelets: a key to higher-dimensional intermittency? Philos. Trans. R. Soc. Lond. Ser. A: Math. Phys. Eng. Sci. **357**(1760), 2495–2509 (1999)
14. Candès, E.J., Donoho, D.L.: New tight frames of curvelets and optimal representations of objects with piecewise c^2 singularities. Commun. Pure Appl. Math. **57**(2), 219–266 (2004)
15. Zhang, C., Chen, T.: Spectral analysis for sampling image-based rendering data. IEEE Trans. Circuits Syst. Video Technol. **13**(11), 1038–1050 (2003)
16. Chai, J.X., Tong, X., Chan, S.C., Shum, H.Y.: Plenoptic sampling. In: 27th Annual Conference on Computer Graphics and Interactive Techniques, SIGGRAPH 2000, pp. 307–318 (2000)
17. Chan, S.H., Wang, X., Elgendy, O.A.: Plug-and-play ADMM for image restoration: fixed-point convergence and applications. IEEE Trans. Comput. Imaging **3**(1), 84–98 (2017)

18. Do, M.N., Marchand-Maillet, D., Vetterli, M.: On the bandwidth of the plenoptic function. IEEE Trans. Image Process. **21**(2), 708–717 (2012)
19. Do, M.N., Vetterli, M.: The contourlet transform: an efficient directional multiresolution image representation. IEEE Trans. Image Process. **14**(12), 2091–2106 (2005)
20. Genzel, M., Kutyniok, G.: Asymptotic analysis of inpainting via universal shearlet systems. SIAM J. Imaging Sci. **7**(4), 2301–2339 (2014)
21. Georgiev, T., Intwala, C.: Light field camera design for integral view photography. Adobe Technical report (2006)
22. Gilliam, C., Dragotti, P., Brookes, M.: On the spectrum of the plenoptic function. IEEE Trans. Image Process. **23**(2), 502–516 (2014)
23. Gilliam, C., Dragotti, P.L., Brookes, M.: A closed-form expression for the bandwidth of the plenoptic function under finite field of view constraints. In: IEEE International Conference on Image Processing (ICIP), pp. 3965–3968, September 2010
24. Gortler, S.J., Grzeszczuk, R., Szeliski, R., Cohen, M.F.: The lumigraph. In: 23rd Annual Conference on Computer Graphics and Interactive Techniques, SIGGRAPH 1996, pp. 43–54 (1996)
25. Heber, S., Pock, T.: Convolutional networks for shape from light field. In: IEEE Conference on Computer Vision and Pattern Recognition (CVPR), pp. 3746–3754, June 2016
26. Heber, S., Yu, W., Pock, T.: Neural EPI-volume networks for shape from light field. In: IEEE International Conference on Computer Vision (ICCV), pp. 2271–2279, October 2017
27. Heyden, A., Pollefeys, M.: Multiple view geometry. Emerg. Top. Comput. Vis. **3**, 45–107 (2005)
28. Hirschmuller, H.: Stereo processing by semiglobal matching and mutual information. IEEE Trans. Pattern Anal. Mach. Intell. **30**(2), 328–341 (2008)
29. Honauer, K., Johannsen, O., Kondermann, D., Goldluecke, B.: A dataset and evaluation methodology for depth estimation on 4D light fields. In: Lai, S.-H., Lepetit, V., Nishino, K., Sato, Y. (eds.) ACCV 2016. LNCS, vol. 10113, pp. 19–34. Springer, Cham (2017). https://doi.org/10.1007/978-3-319-54187-7_2
30. Hosni, A., Rhemann, C., Bleyer, M., Rother, C., Gelautz, M.: Fast cost-volume filtering for visual correspondence and beyond. IEEE Trans. Pattern Anal. Mach. Intell. **35**(2), 504–511 (2013)
31. Ihm, I., Park, S., Lee, R.K.: Rendering of spherical light fields. In: Fifth Pacific Conference on Computer Graphics and Applications, pp. 59–68, October 1997
32. Jeon, H., et al.: Accurate depth map estimation from a lenslet light field camera. In: IEEE Conference on Computer Vision and Pattern Recognition (CVPR), pp. 1547–1555, June 2015
33. Kalantari, N.K., Wang, T.C., Ramamoorthi, R.: Learning-based view synthesis for light field cameras. ACM Trans. Graph. (TOG) **35**(6), 1–10 (2016)
34. Kim, C., Zimmer, H., Pritch, Y., Sorkine-Hornung, A., Gross, M.: Scene reconstruction from high spatio-angular resolution light fields. ACM Trans. Graph. (TOG) **32**(4), 1–12 (2013)
35. Krishnan, D., Fergus, R.: Fast image deconvolution using hyper-laplacian priors. In: Advances in Neural Information Processing Systems, vol. 22, pp. 1033–1041 (2009)
36. Kutyniok, G., Lemvig, J., Lim, W.Q.: Shearlets: Multiscale Analysis for Multivariate Data. Springer, Heidelberg (2012). https://doi.org/10.1007/978-0-8176-8316-0
37. Kutyniok, G., Lim, W.Q.: Compactly supported shearlets are optimally sparse. J. Approx. Theory **163**(11), 1564–1589 (2011)

38. Lee, H., Battle, A., Raina, R., Ng, A.Y.: Efficient sparse coding algorithms. In: Proceedings of the 19th International Conference on Neural Information Processing Systems, NIPS 2006, pp. 801–808. MIT Press (2006)
39. Levin, A., Lischinski, D., Weiss, Y.: A closed-form solution to natural image matting. IEEE Trans. Pattern Anal. Mach. Intell. **30**(2), 228–242 (2008)
40. Levin, A., Lischinski, D., Weiss, Y.: Colorization using optimization. ACM Trans. Graph. (TOG) **23**(3), 689–694 (2004)
41. Levoy, M., Hanrahan, P.: Light field rendering. In: 23rd Annual Conference on Computer Graphics and Interactive Techniques, pp. 31–42 (1996)
42. Lim, W.Q.: Nonseparable shearlet transform. IEEE Trans. Image Process. **22**(5), 2056–2065 (2013)
43. Lin, Z., Shum, H.Y.: A geometric analysis of light field rendering. Int. J. Comput. Vis. **58**(2), 121–138 (2004)
44. Mallat, S.: A Wavelet Tour of Signal Processing: The Sparse Way. Academic Press, Cambridge (2008)
45. McMillan, L., Bishop, G.: Plenoptic modeling: an image-based rendering system. In: 22nd Annual Conference on Computer Graphics and Interactive Techniques, SIGGRAPH 1995, pp. 39–46 (1995)
46. Ng, R., Levoy, M., Brédif, M., Duval, G., Horowitz, M., Hanrahan, P., et al.: Light field photography with a hand-held plenoptic camera. Comput. Sci. Techn. R. (CSTR) **2**(11), 1–11 (2005)
47. Overbeck, R.S., Erickson, D., Evangelakos, D., Pharr, M., Debevec, P.: A system for acquiring, processing, and rendering panoramic light field stills for virtual reality. ACM Trans. Graph. (TOG) **37**, 1–15 (2018)
48. Sahin, E., Vagharshakyan, S., Mäkinen, J., Bregovic, R., Gotchev, A.: Shearlet-domain light field reconstruction for holographic stereogram generation. In: IEEE International Conference on Image Processing (ICIP), pp. 1479–1483 (2016)
49. Shen, Z., Toh, K., Yun, S.: An accelerated proximal gradient algorithm for frame-based image restoration via the balanced approach. SIAM J. Imaging Sci. **4**(2), 573–596 (2011)
50. Shi, L., Hassanieh, H., Davis, A., Katabi, D., Durand, F.: Light field reconstruction using sparsity in the continuous fourier domain. ACM Trans. Graph. (TOG) **34**(1), 1–13 (2014)
51. Shin, C., Jeon, H., Yoon, Y., Kweon, I.S., Kim, S.J.: EPINET: a fully-convolutional neural network using epipolar geometry for depth from light field images. In: 2018 IEEE/CVF Conference on Computer Vision and Pattern Recognition, pp. 4748–4757, June 2018
52. Shum, H.Y., He, L.W.: Rendering with concentric mosaics. In: 26th Annual Conference on Computer Graphics and Interactive Techniques, SIGGRAPH 1999, pp. 299–306 (1999)
53. Tao, M.W., Hadap, S., Malik, J., Ramamoorthi, R.: Depth from combining defocus and correspondence using light-field cameras. In: IEEE International Conference on Computer Vision (ICCV), pp. 673–680, December 2013
54. Vagharshakyan, S., Bregovic, R., Gotchev, A.: Accelerated shearlet-domain light field reconstruction. IEEE J. Sel. Top. Signal Process. **11**(7), 1082–1091 (2017)
55. Vagharshakyan, S., Bregovic, R., Gotchev, A.: Light field reconstruction using shearlet transform. IEEE Trans. Pattern Anal. Mach. Intell. **40**(1), 133–147 (2018)
56. Vagharshakyan, S.: Densely-sampled light field reconstruction. Ph.D. thesis, Tampere University (2020)
57. Vaish, V., Adams, A.: The (new) stanford light field archive (2008). http://lightfield.stanford.edu

58. Wanner, S., Goldluecke, B.: Variational light field analysis for disparity estimation and super-resolution. IEEE Trans. Pattern Anal. Mach. Intell. **36**(3), 606–619 (2014)
59. Wen, Z., Goldfarb, D., Yin, W.: Alternating direction augmented lagrangian methods for semidefinite programming. Math. Program. Comput. **2**(3–4), 203–230 (2010)
60. Wilburn, B., et al.: High performance imaging using large camera arrays. ACM Trans. Graph. (TOG) **24**(3), 765–776 (2005)
61. Wilburn, B.S., Smulski, M., Lee, H.H.K., Horowitz, M.A.: Light field video camera. In: Media Processors 2002, vol. 4674, pp. 29–37 (2001)
62. Wood, D.N., et al.: Surface light fields for 3D photography. In: 27th Annual Conference on Computer Graphics and Interactive Techniques, SIGGRAPH 2000, pp. 287–296 (2000)
63. Wu, G., Liu, Y., Fang, L., Dai, Q., Chai, T.: Light field reconstruction using convolutional network on EPI and extended applications. IEEE Trans. Pattern Anal. Mach. Intell. **41**(7), 1681–1694 (2018)
64. Wu, G., Zhao, M., Wang, L., Dai, Q., Chai, T., Liu, Y.: Light field reconstruction using deep convolutional network on EPI. In: IEEE Conference on Computer Vision and Pattern Recognition (CVPR), pp. 1638–1646, July 2017
65. Yu, Z., Guo, X., Ling, H., Lumsdaine, A., Yu, J.: Line assisted light field triangulation and stereo matching. In: IEEE International Conference on Computer Vision (ICCV), pp. 2792–2799, December 2013

Multiview Panorama Alignment and Optical Flow Refinement

Moritz Mühlhausen[(✉)] and Marcus Magnor

TU Braunschweig, Braunschweig, Germany
{muehlhausen,magnor}@cg.cs.tu-bs.de
https://graphics.tu-bs.de

Abstract. Current techniques for "RealVR" experiences are usually limited to a small area around the capture setup. Simple linear blending between several viewpoints will disrupt the virtual reality (VR) experience and cause a loss of immersion for the user. To obtain smoother transitions, optical flow based warping between viewpoints can be utilized. Therefore, the panorama images of these viewpoints do not only need to be upright adjusted but also their viewing direction need to be aligned first. As panoramas for VR are usually of high resolution for high quality results in every direction, the optical flow in a high resolution is also indispensable.

This chapter gives an overview of how to align several viewpoints to a common viewing direction and obtain high resolution optical flow in between.

Keywords: Panorama images · Optical flow · Panorama alignment

1 Introduction

Real VR tries to map the real world into the VR world making it possible to experience a place and moment from anywhere at anytime. In contrast to photography with a fixed viewpoint, users should be able to move freely and perceive the scene naturally. The advent of head-mounted displays (HMDs) [19,32,34] has greatly enhanced the immersion of virtual scenes. Instead of observing through a fixed screen, HMDs perceive the users head-movement and can react accordingly, which enables a more natural way of perceiving VR.

A standard method to encode a scene are spherical panoramas, capturing all view directions from a single point in space. HMDs display a part of the panorama according to the users' view direction. However, visual exploration in natural environments also involves small head-movements and not only different view directions. Including this motion parallax to real VR more information about the underlying scene is necessary. Additional depth information can be utilized to create a rough 3D-reconstruction [44], which makes rendering of new viewpoints possible. Due to disocclusions of unseen parts artifacts are indispensable, getting worse the further the viewpoints moves. This can be counteracted by

© Springer Nature Switzerland AG 2020
M. Magnor and A. Sorkine-Hornung (Eds.): Real VR, LNCS 11900, pp. 96–108, 2020.
https://doi.org/10.1007/978-3-030-41816-8_4

filling these holes using information from other viewpoints. However, while most stitching software for panoramas already include an Upright Adjustment [22] to level the horizon, they are stitched independently, leaving the relative orientation of several panoramas remain unknown.

With aligned panoramas a transition between neighboring viewpoints is needed. Google Street View [3] transitions between viewpoints by blurring and fading the images. Utilizing optical flow Image based Rendering or 3D reconstruction techniques are possibilities to acquire smoother transitions. State-of-the-art optical flow approaches are based on deep learning, limiting image sizes due to memory restrictions and a fixed receptive field. This chapter gives an overview of how several panoramas can be aligned and high resolution optical flow can be estimated in between.

2 Rotational Alignment of Multi-View Spherical Panoramas

Fig. 1. The effect of *Upright Adjustment* and *Rotational Alignment*. The left column shows the reference panorama. Top: Input panorama pair with arbitrary orientations. Middle: After *Upright Adjustment* y of their respective coordinate systems are aligned. Bottom: *Rotational Alignment* aligns x and z to the reference panorama.

Within the last years the use of panorama images and videos has steadily increased fueled by innovation in hardware technology. Google and Facebook added the possibility to share and view panorama images to their platforms and several affordable hand-held panorama cameras have been released. Even mobile devices possess the ability to capture panorama images, making them ubiquitous.

With this growing interest applying state-of-the-art computer vision algorithms to panoramas become essential. Without precise leveling of the cameras during acquisition, the acquired images have wavy horizons and slanted objects due to camera tilts. Such misorientations are not only unpleasant for viewing the panoramas in head-mounted displays (HMDs) but are usually not anticipated by algorithms for standard images. Hence, the first step is to resolve these misorientations in panorama images.

This problem has been addressed before [22,26] by introducing *Upright Adjustment* techniques, which level the horizon in photographs and panorama images. While this makes the adaptation of single image algorithms to panoramas easier, the next step is to extend algorithms for multiple images or image sequences like motion estimation, image-based rendering [40], video stabilization [25], and 3D reconstruction. For this step another alignment problem arises: the cameras do not only need to be leveled properly, but also the relative orientation needs to be known. A closely related topic is 3D camera calibration, which consists of finding the rotation as well as the translation between several cameras [28]. Here, the focus lies only on the rotational component between panoramas, exploiting already known information from the *Upright Adjustment*.

In this section a technique for *Upright Alignment* of spherical panoramas, a combination of *Upright Adjustment* and *Rotational Alignment*, is presented. This is an important preprocessing step in order to apply various multi-view image computer vision algorithms to panoramas. For this purpose the *Upright Adjustment* method of Jung *et al.* [22] is adopted to calibrate the initial orientations of spherical panoramas independently. Assuming correct *Upright Adjustment*, only a rotation around the north pole is left for full alignment. This *Rotational Alignment* problem is addressed by matching horizontal vanishing points in multi-view panoramas. An overview for this is shown in Fig. 1 which highlights the effects of both steps.

2.1   Related Work

Estimating the rotation in conventional and panorama images has been researched extensively, especially in the context of 3D camera registration. The broad research on this and related topics can be divided into three main categories.

Feature Matching. Most of the existing methods are based on epipolar geometry and matching feature points, like scale-invariant feature transform (SIFT). These methods utilize point correspondences between images for rotation estimation, which has been shown to be possible up to scale and a four-fold ambiguity given eight point correspondences [17]. This has been used for tasks like 3D reconstruction for conventional cameras [1,2] and simultaneous localization and mapping (SLAM) algorithms for conventional [24] as well as panorama cameras [27]. Cubic panorama pairs can be aligned to their respective epipole [15,23] using SIFT feature points on each side of the panorama. However, these approaches align only a pair of images towards their epipole, making them unsuited for more than two images. This limitation was addressed by Saheli *et al.* [38] to align complete cubic panorama image data sets to a common direction. Although feature matching methods can produce impressive results, they suffer from various limitations. The matching step can be difficult due to illumination changes, repeating textures, mirrors, or other kind of ambiguities within the images. Moreover, they are time consuming and are indirect as they compute the complete motion, consisting of rotation and translation, even when only the rotation is desired.

Featureless Approaches. These methods do not rely on feature correspondences, instead they exploit different image statistics. For parabolic catadioptric images Makadia *et al.* [29] propose a method involving spherical Fourier transform. They convert the image into the frequency domain and obtain the rotation from the conservation of harmonic coefficients in the rotational shift theorem. However, the frequency domain is sensitive to translation and non-static objects, making the correlation between moved cameras or frames of dynamic scenes difficult. Gurrieri *et al.* [16] align cylindrical panoramas based on dense disparity maps. They first perform a rough alignment of the panoramas by finding the most similar patch to a central region. Afterwards they identify and classify patterns in the disparity maps within this region for further alignment. Since computing disparity maps is error-prone to misaligned images, this method relies strongly on the exhaustive search in the first step.

Vanishing Points. The last category of methods utilize vanishing points for rotation estimation. Vanishing points are intersections of parallel lines in the world projected in an image. They correlate to points at infinity and therefore their position depends only on the rotation and they are independent of translations. This idea has been used for tasks like 3D reconstruction [10] and camera calibration [35]. Moreover, they have been used for camera orientation estimation for conventional images [30] and panorama images [4,6]. While some approaches work on edge pixels directly [4,30] to estimate vanishing points, others use extracted lines [6]. All of these methods work best when satisfying the *Manhattan World Assumption* [13], which states that scenes are built in a cartesian grid, so that only a single dominant orientation is assumed. Hence, scenes which satisfy this assumption have at most three vanishing points, two horizontal and one vertical. The presented alignment approach also belongs to this category, but instead of restricting the vanishing point to match an orthonormal coordinate system [6], vanishing points between image pairs are matched. Therefore, the restriction is loosen to the *Atlanta World Assumption* [39], which allow more than a single orientation.

2.2   Upright Adjustment

This *Rotational Alignment* approach adopts the *Upright Adjustment* of Jung *et al.* [22], which updates the position of the north pole for a single image in an iterative process. A cost function is formulated to find the subsequent north pole position $\boldsymbol{P}$:

$$E(\boldsymbol{P}) = \alpha \sum_i (\boldsymbol{v_i} \cdot \boldsymbol{P})^2 + \beta \sum_j (\boldsymbol{h_j} \cdot \boldsymbol{P})^2 + \lambda (1 - \boldsymbol{y} \cdot \boldsymbol{P})^2 \tag{1}$$

Fig. 2. A synthetic scene highlighting the found great circles (green) and corresponding vanishing points (red). The *Upright Adjustment* step aligns these vanishing points to the horizon, while the *Rotational Alignment* aligns them between several panoramas.

Here, v_i are unit vectors perpendicular to great circles from vertical lines and h_i are unit vectors from horizontal vanishing points, computed from horizontal line great circles. To prevent drastic change in a single iteration, the last term penalizes the deviation to the old north pole y. For the weighting parameters α, β and λ, we adopt $\alpha = 1.0, \beta = 0.5$ and $\lambda = 10.0$. Figure 2 displays the found great circles and corresponding vanishing points in one iteration for a synthetic scene.

The recovery of horizontal and vertical great circles, as well as the vanishing point detection, are utilizing a spherical Hough transformation. First, line segments are detected with an arbitrary line detection algorithm, like *LSD* [42]. These line segments are categorized to be either horizontal or vertical. For each line segment the corresponding great circle is accumulated in spherical Hough space to identify the best great circles. These great circles are rasterized in spherical Hough space to find vanishing points.

With these information new north poles are computed subsequently, rotating the image after each iteration to obtain new great circles and vanishing points. Ending when the difference between y and P becomes sufficiently small, taking P as the final north pole.

2.3   Rotational Alignment

The *Rotational Alignment* aligns two upright adjusted images, i.e. a panorama I is aligned to a reference panorama $\widehat{I}$. However, this approach can handle any number of panoramas, by subsequently aligning all panoramas to the same reference $\widehat{I}$.

After the *Upright Adjustment* step the panoramas are properly leveled. The horizontal vanishing points found in the last iteration are kept from the last iteration. While arbitrary vanishing points are found and used in the *Upright Adjustment*, only the most dominant ones are used for the *Rotational Alignment*, i.e. all vanishing points with Hough weights below a percental threshold of the best weight are ignored. Specifically, all vanishing points with weights below 0.9 are ignored and at most four opposing vanishing point pairs are used. Moreover, vanishing point search is restricted to the leveled horizon, reducing their dimension to 1D. These dominant vanishing points are usually more precise ones in the image, hence aligning the images accordingly increases accuracy.

For *Rotational Alignment* a single pair of corresponding vanishing needs to be found and a new horizontal position to every pixel (n, m) of the image assigned. However, points at infinity can be occluded by closer objects within one image. Hence, the surroundings of corresponding vanishing points can be very different, making matching difficult. Therefore, instead of matching the vanishing points directly, the whole rotated images given a corresponding vanishing point pair can be compared. Assuming a vanishing point $\hat{h}_i \in \hat{H}$ of the reference image $\hat{I}$ to correspond to $h_j \in H$ in the current image I, I needs to be rotated by $\hat{h}_i - h_j$ around the north pole to obtain $I'_{\hat{h}_i, h_j}$.

$$I'_{\hat{h}_i, h_j}(n, m) = I(n, m - (\hat{h}_i - h_j)) \tag{2}$$

Then, the obtained image can be compared with $\hat{I}$ to check whether or not the points actually correspond. Testing with all vanishing point pairs $\hat{h}_i, h_j$, the best match is kept. This is similar to the coarse alignment of Gurrieri *et al.* [16]. Yet, this approach only needs to check a few rotations, instead of a complete search over the width of the image. Moreover, unless only different vanishing points are found, at least one of these rotations is correct. The *Structural Similarity (SSIM)* is used for comparison instead of plain pixel values:

$$\max_{\hat{h}_i \in \hat{H}, h_j \in H} \left\| \text{SSIM}(\hat{I}, I'_{\hat{h}_i, h_j}) \right\|_2^2 \tag{3}$$

Here, $\hat{H}$ is the set of the dominant vanishing points in the reference panorama $\hat{I}$ and accordingly H is the set of dominant vanishing points in I. $\|\cdot\|_2^2$ is the squared norm, so the squared sum of the *SSIM* over every channel of the image is taken.

3   Iterative Optical Flow Refinement

Optical flow estimation find its application in several real-world problems like video encoding, autonomous driving and image-based rendering. As a classical computer vision technique of high relevance, new approaches are published regularly. A couple of years ago convolutional neural networks (CNNs) started to outperform traditional techniques [14] on several benchmarks [7,41]. While this shift of paradigm improved the quality of estimation, CNNs come with some limitations. First, because optical flow is a complex problem which involves scene understanding, these networks need many parameters which not only makes training difficult, but also results in strict memory requirements. Furthermore, the receptive fields of CNNs are fixed by the architecture, limiting the maximum perceivable displacement. Moreover, CNNs are biased by the training data, resulting in unreliable estimation if displacements are larger than seen in the training data, even if they are within the receptive field. Especially with the current advent of consumer grade cameras, which can already capture very high resolution images, these problems become relevant. Also for panoramas which are usually of high resolution to ensure high quality in each viewing direction.

A naive solution would be to down-sample the input images, compute low resolution flow, and finally up-sample the flow to the necessary image resolution. However, following this approach fine structures of the panoramas will be lost. Cutting images into tiles on a regular grid can be used in order to keep more details. This reduces the memory footprint of each computation, but objects in a tile can move independently which can not be represented by a one to one relation.

A pyramidal approach of flow estimation [33] at multiple increasing image resolutions overcomes these problems. It is a combination of these naive solutions: First, flow is calculated for down-sampled input images to identify image patches with similar displacement. The flow between these patches is merged into a complete flow image and passed to the next iteration. This process is repeated until the full resolution is reached.

3.1 Related Work

Optical flow is a classical computer vision task since the initial formulation by Horn and Schunck in the 1980s [18]. Many benchmarks [5,9,31] to measure and compare optical flow approaches have been established over the years. Shortly after the introduction of deep learning to optical flow estimation [21], CNNs have replaced traditional methods in the highest ranks in these benchmarks [7,41]. However, current benchmarks only contain low resolution images making comparison and training on high resolution images difficult.

The idea of image pyramids have been utilized for other computer vision tasks for a long time [8]. Although many CNNs use image pyramids as an internal part of the network architecture [20,21,36,41], the amount of displacement that networks can reliable calculate is still limited as the receptive field is based on the fixed pyramid levels. Retraining would be necessary to adapt the networks, which requires much time and new data. While CNNs for panoramas were introduced [11,12], there are no dedicated optical flow CNNs for panoramas yet.

One popular method to post-process optical flow is to create dense flow fields from sparse flow information [37]. Other techniques focus on refining dense flow values by using semantic scene information like planar assumptions [43] for street scenes like the KITTI dataset [31]. In contrast to these refinement methods, the iterative optical flow refinement computes dense flow as input and computes high resolution flow without further assumptions.

3.2   Iterative Flow Refinement

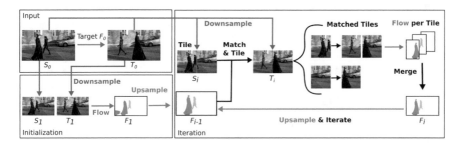

Fig. 3. The pipeline of the Iterative Flow Refinement. Estimating the flow between two high resolution input images S_0 and T_0. First, these images are downsampled and flow is computed between them with any flow estimator. Then, the images are iteratively upsampled and tiled in an image pyramid manner. During each iteration the images are up-sampled and image tiles are matched based on the previous flow. Flow is computed between matching tiles, merged, up-sampled, and passed to the next iteration until full image resolution is reached.

An arbitrary flow estimation CNN C as well as a source S_0 and target T_0 image pair are used as input. The output is the flow F_0 from S_0 to T_0 respecting the resolution of the input images. After an initialization step, flow estimation is performed iteratively at multiple increasing image resolutions in a pyramidal style. To overcome displacement and memory restrictions the images are tiled in several patches and estimate the flow between them with C. The tile size u_s can be defined by the user according to the available GPU memory or the training data. Each iteration i ends with combining all estimated flow tiles into F_i, upsampled, and passed to the next iteration. Figure 3 shows an overview of the iterative optical flow refinement approach.

Initialization. The initialization step is used to obtain global optical flow information between the input images S_0 and T_0. These are used to guide the tiling in the first iteration. Therefore, the input images are downsampled to fit onto a single tile, S_1 and T_1. These images are passed to an arbitrary flow estimator C computing the flow F_1. Due to the downsampling these input images should respect the receptive field of C and hence provide meaningful global optical flow information. Although flow information of fine structures are missing, they will be retained incrementally during the iteration steps.

Iteration. The inputs for each iteration i are S_0, T_0 as well as the flow F_{i-1} of the previous level. Each iteration consists of the several steps: Scaling of S_0, T_0 and F_{i-1}, tiling the scaled images, computing flow tiles for all pairs using C, and finally merging the flow tiles to obtain the complete flow F_i. First, the input images are downsampled to S_i and T_i, depending on a scaling factor u_f per pyramid level. A default factor of 2 has shown good results in practice, therefore,

S_i and T_i are twice the width and height of S_{i-1} and T_{i-1}. Additionally, F_{i-1} is upsampled to match their size. The flow values are scaled accordingly.

Next, the source image S_i is tiled on a regular grid according to its width $S_{i,x}$ and height $S_{i,y}$, the tile size u_s and an overlap factor u_o. The tiles' overlap is needed to increase the similarity of the estimated flow in border regions and enable smooth blending when combining the flow. K tiles, $s_1^i, \ldots, s_K^i$ of S_i are cut, with K defined as:

$$K = \lceil S_{i,x}/(u_{s,x} - 2 \cdot u_{o,x}) \rceil \cdot \lceil S_{i,y}/(u_{s,y} - 2 \cdot u_{o,y}) \rceil \tag{4}$$

The target image T_i is not tiled regularly, as objects could move out of the tile. Furthermore, if several objects move in opposing directions, it may not be possible to capture all objects in a single tile. To handle cases like that, flow clusters are generated depending on k-means cluster on F_{i-1}. To determine the necessary number of clusters an elbow method with a maximum of $N = 10$ can be used, the accordings cluster labels are stored in M_i. For each cluster n, one target tile $t_{(k,n)}^i$ is created. The position of this target tile is determined by the mean flow $o_{(k,n)}^i$ of its respective cluster n. $o_{(k,n)}^i$ is added to the initial position obtained from s_k^i. Then, all resulting source-target tile pairs $(s_k^i, t_{(k,n)}^i)$ are passed to the chosen flow estimator C.

At last, resulting flow tiles $f_{(k,n)}^i$ are merged into F_i. For this purpose first one combined flow tile f_k^i for each source tile s_k^i is created:

$$f_k^i = \sum_{n=1}^{N} (f_{k,n}^i + o_{(k,n)}^i) \circ m_{(k,n)}^i,$$

where $m_{(k,n)}^i$ is a mask based on M_i indicating which pixels belong to cluster n. Since the target tiles are moved, this offset $o_{(k,n)}^i$ is added to account for global flow information. After all source tiles have complete flow information they are merged into the current flow F_i. To obtain smooth results, for each f_k^i a centered Gaussian kernel is applied as a weighting factor. Normalizing the weights, the flow estimates are blended in the overlapping regions. F_i is then passed as input to the next iteration. Once the desired resolution is computed, this iteration stops.

Panorama Images. This approach has also shown useful for handling spherical panorama images as input. Next to the challenges arising from large displacements and memory requirements, the wrapping at the borders of panorama images needs to be addressed correctly. In full panorama images, objects can not move out of the visible area but by occlusion. Instead, they reenter the image at a different position. As this is not anticipated by standard flow estimators, the flow of objects that move across image borders is not computed correctly.

For the initial down-sampled complete flow computation, a more than full panorama is used, i.e. $400° \times 200°$, showing doubling some parts in the image. This allows the network to identify global movements across the original image borders. For the iteration steps, the tiling can be used to handle the wrapping

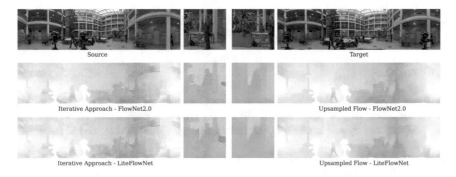

Fig. 4. Comparison between the flow computed by the iterative approach and upsampled flow (between downsampled versions of the input). FlowNet 2.0 [21] and Lite-FlowNet [20] were used as flow estimators.

of panoramas and create continuous tiles, correctly matching objects across borders. Two wrapping cases exist: Tiles move across the x or the y border. If tiles move across the x border they simply reenter the image at the opposite x border. Therefore, a modulo-operation on the x coordinates is sufficient to find the correct position. However, if tiles move across the y border they reenter at the same border but their x coordinates are shifted by half the size of the original 360° panorama. Moreover, they are turned upside down after reentry. The flow is adjusted accordingly in the merging step. Figure 4 shows a comparison between a naive upsampling and this iterative approach for two different flow estimators.

4   Conclusion

This chapter discusses important steps towards seamless and smooth transitions between different panoramic viewpoints of RealVR scenes. The main idea is to estimate optical flow between panoramas and apply optical flow based warping as transitions. While usually panoramas are upright adjusted during the stitching process, i.e. the horizon is straightened in the center, for warping the panoramas viewing directions also need to be aligned. The presented *Rotational Alignment* approach utilizes vanishing points which most panorama stitching approaches already compute and use for *Upright Adjustment*. Therefore, this alignment of several panoramas does not rely on additional information, resulting in minimal overhead. Matching found vanishing points between panoramas and rotating them accordingly results in aligned viewing directions. However, to ensure a high quality of realism in VR, the panoramas need a very high resolution as each viewing direction requires a decent resolution. As state-of-the-art optical flow estimators are not suitable and trained for handling high resolutions like these, an iterative approach in a pyramidal matter is presented. This ensures that fine structures within the panoramas are also reflected in the estimated optical flow. Furthermore, the iterative approach is independent of the estimator, making it applicable to any optical flow approaches in the future.

Acknowledgements. The authors gratefully acknowledge funding by the German Science Foundation (DFG MA2555/15-1 "Immersive Digital Reality").

References

1. Agarwal, S., et al.: Building Rome in a day. Commun. ACM **54**(10), 105–112 (2011)
2. Akbarzadeh, A., et al.: Towards urban 3D reconstruction from video. In: Third International Symposium on 3D Data Processing, Visualization, and Transmission, pp. 1–8. IEEE (2006)
3. Anguelov, D., et al.: Google street view: capturing the world at street level. Computer **43**, 32–38 (2010). http://ieeexplore.ieee.org/xpls/abs_all.jsp?arnumber=5481932&tag=1
4. Antone, M.E., Teller, S.: Automatic recovery of relative camera rotations for urban scenes. In: Proceedings IEEE Conference on Computer Vision and Pattern Recognition, 2000, vol. 2, pp. 282–289. IEEE (2000)
5. Baker, S., Scharstein, D., Lewis, J., Roth, S., Black, M.J., Szeliski, R.: A database and evaluation methodology for optical flow. Int. J. Comput. Vis. **92**(1), 1–31 (2011)
6. Bazin, J.C., Demonceaux, C., Vasseur, P., Kweon, I.: Rotation estimation and vanishing point extraction by omnidirectional vision in urban environment. Int. J. Robot. Res. **31**(1), 63–81 (2012)
7. Behl, A., Hosseini Jafari, O., Karthik Mustikovela, S., Abu Alhaija, H., Rother, C., Geiger, A.: Bounding boxes, segmentations and object coordinates: how important is recognition for 3D scene flow estimation in autonomous driving scenarios? In: IEEE International Conference on Computer Vision (ICCV), pp. 2574–2583 (2017)
8. Burt, P., Adelson, E.: The Laplacian pyramid as a compact image code. IEEE Trans. Commun. **31**(4), 532–540 (1983)
9. Butler, D.J., Wulff, J., Stanley, G.B., Black, M.J.: A naturalistic open source movie for optical flow evaluation. In: Fitzgibbon, A., Lazebnik, S., Perona, P., Sato, Y., Schmid, C. (eds.) ECCV 2012. LNCS, vol. 7577, pp. 611–625. Springer, Heidelberg (2012). https://doi.org/10.1007/978-3-642-33783-3_44
10. Cipolla, R., Drummond, T., Robertson, D.P.: Camera calibration from vanishing points in image of architectural scenes. In: BMVC, vol. 99, pp. 382–391 (1999)
11. Cohen, T., Geiger, M., Köhler, J., Welling, M.: Convolutional networks for spherical signals. In: ICML Workshop on Principled Approaches to Deep Learning (2017)
12. Cohen, T.S., Geiger, M., Köhler, J., Welling, M.: Spherical CNNs. In: International Conference on Learning Representations (ICLR) (2018)
13. Coughlan, J.M., Yuille, A.L.: Manhattan world: compass direction from a single image by Bayesian inference. In: The Proceedings of the Seventh IEEE International Conference on Computer Vision, 1999, vol. 2, pp. 941–947. IEEE (1999)
14. Dosovitskiy, A., et al.: FlowNet: learning optical flow with convolutional networks. In: IEEE International Conference on Computer Vision (ICCV), pp. 2758–2766 (2015)
15. Fiala, M., Roth, G.: Automatic alignment and graph map building of panoramas. In: IEEE International Workshop on Haptic Audio Visual Environments and their Applications, 2005, p. 6. IEEE (2005)
16. Gurrieri, L.E., Dubois, E.: Optimum alignment of panoramic images for stereoscopic navigation in image-based telepresence systems. In: 2011 IEEE International Conference on Computer Vision Workshops (ICCV Workshops), pp. 351–358. IEEE (2011)

17. Hartley, R., Zisserman, A.: Multiple View Geometry in Computer Vision. Cambridge University Press, Cambridge (2003)
18. Horn, B.K., Schunck, B.G.: Determining optical flow. Artif. Intell. **17**(1–3), 185–203 (1981)
19. HTC: Discover virtual reality beyond imagination. https://www.vive.com/uk/
20. Hui, T.W., Tang, X., Loy, C.C.: LiteFlowNet: a lightweight convolutional neural network for optical flow estimation. In: IEEE Conference on Computer Vision and Pattern Recognition (CVPR), pp. 8981–8989 (2018)
21. Ilg, E., Mayer, N., Saikia, T., Keuper, M., Dosovitskiy, A., Brox, T.: FlowNet 2.0: evolution of optical flow estimation with deep networks. In: IEEE Conference on Computer Vision and Pattern Recognition (CVPR), pp. 1647–1655 (2017)
22. Jung, J., Lee, J.Y., Kim, B., Lee, S.: Upright adjustment of 360 spherical panoramas. In: 2017 IEEE Virtual Reality (VR), pp. 251–252. IEEE (2017)
23. Kangni, F., Laganiere, R.: Epipolar geometry for the rectification of cubic panoramas. In: The 3rd Canadian Conference on Computer and Robot Vision, 2006, p. 70. IEEE (2006)
24. Karlsson, N., Di Bernardo, E., Ostrowski, J., Goncalves, L., Pirjanian, P., Munich, M.E.: The vSLAM algorithm for robust localization and mapping. In: Proceedings of the 2005 IEEE International Conference on Robotics and Automation, ICRA 2005, pp. 24–29. IEEE (2005)
25. Kopf, J.: 360 video stabilization. ACM Trans. Graph. (TOG) **35**(6), 195 (2016)
26. Lee, H., Shechtman, E., Wang, J., Lee, S.: Automatic upright adjustment of photographs with robust camera calibration. IEEE Trans. Pattern Anal. Mach. Intell. **36**(5), 833–844 (2014)
27. Lemaire, T., Lacroix, S.: SLAM with panoramic vision. J. Field Robot. **24**(1–2), 91–111 (2007)
28. Luong, Q.T., Faugeras, O.: The geometry of multiple images. MIT Press Boston **2**(3), 4–5 (2001)
29. Makadia, A., Daniilidis, K.: Rotation recovery from spherical images without correspondences. IEEE Trans. Pattern Anal. Mach. Intell. **28**(7), 1170–1175 (2006)
30. Martins, A.T., Aguiar, P.M., Figueiredo, M.A.: Orientation in Manhattan: equiprojective classes and sequential estimation. IEEE Trans. Pattern Anal. Mach. Intell. **27**(5), 822–827 (2005)
31. Menze, M., Geiger, A.: Object scene flow for autonomous vehicles. In: IEEE Conference on Computer Vision and Pattern Recognition (CVPR), pp. 3061–3070 (2015)
32. Microsoft: Microsoft hololens — mixed reality technology for business. https://www.microsoft.com/en-us/hololens
33. Mühlhausen, M., Wöhler, L., Albuquerque, G., Magnor, M.: Iterative optical flow refinement for high resolution images. In: Proceedings of IEEE International Conference on Image Processing (ICIP) (September 2019)
34. Oculus: Oculus rift. https://www.oculus.com/rift/
35. Orghidan, R., Salvi, J., Gordan, M., Orza, B.: Camera calibration using two or three vanishing points. In: 2012 Federated Conference on Computer Science and Information Systems (FedCSIS), pp. 123–130. IEEE (2012)
36. Ranjan, A., Black, M.J.: Optical flow estimation using a spatial pyramid network. In: IEEE Conference on Computer Vision and Pattern Recognition (CVPR), pp. 2720–2729 (2017)
37. Revaud, J., Weinzaepfel, P., Harchaoui, Z., Schmid, C.: EpicFlow: edge-preserving interpolation of correspondences for optical flow. In: IEEE Conference on Computer Vision and Pattern Recognition (CVPR), pp. 1164–1172 (2015)

38. Salehi, S., Dubois, E.: Alignment of cubic-panorama image datasets using epipolar geometry. In: 2011 IEEE International Conference on Acoustics, Speech and Signal Processing (ICASSP), pp. 1545–1548. IEEE (2011)
39. Schindler, G., Dellaert, F.: Atlanta world: an expectation maximization framework for simultaneous low-level edge grouping and camera calibration in complex man-made environments. In: Proceedings of the 2004 IEEE Computer Society Conference on Computer Vision and Pattern Recognition, CVPR 2004, vol. 1, p. I. IEEE (2004)
40. Shum, H.Y., Chan, S.C., Kang, S.B.: Image-Based Rendering. Springer, Heidelberg (2008)
41. Sun, D., Yang, X., Liu, M.Y., Kautz, J.: PWC-Net: CNNs for optical flow using pyramid, warping, and cost volume. In: IEEE Conference on Computer Vision and Pattern Recognition (CVPR), pp. 8934–8943 (2018)
42. Von Gioi, R.G., Jakubowicz, J., Morel, J.M., Randall, G.: LSD: a fast line segment detector with a false detection control. IEEE Trans. Pattern Anal. Mach. Intell. **32**(4), 722–732 (2010)
43. Xu, J., Ranftl, R., Koltun, V.: Accurate optical flow via direct cost volume processing. In: IEEE Conference on Computer Vision and Pattern Recognition (CVPR), pp. 1289–1297 (2017)
44. Zhou, T., Tucker, R., Flynn, J., Fyffe, G., Snavely, N.: Stereo magnification: learning view synthesis using multiplane images. In: SIGGRAPH (2018)

Image-Based Scene Representations
for Head-Motion Parallax
in 360° Panoramas

Tobias Bertel[1]([✉]) [ID], Feng Xu[2] [ID], and Christian Richardt[1] [ID]

[1] University of Bath, Bath, UK
T.B.Bertel@bath.ac.uk, christian@richardt.name
[2] Tsinghua University, Beijing, China
feng-xu@tsinghua.edu.cn
https://richardt.name/

Abstract. Creation and delivery of "RealVR" experiences essentially consists of the following four main steps: capture, processing, representation and rendering. In this chapter, we present, compare, and discuss two recent end-to-end approaches, Parallax360 by Luo *et al.* [9] and MegaParallax by Bertel *et al.* [3]. Both propose complete pipelines for RealVR content generation and novel-view synthesis with head-motion parallax for 360° environments.

Parallax360 uses a robotic arm for capturing thousands of input views on the surface of a sphere. Based on precomputed disparity motion fields and pairwise optical flow, novel viewpoints are synthesized on the fly using flow-based blending of the nearest two to three input views which provides compelling head-motion parallax.

MegaParallax proposes a pipeline for RealVR content generation and rendering that emphasizes casual, hand-held capturing. The approach introduces view-dependent flow-based blending to enable novel-view synthesis with head-motion parallax within a viewing area determined by the field of view of the input cameras and the capturing radius.

We describe both methods and discuss their similarities and differences in corresponding steps in the RealVR pipeline and show selected results. The chapter ends by discussing advantages and disadvantages as well as outlining the most important limitations and future work.

Keywords: 360° scene capture · Scene representation · Head-motion parallax · Image-based rendering · Novel-view synthesis

1 Introduction

A very important aspect to provide *immersive* VR experiences is head-motion parallax. *Motion parallax* occurs whenever we move our head, e.g. when looking around, driving a car, or riding a train. When riding a train and looking out of the window, you notice that closer objects will pass much faster than objects

© Springer Nature Switzerland AG 2020
M. Magnor and A. Sorkine-Hornung (Eds.): Real VR, LNCS 11900, pp. 109–131, 2020.
https://doi.org/10.1007/978-3-030-41816-8_5

farther away, such as a mountain in the distance. This effect is called motion parallax and is an essential monocular depth cue for the human visual system.

This chapter presents two recent methods that build upon an image-based scene representation containing dense imagery and which are able to provide head-motion parallax in real-world environments by employing a flow-based view synthesis.

On one hand, Parallax360 [9] supports full head-motion parallax and relies on a non-casual capturing and time-consuming processing stage. On the other hand, MegaParallax [3] provides restricted head-motion parallax and builds on a casual capturing stage and an additional step for extrinsic calibration via Structure-from-Motion (SfM) [17] and frame registration. Both methods use optical flow to establish dense (per-pixel) correspondences between *reference viewpoints* or *key frames*. Lastly, both approaches employ different *flow-based* blending procedures which allow to render novel viewpoints in high-quality and in real-time.

Creating content for real-world VR applications is a very interesting research field. One day, VR content will be as ordinary as an image or a video are today.

2   Related Work

Image-based rendering (IBR) or novel-view synthesis at its core can be formulated as follows: *Given a set of reference views of a scene, how can novel views be inferred from them?* Since it is not practical to sample the space of possible viewpoints (plenoptic function [1]) very densely, e.g. using light fields [8], novel or missing viewpoints have to be predicted or interpolated sufficiently fast at runtime to change virtual viewpoints smoothly. IBR methods have been commonly categorized according to the type of geometry used by the representation to perform novel-view synthesis (see Sect. 2.2 later in this chapter).

The state of the art for capturing and displaying 360° real-world environments in terms of visual quality and correctness is based on *explicit* scene reconstruction [6,7]. However, 3D reconstruction of arbitrary environments with a single moving camera is extremely challenging. To give an example, dynamic objects like cars, people, animals, plants, etc. may move during the capture. Furthermore, shiny or specular scene objects, such as cars, metals, polished surfaces, glass, water, etc. have a view-dependent appearance which leads to incorrect feature matches and thus to erroneous 3D reconstructions.

The commercial standard for real-world VR content generation, transmission, and playback [2,16] is based on omnidirectional stereo [14,15], which is *not* relying on any explicit geometry reconstruction, but image stitching techniques [21] tweaked with *implicit* geometry, such as optical flow. The most promising work with respect to VR video was recently published by Facebook [13] and is based on IBR with explicit geometry.

The subject of 3D reconstruction is not discussed in this chapter. The reader finds excellent information about that in Peter Hedman's chapter in this very book. The presented approaches explicitly avoid 3D reconstruction by relying on densely sampled imagery. The set of all reference viewpoints and their corresponding pixels can be seen as a large database of light rays, assuming an infinitely small aperture as its the case in pinhole images. Only the most relevant work to understand and motivate Parallax360 and MegaParallax is addressed in the remainder of this section.

2.1   The Plenoptic Function

The plenoptic function [1] describes the incident radiance at a 3D point (x, y, z) from a certain direction (θ, ϕ), in 2D spherical coordinates, with wavelength λ at time t. Thus overall, the function has 7 dimensions. The wavelength is usually discretized in a 3-channel RGB texture, and it is assumed in this chapter that time is fixed. The plenoptic function thus becomes a 5D function depending on space (3D) and direction (2D): $\mathbf{L}(x, y, z, \theta, \phi)$.

Every pinhole image taken of the real-world represents a finite set of samples of the plenoptic function assuming the optical center of the camera as (x, y, z) and the field of view as a range over θ and ϕ. The fundamental goal of all image-based rendering approaches is to reconstruct the plenoptic function $\mathbf{L}$ *continuously* given only finitely many samples of it.

Plenoptic Modelling. [10] is an IBR framework describing (1) sampling, (2) reconstruction, and (3) resampling of the plenoptic function to create novel viewpoints from a set of monoscopic cylindrical panoramas. Novel viewpoints show correct perspectives and visibility without reconstructing any scene geometry explicitly, but only estimating optical flow between the reference images. The downsides of the method are the non-casual capture of cylindrical images and the required density of viewpoints to keep optical flow estimation reliable.

Light Field Rendering. [8] presents a 4D representation of the 5D plenoptic function called a light field by parameterizing plenoptic samples using rays connecting two planes that can be described by two 2D coordinates from the respective planes. Their input images are sampled so densely that reconstructing a desired viewpoint is performed by solely looking up and bilinearly (or quadrilinearly, if a focal plane is used additionally to the camera plane) blending reference pixels. The main downside of the method is the large memory footprint of light fields. Dozens of images captured with a gantry are necessary to obtain a viewing space of a few centimeters, in which head-motion is supported.

Rendering with Concentric Mosaics. [19] present a 3D representation of the 5D plenoptic function which is limited to translation in a plane. Multiple concentric circles are sampled using a *slit-image* approach as often used in the image stitching community [14,15,21]. Every slit image is naturally described by radius, rotation angle, and vertical elevation. A desired viewpoint is synthesized by mosaicking reference slit images. This work was the first to report the effect of *vertical distortion*, which occurs if a desired viewpoint is stitched with slit images that were captured far away from the desired optical center. The suggestion to use a constant-depth proxy to address vertical distortion can be seen as constant composition surface in image stitching algorithms [21].

Vertical distortion and the non-casual, time-consuming capturing process are the main downsides of this method.

2.2   Image-Based Rendering (IBR)

Approaches all aim for reconstructing the plenoptic function continuously given a finite set of reference viewpoints and estimated *correspondences* among these viewpoints. IBR methods can be categorized according to the type of geometry which is contained in the representation and used in the view synthesis stage [18]. We will highlight relevant aspects of IBR in this chapter which give important motivation and context for the presented papers.

No Geometry. Light field rendering [8] and concentric mosaics [19] do not rely on any reconstructed geometry to synthesize novel viewpoints.

Implicit Geometry. Pixel correspondences between a pair of images implicitly model geometric relations among the depicted scene objects. Motion vectors of close objects will have a larger magnitude than objects farther away due to motion parallax. Plenoptic modelling [10] uses optical flow between reference views to establish dense pixel correspondences needed for rendering. Megastereo [15] utilizes a casual capturing setup and performs flow-based blending in order to mosaic omnidirectional stereo panoramas [14] assuming a constant-depth composition surface.

The papers we focus on in this chapter are both IBR methods relying on *implicit* geometry.

Explicit Geometry. As soon as an IBR approach relies on geometry, e.g. in the form of depth maps or a global scene proxy or mesh, it is called *explicit*. The main idea of these methods is that desired viewpoints can be estimated by *reprojecting* reference views into the desired view using the scene geometry.

Unstructured Lumigraph Rendering (ULR) [4] postulates desirable properties any IBR system should have. If given a sufficient amount of images, it turns into lumigraph rendering [5]. Otherwise, if given an unstructured set of input images with a high-quality geometric proxy, it turns into view-dependent texture mapping.

Overbeck *et al.* present a end-to-end VR pipeline for full head-motion parallax [12]. The capture is non-casual and rendering involves explicit geometry in the form of depth maps. The results are visually outstanding, but the representation is large.

It was shown that image edges must align well with explicitly reconstructed geometry in order to minimize visual artefacts along depth edges when performing novel-view synthesis [7]. Hedman *et al.* further show how to reconstruct a set of casually captured fish-eye images into global scene proxies and statically texture them by proposing a state-of-the-art plane-sweep algorithm and efficient cost-volume filtering [6].

2.3 Learning-Based Approaches

Deep neural networks define the state of the art for many computer vision tasks, e.g. optical flow estimation, segmentation, classification, depth prediction from single images, and many more. The essence of all learning-based approaches is *data*. Many of the most successful networks are trained in a *supervised* manner, meaning that ground-truth labels for the training data are required. For example, to train a supervised cat detector, a network might see a set of images containing cats and images containing no cats. For each incorrect prediction in an epoch (iterating once through the entire training dataset), a loss is accumulated which informs the neural network about its mistakes, i.e. wrong predictions. *Unsupervised* learning approaches train on unlabeled data and try to infer more general structures inherent in the observed data.

The most promising learning-based approaches used for IBR rely on physically motivated *models*[1] which can be trained to obtain powerful scene representations such as multiplane images (MPIs) as introduced by Zhou *et al.*'s stereo magnification work [22]. The authors train a network from data which is mined from YouTube videos and fully automatic scene reconstructions using SfM, with the goal of extrapolating novel viewpoints beyond the baseline of a stereo image captured with a dual camera of a smartphone. The core idea of the MPI representation is that a scene volume can be modeled by a set of fronto-parallel semi-transparent layers[2] which can be rendered from novel viewpoints.

The current state of the art of learned image-based representations suitable for head-motion parallax is local light field fusion [11]. The method generates *local* light fields by taking a set of casually captured images as input and predicting MPIs for each image with its four closest neighbors. At runtime, neighboring light fields are *fused* to continuously render novel viewpoints. The biggest limitations of the representation are its size and its current restriction to indoor environments.

3 Methods

This section gives an overview of the presented methods, which both rely on a dense sampling of key frames or reference viewpoints captured with a single moving camera. In both works, novel views are synthesized by combining viewpoints using some sort of flow-based blending *without* relying on any type of explicit geometry like depth maps or meshes. Both methods assume that all input views share the same intrinsic calibration and both register the central rays of captured viewpoints to *radial* directions of a camera manifold, i.e. a circle or a sphere, which is technically done by parameterizing the optical center and central ray using polar or spherical coordinates respectively.

---

[1] E.g. a model aiming to minimize the reprojection error of a set of images as commonly used in bundle-adjustment.

[2] This concept was first used by Walt Disney in the early stages of cartoon productions when artists moved semi-transparent layers relatively to each other to create new scenes.

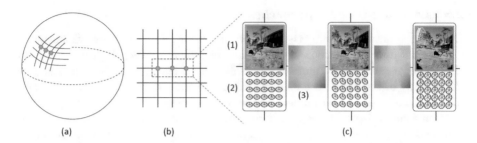

Fig. 1. Parallax360 representation: (a) Sampling sphere with three key frames (in orange), (b) key frames on longitude/latitude grid, (c) three main components: (1) key frames, (2) curve-based disparity motion fields, and (3) optical flow between key frames.

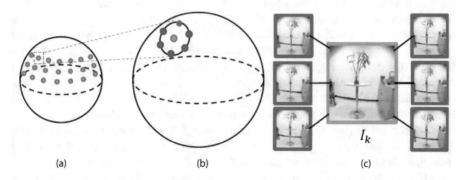

Fig. 2. Parallax360 capture: (a) key frames, (b) disparity motion fields to 6-node ring neighborhood, (c) zoom in to (b).

3.1 Parallax360

The scene representation of Parallax360 consists of uniformly sampled key frames on a sphere (see Fig. 1 (a)), captured using a robot arm (hence no extrinsic calibration is needed), disparity motion field for each key frame, calculated with the relative frames around the key frames, as well as dense bidirectional optical flow between key frames. A novel viewpoint is synthesized by determining the K nearest key frames (in practice $K = 2, 3$), followed by a patch-wise flow-based warping operation concluded by an alpha-blending step.

Capture. A *robot arm* captures thousands of plenoptic samples (pinhole images) and support images in a 6-node ring neighborhood (relative frames), as shown in Fig. 2, along the radial directions of a spherical surface. Since the robot's positioning is very accurate, there is no need for external calibration, i.e. reconstruction of camera geometry, after the capturing procedure. The capturing process for Parallax360 datasets is non-casual and time-consuming, e.g. capturing a dataset (key frames and relative frames) is done in almost 2 h.

Processing. The core of the Parallax360 processing is the computation of *curve-based* disparity motion fields and pairwise optical flow used for novel-view synthesis. Each disparity motion field $\mathbf{f}_1, \ldots, \mathbf{f}_6$ is computed from a set of 7 frames: 1 key frame and its 6 relative frames (see Fig. 2(b,c)). Flow vectors $\mathbf{f}_i(\mathbf{p})$ per pixel $\mathbf{p}$ are aggregated into image patches $\mathbf{P}$ of size 8×8 pixels by averaging them. The 6 initial disparity motion fields of a key frame are converted into a curve-based motion representation, modeled by a fitted ellipse and 6 polar angles (see Fig. 3(e)). For every patch $\mathbf{P}$ of a key frame, an ellipse $\mathbf{E}_P{}^3$ is computed by least-squares fitting. Five 2D points are needed for describing an ellipse as a quadric surface, and six motion vectors to relative frames are available. The endpoints of the motion vectors originating from the center of a patch are used to fit the ellipse. The motion field generation takes up to 24 h for a single dataset on a quad-core computer.

Representation. The fundamental component of Parallax360 datasets is the *curve-based* motion representation (see Fig. 3). The parameters of the fitted ellipse $\mathbf{E_P}$ and polar angles $\theta_{\mathbf{P}}^i$ are used to encode the magnitudes and directions of the motion vectors respectively. Every patch $\mathbf{P}$ of each key frame is associated with a fitted ellipse and 6 polar angles. The authors state that the estimation errors of the individual motion vectors can be alleviated by fitting the ellipse to the endpoints of the motion vectors. Key and relative frames are parameterized in spherical coordinates.

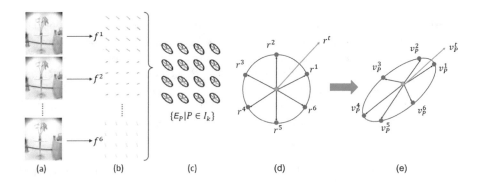

(a)   (b)   (c)   (d)   (e)

Fig. 3. Parallax360 disparity motion fields (a,b) and curve-based motion fields (c,d,e): (a) Relative frames, (b) corresponding motion fields, (c) disparity motion curves, (d) key and relative frames $\mathbf{r}^i$, (e) motion vectors $\mathbf{v_P^i}$ for a patch $\mathbf{P}$.

---

[3] The ellipse is denoted $\mathbf{C}_P$ in the original paper, but this conflicts with the camera centers $\mathbf{C}_i$ used in MegaParallax.

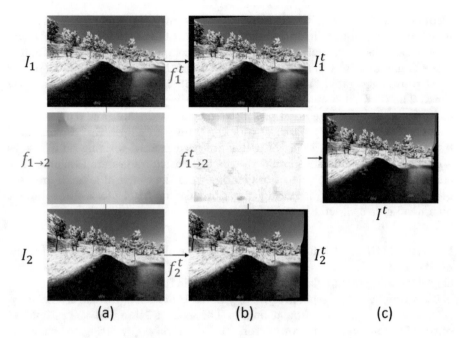

Fig. 4. Parallax 360 view synthesis: (a) Two closest key frames $\mathbf{I}_1, \mathbf{I}_2$ and optical flow $\mathbf{f}_{1\rightarrow2}$, (b) key frames warped $\mathbf{I}_1^t, \mathbf{I}_2^t$ into the target viewpoint $\mathbf{r}^t$ and blending motion field $\mathbf{f}_{1\rightarrow2}^t$, (c) image of target viewpoint $\mathbf{I}^t$.

Rendering. A target viewpoint $\mathbf{r}^t$ in Parallax360 is assumed to be tangential[4] to the spherical imaging surface exactly like the key frames. The authors consider the two or three closest key frames to synthesize a novel viewpoint (see Fig. 4).

For each key frame, the direction of the target viewpoint $\mathbf{r}^t$ can be described by the two closest motion vectors expressed by the ellipse $\mathbf{E_P}$ and the polar coordinates θ_P of the nearest two relative frames, e.g. $\mathbf{r}^1$ and $\mathbf{r}^2$ in Fig. 3(d). $\mathbf{r}^t$ can thus be written as a convex combination of polar coordinates:

$$\theta(r^t) = \alpha\theta_{\mathbf{P}}^1 + \beta\theta_{\mathbf{P}}^2 \tag{1}$$

$\alpha + \beta = 1$ and $\theta(\mathbf{r}^t)$ denotes the polar angle of the 2D vector $\mathbf{r}$. For a patch $\mathbf{P}$ in the key frame, the motion vector is computed by using

$$\mathbf{v}_{\mathbf{P}}^t = \frac{\|\mathbf{r}^t\|}{\|\mathbf{r}^1\|} \cdot \mathbf{E_P}(\alpha\theta_{\mathbf{P}}^1 + \beta\theta_{\mathbf{P}}^2). \tag{2}$$

Here, $\mathbf{E_P}(\theta)$ is a motion vector from the center of the ellipse to the point on the ellipse with polar angle θ. The parameters α and β are further used to synthesize *intermediate* target images $\mathbf{I}_k^t, k \in \{1, 2, 3\}$ by warping patches of the corresponding key frames:

$$\mathbf{I}_k^t(\mathbf{p}) = \mathbf{I}_k\left((\mathbf{f}_k^t)^{-1}(\mathbf{p})\right), \tag{3}$$

---

[4] Image planes are tangential to the sphere meaning orthogonal to the surface normal.

where $(\mathbf{f}_k^t)^{-1}$ maps the pixels of the target frame $\mathbf{I}^t$ into the k-th key frame $\mathbf{I}_k$. Note that the representation is based on image patches $\mathbf{P}$ but the target frame $\mathbf{I}^t$ is synthesized per pixel. The aggregated or patched motion vectors are smoothly propagated per pixel by using bilinear interpolation.

To avoid computing the flow field online for blending the intermediate images, Parallax360 uses the following strategy:

1. Map pixels from the target view $\mathbf{I}^t$ into the key frame $\mathbf{I}_i$ by applying the inverse of the disparity motion field $\mathbf{f}_i^t$,
2. apply the pairwise motion field $\mathbf{f}_{i\to k}$ to key frame $\mathbf{I}_k$,
3. use $\mathbf{f}_k^t$ to end up in the coordinates of the target image $\mathbf{I}_k^t$:

$$\mathbf{f}_{i\to k}^t = \mathbf{f}_k^t \oplus \mathbf{f}_{i\to k} \oplus (\mathbf{f}_i^t)^{-1}, \tag{4}$$

where $\oplus$ denotes the operator to concatenate mappings. With this strategy, we leverage the pre-computed optical flow $\mathbf{f}_{1\to 2}$ to achieve real-time rendering of $\mathbf{I}^t$.

Note that it is useful to think about the rendering as a *backward warping* process, in which the target image plane is the novel viewpoint $\mathbf{r}^t$ and the source plane is one of the nearest key frames $\mathbf{I}_k$. Since the novel viewpoint can be expressed in each patch of each key frame by using the fitted ellipse $\mathbf{E}_k$ and a polar angle, intermediate images can be created according to Eq. 3. In order to blend smoothly, optical flow is approximated for the intermediate images $\mathbf{I}_k^t$ as shown in Eq. 4 and used for *flow-based* blending. The authors report *ghosting* artifacts (see Fig. 7 right) when not using the flow field $\mathbf{f}_{1\to 2}^t$. The issue becomes more severe for challenging viewpoints that contain scene objects close to the camera because of their different perspectives in the key frames.

3.2   MegaParallax

The scene representation of MegaParallax consists of casually captured key frames on a circle (see Fig. 5, Capture), e.g. hand-held using a consumer camera or mobile device, extrinsic calibration obtained by SfM, and bidirectional optical flow between the key frames.

A novel viewpoint is synthesized by reconstructing individual camera rays of a desired viewpoint. First, for each ray, the enclosing pair of key frames is determined. Second, the ray reconstruction itself uses a flow-based blending of a pair of pixels, stemming from the camera pair (one pixel per camera), which correspond according to a simple proxy geometry, e.g. a plane parallel to the desired camera's image plane, but much farther away (see Fig. 8).

Capture. MegaParallax datasets share exactly the same input requirement as suggested in Megastereo [15]. *Hand-held* cameras can be used to acquire datasets for 360° stereo panoramas. The suitability of the captured video to get successfully processed into a Megastereo or MegaParallax dataset is fundamentally determined by the quality of the extrinsic calibration. The capturing procedure itself takes only about 10 s.

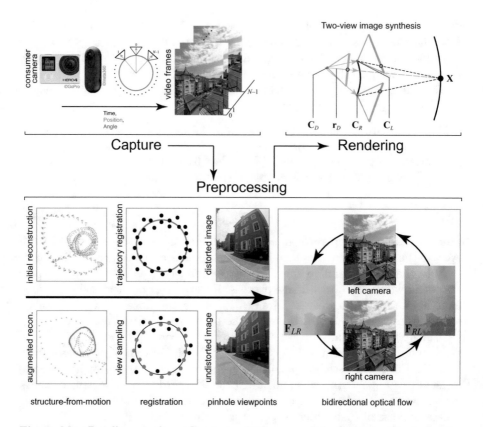

Fig. 5. MegaParallax pipeline: **Capture:** Video recorded along circular trajectory. **Preprocessing:** Estimate extrinsics, fit ideal trajectory, allows simple key frame registration via polar coordinates, undistort key frames, bidirectional flow for each pair of neighboring cameras. **Rendering:** Viewing rays are reconstructed using view-dependent flow-based blending.

There is active research that focuses on making the reconstruction of the desired egocentric camera paths more robust [20]. The dominance of rotation compared to translation makes egocentric camera paths very hard to reconstruct.

Processing. As shown in Fig. 5, the processing involves the following five steps:

1. Estimate camera extrinsics using SfM, e.g. COLMAP [17],
2. fit a circle to the optical centers,
3. register viewpoints (a.k.a. input, reference or key frames) to the circle identifying the optical axis of each viewpoint with a polar angle ϕ,
4. undistort images to obtain pinhole images, and lastly
5. compute bidirectional optical flow for each reference frame towards its left and right neighbors.

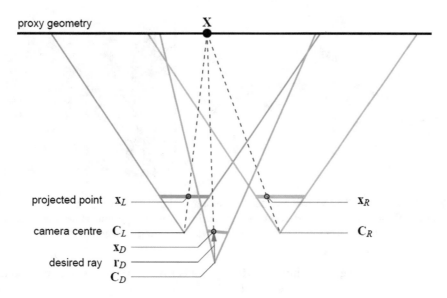

Fig. 6. MegaParallax view synthesis: The camera ray $\mathbf{x}_D$ is reconstructed by projecting a world point $\mathbf{X}$ into the surrounding pair of cameras $\mathbf{C}_L$ and $\mathbf{C}_R$.

The bottleneck of this stage is the estimation of the camera extrinsics (1) since the specific egocentric, inside-out camera path makes the reconstruction very challenging. Bertel *et al.* perform the extrinsic reconstruction in two passes. The first pass is performed on a subset of frames to increase the baselines between neighboring pairs of cameras. The second pass registers the remaining frames to the reconstruction from the first step. The viewpoints are picked by uniformly sampling polar angles induced by the circle. Estimating the extrinsics, i.e. performing a sparse SfM reconstruction, for a dataset takes between 30 and 60 min. The used two-pass strategy[5] allows for quick reconstructions. A few iterations of bundle adjustment can be applied to refine the final reconstruction. Finally, computing optical flow (5) is reliable as long imaged scenes are mostly diffuse and static, and source and target images are sufficiently close, i.e. having a small baseline and share similar orientations.

Representation. The representation of a MegaParallax dataset is very simple. The following data must be provided for each viewpoint at runtime: (1) the corresponding reference frame $\mathbf{I}_k$ and flow fields to left and right neighbor frames ($\mathbf{F}_{k \to k-1}$ and $\mathbf{F}_{k \to k+1}$ respectively), and (2) the projection matrix. The fitted circle and a linear array indexed by the polar coordinates of the viewpoints are needed to enable fast lookup operations at runtime.

A static cylindrical or dynamic planar scene geometry is taken as proxy geometry for the rasterization pipeline of OpenGL. The cylinder mimics previous

---

[5] Originally proposed in Marc Pollefeys' PhD thesis.

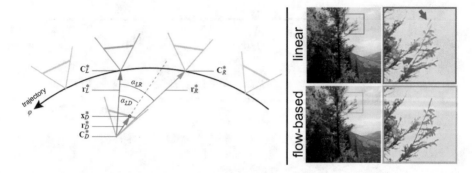

Fig. 7. MegaParallax view-dependent blending weight and ghosting: **Left:** View-dependent blending weight determined by desired camera ray and enclosing camera pair. **Right:** Flow-based blending is used to avoid ghosting artefacts.

panorama stitching algorithms [14, 15, 21] whereas a fronto-parallel plane in front of a desired viewpoint has been used in light field rendering [8].

Rendering. The rendering procedure used in MegaParallax is depicted in Fig. 6. A pixel $\mathbf{x}_D$ in the desired view is a convex combination of pixels $\mathbf{x}_L$ (left viewpoint) and $\mathbf{x}_R$ (right viewpoint):

$$\mathbf{I}_D(\mathbf{x}_D) = (1 - \alpha) \cdot \mathbf{I}_L(\mathbf{x}_L) + \alpha \cdot \mathbf{I}_R(\mathbf{x}_R), \tag{5}$$

the blending weight α depends on the relative angle α_{LD} between the vectors $\mathbf{r}_L^*$ and $\mathbf{r}_R^*$ connecting the optical centers of the left $\mathbf{C}_L$ and right $\mathbf{C}_R$ viewpoints with the optical center of the desired viewpoint and the desired camera ray (see Fig. 7, left). Note that the blending weights – and hence overall color – are computed independently per pixel of the desired viewpoint, which allows for extrapolation of novel viewpoints.

The use of an inaccurate proxy geometry may produce large reprojection errors, which reveal themselves as blurry artefacts or texture misalignments, such as ghosting (see Fig. 7, right). Megastereo [15] proposes flow-based ray interpolation to overcome these artefacts.

MegaParallax proposes *view-dependent* flow-based blending, which is not solely restricted to a fixed viewing circle as applied in Megastereo's casual ODS approach. To alleviate ghosting artefacts, MegaParallax uses *flow-corrected* pixel coordinates $\mathbf{x}_L^*$ and $\mathbf{x}_R^*$ to sample source pixels from the left $\mathbf{I}_L$ and right $\mathbf{I}_R$ reference images, respectively, to synthesize a pixel $\mathbf{x}_D$ in the desired image $\mathbf{I}_D$:

$$\mathbf{I}_D(\mathbf{x}_D) = (1 - \alpha) \cdot \mathbf{I}_L(\mathbf{x}_L^*) + \alpha \cdot \mathbf{I}_R(\mathbf{x}_R^*). \tag{6}$$

The flow-corrected pixel coordinates are obtained as follows:

1. A plane-induced displacement between the projections $\mathbf{x}_L$ and $\mathbf{x}_R$ is performed:

$$\mathbf{v}_{LR} = \mathbf{x}_R - \mathbf{x}_L \quad \text{and} \quad \mathbf{v}_{RL} = \mathbf{x}_L - \mathbf{x}_R. \tag{7}$$

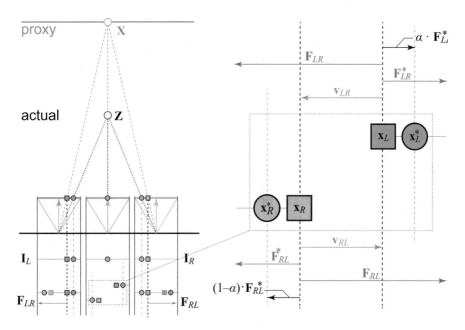

Fig. 8. MegaParallax's view-dependent flow-based blending enables motion parallax without ghosting artefacts. More description in the text.

2. The motion-corrected flow vectors are obtained using:

$$\mathbf{F}^*_{LR}(\mathbf{x}_L) = \mathbf{v}_{LR} - \mathbf{F}_{LR}(\mathbf{x}_L) \quad \text{and} \tag{8}$$

$$\mathbf{F}^*_{RL}(\mathbf{x}_R) = \mathbf{v}_{RL} - \mathbf{F}_{RL}(\mathbf{x}_R). \tag{9}$$

3. Scaling these displacements yields the flow-corrected image coordinates:

$$\mathbf{x}^*_L = \mathbf{x}_L + \alpha \cdot \mathbf{F}^*_{LR}(\mathbf{x}_L) \quad \text{and} \tag{10}$$

$$\mathbf{x}^*_R = \mathbf{x}_R + (1 - \alpha) \cdot \mathbf{F}^*_{RL}(\mathbf{x}_R). \tag{11}$$

Note that view-dependent flow-based blending resolves ghosting in the desired viewpoints, but does not necessarily produce correct perspectives in all cases due to vertical distortion. The scaled displacements $\alpha \cdot \mathbf{F}^*_{LR}$ and $(1 - \alpha) \cdot \mathbf{F}^*_{RL}$ only push the initial projections $\mathbf{x}_L$ and $\mathbf{x}_R$ in the *correct* directions, as illustrated in Fig. 8. The method works well if the angular baseline[6] between images is sufficiently small with respect to the closest scene object, and optical flow is sufficiently smooth.

The rendering speed is very fast (>200 fps) since all flow-fields are precomputed and thus only light-weight computations, mostly texture lookups, need to be performed at runtime. The rendering strategy delivers high-quality results

---

[6] Angle between neighboring viewpoints, e.g. 180 viewpoints sampled uniformly on a circle yields an angular baseline of 2°.

and supports desired views with wide field of views by design. The per-pixel blending allows for view extrapolation, which occurs whenever a viewpoint is synthesized *within* the camera circle. This can be seen at best in the supplemental video of MegaParallax[7] when translational camera motion is compared against Parallax360.

4 Results

This section shows some selected results shown in the presented papers. Luo *et al.* show comparisons between omnidirectional stereo (ODS) panoramas [14, 15] and Parallax360 in Fig. 9. The first row depicts two viewpoints (left and right view) with different head orientations obtained from a stereo panorama. The second row shows close-ups of the rectangles depicted in the first row. Note that there is no relative motion between scene objects. The third row shows two stereo viewpoints obtained by Parallax360. The fourth row shows close-ups in spirit of the second row. ODS panoramas provide binocular disparity for head rotation but do not support head translation and thus neither support motion parallax by design. Note the relative displacements of the trees observed in the fourth row of Fig. 9, caused by motion parallax.

Bertel *et al.* show comparisons between Unstructured Lumigraph Rendering (ULR) [4], Megastereo [15], and MegaParallax in Fig. 10. First row: ULR provides motion parallax, but leads to blurry rendering artefacts (ghosting) which is expected when using an inaccurate scene proxy. Second row: Megastereo shows no motion parallax, but the viewpoints show visually crisp results (no ghosting). Third row: MegaParallax combines the best of both approaches, namely motion parallax without introducing ghosting artefacts.

5 Discussion

We now discuss the most important aspects of the two methods described in this chapter and focus on the need of compelling visual content that is suitable for RealVR experiences, i.e. content that provides head-motion parallax at runtime.

5.1 Capturing

Parallax360 uses a robot arm to capture thousands of input images. The capturing procedure takes less than two hours. MegaParallax, on the other hand, needs only hundreds of input images and the capturing takes about 10 s. The input images are extracted from a continuous sweep of a hand-held camera (see Fig. 5 Capture). However, note that Parallax360 densely captures a spherical imaging surface (see Fig. 2), while MegaParallax just captures one single circle.

The fundamental trade-off here is that casual captures take much less time than fully controlled captures. However, this comes at the cost of a more difficult

---

[7] https://richardt.name/megaparallax.mp4.

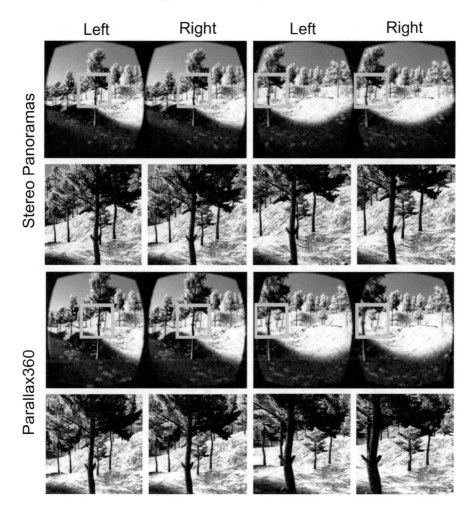

Fig. 9. Parallax360 results: A comparison between stereo panoramas and Parallax360 results. More description in the text.

estimation of the camera path, e.g. by determining extrinsic calibration of video frames using SfM or SLAM.

Finding capturing procedures and flexible models to represent RealVR experiences is very exciting research since it combines many areas from computer vision and computer graphics.

5.2 Processing

Parallax360 does not rely on estimating camera extrinsics because of the fully controlled capture procedure using a robot arm. The core of its representation are curve-based disparity motion fields (see Fig. 3), which are computed by pro-

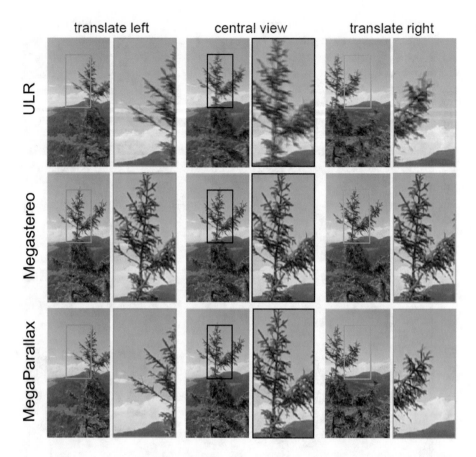

Fig. 10. MegaParallax results: Comparison between ULR (motion parallax but blurry), Megastereo (no motion parallax but crisp) and MegaParallax (motion parallax and crisp). More description in the text.

cessing disparity information obtained by optical flow between key frames and associated neighboring relative frames.

MegaParallax relies on the estimation of camera extrinsics. The ability to create datasets of sufficient quality converges with the problem to reconstruct scenes from a egocentric inside-out video. Once a camera path reconstruction of sufficient quality is obtained, it is straightforward to fit a circle to the estimated viewpoint centers, register viewpoints via polar angles induced by the circle, and to compute bidirectional optical flow between neighboring viewpoints (see Fig. 5 Preprocessing).

Note that both methods demonstrate that optical flow works reliably if source and target images are *sufficiently* close to each other. An important remark is that the degree of closeness depends on the depth distribution of the scene.

The closer scene objects come to a viewpoint, the bigger their disparity (motion parallax), when projecting them into a pair of neighboring frames or viewpoints.

While computing the curved motion fields can take up to 24 h on a quad-core PC, and thus dominates the Parallax360 preprocessing time, SfM and optical flow computation takes less than 2 h in MegaParallax.

5.3   Representation

Parallax360 computes the 5 parameters of an ellipse and 6 polar angles for every patch of every key frame to encode curve-based motion fields (see Fig. 3). Key frames as well as novel viewpoints are defined *on* the spherical imaging surface that was sampled during capturing (see Figs. 1 and 2). The viewing direction of a key or target frame is fully determined by the spherical coordinates modeling its central ray, i.e. a ray originating at the sphere's center and thus intersecting the spherical surface in normal direction (a.k.a. radial direction).

MegaParallax needs to estimate camera extrinsics per frame or viewpoint. Every viewpoint is registered with a circle fitted to the optical centers of cameras. For each pair of neighboring cameras, bidirectional flow is computed (see Fig. 5, Preprocessing). In summary, for each key frame (viewpoint), a projection matrix is stored, as well as a polar angle and dense optical flow to its left and right neighbor.

The advantage of dense image representations is that no explicit scene geometry needs to be known to synthesize novel viewpoints. Nevertheless, this statement is not complete, since the quality of novel viewpoints depends heavily on the quality of correspondences between the images. This, in turn, varies with the nature of the scene to be captured. Note that visibility does not need to be modeled in dense image-based representations, view synthesis comes down to lookups and blendings and does not rely on reprojection over scene geometry.

5.4   Rendering

Synthesizing a novel viewpoint in Parallax360 (see Fig. 4) is based on representing the target viewpoint with respect to its two or three closest key frames. The disparity motion fields of the key frames are then used to create intermediate target viewpoints by warping key frames *towards* the target viewpoint (see Fig. 4(b) and Eq. 3). The target viewpoint is created by flow-based blending of the intermediate viewpoints, whose flow can be obtained from the disparity motion fields and the dense flow fields between key frames (see Eq. 4). Note that while the synthesis runs per pixel, the representation is based on image patches. Furthermore, novel viewpoints are always *interpolations* of existing pairs of key frames on a per-patch level.

View synthesis in MegaParallax (see Figs. 6 and 8) is achieved by reconstructing individual camera rays, which leads to panoramic field of views and *extrapolation* of the captured viewpoints instead of only interpolation.

The most important aspect of flow-based blending is that *close* scene objects will project farther away from the centers of the source images, which introduces

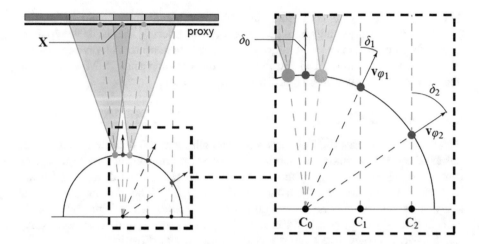

Fig. 11. MegaParallax viewing space analysis: **Left:** Blending performance according to central ray of the desired viewpoint, e.g. $\mathbf{C}_0$ placed at the center of the circle. **Right:** Translating the desired viewpoint ($\mathbf{C}_1$, $\mathbf{C}_2$) causes slanted angles with the circle, e.g. δ_1 and δ_2. If δ_i exceeds the field of view of the reference viewpoint, the ray reconstruction fails.

errors. This is very similar to the case of panorama stitching algorithms which mosaic vertical image strips into a single equirectangular image in 2D [14,15,21]. Nearby scene objects in the real world get *vertically distorted* [19] when packed into equirectangular images. They get literally *squeezed* horizontally which is desired in 360° panorama stitching algorithms, but unwanted in image-based rendering applications, in which correct perspectives in desired viewpoints are essential to immerse consumers into "RealVR" experiences.

5.5   Viewing Space

The Parallax360 approach synthesizes novel viewpoints *on* the spherical imaging surface, which is sampled during the capture process. Novel viewpoints are synthesized using flow-based image interpolation. To enable head-motion parallax within the sphere, the initial target viewpoints need to be *extended*.

A viewpoint extension uses a homography and a scaling operation to adjust a synthesized viewpoint to approximate a desired viewpoint. The homography applies scaling to account for the expected change in parallax when moving forward or backward. Since this operation does not provide plausible motion parallax, we think that Parallax360 provides real head-motion parallax only on the surface of the sphere and not within. Nevertheless, the method supports arbitrary head-motions, but provides only restricted motion parallax when viewpoints need to be extended. The method employs a diameter of 1.25 m for the spherical imaging surface and shows compelling results for head-motion parallax in 360° environments. Nevertheless, the actual viewing space within the capturing sphere is not further evaluated.

Fig. 12. Top row, Parallax360 limitation: Sequence of viewpoints with incorrect motion fields produce interpolation artefacts. Bottom row, MegaParallax limitation: The desired viewpoint is translated from the center of the circle to the left, outside the supported viewing space.

MegaParallax operates *within* a circle, in comparison to Parallax360 which operates *on* the surface of a sphere. The translational freedom is restricted by (see Fig. 11):

1. The radius of the circle,
2. the density of reference viewpoints, and
3. their field of view shared with neighboring views.

The field of view of the desired viewpoint has an impact as well, but this parameter is kept fixed for each dataset. The actual viewing area is described by a concentric circle which supports high-quality view synthesis within a radius of roughly factor 2 of the capturing circle's radius depending on the quality of the extrinsic calibration (for more details, please refer to Bertel *et al.* [3], Sect. 8, Fig. 14). As an example, hand-held datasets have a circle radius of roughly 0.8 m which leads to a viewing area radius of 0.4 m.

5.6   Limitations

The main limitations of Parallax360 are:

1. A time consuming capture and preprocessing stage and
2. view synthesis technically only on the surface of the imaging surface leading to view interpolation and incorrect motion parallax when moving inside the sphere.

Note that the quality of the view interpolation depends on the quality of the precomputed optical flow fields. The main limitations of MegaParallax are:

1. Only head-motion parallax inside the capture circle,
2. vertical distortion caused by using an inaccurate scene proxy, and
3. fragile extrinsic estimation, which makes datasets from complex environments, such as specular or dynamic scenes or scenes with large depth variation, very challenging to reconstruct.

View synthesis fails in both approaches if a desired ray cannot be reconstructed from a determined pair of cameras (or triplet of key frames) due to insufficient field of view as discussed in Sect. 5.5. This results visually in black stripes as seen in the bottom row in Fig. 12. From left to right: (1) The desired viewpoint placed at the center of the circle. (2) Viewpoint translates to the left. Camera rays on the right start retrieving black pixels because of slanted angles δ. (3) Translating further to the left causes more ray reconstructions to fail.

Another limitation shared by Parallax360 and MegaParallax is the dependency on sufficiently good flow fields. Optical flow can become unreliable in certain situations, e.g. when estimating correspondences in regions with repetitive textures (see Fig. 12, top row).

It is worth noting that Parallax360 does not struggle with specular scenes because of the fully controlled capturing which is very similar in spirit to light field rendering [8]. Parallax360 does not suffer from vertical distortion since target viewpoints are created by blending warped key frames. The warping happens on the spherical surface and on a per patch-level within each key frame. Since *similar* perspective images are warped and blended, resulting viewpoints exhibit plausible perspectives. Note that this only works if the key frames are captured sufficiently dense with respect to the closest object[8] in the scene.

This is not the case for MegaParallax, which performs independent, per-ray reconstructions which can lead to cases in which a single viewpoint is synthesized by dozens of pairs of reference viewpoints which all show different perspectives, but cover a larger field of view. Since there is no accurate scene proxy to reproject reference viewpoints in 3D Euclidean space, vertical distortion becomes visible in desired viewpoints (see how the hand-rail bends in Fig. 8 of [3]).

6   Conclusion

Both Parallax360 and MegaParallax propose image-based scene representations and use implicit geometry, i.e. optical flow, to render novel viewpoints using a variant of flow-based blending. The absence of explicit geometry is compensated by a large number and high density of reference views, which are necessary to (1) compute flow fields reliably and (2) perform view interpolation while maintaining plausible perspectives. Both methods share time-consuming preprocessing stages, which enable real-time rendering algorithms based primarily on texture lookups and only light-weight computations at runtime.

---

[8] Assuming a uniform distribution of reference viewpoints.

The main advantage of the presented methods is the high visual quality of their results, particularly for the outdoor environments shown in this chapter (see Figs. 9 and 10), which are known to be very difficult to reconstruct explicitly. Especially fine geometry like plants or trees are very challenging, but supported well in the results.

The main issues with MegaParallax are (1) vertical distortion that is caused by a constant scene depth assumption (as in concentric mosaics [19]) and (2) a viewing space restricted to a circle. The viewing space could be extended easily by using reference viewpoints with a wider field of view or providing explicit scene geometry to allow small off-plane movements and rotations. For Parallax360, the time-consuming capturing and processing stages as well as its viewpoint extension to render viewpoints within the sphere are its main issues.

While image-based rendering methods relying on explicit geometry produce the visually most compelling results for many environments, they rely on a successful estimation of scene geometry, which is hard to guarantee in arbitrary situations (see Fig. 9 in [3]). The quality of the results mainly depends on the quality of the estimated geometry.

The interplay of capturing, processing, representation, and rendering is vital to understand design decisions in "RealVR" pipelines. Since representations have to adopt to the nature of scene objects which shall be modeled, e.g. diffuse architecture vs. shiny cars, or hairy cats vs. thin twigs and leaves, more flexible representations have to be found to faithfully capture and represent the real world in all its beauty and visual fidelity.

To represent a real-world scene in all its complexity using only a sparse number of viewpoints, it seems natural to us that hybrid representations have to evolve, which combine the advantages of implicit and explicit geometry as well as learning-based approaches, such as multiplane images. The representations of the presented methods could be compressed by modeling static and diffuse parts of the scene with static geometry, since it is not necessary to store dozens of largely redundant images of a scene, which does not contain view-dependent effects.

We currently see the biggest demand in more robust and reliable methods for 2D and 3D scene understanding and scene reconstruction in particular. This will automatically provide better correspondences and thus more robust and more compact scene representations, which can be tweaked to perform excellently for special types of scenes. Finding a scene representation that is sufficiently flexible to model the real world has been a difficult challenge in computer graphics research for decades. Requiring that this representation should be *extractable* from a sparse set of viewpoints, ideally casually captured, makes novel-view synthesis for "RealVR" a very challenging and multi-disciplinary research topic.

Acknowledgements. This work was supported by EU Horizon 2020 MSCA grant FIRE (665992), the EPSRC Centre for Doctoral Training in Digital Entertainment (EP/L016540/1), RCUK grant CAMERA (EP/M023281/1), the NSFC (No. 61671268, 61672307, 61727808), the National Key Technologies R&D Program of China (No. 2015BAF23B03), a UKRI Innovation Fellowship (EP/S001050/1), a Rabin Ezra Scholarship and an NVIDIA Corporation GPU Grant.

References

1. Adelson, E.H., Bergen, J.R.: The plenoptic function and the elements of early vision. In: Computational Models of Visual Processing, pp. 3–20. MIT Press (1991)
2. Anderson, R., et al.: Jump: virtual reality video. ACM Trans. Graph. **35**(6), 1–13 (2016). https://doi.org/10.1145/2980179.2980257. Article no. 198, Proceedings of SIGGRAPH Asia
3. Bertel, T., Campbell, N.D.F., Richardt, C.: MegaParallax: casual 360° panoramas with motion parallax. IEEE Trans. Visual Comput. Graph. **25**(5), 1828–1835 (2019). https://doi.org/10.1109/TVCG.2019.2898799
4. Buehler, C., Bosse, M., McMillan, L., Gortler, S., Cohen, M.: Unstructured Lumigraph rendering. In: Proceedings of the Annual Conference on Computer Graphics and Interactive Techniques (SIGGRAPH), pp. 425–432 (2001). https://doi.org/10.1145/383259.383309
5. Gortler, S.J., Grzeszczuk, R., Szeliski, R., Cohen, M.F.: The Lumigraph. In: Proceedings of the Annual Conference on Computer Graphics and Interactive Techniques (SIGGRAPH), pp. 43–54, August 1996. https://doi.org/10.1145/237170.237200
6. Hedman, P., Alsisan, S., Szeliski, R., Kopf, J.: Casual 3D photography. ACM Trans. Graph. **36**(6), 1–15 (2017). https://doi.org/10.1145/3130800.3130828. Article no. 234, Proceedings of SIGGRAPH Asia
7. Hedman, P., Ritschel, T., Drettakis, G., Brostow, G.: Scalable inside-out image-based rendering. ACM Trans. Graph. **35**(6), 1–11 (2016). https://doi.org/10.1145/2980179.2982420. Article no. 231, Proceedings of SIGGRAPH Asia
8. Levoy, M., Hanrahan, P.: Light field rendering. In: Proceedings of the Annual Conference on Computer Graphics and Interactive Techniques (SIGGRAPH), pp. 31–42, August 1996. https://doi.org/10.1145/237170.237199
9. Luo, B., Xu, F., Richardt, C., Yong, J.H.: Parallax360: stereoscopic 360° scene representation for head-motion parallax. IEEE Trans. Visual Comput. Graph. **24**(4), 1545–1553 (2018). https://doi.org/10.1109/TVCG.2018.2794071
10. McMillan, L., Bishop, G.: Plenoptic modeling: an image-based rendering system. In: Proceedings of the Annual Conference on Computer Graphics and Interactive Techniques (SIGGRAPH), pp. 39–46 (1995). https://doi.org/10.1145/218380.218398
11. Mildenhall, B., et al.: Local light field fusion: practical view synthesis with prescriptive sampling guidelines. ACM Trans. Graph. **38**(4), 1–14 (2019). https://doi.org/10.1145/3306346.3322980. Article no. 29, Proceedings of SIGGRAPH
12. Overbeck, R.S., Erickson, D., Evangelakos, D., Pharr, M., Debevec, P.: A system for acquiring, compressing, and rendering panoramic light field stills for virtual reality. ACM Trans. Graph. **37**(6), 1–15 (2018). https://doi.org/10.1145/3272127.3275031. Article no. 197, Proceedings of SIGGRAPH Asia
13. Parra Pozo, A., et al.: An integrated 6DoF video camera and system design. ACM Trans. Graph. **38**(6), 1–16 (2019). https://doi.org/10.1145/3355089.3356555. Article no. 216, Proceedings of SIGGRAPH Asia
14. Peleg, S., Ben-Ezra, M., Pritch, Y.: Omnistereo: Panoramic stereo imaging. IEEE Trans. Pattern Anal. Mach. Intell. **23**(3), 279–290 (2001). https://doi.org/10.1109/34.910880
15. Richardt, C., Pritch, Y., Zimmer, H., Sorkine-Hornung, A.: MegaStereo: constructing high-resolution stereo panoramas. In: Proceedings of the International Conference on Computer Vision and Pattern Recognition (CVPR), pp. 1256–1263 (2013). https://doi.org/10.1109/CVPR.2013.166

16. Schroers, C., Bazin, J.C., Sorkine-Hornung, A.: An omnistereoscopic video pipeline for capture and display of real-world VR. ACM Trans. Graph. **37**(3), 1–13 (2018). https://doi.org/10.1145/3225150. Article no. 37

17. Schönberger, J.L., Frahm, J.M.: Structure-from-motion revisited. In: Proceedings of the International Conference on Computer Vision and Pattern Recognition (CVPR), pp. 4104–4113 (2016). https://doi.org/10.1109/CVPR.2016.445

18. Shum, H.-Y., Chan, S.-C., Kang, S.-B.: Image-Based Rendering. Springer, Heidelberg (2007). https://doi.org/10.1007/978-0-387-32668-9

19. Shum, H.Y., He, L.W.: Rendering with concentric mosaics. In: Proceedings of the Annual Conference on Computer Graphics and Interactive Techniques (SIGGRAPH), pp. 299–306, August 1999. https://doi.org/10.1145/311535.311573

20. Sweeney, C., Holynski, A., Curless, B., Seitz, S.M.: Structure from motion for panorama-style videos (2019). arXiv:1906.03539

21. Szeliski, R.: Image alignment and stitching: a tutorial. Found. Trends Comput. Graph. Vis. **2**(1), 1–104 (2006). https://doi.org/10.1561/0600000009

22. Zhou, T., Tucker, R., Flynn, J., Fyffe, G., Snavely, N.: Stereo magnification: learning view synthesis using multiplane images. ACM Trans. Graph. **37**(4), 1–12 (2018). https://doi.org/10.1145/3197517.3201323. Article no. 65, Proceedings of SIGGRAPH

Viewpoint-Free Photography
for Virtual Reality

Peter Hedman[(⊠)][iD]

University College London, London, UK
p.hedman@cs.ucl.ac.uk
http://www.phogzone.com

Abstract. Viewpoint-free photography, i.e., interactively controlling
the viewpoint of a photograph after capture, is a central challenge for real
virtual reality (VR) experiences. In this chapter, we present algorithms
that enable viewpoint-free photography from casual capture, i.e., footage
easily captured with consumer cameras. We build on extensive work in
image-based rendering, which often focuses on full or near-interpolation,
where output viewpoints lie directly between captured images, or nearby.
However, for 6-DOF VR experiences, it is essential to create viewpoint-
free photos with a wide field-of-view and sufficient positional freedom to
cover the range of motion a user might experience.

We focus on two VR experiences:

(1) Seated experiences, where the user can lean in different directions.
    Since the scene is only observed from a small range of viewpoints, we
    focus on easy capture—showing how to turn panorama-style capture
    into 3D photos, a simple representation for viewpoint-free photos,
    and also how to significantly speed up processing times.

(2) Room-scale experiences, where the user can explore vastly different
    perspectives. This is challenging: More input footage is needed, main-
    taining real-time display rates becomes difficult, view-dependent
    appearance and object backsides need to be modelled, all while pre-
    venting noticeable mistakes. We address these challenges by: (1) cre-
    ating refined geometry for each input photograph, (2) using a fast
    tiled rendering algorithm to achieve real-time display rates, and (3)
    using a convolutional neural network to hide visual mistakes during
    compositing.

Overall, we provide evidence that viewpoint-free photography is feasible
from casual capture—for both seated and room-scale VR experiences.

Keywords: 3D photography · Image-based rendering · Free-viewpoint

1 Introduction

Imagine if you could visually capture any place, in a way that allows anyone
to immersively re-experience the sensation of being there. This goal lies at the
intersection of art and science, and is something we have been working toward for
centuries. Already in the 15th century, realistic paintings painstakingly captured

© Springer Nature Switzerland AG 2020
M. Magnor and A. Sorkine-Hornung (Eds.): Real VR, LNCS 11900, pp. 132–166, 2020.
https://doi.org/10.1007/978-3-030-41816-8_6

effects such as perspective, illumination and even complex reflections of mirrors. With the advent of photography, it became possible to easily capture images with this degree of realism. Since then, we have captured a much greater amount of realistic content, giving us a rich visual history of the 20$^\text{th}$ century. Today, you can capture photos of places you visit, share them with friends and family, so they feel more connected to you, or preserve your personally treasured places as visual memories.

However, photos only capture a single perspective and cannot fully convey the experience of a place. Modern VR headsets with positional tracking, such as the Oculus Rift and HTC Vive, enable much more immersive experiences. For example, *seated VR* is where the user can lean in different directions and peek behind corners, and *room-scale VR* is where the user can freely walk around the room and view the scene from vastly different perspectives. However, there is not yet a way to easily capture real places for these experiences. Such technology would allow everyone to experience hard to reach places, such as the wreck of the Titanic or the peaks of Mount Everest. It also has commercial applications, for example in real estate, where it is useful to present property on sale in realistic 3D [2], or for video game development where 3D asset creation is costly [1]. Finally, this would enable people to capture places of personal or cultural importance, and share these with friends, or preserve them as digital memories.

1.1   Goals

Our focus is on easily capturing real places for realistic display in VR. We call this *viewpoint-free photography*, i.e. capturing a real place without fixing the viewpoint in advance, and strive toward four goals: (1) ease of capture, (2) sufficient range of motion, (3) high quality (realism), and (4) real-time display rates.

Specifically, we only use off-the-shelf hardware, and look for approaches that can capture a real place in a short amount of time (1). The resulting viewpoint-free photos should allow the user sufficient range of motion for either a seated VR or a room-scale VR experience (2) without noticing mistakes whose appearance in the photos significantly differ from reality (3). Finally, to allow interactive exploration in VR, we investigate approaches that can quickly display 2D images at novel viewpoints at real-time rates of 30 images per second or more (4).

1.2   Context

We make heavy use of recent advances in the closely related, but subtly different, field of 3D reconstruction from images (or *multi-view stereo, MVS*) [23,59,65]. While our focus is on accurately capturing the appearance of the scene, MVS is less concerned with appearance and works towards accurate 3D geometry. Instead, our work sits in the space of image-based rendering (IBR), which covers all methods that synthesize images from a collection of input photos in a scene.

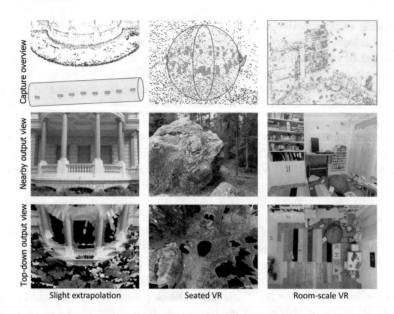

Fig. 1. Left-to-right: Image-based rendering for slight view extrapolation (Soft 3D [56]), viewpoint-free photography for seated VR (Sects. 3 and 4), viewpoint-free photography for room-scale VR (Sects. 5 and 6). The top row shows the input photo locations in red and the range of motion enabled by each method is visualized in green. Note that the left column is not directly suitable for VR experiences—it does not capture the entire scene, as the input photos all face the same way. All methods look great when staying close to the input photos (middle row), but only our approach for room-scale VR is able to maintain high-quality results with a difficult top-down view, which is far away from the input photos (bottom row).

In this chapter, we target easy-to-capture VR experiences. In particular, the rotational range of motion in VR headsets is immense: the user can rotate freely and look in all directions, making it essential to create viewpoint-free photos with a wide field-of-view (FOV). As Fig. 1 (left) shows, earlier methods for easy-to-capture IBR are generally limited to narrow FOV experiences.

In Sects. 3 and 4, we target seated VR experiences with a limited range of motion, see Fig. 1 (middle). This simplifies the representation and reconstruction problem, as the scene is only ever observed from a small range of viewpoints. For example, the user only ever sees the front facing side of objects in the scene and the view-dependent appearance of materials becomes less important to preserve. We thus focus on ease of capture (goal 1), showing how to turn panorama-style capture into *3D photos*, a simple representation for viewpoint-free photos (Sect. 3), and also how to significantly speed up processing (Sect. 4).

In Sects. 5 and 6, we target room-scale VR experiences where the user is free to explore the scene without constraints, see Fig. 1 (right). In this setting, we have to capture more data from different viewpoints in the scene, so instead of focusing on ease-of-capture, we place our effort on realism, quality (goal 3), and real-time display rates (goal 4). In particular, maintaining real-time display rates becomes difficult with more data, we also have to pay attention to view-dependent appearance, build a representation for the backsides of objects, and also make sure that there are no noticeable mistakes in the locations the user might visit.

2   Background

Our work builds on a long tradition of 3D reconstruction from images [22] and IBR [68]. MVS algorithms (e.g., [23,26,37]) perform automatic 3D geometry reconstruction from unstructured photo collections. Approaches based on Delaunay tetrahedralization (e.g., [37,45]) generate impressive 3D models, even in the presence of traditionally hard cases such as large textureless regions. In parallel, other methods improve the quality of individual depth maps by enforcing smoothness in image-space [33,63]. Recently, Patch-Match based algorithms such as COLMAP [65] have been the most accurate in benchmark tests [41,66].

However, for viewpoint-free photography we need a representation for the visual information in the scene, which often has to describe more than geometry: view-dependent materials, reflections, refractions, and light scattering through participating media (*e.g.* light cones in fog). Here we review several representations for viewpoint-free photos, and evaluate them in the context of our goals.

2.1   Artifacts

To concretely discuss both quality and realism (goal 3), we pay attention to common visible mistakes, or so-called *artifacts*. See Fig. 2 for examples:

Floating geometry: Some stereo matching approaches incorrectly reconstruct nearby depth for regions where photoconsistency is unreliable, resulting in "floating" pieces of geometry.

Misaligned occlusion edges: Many 3D reconstruction methods inflate or erode objects in the scene. This causes misalignment between the scene geometry and the input photographs at occlusion edges.

Foreground bleeding: Inaccurate foreground geometry can lead to ghosting, where the color of foreground objects is projected onto the background.

Color seams: These are often caused by misalignment, different resolutions, and shifts in colors for the same (or neighboring) content across input photos.

Missing highlights: Highlights are important. However, it may be more visually pleasing to discard highlights that cannot be convincingly be reproduced.

Finally, the output imagery needs to be temporally stable.

Fig. 2. Common artifacts for viewpoint-free photography methods.

2.2   Representations

Panoramas. Using 360 cameras, it is now easy to capture $360° × 180°$ panoramas. Such panoramas can also be stitched from multiple normal photos, albeit with risk of misalignment artifacts such as seams or ghosting. These can be alleviated with seam-hiding [4,44], or warp-deformations [48,57,81]. However, panoramas provide no range of motion as they only capture a single viewpoint (goal 2).

Stereo panoramas provide binocular depth cues [6,36,42,55,61]. Unfortunately, this representation has drawbacks in VR [6]:

1. non-linear perspective: straight lines in the scene are rendered as bent;
2. the lack of realistic motion parallax as the head is turned;
3. incorrect stereo parallax away from the equator, most noticeable as the distance to the floor appearing "at infinity", resulting in unpleasant vertigo;
4. the inability to tilt the head sideways and obtain correct binocular parallax;
5. un-specified behavior at the poles: a simple 180 vertical sweep leaves gaps.

Color-and-depth panoramas support viewpoint changes [35]. However, using only a single depth channel exposes artifacts at depth discontinuities, *e.g.* long stretched triangles or holes. Layered depth panoramas address this [82], but cannot represent sloped surfaces as the layers are not connected.

Light Fields. Light fields are high-quality viewpoint-free photos that capture view-dependent effects, but require a lot of storage. In the general case, these representations are five dimensional—a 3D grid of 2D input photos. Early approaches [28,46] reduced this to four dimensions if the viewing volume contains empty space, three dimensions if the output camera is constrained to a plane [69]. Unfortunately, these representations have a limited range of motion (goal 2), and require a many of input photos, making capture tedious and time consuming (goal 1). This can be alleviated with hybrid techniques that synthesize in-between views using image warping [14,28,32], or CNN-based approaches [39,71]. However, these focus on object capture, resulting in small light fields with a limited field-of-view. It is possible to build larger, panoramic light fields from hand-held footage [10], and room-scale light fields with robot capture [5], by restricting the output camera to a plane. Recent methods combine modern MVS methods with motorized rig capture to build light fields suitable for seated VR experiences [53].

Global Texture. It is useful to incorporate geometry into viewpoint-free photos. For example, by overlaying a *texture map*, on top of the reconstructed geometry in the scene. This texture map is commonly obtained by projecting input photos onto the scene geometry and resolving alignment artifacts using *e.g.* seam-hiding stitching [74], warp deformations [83], or super-resolution techniques [27]. This representation can be rendered from any viewpoint using standard graphics engines, resulting in real-time display rates (goal 4) and, in theory, a large range of motion (goal 2). However, quality heavily depends on the reconstructed geometry and a single texture cannot represent view-dependent effects. Even with perfect geometry this looks artificial, as highlights are static or missing.

View-Dependent Textures. Applying *view-dependent textures* onto scene geometry has potential for higher realism. Early approaches used either a few input photos captured by hand [15], or an abundance of photos from a capture rig [76]. The Unstructured Lumigraph [11] algorithm works with any number of input photos, and generalizes into a light field representation if enough photos are used. While these representations reproduce view-dependent effects, they depend on the accuracy of the reconstructed geometry. Some artifacts from inaccurate geometry, such as ghosting can be alleviated with soft visibility [58] and image-warping techniques [16]. However, artifacts are still visible at misaligned occlusion edges.

Per-Input-View Geometry. Tailoring custom geometry for each input photo makes it easier to align with image content. This has lead to representations that use *per-input-view geometry* to warp input photos into the output view, forming the image as a view-dependent blend of the warped photos. This was first shown in synthetic scenes with accurate geometry [13], and later extended to real photos [49]. Recent approaches improve quality for real scenes by enforcing smooth pixel motion when warping photos, except at occlusion boundaries [12,52,70,84]. However, rendering with per-input-view geometry becomes expensive in large scenes with several input photos. This limits range of motion, and most approaches use few input cameras and show only slight view extrapolation [12,43,52]. Furthermore, these redundant representations for geometry introduce more opportunities for mistakes. This often results in floating geometry, and does not completely eliminate foreground bleeding and misaligned occlusion edges.

Output-View-Dependent Geometry. Instead of computing geometry for each *input* view, some representations tailor geometry for every *output* view. Image priors can be used to guide reconstruction in a way that produces more plausible rendered images. The priors can be encoded as a dictionary of patches from input photos [18,77–79], or as a CNN [19]. Unfortunately these approaches are not interactive, as building geometry for each output view is expensive.

Soft3D [56] computes a *soft* 3D reconstruction of the scene, encoded as a plane sweep volume, and produces output images by marching through this representation. This produces high quality results close to input photos, but only supports a limited range of motion before discretization artifacts occur.

3   Casual 3D Photography

In this section, we present a technology which creates viewpoint-free photos for seated VR experiences. We describe a suitable representation and introduce reconstruction algorithms specifically designed for easy capture. We do not require the user to capture a scene from all angles, but just an arc around a single viewpoint. A person captures a scene by moving a hand-held camera sideways at about a half arm's length, while taking a series of still images (Fig. 3, left). The capture is unstructured, i.e. the motion does *not* have to be precisely executed, and takes just seconds to a few minutes, depending on the desired amount of coverage. Given this input, our algorithm automatically reconstructs

Panorama-style   Color   Depth   Normal map   Geometry-aware effects
capture |————— Reconstruction —————|

Fig. 3. Using casually captured smart phone or DSLR images as input, our algorithm reconstructs a viewpoint-free photo suitable for seated VR experiences. The result is a *3D photo*, i.e. a multi-layered panoramic mesh with reconstructed surface color, depth, and normals. 3D photos can also be viewed on a regular mobile device or in a Web browser, and the reconstructed depth and normals allow interacting with the scene through geometry-aware effects.

a *3D photo*, i.e. a textured, panoramic, multi-layered geometric mesh representation for viewpoint-free photos specifically designed for seated VR (Fig. 3, middle). This representation can be rendered using standard graphics engines.

The mature field multi-view stereo (MVS) has seen over 30 years of research, and several high quality and actively maintained software packages implementing state-of-the-art algorithms are available (see Sect. 2). However, applying these algorithms directly in our scenario produces unsatisfactory results, for the following reasons: (1) our casually captured images violate many common assumptions in MVS algorithms leading to geometric artifacts: they are captured with a narrow baseline, and our scenes are often not fully static and contain large textureless areas; (2) the geometry produced by MVS algorithms is not optimized for a specific viewpoint and often lacks completeness and detail. Our approach uses state-of-the-art reconstruction algorithms as core components, but through several technical innovations, we make them work robustly in our scenario.

We have applied our algorithm to numerous 3D photos captured with DSLRs and cell phone cameras. Among these are indoor and outdoor as well as man-made and natural scenes. We compare our 3D photos extensively with results obtained with existing state-of-the-art reconstruction algorithms.

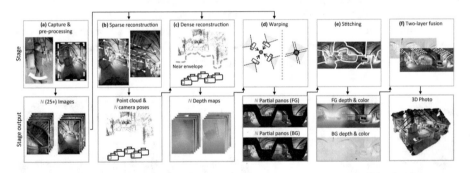

Fig. 4. Algorithm breakdown, with corresponding outputs: **(a)** Capture and pre-processing; **(b)** Sparse reconstruction; **(c)** Dense reconstruction; **(d)** Warping into a central panorama; **(e)** Parallax-tolerant stitching; **(f)** Two-layer fusion.

3.1 Method

One of our primary goals is to make capture easy for inexperienced users: it be hand-held, should not take too long, and should work with existing, low-cost cameras. This influenced many of the design decisions further down the pipeline.

We represent a 3D photo in a single-viewpoint panoramic projection that is discretized into a pixel grid. While we use an equirectangular projection in our representation, other sensible choices, such as a cube map, would also be possible. Every pixel can hold up to two layers of "nodes" that store RGB radiance, normal vector, and depth values. This resembles layered depth images [67]. However, in addition to the layered nodes, we also store the connectivity between and among the two layers, in a manner similar to that of [85]. Our representation has several advantages: (1) the panoramic domain has an *excellent resolution trade-off* for rendering from a specific viewpoint, since it provides automatic level-of-detail where further away geometry is represented more coarsely; (2) it can be *stored compactly* using standard image coding techniques and tiled for network delivery; (3) the two layers can represent color and geometric *details at disocclusions*; (4) the *connectivity* enables converting the 3D photo into a dense mesh that can be rendered without gaps and easily simplified for low-end devices.

Our input is set of casually captured photos (Fig. 4(a)) and we use an existing structure from motion algorithm [64] to estimate the camera poses and a sparse geometric representation of the scene (Fig. 4(b)). Our technical innovations concentrate in the following three stages: reconstruction (Fig. 4(c)), Parallax-tolerant stitching (Fig. 4(d–e)), and Two-Layer Fusion (Fig. 4(f)).

Dense Reconstruction. Taking the sparse reconstruction as a starting point, we first compute complete depth maps for the input images. We propose a novel prior, called the *near envelope*, that constrains the depth using a conservatively but tightly estimated lower bound. This prior results in highly improved reconstructions in our setting, and can be used with any MVS algorithm that builds a cost volume. The idea behind the prior is to propagate a conservative lower depth bound from confident to the less confident pixels. The prior effectively discards a large fraction of erroneous near-depth hypotheses from the cost volume, and causes the optimizer to reach a better solution, see Fig. 5.

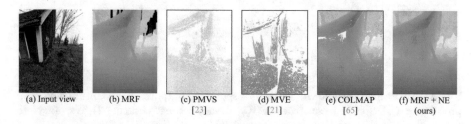

| (a) Input view | (b) MRF | (c) PMVS [23] | (d) MVE [21] | (e) COLMAP [65] | (f) MRF + NE (ours) |

Fig. 5. Existing state-of-the-art MVS algorithms (b–e) often produce incomplete and noisy depth maps for our casually captured data. Injecting our near-envelope prior into the MRF baseline algorithm shown in (b) produces superior results (f).

Parallax-Tolerant Stitching. The next goal is to merge the depth images into the final representation. We forward-warp the depth images into the panoramic domain, for each image generating a *front warp* using a standard depth test and a *back warp* using an inverted depth test. Next, we merge these images into a front and back stitch, respectively (Fig. 6). This involves solving a discrete pixel labeling problem, where each pixel i in the panorama chooses the label α_i from one of the warped sources. There are a number of different data and smoothness

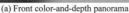
(a) Front color-and-depth panorama   (b) Front detail   (c) Back detail

Fig. 6. Our algorithm first stitches a color-and-depth panorama for the front-surfaces (a). Its depth is used as constraint, when subsequently stitching the back-surface panorama (c, only detail shown). Note the eroded foreground objects when comparing the back and front details (b–c).

constraints that have to be considered and are sometimes conflicting. We first stitch the front, and subsequently the back-surface panorama by optimizing an Markov random field (MRF) with the following terms:

1. Geometric consistency [75], ensuring that the 3D location of the label is consistent across multiple depth maps.
2. Triangle stretch, which penalizes long stretched triangles connecting foreground objects with the background.
3. A depth term, which teases apart the foreground and background panormas.
4. Seam hiding pairwise terms [44] for both colors and depth, dicsouraging the visible seams in the resulting color-and-depth panorama.

When stitching front surfaces, we use the depth term to encourage depths that are consistent among many views. When stitching back surfaces, we use a different depth term that discourages pixels in front of the front stitch.

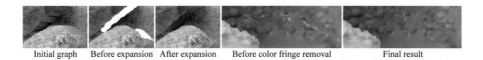
Initial graph   Before expansion   After expansion   Before color fringe removal   Final result

Fig. 7. Steps of two-layer fusion.

Two-Layer Fusion. Our next goal is to the fuse front and back stitch into the final two-layer representation, to produce a light-weight mesh representation of the scene that is easy to render on a wide variety of devices. As shown in Fig. 7, we fuse the two layers by (1) resolving which pixels should be connected as part of the same surfaces and where there should be gaps (2) removing color fringes and allows for seamless texture filtering across layers, (3) identifying and discarding redundant parts of the background layer, (4) hallucinating unseen geometry by extending the background layer.

3.2   Results and Evaluation

All our 3D photos can be seen in supplemental material[1]. 14 were captured with a DSLR camera and 5 with a cell phone. The scenes span man-made and natural environments, both indoors and outdoors. They contain many difficult-to-reconstruct elements, such as water surfaces, swaying trees, and moving cars and people. We compare with the following end-to-end reconstruction systems:

PMVS: We reconstruct a semi-dense point cloud with PMVS [23] and then use Screened Poisson Surface Reconstruction [40] to create a watertight surface.

MVE: We use the Multi-View Environment [21] implementations of Goesele et al.'s [26] semi-dense reconstruction and Floating Scale Surface Reconstruction for meshing [20].

GDMR: The Global, Dense Multiscale Reconstruction method [73] starts from the same semi-dense reconstruction as MVE, but provides an alternative surface reconstruction and texturing method.

COLMAP: COLMAP 2.1 [64,65] provides an end-to-end pipeline for sparse reconstruction, depth map computation, and fusion.

PhotoScan: Agisoft PhotoScan[2] is a commercial 3D reconstruction pipeline.

Capturing Reality: This[3] is another state-of-the-art 3D reconstruction pipeline.

As some of these produce relatively coarse textures, we also experimented with the following alternative texturing methods, in addition to whatever native textures each system produces:

TexRecon [74]: This method produces a high-quality texture for a given 3D model and registered input images.

Unstructured Lumigraph Rendering (ULR) [11]: This method uses the 3D model as a geometric proxy for Image-Based Rendering.

| (a) | (b) | (c) | (d) | (e) | (f) | (g) | (h) |
| Reference | Our result | Capturing reality | Photoscan | GDMR, TexRecon | COLMAP 2.1, TexRecon | PMVS, TexRecon | MVE, TexRecon |

Fig. 8. Rendered results and corresponding rephotography errors in the Church scene. Dark regions have lower error. Refer to the supplemental web page at http://vis.cs.ucl.ac.uk/Download/G.Brostow/Casual3D for a convenient side-by-side visual inspection of results in all scenes.

---

[1] http://vis.cs.ucl.ac.uk/Download/G.Brostow/Casual3D.

[2] http://www.agisoft.com/.

[3] http://www.capturingreality.com/.

Qualitative Comparison. See Fig. 8 for a visual comparison from the rephotography evaluation. We also provide videos with scripted camera paths for all scenes and all methods in the supplementary material. A major limitation of most systems we compare with is that they do not produce complete results. Most methods do not reconstruct far regions or texture-less areas, due to reliability thresholds in the depth estimation. Our technique produces more complete results and relies on MRF-based smoothing to fill in unreliable or ambiguous regions.

Some systems produce only relatively coarse vertex color textures. TexRecon [74] improves the texturing at the expense of making the results less complete, as it removes uncertain triangles. Another alternative is ULR [11] which is very good at optimizing the reprojection error. However, since texturing is view-dependent, this introduces visibly moving texture seams when the camera moves.

Performance. All 3D photos were reconstructed on a single 6-Core Intel Xeon PC with an NVIDIA Titan X GPU and 256 GB of memory. Reconstruction takes 4 h and 55 min for a representative DSLR capture with 54 input images at 1350×900 and an output color-and-depth panorama size of 8192×4096 pixels. While our implementation is slow, there is significant room for improvement. The two bottlenecks are the sparse and the dense scene reconstruction steps, with 40 min spent on sparse reconstruction and 3 h spent on dense reconstruction. Both steps can be sped up significantly as shown in Sect. 4.

Limitations. Our system inherits some limitations from the underlying reconstruction algorithms. For example, the stereo algorithm may fail to reconstruct shiny and reflective surfaces (e.g., British Museum), as well as dynamically moving objects such as people (e.g., Pike Place, Gum Wall).

3.3   Conclusions

In this section, we discussed a system that constructs a *3D photo*, a seamless two-layer representation for viewpoint-free photos from sequences of casually acquired input photos. This brings us closer to our goal of easy capture: we can apply our algorithm to *casually* captured images that violate common assumptions of MVS algorithms. Most of our scenes contain difficult to reconstruct elements, such as dynamic objects (people, swaying trees), shiny materials (lake surface, windows), and textureless surfaces (sky, walls). That we nevertheless reconstruct relatively artifact-free scenes speaks for the robustness of our approach.

However, our system requires several hours of processing. Speeding this up would make capture even easier: if users could see the final 3D photo still on-set, they can spot mistakes and adjust their capture accordingly. In the next section, we address this with a much faster method to reconstruct 3D photos.

4   Instant 3D Photography

| Dual camera phone | Input: 34 color-and-depth photos, captured in 34.0 s. | 3D photo (color, depth, and a 3D effect), generated in 34.7 s. |

Fig. 9. Our work enables practical and casual free-viewpoint photography with dual-camera phones. Like Sect. 3, we target seated VR experiences and use the *3D photo* representation. *Left:* A burst of input color-and-depth image pairs captured with a dual camera cell phone at a rate of one image per second. *Right:* 3D photo generated with our algorithm in about the same time it took to capture. The geometry is highly detailed and enables viewing with binocular and motion parallax in VR, as well as 3D effects that interact with the scene.

We continue our work on creating viewpoint-free photos for seated VR experiences. Like in Sect. 3, we focus on easy capture and use the *3D photo* representation: a textured, multi-layered 3D mesh that can be rendered with standard graphics engines. Unlike Sect. 3, the system here is specifically designed with processing speed in mind and runs several orders of magnitude faster. The drawback is that, when compared to Sect. 3, this approach has a slightly reduced range-of-motion.

As stated in Sect. 1.1, we are looking for a method that does not require expensive hardware and is easy to use. Yet, it should create high-quality viewpoint-free photos suitable for seated VR experiences with both binocular and head-motion parallax. In this section we focus on fast processing times, on the order of seconds at most. We present a new algorithm that constructs 3D photos from sequences of color-and-depth photos produced from small-baseline stereo dual camera cell phones, such as recent iPhones. Depth reconstruction is essentially free since it is integrated into native phone OS APIs and highly optimized.

In contrast to Sect. 3, which requires several hours to process a scene, our method is fast and processes approximately one input image per second on a laptop PC, about the same time it takes to capture. We found that as our system became faster, it made our own behavior with regards to capture more opportunistic: we were suddenly able to capture spontaneously on the go and even perform multiple captures in the same scene to try different viewing angles. We demonstrate our algorithm on a wide variety of captured scenes, including indoor, outdoor, urban, and natural environments at day and night time.

4.1   Dual Lens Depth Capture

Dual lens cameras capture synchronized small-baseline stereo image pairs for the purpose of reconstructing an aligned color-and-depth image using depth-from-stereo algorithms [72]. Depth reconstruction is typically implemented in system-level APIs and highly optimized. Several recent phones feature dual cameras, including the iPhone 7 Plus, 8 Plus, X, and Samsung Note 8. Such devices are already in the hands of tens of millions of consumers.

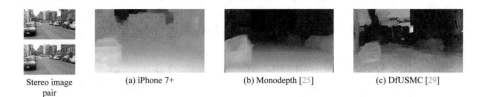

Stereo image   (a) iPhone 7+   (b) Monodepth [25]   (c) DfUSMC [29]
pair

Fig. 10. Depth maps from various algorithms. Note the relative scale differences and low-frequency deformations. (a) Small baseline stereo depth from the native iOS algorithm on an iPhone 7+. (b) Single image CNN depth map [25]. (c) Depth from accidental motion result [29] (for this we used a short video clip as input).

The small baseline is both a blessing and a curse: the limited search range enables quickly establishing correspondence but also makes triangulation less reliable and causes large uncertainty in the estimated depth. For this reason, most algorithms employ aggressive edge-aware filtering [9,30], which yields smoother depth maps with color-aligned edges, but large low-frequency error in the absolute depth values. In addition, the dual lenses on current phones constantly move and rotate due to optical image stabilization, changes in focus, and even gravity[4]. This introduces a non-linear and spatially-varying transformation of disparity that adds to the low-frequency error from the filtering mentioned above.

Figure 10 shows depth maps reconstructed using different stereo algorithms on this kind of data. As revealed in the figure, there are significant low-frequency errors in the depth maps. An important detail is that many small baseline stereo methods (including on the iPhone) do *not* estimate absolute depth, but instead produce *normalized* depth maps. Aligning such depth maps involves estimating scale factors for each of them, or, in fact, even more complicated transformations.

4.2   Method

Our algorithm proceeds in five stages: Capture, Deformable Depth Alignment, Stitching, Color Harmonization, and Multi-layer Mesh Generation.

---

[4] See http://developer.apple.com/videos/play/wwdc2017/507 at 17:20–20:50, Slides 81–89.

Capture. Our input is a sequence of aligned color-and-depth image pairs, which we capture from a single vantage point on a dual lens camera phone (iPhone 7 Plus) using a custom burst capture app. The capture motion resembles panorama capture: the camera is pointed outwards while holding the device at half-arms' length and scanning the scene in an arbitrary up-, down-, or sideways motion. Unfortunately, the field-of-view of the iPhone 7 Plus camera is narrow in depth capture mode (37° vertical), so we need to capture more images than we would with other cameras. A typical scene contains between 20 and 200 images with a color resolution of 720 × 1280 pixels and a depth resolution of 432 × 768 pixels. We enable auto-exposure to capture more dynamic range. We also record the device orientation estimate provided by the IMU.

Deformable Depth Alignment. We align the depth maps by minimizing the distance between reprojected feature point matches, which have been established using standard methods. Due to the small camera baseline and resulting triangulation uncertainty, the input depth maps are not very accurate, and it is not possible to align them well using global transformations—see Fig. 11. We resolve this problem using a novel optimization method that jointly estimates the camera poses as well as spatially-varying adjustment maps that are applied to deform the depth maps and bring them into good alignment.

Our deformation model applies an affine transformation (i.e. scale and offset) of pixel disparities (inverse depths). For each image, we use a regular 5 × 5 grid of scale and offset coefficients that are bilinearly interpolated across the image. We model this as a non-linear least squares problem with the following terms:

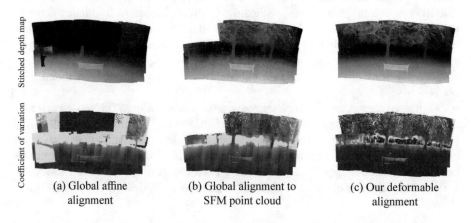

(a) Global affine alignment

(b) Global alignment to SFM point cloud

(c) Our deformable alignment

Fig. 11. Aligning depth maps with low-frequency errors: (a) Our algorithm with a global affine model. Many depth maps got pushed to infinity. (b) Aligning each depth map *independently* to a high-quality reconstruction. The result is better, but contains many visible seams and floaters due to the impossibility to fit the inaccurate depth maps with simple global transformations. (c) Our algorithm with the spatially-varying affine model yields excellent alignment.

1. A robust reprojection loss to reduce sensitivity to outlier matches,
2. a smoothness cost between neighboring grid values, and
3. a regularization term that keeps the overall scale in the scene constant.

We initialize the camera rotations using the IMU orientations, and the locations by pushing them forward onto the unit sphere. We use the Ceres library [3] to minimize our cost function with the Levenberg-Marquardt algorithm.

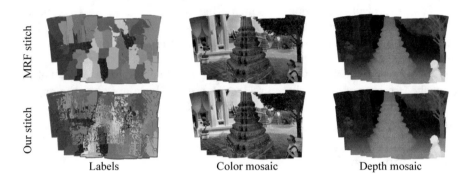

Fig. 12. MRF stitching (runtime 3.25 min) vs. our algorithm (runtime 0.5 sec).

Stitching. Next, we stitch the aligned color-and-depth photos into a panoramic mosaic. Usually this is formulated as a labeling problem and solved using discrete optimization methods. However, optimizing label smoothness, e.g., using MRF solvers, is very slow. Using a carefully designed data term and the high quality of our depth alignment, we replace label smoothness optimization with independently optimizing every pixel, after filtering the data term in a depth-guided manner [34]. This is an order of magnitude faster, and achieves visually similar results.

A "good" source for the target pixel should satisfy a number of constraints, which we formulate as penalties in our data term:

1. A depth consensus penalty similar to Sect. 3,
2. a penalty which prefers pixels from the image center where depth is more reliable and there is more space for seam-hiding feathering, and
3. a penalty that avoids overexposed source pixels.

In Fig. 12 we compare our result with an MRF solution using the color and disparity smoothness from Sect. 3. While our stitch has more frequent label changes the stitched color and depth mosaics are visually very similar.

Color Harmonization. Since we capture with auto-exposure, we now align exposures to create a seamless panorama. Following Reinhard et al. [60], we convert the images to the channel-decorrelated CIELAB color space, and process each channel independently. We solve a linear system to compute global affine color-channel adjustments (i.e., scale and offset) for each source image, such that the adjusted colors in the overlapping regions agree. We further reduce visible seams by feathering the label region boundaries with a wide radius of 50 px.

Multi-layer Mesh Generation. As the last stage, we convert the panorama into a multi-layered and textured mesh that can be rendered using standard graphics engines. We tear the mesh at strong depth edges and extend the back-side into the occluded regions, hallucinating new color and depth values in occluded areas. Our solution resembles the "two-layer merging" in Sect. 3. However, an important difference is that we do not produce back-surface stitches, since the baseline is too small to reconstruct significant content in occluded regions. If scenes were captured with a wider baseline and/or a wider field-of-view the two-layer stitch-and-merge algorithm could be adapted at the expense of slower runtime. As a final step, we simplify the mesh and compute a texture atlas.

4.3   Results and Limitations

We have captured dozens of scenes with an iPhone 7 Plus—see Fig. 13, as well as supplemental material[5]. These scenes span a wide range of environments (indoor and outdoor, urban and natural) and capture conditions (day and night, bright and overcast). The scenes we captured range from about 20 to 200 source images, and their horizontal field-of-view ranges from 60° to 360°.

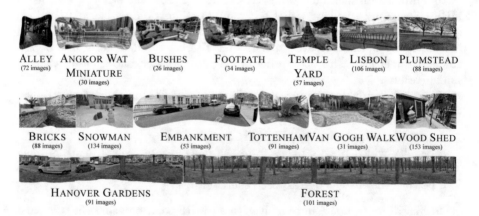

Fig. 13. Some of the datasets shown in this section, video, and supplementary material (http://visual.cs.ucl.ac.uk/pubs/instant3d/supplemental). The bottom row shows 360° panoramas.

---

[5] http://visual.cs.ucl.ac.uk/pubs/instant3d/supplemental.

SfM and MVS Comparison. We tested standard SfM algorithms on our datasets. When processing our 25 datasets with COLMAP's SfM algorithm [64] 7 scenes failed entirely, in 7 more not all cameras were registered, and there was 1 were all cameras registered but the reconstruction was an obvious catastrophic failure. This high failure rate underscores the difficulty of working with small baseline imagery. We also compare with MVS systems: the commercial Capturing Reality system [59] and Casual 3D photography described in Sect. 3. Capturing Reality's reconstruction speed is impressive for a full MVS algorithm, but due to the small baseline it is only able to reconstruct foreground. Casual 3D produces comparable quality to ours, but at much slower speed. Figure 14 shows an example scene, and supplemental material shows video comparisons in more scenes.

| (a) RealityCapture (2.1 minutes) | (b) Casual 3D (1.8 hours) | (c) Our result (34.7 seconds) |

Fig. 14. Comparison with MVS systems: (a) Capturing Reality is fast, but the reconstruction breaks down a few meters away from the vantage point due to triangulation uncertainty. (b) Casual 3D produced a high quality result, but it is slow. (c) Our result has even better quality, and was computed over **200×** faster.

Performance. All scenes were processed with a PC with 3.4 GHz 6-core Intel Xeon E5-2643 CPU and a NVIDIA Titan X GPU and 64 GB of memory. Our implementation mostly consists of unoptimized CPU code, the GPU is only (insignificantly) used for warping. We also tested on a slower 14" laptop with a 3.3 GHz 4-core Intel i7-7700HQ CPU and a NVIDIA GTX 1060 GPU. Table 1 shows a timing breakdown on both systems for an example scene. While our algorithm is already fast, there are significant further optimizations on the table. The alignment optimization could be sped up by implementing a custom solver, tailored to this particular problem. Our warping algorithm is implemented in a wasteful way, properly rewriting this GPU code would make this practically free. Stitching could also be moved to the GPU for a significant speed-up.

Limitations. The iPhone camera has a very narrow field-of-view in depth capture mode, with a wider field-of-view we would need to capture considerably fewer images to achieve the same amount of overlap. At the same time the baseline would increase, making the reconstruction problem easier. Our results exhibit similar artifacts as other 3D reconstruction systems, e.g. floating geometry, incorrect depth in untextured regions, and ghosting on dynamic objects. Compared to existing systems these are reduced (Fig. 14), but still present. We suggest watching the video comparison in supplementary material.

Table 1. Breakdown of performance for the 34-image scene from Fig. 9.

Stage	Desktop timing	Laptop timing
Feature extraction and matching	6.6 s	7.0 s
Deformable alignment	9.8 s	10.2 s
Warping	6.6 s	5.1 s
Stitching	2.7 s	2.6 s
Color harmonization	1.6 s	1.8 s
Multi-layer computation	1.0 s	1.1 s
Mesh simplification	3.1 s	3.5 s
Texture atlas generation	3.3 s	3.7 s
Total	**34.7 s**	**35.0 s**

4.4   Conclusions

We have presented a fast end-to-end algorithm that creates viewpoint-free photos for seated VR from a sequence of color-and-depth images. This provides a speed-up of two orders of magnitude compared to Sect. 3. The availability of a fast capture and reconstruction system has made the way we capture scenes more opportunistic and impulsive. Almost all of the scenes in this section have been captured spontaneously without planning, e.g. while travelling. This concludes our investigation into seated VR experiences. We now shift our focus towards the challenges with viewpoint-free photography for room-scale VR experiences.

5   Scalable Free-Viewpoint Image-Based Rendering

In this section, we present a viewpoint-free photography approach for room-scale VR experiences. Compared to seated VR experiences this introduces several new challenges. For example, the 3D photo representation in the previous two sections only captures the front-facing side of the scene and is not suitable for room-scale VR exploration, where the user is free to walk behind objects. As an alternative, we can use modern multi-view stereo (MVS) tools to obtain complete, two-sided 3D reconstructions with texture [59]. However, these reconstructions can appear blobby and seldom align with image edges. Even with perfect geometry this looks artificial, as highlights are baked in or missing completely.

A key to recent success in IBR is the use of *per-view input image information*, using representations such as custom meshes and super-pixel over-segmentation, which preserve depth boundaries even with imperfect 3D reconstructions. However, the number of images required for room-scale VR exploration is very high, making per-view geometry costly. While MVS algorithms now provide impressive 3D reconstructions, they seldom achieve the quality required for realistic viewpoint-free photography. We improve this with a new per-view geometry refinement method that combines two different MVS reconstructions with complementary accuracy vs. completeness tradeoffs.

This section addresses two key challenges for room-scale viewpoint-free photography: (1) how to combine a global 3D mesh with per-view geometry, and (2) how to render high-quality novel views using this geometry, while maintaining real-time display rates.

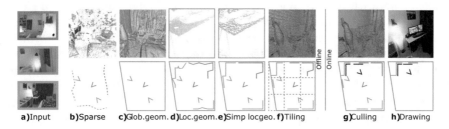

a)Input   b)Sparse   c)Glob.geom. d)Loc.geom.e)Simp locgeo. f)Tiling   g)Culling   h)Drawing

Fig. 15. Overview. (**a**) Input: Unstructured photos. (**b**) Sparse reconstruction. (**c**) 3D reconstruction of global geometry. (**d**) Creating refined per-input-view meshes. (**e**) Mesh simplification. (**f**) The per-input-view meshes are partitioned into tiles. (**g**) At run-time, the per-view meshes are culled, leaving only those relevant for the novel view (the black camera). (**h**) Rendering with view-dependent blending.

5.1 Method

Unlike traditional methods for 3D reconstruction [59,65] and texturing [74,83], we aim to reproduce view-dependent appearance such as highlights, and to render accurate images even in regions where a global 3D reconstruction has missing or inaccurate data. See Fig. 15 for an overview of our pipeline.

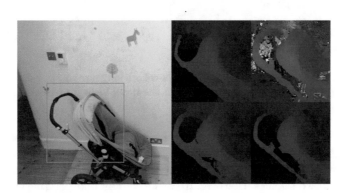

Fig. 16. Merging globally and locally accurate depth maps leads to improved occlusion edge handling and artifact minimization. **Left:** Reference image **Top middle:** Globally complete RealityCapture mesh. **Top right:** Locally accurate COLMAP depth map. **Bottom middle:** Fused COLMAP and RealityCapture depth maps. **Bottom right:** Our refined depth map.

3D Reconstruction. Our method takes as input camera poses for the input photos, estimated by a structure-from-motion package [64], as well as a global 3D reconstruction of the scene, computed with commercial multi-view stereo package [59]. Note, that these inputs are not sufficient for high quality with view-dependent textures (e.g., [11,16]), since object boundaries in the photographs seldom align with the global geometry. Rather than relying on improved global geometry, we make a deliberate trade-off: To respect object boundaries we sacrifice global agreement and create per-view geometry for each input photograph.

As Fig. 16 shows, we achieve this by creating combined depth maps from two complementary MVS methods: COLMAP [65] with better detail accuracy, and RealityCapture [59] with better global completeness. We then refine occlusion edges using PatchMatch optimization [8,50] to search for more photoconsistent depths at every pixel. To limit noise where photoconsistency is ambiguous, we penalize depths that are far away from the surfaces in the combined depth maps. Next, we convert the refined depth maps into simplified meshes for efficient rendering. We convert every pixel in the depth map to a 3D vertex and form a grid mesh by connecting neighboring vertices with triangles. To avoid connecting foreground and background layers at occlusion boundaries, we do not create triangles at edges where the depth difference is large. Finally, we simplify the meshes [24], using custom simplification costs to preserve detail in foreground regions and at occlusion boundaries.

Now, we can render high-quality images by projecting per-view geometries into the novel view, and compositing them with view-dependent blending.

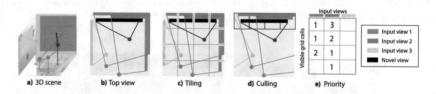

Fig. 17. The tiling procedure, for a 3D scene with a single room, acquired from three input views *(yellow, red, blue)* to rendered in the novel view (in black).

Rendering. Even with high-quality geometry, hundreds of input photographs are required to faithfully reproduce the view-dependent appearance of indoor scenes during free view-point navigation, given the many occlusions and large parallax at close distances. However, iterating over all photographs when rendering novel views is very expensive, especially when each photograph corresponds to a complex per-view mesh. To overcome this problem, we present a culling strategy with two elements: a tiling data structure to only render potentially visible geometry, and worst-case blend weight bounds to avoid rendering per-view geometry likely to be discarded during view-dependent blending.

We partition the scene into a regular 3D grid as shown in Fig. 17. As a pre-process (Fig. 17(c)), we associate all triangles in the input views with the grid cells they intersect. We refer to the unique pairing of a grid cell with an input view as an *input tile*, i.e. the collection of triangles from a single input view that intersect a grid cell. At run-time, we save effort by only rendering input tiles visible to the novel-view (tiling and culling). In Fig. 17(d), this allows us to ignore the yellow view altogether as well as parts of the red and blue views.

However, because of view-dependent blending, only a few visible input tiles will actually contribute to the final image. We therefore strive to render a small subset of the input tiles that ensures a high blend weight for all pixels in the novel view. To achieve this, we sort the input tiles according to an aggregate, worst-case blend weight estimated for the entire tile. We then draw only the tiles which will contribute the most to the output image, based on the estimated worst-case blend weights. The exact number varies between grid cells, as we stop drawing input tiles when we determine that a cell has been sufficiently covered. Predicting worst-case blend weights is crucial for performance, as it focuses the rendering effort on the input tiles that actually affect the final image.

5.2   Results

We compare with existing baseline algorithms, using published code wherever possible. Here and in the supplemental material, we provide qualitative comparisons of our rendering phases, and quantitative results for speed tests. We captured scenes with a digital camera (Sony NEX-C3 at 1228×816 or Canon

Fig. 18. Four example scenes, comparing our system with ULR [11], Selective IBR [52], and the global mesh from RealityCapture [59].

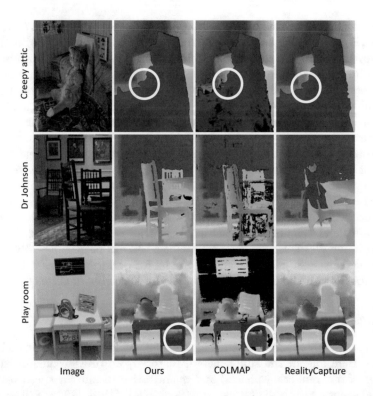

Image   Ours   COLMAP   RealityCapture

Fig. 19. Left-to-right: Input photograph; Our refined depth maps; Global reconstruction [59]; COLMAP [65]. Our refined depth maps combine the best of both; complete reconstructions that align with image edges (see the white circles).

EOS 550D at 1296 × 864), taking 150-300 RAW photos per scene. During preprocessing, we color-harmonized the images using Adobe Lightroom. In Figs. 18 and 19, and the supplemental material[6] we show the following scenes:

CREEPY ATTIC: A small $(5 \times 4 \times 4 \text{ m}^3)$, old, attic with textiles and artwork.
DORM ROOM: A small $(4 \times 4 \times 5 \text{ m}^3)$ student bedroom with textureless walls.
DR JOHNSON: A large $(16 \times 6 \times 5 \text{ m}^3)$ scene in a preserved 17th century house.
PLAYROOM: A medium-sized $(6 \times 6 \times 5 \text{ m}^3)$ living room cluttered with toys.

In supplemental material, we also show comparisons in a collection of standard IBR scenes from [12], as well as some of our own outdoor scenes.

Rendering Comparison. In the supplemental material and Fig. 18 we compare with the global mesh reconstructed by the state-of-the-art commercial multiview stereo tool RealityCapture [59], Selective IBR [52], and also to ULR [11] with improved visibility akin to floating textures [16].

---

[6] http://team.inria.fr/graphdeco/deep-blending, listed as "Heuristic Blending".

Compared to [52], our mesh-based approach tends to preserve complex shape boundaries better since super-pixels are warped independently in their method. This can be seen in PLAYROOM, where the toy radio gets broken up, and also in DR JOHNSON, where the painting on the wall has visible seams. Compared to the global mesh from RealityCapture, our geometry refinement approach helps preserve the shape of hard-to-reconstruct objects better. This can for example be seen on the lamps in both CREEPYATTIC and DORM ROOM. Compared to ULR, our refined geometry results in significantly fewer foreground bleeding artifacts (e.g. CREEPYATTIC, PLAYROOM and DORM ROOM) and also preserves the shape of hard-to-capture objects like the chandelier in DR JOHNSON.

Geometry Comparison. In Fig. 19 we compare the geometry reconstructions from different components of our system. We see that the global reconstruction from RealityCapture [59] is complete but tends to over- or underestimate the size of foreground objects. We also include COLMAP [65], which preserves details better than the global reconstruction, but is often incomplete (shown as black) in textureless areas. The geometry produced by our local per-view refinement is complete and aligns well with image edges. Note how it corrects occlusion boundaries grossly misestimated in the global reconstructions (circled in white): The hand of the doll in CREEPY ATTIC; the eroded chair in DR JOHNSON and the rounded corners on the chair in PLAY ROOM. These boundaries are important for IBR, as getting them wrong causes foreground bleeding.

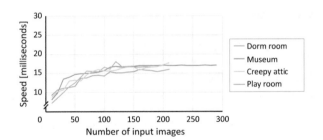

Fig. 20. Performance scaling at 1080p with Nvidia GTX Titan X. We fix the camera position in each scene and measure performance of our tiled rendering as the number of input images increases.

Performance. In these experiments we use the geometry from [31]. This may impact the performance per scene, but has a minimal effect on the relative measurements we emphasize here. We measured the average frame time at 1080p in each scene as the virtual camera moves along a predetermined path. Tiling provides a speedup of 2× to 4× depending on the scene and hardware. Without tiling, rendering takes 35–60 ms on our high-end machine (Desktop PC; Nvidia GTX Titan X), and 220–388 ms on the low-end machine (Laptop; Nvidia GTX 660M). With tiling, this is reduced to 15–18 ms and 60–120 ms, respectively. Figure 20 shows that performance scales sub-linearly with the number of input images and the frame time plateaus after 150 images.

Fig. 21. Typical artifacts with our approach. **Left-to-right:** Incorrect occlusion boundaries, broken highlights, foreground bleeding.

5.3 Conclusion

We have presented a novel approach to viewpoint-free photography for room-scale VR experiences which achieves several of the goals in Sect. 1.1: it works with an unstructured collection of photos as input (goal 1 - ease of capture), supports a large range of motion (goal 2), and maintains real-time display rates—even for large scenes (goal 4). However, while this method preserves occlusion boundaries and view-dependent effects, it struggles to consistently achieve high quality results (goal 3). See Fig. 21 for examples. In the next section we address this, using a convolutional neural network to alleviate artifacts during the blending.

6 Deep Blending

In the previous section, we presented an approach for viewpoint-free photography suitable for room-scale VR experiences. However, like many other Image-Based Rendering (IBR) methods [52,56], this approach still suffers from many visible artifacts, especially when moving far from the input photos. In general, novel views are synthesized in IBR by combining warped pixels from input photos; output quality depends on the computation of visibility in the presence of *inaccurate geometry* and on the *blending* method.

With only few exceptions (e.g. [47]), previous solutions use heuristic blending to handle geometric inaccuracies, and to correct image seams and ghosting due to view-specific differences in the combined images. Blending needs to correct for artifacts due to incorrect *occlusion edges*, *visible seams* due to *texture stretch/misalignment*, and *lack of color harmonization*, as well as view-dependent effects from highlights, different exposures, and unsuitable camera selection. These complex, often contradictory requirements have led prior work to develop case-specific, hand-crafted heuristics that always fail for some configurations. We build on the system in Sect. 5 with the following contribution: a deep convolutional neural network solution to the blending problem. Our main insight is that a data-driven solution is currently a better strategy to effectively satisfy these challenging requirements. We introduce a *deep blending* algorithm, leveraging convolutional neural networks (CNNs) that learn *blending weights* that will most reasonably approximate real imagery for novel view synthesis.

Our solution provides realistic image-based rendering across the variety of scenes attempted by the IBR community so far, and it gracefully degrades in quality when the geometric reconstruction fails completely or exposure differences are too pronounced. For a majority of the scenes tested – both outdoors and indoors – our method achieves excellent quality for free-viewpoint navigation, while also being capable of achieving interactive frame-rates.

6.1   Method

Deep learning has demonstrated the ability to perform very complex image transformation tasks and is thus an ideal candidate for solving the IBR blending problem. We train a convolutional neural network (CNN) to generate *blending weights* that are then used to combine reprojected contributions from different input images. Our goal is to evaluate the feed-forward CNN in an interactive renderer, imposing strict constraints on network architecture, input layers, and the renderer. Generating sufficient training data is also challenging. Finally, care must be taken when defining the training loss: we want to produce images that are as realistic as possible, avoiding temporal artifacts such as flickering.

Our input is a set of input photographs of a scene and a global 3D reconstruction of the scene. We use the approach from Sect. 5 to create high quality per-view meshes that respect occlusion edges as much as possible.

Network Architecture and Inputs. To allow a per-frame interactive rendering loop that includes a CNN evaluation, we choose a U-net [62] architecture (Fig. 23), and generate a fixed set of inputs to the CNN. For rendering, we build on Sect. 5, which at each output pixel selects a variable number of input photos to blend into a final image. In our rendering loop, we use the blend weights to rank these per-pixel selections to generate a fixed number of *mosaics* that are blended into the novel view. As Fig. 22 shows, each pixel of the first mosaic contains the color value of the best selected pixel, the second mosaic contains the second best, and so on. In the case of missing geometry, we fill holes in the input mosaics with a rendered view of the textured global mesh. These four mosaics, together with a view of the global mesh, form the input layers to our network.

Network Training. Training data for our supervised learning of the CNN weights is non-traditional: the same photo serves, at times, as one of the *inputs* to the mosaic-building step, or it is held-out so it can serve as the ground truth *output* that the network tries to reconstruct from mosaics of other input photos. We generate a large dataset of input images through round-robin use of this hold-out strategy, and through data augmentation.

We collected a total of 19 scenes from different sources: 7 scenes from Chaurasia et al. [12], 4 scenes from Sect. 5, 1 scene from the Eth3D benchmark [66], and 7 new scenes which we have captured ourselves. Each scene contains between 12 and 418 input images, with resolution varying from 1228×816 to 2592×1944. There are 5 indoors scenes, and 5 scenes containing a significant amount of vegetation.

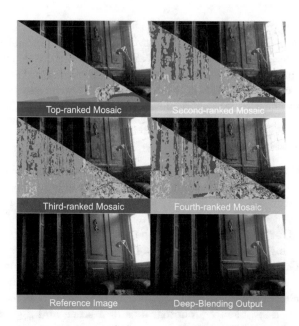

Fig. 22. Example mosaics are shown in the first two rows. The top right halves show the color mosaic, while the bottom left halves visualize the selection, with each input shown in a different color. Weighted blending outputs from our network (bottom right) are trained by minimizing their difference with real images (bottom left). Our network also blends an RGB view of the global mesh (not shown).

In total, we have 2630 images, and we use data augmentation to mitigate the risk of overfitting by taking random 256×256 crops of the images and performing random rotations and horizontal/vertical flips.

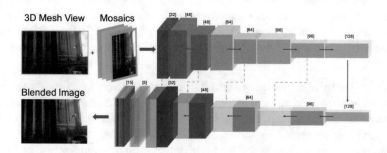

Fig. 23. Network architecture. Each block is a 3×3 convolution followed by a ReLU, with the output channels shown in brackets. Skip connections are shown with dotted lines. A softmax is used at the end to obtain per-pixel blend weights, forming output image as the per-pixel weighted sum of the five network inputs.

To achieve good visual quality and overcome alignment issues we use a perceptually-motivated loss [38]. For temporal stability, we introduce an auxiliary loss, based on a small window of camera motion. As training data, we generate small 2-frame clips, which start from a reference camera pose and move slightly in a random direction. During training, we run the network twice to generate outputs for both the frames in the clip, compensate for motion using the estimated geometry, and introduce a loss between the motion-compensated outputs.

The test results we show are samples (novel viewpoints) never seen in training.

6.2   Results

In Fig. 24 and supplemental material[7], we compare with other IBR systems:

RealityCapture: The textured mesh from [59].
Selective IBR: The superpixel IBR approach by [52] using the RealityCapture mesh as input geometry.
ULR: Unstructured Lumigraph Rendering [11] with soft visibility [16] and the RealityCapture mesh as the geometry proxy.

Fig. 24. Results. **Left:** Full novel view from our solution, followed by a crop. The remaining three columns show other methods: Textured Mesh-based rendering, Selective IBR [52], ULR [11] with soft visibility [16], InsideOut [31], and Soft3D [56]. Only some methods shown per row; videos of all methods are available in supplemental material: http://team.inria.fr/graphdeco/deep-blending.

---

[7] http://team.inria.fr/graphdeco/deep-blending.

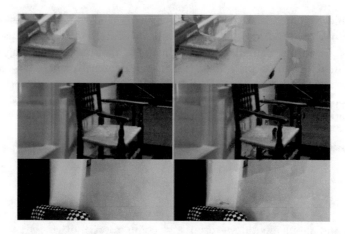

Fig. 25. Our blending network (left) vs. heuristic blending from Sect. 5 (right).

Soft3D: The novel view synthesis algorithm by [56], using their custom soft 3D reconstructions.

InsideOut: The indoor IBR system by [31] using their custom depth-sensor based 3D reconstructions. Note that this is different from the system described in Sect. 5, which uses improved reconstruction and blending techniques, and does not rely on depth sensor data.

Heuristic blending: In Fig. 25, we compare with the heuristic blending used in Sect. 5, isolating the effect of blending.

Except for InsideOut, which uses the original reconstructions with depth-sensor data, all methods use the same camera registration and calibration produced by COLMAP. The full set of videos with paths from all these scenes and comparisons with other methods is in supplemental material.

Network Evaluation. In supplemental material, we also provide a large number of videos showing different ablations in data or method:

Training scenes. In supplemental material, we show the effect of running our network in 5 scenes it did not see during training (hold-one-out). The results are similar to training with the scene. We also test training on only one scene (single-scene), which tends to reduce temporal stability.

Loss. In supplemental material, we also show the effect of our perceptual loss vs. an L_1 loss, as well as results of our network trained without the temporal loss; these exhibit strong inter-frame intensity flicker in many of the sequences.

Image regression. We tested directly regressing (predicting) the output image rather than blend weights. Like [7], we observe that this works well, but network convergence is much slower.

Number of mosaics. We show n results using only the top 1 or 2 mosaics as network input. While more mosaics leads to smoother view transitions, we observe diminishing return with more mosaics – each additional mosaic contributes to smaller details, mostly along surface boundaries.

Table 2. Average runtimes (ms/frame) over 100 frames for our IBR system.

Scene	Non-network runtime	Total runtime	Scene	Non-network runtime	Total runtime
Museum-1	6.2	26.2	Hugo-1	14.1	35.6
Creepy Attic	7.1	26.8	Night Snow	15.3	33.0
Dr Johnson	12.4	33.6	Boats	19.7	47.6

Performance. In Table 2, we evaluate the runtime performance of our interactive renderer at 1280×720 on a system with a 3.47 GHz Intel Xeon CPU and an NVIDIA GTX 1080Ti GPU. (Note that the supplemental videos are rendered offline at 1920×1080.) For smaller scenes, especially indoors, our implementation achieves 30 Hz, which falls off gradually as scene complexity increases. For large outdoor scenes, the bottleneck is the voxel-wise camera selection.

6.3   Conclusions

We have extended the system in Sect. 5 with a deep blending network, demonstrating that it is possible to learn blending weights for viewpoint-free photography while maintaining interactive display rates. This shows promise as a solution for room-scale VR experiences. It achieves all the goals from Sect. 1.1, it works with easy-to-capture photos as input (goal 1), supports free-viewpoint rendering with a large range of motion (goal 2), suppresses artifacts and maintains high-quality results (goal 3). Achieving real-time performance (goal 4), especially in the context of stereo viewing for VR (i.e. at least 90 fps) is possible, but requires performance improvements. We believe this can be addressed with careful code optimization and upgraded hardware: a dual-GPU system would render the views for both eyes in parallel, and next generation GPUs provide further speedups.

7   Conclusions and Future Work

In this chapter, we explored methods to easily capture and digitally preserve a real place, so it can later be revisited realistically in VR. We call this *viewpoint-free photography* and explored two common VR experiences: (1) seated VR, where the viewpoint is mostly stationary, but the user can peek behind corners, and (2) room-scale VR, where the user can freely explore the scene. We can gain further insights by revisiting our goals from Sect. 1.1: (1) ease of capture, (2) sufficient range of motion, (3) high quality (realism), and (4) real-time display rates. While it is certainly possible that no approach can simultaneously maximize all goals, we believe improvements can still be made towards each goal without sacrificing the others. We discuss a few such improvements below.

Ease of Capture. 360 cameras, such as the Ricoh Theta[8], could drastically reduce the number of input images, as they capture a much larger view of the scene compared to normal photos. Implicitly, the methods presented in this chapter assume crisp, noise-free images without rolling shutter distortion. This makes capture tedious in low-light conditions, requiring patience and a steady hand. A system that remains robust to this type of noise, blur and distortion would facilitate truly casual capture, enabling the user to quickly and carelessly capture viewpoint-free photos by waving a camera around in the scene.

Range of Motion. We used panorama-style input footage only for seated VR experiences. Foreseeably, it would be possible to extend the range of motion by hallucinating the unobserved regions in the scene. Using e.g., inpainting techniques to fill in both geometry [17] and colors [8,54]. This would lead towards bridging the gap between seated and room-scale VR experiences.

High Quality. Our viewpoint-free photos preserve view-dependent effects by blending between highlights in the captured footage. This works for rough highlights that have been captured sufficiently, but is unconvincing for sharp highlights on mirror-like surfaces. This could be addressed with an approach that explicitly recreates the motion of highlights on surfaces in the scene [43]. We have not addressed viewpoint-free photography for transparent objects: a formidable problem which would require rethinking both the reconstruction [80] and rendering components [56] of our methods. Furthermore, our methods are designed to capture *places* rather than *moments* and struggle with large changes in scene appearance or many moving objects, such as a crowd of people.

Real-Time Display Rates. While all approaches in this chapter facilitate real-time display rates, we never pay close attention to the hardware which is used for rendering. This comes to a head in Sect. 6, where a modern dual-GPU computer would be needed. However, many current and future headsets work with much less powerful hardware—especially untethered headsets[9]. Maintaining real-time display rates on such limited hardware poses an interesting challenge. This opens up many exciting avenues for future work, e.g. more efficient acceleration structures, network compression [51] or precomputation [28,46].

References

1. CR-Play. http://www.cr-play.eu. Accessed 15 Oct 2016
2. Immersive 3D Spaces for real-world applications—Matterport. http://matterport.com/. Accessed 15 Oct 2016
3. Agarwal, S., Mierle, K., et al.: Ceres solver (2017). http://ceres-solver.org. Accessed 01 Oct 2018
4. Agarwala, A., et al.: Interactive digital photomontage. ACM Trans. Graph. **23**(3), 294–302 (2004)

---

[8] https://theta360.com.

[9] https://www.oculus.com/quest/.

5. Aliaga, D.G., Funkhouser, T., Yanovsky, D., Carlbom, I.: Sea of images. In: Vis, pp. 331–338. IEEE (2002)
6. Anderson, R., et al.: Jump: virtual reality video. ACM Trans. Graph. **35**(6), 1–13 (2016)
7. Bako, S., et al.: Kernel-predicting convolutional networks for denoising Monte Carlo renderings. ACM Trans. Graph. **36**(4), 97 (2017)
8. Barnes, C., Shechtman, E., Finkelstein, A., Goldman, D.B.: Patchmatch: a randomized correspondence algorithm for structural image editing. ACM Trans. Graph. **28**(3), 24:1–24:11 (2009)
9. Barron, J.T., Malik, J.: Shape, illumination, and reflectance from shading. IEEE Trans. Pattern Anal. Mach. Intell. **37**(8), 1670–1687 (2015)
10. Bertel, T., Campbell, N.D.F., Richardt, C.: Megaparallax: casual 360° panoramas with motion parallax. IEEE TVCG **25**, 1828–1835 (2019)
11. Buehler, C., Bosse, M., McMillan, L., Gortler, S., Cohen, M.: Unstructured lumigraph rendering. In: SIGGRAPH, pp. 425–432. ACM (2001)
12. Chaurasia, G., Duchene, S., Sorkine-Hornung, O., Drettakis, G.: Depth synthesis and local warps for plausible image-based navigation. ACM Trans. Graph. **32**(3), 30:1–30:12 (2013)
13. Chen, S.E., Williams, L.: View interpolation for image synthesis. In: SIGGRAPH, pp. 279–288. ACM (1993)
14. Davis, A., Levoy, M., Durand, F.: Unstructured light fields. Comp. Graph. Forum **31**(2), 305–314 (2012)
15. Debevec, P., Yu, Y., Borshukov, G.: Efficient view-dependent image-based rendering with projective texture-mapping. In: Drettakis, G., Max, N. (eds.) Rendering Workshop, pp. 105–116. Springer, Heidelberg (1998). https://doi.org/10.1007/978-3-7091-6453-2_10
16. Eisemann, M., et al.: Floating textures. Comput. Graph. Forum **27**(2), 409–418 (2008)
17. Firman, M., Aodha, O.M., Julier, S., Brostow, G.J.: Structured prediction of unobserved voxels from a single depth image. In: CVPR, pp. 5431–5440. IEEE (2016)
18. Fitzgibbon, A., Wexler, Y., Zisserman, A.: Image-based rendering using image-based priors. Int. J. Comput. Vis. **63**(2), 141–151 (2005)
19. Flynn, J., Neulander, I., Philbin, J., Snavely, N.: DeepStereo: learning to predict new views from the world's imagery. In: CVPR, pp. 5515–5524. IEEE, June 2016
20. Fuhrmann, S., Goesele, M.: Floating scale surface reconstruction. ACM Trans. Graph. **33**(4) (2014). Article no. 46
21. Fuhrmann, S., Langguth, F., Goesele, M.: MVE: a multi-view reconstruction environment. In: Proceedings of the Eurographics Workshop on Graphics and Cultural Heritage (GCH 2014), pp. 11–18 (2014)
22. Furukawa, Y., Hernández, C.: Multi-view stereo: a tutorial. Found. Trends. Comput. Graph. Vis. **9**(1–2), 1–148 (2015)
23. Furukawa, Y., Ponce, J.: Accurate, dense, and robust multiview stereopsis. IEEE Trans. Pattern Anal. Mach. Intell. **32**(8), 1362–1376 (2010)
24. Garland, M., Heckbert, P.S.: Surface simplification using quadric error metrics. In: SIGGRAPH, pp. 209–216. ACM (1997)
25. Godard, C., Mac Aodha, O., Brostow, G.J.: Unsupervised monocular depth estimation with left-right consistency. In: CVPR (2017)
26. Goesele, M., Snavely, N., Curless, B., Hoppe, H., Seitz, S.M.: Multi-view stereo for community photo collections. In: ICCV, pp. 1–8. IEEE (2007)

27. Goldlücke, B., Aubry, M., Kolev, K., Cremers, D.: A super-resolution framework for high-accuracy multiview reconstruction. Int. J. Comput. Vis. **106**(2), 172–191 (2014)
28. Gortler, S.J., Grzeszczuk, R., Szeliski, R., Cohen, M.F.: The lumigraph. In: SIGGRAPH, pp. 43–54. ACM (1996)
29. Ha, H., Im, S., Park, J., Jeon, H.G., Kweon, I.S.: High-quality depth from uncalibrated small motion clip. In: CVPR (2016)
30. He, K., Sun, J., Tang, X.: Guided image filtering. In: Daniilidis, K., Maragos, P., Paragios, N. (eds.) ECCV 2010. LNCS, vol. 6311, pp. 1–14. Springer, Heidelberg (2010). https://doi.org/10.1007/978-3-642-15549-9_1
31. Hedman, P., Ritschel, T., Drettakis, G., Brostow, G.: Scalable inside-out image-based rendering. ACM Trans. Graph. **35**(6), 231:1–231:11 (2016)
32. Heigl, B., Koch, R., Pollefeys, M., Denzler, J., Van Gool, L.: Plenoptic modeling and rendering from image sequences taken by a hand-held camera. In: Förstner, W., Buhmann, J.M., Faber, A., Faber, P. (eds.) Mustererkennung 1999, pp. 94–101. Springer, Heidelberg (1999). https://doi.org/10.1007/978-3-642-60243-6_11
33. Hirschmuller, H.: Stereo vision in structured environments by consistent semi-global matching. In: CVPR, pp. 2386–2393. IEEE (2006)
34. Hosni, A., Rhemann, C., Bleyer, M., Rother, C., Gelautz, M.: Fast cost-volume filtering for visual correspondence and beyond. IEEE Trans. Pattern Anal. Mach. Intell. **35**(2), 504–511 (2013)
35. Im, S., Ha, H., Rameau, F., Jeon, H.G., Choe, G., Kweon, I.S.: All-around depth from small motion with a spherical panoramic camera. In: Leibe, B., Matas, J., Sebe, N., Welling, M. (eds.) ECCV 2016. LNCS, vol. 9907, pp. 156–172. Springer, Heidelberg (2016). https://doi.org/10.1007/978-3-319-46487-9_10
36. Ishiguro, H., Yamamoto, M., Tsuji, S.: Omni-directional stereo for making global map. In: ICCV, pp. 540–547. IEEE (1990)
37. Jancosek, M., Pajdla, T.: Multi-view reconstruction preserving weakly-supported surfaces. In: CVPR, pp. 3121–3128 (2011)
38. Johnson, J., Alahi, A., Fei-Fei, L.: Perceptual losses for real-time style transfer and super-resolution. In: Leibe, B., Matas, J., Sebe, N., Welling, M. (eds.) ECCV 2016, vol. 9906, pp. 694–711. Springer, Heidelberg (2016). https://doi.org/10.1007/978-3-319-46475-6_43
39. Kalantari, N.K., Wang, T.C., Ramamoorthi, R.: Learning-based view synthesis for light field cameras. ACM Trans. Graph. **35**(6), 1–10 (2016)
40. Kazhdan, M., Hoppe, H.: Screened Poisson surface reconstruction. ACM Trans. Graph. **32**(3), 29:1–29:13 (2013)
41. Knapitsch, A., Park, J., Zhou, Q.Y., Koltun, V.: Tanks and temples: benchmarking large-scale scene reconstruction. ACM Trans. Graph. **36**(4), 1–13 (2017)
42. Konrad, R., Dansereau, D.G., Masood, A., Wetzstein, G.: SpinVR: towards live-streaming 3D virtual reality video. ACM Trans. Graph. **36**(6) (2017). Article no. 209
43. Kopf, J., Langguth, F., Scharstein, D., Szeliski, R., Goesele, M.: Image-based rendering in the gradient domain. ACM Trans. Graph. **32**(6), 199:1–199:9 (2013)
44. Kwatra, V., Schödl, A., Essa, I., Turk, G., Bobick, A.: Graphcut textures: image and video synthesis using graph cuts. ACM Trans. Graph. **22**(3), 277–286 (2003)
45. Labatut, P., Pons, J.P., Keriven, R.: Efficient multi-view reconstruction of large-scale scenes using interest points, delaunay triangulation and graph cuts. In: ICCV, pp. 1–8. IEEE (2007)
46. Levoy, M., Hanrahan, P.: Light field rendering. In: SIGGRAPH, pp. 31–42. ACM (1996)

47. Li, W., Li, B.: Joint conditional random field of multiple views with online learning for image-based rendering. In: CVPR. IEEE (2008)
48. Lin, K., Jiang, N., Cheong, L., Do, M.N., Lu, J.: SEAGULL: seam-guided local alignment for parallax-tolerant image stitching. In: Leibe, B., Matas, J., Sebe, N., Welling, M. (eds.) ECCV 2016, vol. 9907, pp. 370–385. Springer, Heidelberg (2016). https://doi.org/10.1007/978-3-319-46487-9_23
49. McMillan, L., Bishop, G.: Plenoptic modeling: an image-based rendering system. In: SIGGRAPH, pp. 39–46. ACM (1995)
50. Michael Bleyer, C.R., Rother, C.: Patchmatch stereo - stereo matching with slanted support windows. In: BMVC, pp. 14.1–14.11 (2011)
51. Molchanov, P., Tyree, S., Karras, T., Aila, T., Kautz, J.: Pruning convolutional neural networks for resource efficient transfer learning. arXiv preprint arXiv:1611.06440 (2016)
52. Ortiz-Cayon, R., Djelouah, A., Drettakis, G.: A Bayesian approach for selective image-based rendering using superpixels. In: 3DV, pp. 469–477. IEEE (2015)
53. Overbeck, R.S., Erickson, D., Evangelakos, D., Pharr, M., Debevec, P.: A system for acquiring, processing, and rendering panoramic light field stills for virtual reality. ACM Trans. Graph. **37**(6), 197:1–197:15 (2018)
54. Pathak, D., Krähenbühl, P., Donahue, J., Darrell, T., Efros, A.: Context encoders: feature learning by inpainting. In: CVPR. IEEE (2016)
55. Peleg, S., Ben-Ezra, M., Pritch, Y.: Omnistereo: panoramic stereo imaging. IEEE Trans. Pattern Anal. Mach. Intell. **23**(3), 279–290 (2001)
56. Penner, E., Zhang, L.: Soft 3D reconstruction for view synthesis. ACM Trans. Graph. **36**(6), 235 (2017)
57. Perazzi, F., et al.: Panoramic video from unstructured camera arrays. Comput. Graph. Forum **34**(2), 57–68 (2015)
58. Pulli, K., Hoppe, H., Cohen, M., Shapiro, L., Duchamp, T., Stuetzle, W.: View-based rendering: visualizing real objects from scanned range and color data. In: Dorsey, J., Slusallek, P. (eds.) Rendering Techniques 1997. Eurographics, pp. 23–34. Springer, Heidelberg (1997). https://doi.org/10.1007/978-3-7091-6858-5_3
59. RealityCapture, C.: RealityCapture (2016). https://capturingreality.com. Accessed 01 Oct 2018
60. Reinhard, E., Ashikhmin, M., Gooch, B., Shirley, P.: Color transfer between images. IEEE Comput. Graph. Appl. **21**(5), 34–41 (2001)
61. Richardt, C., Pritch, Y., Zimmer, H., Sorkine-Hornung, A.: Megastereo: constructing high-resolution stereo panoramas. In: CVPR, pp. 1256–1263 (2013)
62. Ronneberger, O., Fischer, P., Brox, T.: U-net: convolutional networks for biomedical image segmentation. In: Navab, N., Hornegger, J., Wells, W., Frangi, A. (eds.) MICCAI 2015. LNCS, vol. 9351, pp. 234–241. Springer, Heidelberg (2015). https://doi.org/10.1007/978-3-319-24574-4_28
63. Scharstein, D., Szeliski, R.: A taxonomy and evaluation of dense two-frame stereo correspondence algorithms. Int. J. Comput. Vis. **47**(1–3), 7–42 (2002)
64. Schönberger, J.L., Frahm, J.M.: Structure-from-motion revisited. In: CVPR (2016)
65. Schönberger, J.L., Zheng, E., Pollefeys, M., Frahm, J.M.: Pixelwise view selection for unstructured multi-view stereo. In: Leibe, B., Matas, J., Sebe, N., Welling, M. (eds.) ECCV 2016, vol. 9907, pp. 501–518. Springer, Heidelberg (2016). https://doi.org/10.1007/978-3-319-46487-9_31
66. Schöps, T., et al.: A multi-view stereo benchmark with high-resolution images and multi-camera videos. In: CVPR. IEEE (2017)
67. Shade, J., Gortler, S., He, L.W., Szeliski, R.: Layered depth images. In: SIGGRAPH (1998)

68. Shum, H.Y., Chan, S.C., Kang, S.B.: Image-Based Rendering. Springer, Heidelberg (2008). https://doi.org/10.1007/978-0-387-32668-9
69. Shum, H.Y., He, L.W.: Rendering with concentric mosaics. In: SIGGRAPH, pp. 299–306. ACM (1999)
70. Sinha, S.N., Steedly, D., Szeliski, R.: Piecewise planar stereo for image-based rendering. In: ICCV, pp. 1881–1888. IEEE (2009)
71. Srinivasan, P.P., Wang, T., Sreelal, A., Ramamoorthi, R., Ng, R.: Learning to synthesize a 4D RGBD light field from a single image. In: ICCV, vol. 2, p. 6. IEEE (2017)
72. Szeliski, R.: Computer Vision: Algorithms and Applications, 1st edn. Springer, New York (2010)
73. Ummenhofer, B., Brox, T.: Global, dense multiscale reconstruction for a billion points. In: ICCV (2015)
74. Waechter, M., Moehrle, N., Goesele, M.: Let there be color! Large-scale texturing of 3D reconstructions. In: Fleet, D., Pajdla, T., Schiele, B., Tuytelaars, T. (eds.) ECCV 2014. LNCS, vol. 8693, pp. 836–850. Springer, Heidelberg (2014). https://doi.org/10.1007/978-3-319-10602-1_54
75. Wolff, K., et al.: Point cloud noise and outlier removal for image-based 3D reconstruction. In: 3DV, pp. 118–127 (2016)
76. Wood, D.N., et al.: Surface light fields for 3D photography. In: SIGGRAPH, pp. 287–296. ACM (2000)
77. Woodford, O., Fitzgibbon, A.W.: Fast image-based rendering using hierarchical image-based priors. In: BMVC, vol. 1, pp. 260–269 (2005)
78. Woodford, O.J., Reid, I.D., Fitzgibbon, A.W.: Efficient new-view synthesis using pairwise dictionary priors. In: CVPR, pp. 1–8. IEEE (2007)
79. Woodford, O.J., Reid, I.D., Torr, P.H., Fitzgibbon, A.W.: Fields of experts for image-based rendering. In: BMVC, vol. 3, pp. 1109–1108 (2006)
80. Wu, B., Zhou, Y., Qian, Y., Gong, M., Huang, H.: Full 3D reconstruction of transparent objects. ACM Trans. Graph. 37(4), 103:1–103:11 (2018)
81. Zhang, F., Liu, F.: Parallax-tolerant image stitching. In: CVPR, pp. 3262–3269 (2014)
82. Zheng, K.C., Kang, S.B., Cohen, M.F., Szeliski, R.: Layered depth panoramas. In: CVPR, pp. 1–8 (2007)
83. Zhou, Q.Y., Koltun, V.: Color map optimization for 3D reconstruction with consumer depth cameras. ACM Trans. Graph. 33(4), 155:1–155:10 (2014)
84. Zitnick, C.L., Kang, S.B.: Stereo for image-based rendering using image oversegmentation. Int. J. Comput. Vis. 75(1), 49–65 (2007)
85. Zitnick, C.L., Kang, S.B., Uyttendaele, M., Winder, S., Szeliski, R.: High-quality video view interpolation using a layered representation. ACM Trans. Graph. 23(3), 600–608 (2004)

Hybrid Human Modeling: Making Volumetric Video Animatable

Peter Eisert[(✉)] and Anna Hilsmann

Fraunhofer HHI, Berlin, Germany
{peter.eisert,anna.hilsmann}@hhi.fraunhofer.de
www.hhi.fraunhofer.de/vit/cvg

Abstract. Photo-realistic modeling and rendering of humans is extremely important for virtual reality (VR) environments, as the human body and face are highly complex and exhibit large shape variability but also, especially, as humans are extremely sensitive to looking at humans. Further, in VR environments, interactivity plays an important role. While purely computer graphics modeling can achieve highly realistic human models, achieving real photo-realism with these models is computationally extremely expensive. In this chapter, a full end-to-end pipeline for the creation of hybrid representations for human bodies and faces (animatable volumetric video) is investigated, combining classical computer graphics models with image- and video-based as well as example-based approaches: by enriching volumetric video with semantics and animation properties and applying new hybrid geometry- and video-based animation methods, we bring volumetric video to life and combine interactivity with photo-realism. Semantic enrichment and geometric animation ability is achieved by establishing temporal consistency in the 3D data, followed by an automatic rigging of each frame using a parametric shape-adaptive full human body model. For pose editing, we exploit the captured data as much as possible and kinematically deform selected captured frames to fit a desired pose. Further, we treat the face differently from the body in a hybrid geometry- and video-based animation approach, where coarse movements and poses are modeled in the geometry, while very fine and subtle details in the face, often lacking in purely geometric methods, are captured in video-based textures. These are processed to be interactively combined to form new facial expressions. On top of that, we learn the appearance of regions that are challenging to synthesize, such as the teeth or the eyes, and fill in missing regions realistically with an autoencoder-based approach.

Keywords: Volumetric video · Animation · Human modeling · Hybrid modeling

1 Introduction

In recent years, with the advances in augmented and virtual reality, high-quality free viewpoint video has gained a lot of interest. Today, volumetric studios [6,9]

© Springer Nature Switzerland AG 2020
M. Magnor and A. Sorkine-Hornung (Eds.): Real VR, LNCS 11900, pp. 167–187, 2020.
https://doi.org/10.1007/978-3-030-41816-8_7

can create high-quality 3D video content and advanced virtual and augmented reality hardware [5, 7] is able to create highly immersive viewing experiences. However, high-quality immersiveness is usually limited to experience pre-recorded situations. Changing the recorded scene, e.g. the motion and performance of captured persons, and hence, interaction with high-quality volumetric video content is usually not possible. If interaction with virtual characters is envisioned, usually the fall-back solution are synthetic animatable Computer Graphics models. By making captured human performances alterable and editable, we think immersiveness and interactivity a step further. This chapter presents an end-to-end pipeline for the creation of alterable volumetric video content of human performances and reviews different components necessary to achieve this goal. By enriching the captured high-quality data with semantics and animation properties, we allow direct animation of the high-quality real world data itself instead of creating an animatable model that approximates the captured data.

For animation, we present a hybrid example-based approach that exploits the captured content as much as possible to create new animations and motion sequences in a natural way. First, semantic enrichment allows a direct manipulation of the captured volumetric video frames by kinematic animation. Further, we propose to subdivide the captured volumetric video into elementary subsequences to form new animation sequences through appropriate concatenation and interpolation together with kinematic manipulation of the individual frames. As humans are very sensitive to viewing facial expressions, and it is very difficult to represent all fine and subtle details of facial movements in geometry only, we propose a special hybrid geometry-and-video-based approach for the creation of new facial animation sequences. In our approach, the geometry accounts for low-resolution shape adaptation while fine details are captured by video-textures that function as appearance examples to be combined and interpolated to form new facial textures. Regions such as the eyes or the teeth are still difficult to model both in geometry as well as in texture due to e.g. (dis-)occlusion. We address this by learning the appearance of these regions and realistically synthesize them in an autoencoder-based approach if they are missing in the manipulated texture. With the proposed hybrid animation framework, we take advantage of the richness of the captured data that exhibits real deformations and appearances, producing animations with real shapes, kinematics and appearances.

This chapter presents a full end-to-end framework for the creation of animatable volumetric video and steps through the different components in the processing pipeline (Fig. 1). Starting from the capturing of volumetric video data and the processing into a temporal sequence of 3D meshes (Sect. 2), the next step is to make the captured volumetric video stream animatable and alterable. We address this by enriching the captured data with semantics and animation properties by fitting a parametric kinematic human body model to it (Sect. 3). The output of this step is a volumetric video stream with an attached parametric body model. Through the enrichment of the volumetric video data with kinematic information, we can directly manipulate the captured volumetric frames themselves. Section 3.2 discusses hybrid animation frameworks for the modification of the captured volumetric video data. In each building block, we will discuss related works and alternative approaches before going into detail on our proposed procedure. The presented work is based on previous papers [28,30–32,60,61,67] and combines and extends them to build a full framework for the creation of animatable volumetric video (AVV).

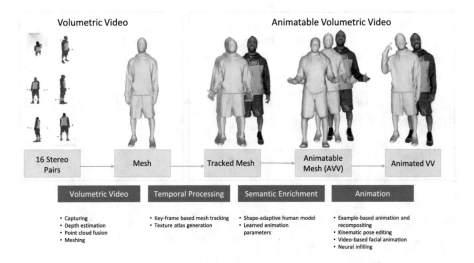

Fig. 1. End-to-end pipeline for the creation of animatable volumetric video content.

2 Volumetric Video

The first step in the processing pipeline towards animatable volumetric video is the capturing of an actor's performance and the computation of a temporal sequence of 3D meshes, usually referred to as Volumetric Video.

2.1 Volumetric Capturing

In recent years, a number of volumetric studios have been created [2,3,6,8,9]. These studios produce high quality free viewpoint video which can be viewed in real-time from a continuous range of viewpoints chosen at any time in playback. Most studios focus on a capture volume that is viewed in 360° from the outside. A large number of cameras are placed around the scene (e.g. in studios from 8i [3], 4dviews [2], uncorporeal [8], or Volucap [9]) providing input for photogrammetric reconstruction of the actors, while Microsoft's Mixed reality Capture Studios [6] rely on active depth sensors for geometry acquisition. In order to separate the scene from the background, all studios are equipped with green screens for chroma keying, wheras Volucap [9] uses a bright backlit background to avoid green spilling effects in the texture.

For our system, we have setup a studio with 32 cameras and 120 LED panels for full 360° acquisition as shown in Fig. 2. The cameras are equipped with high-quality sensors offering 20 MPixel resolution at 30 frames per second, which enables pure image-based 3D reconstruction with high texture resolution. They are grouped into 16 stereo pairs, positioned in 3 rings of different height. From each stereo system, depth maps are computed, which are then fused into complete 3D models [28,66]. Shape estimation is supported by a visual hull formed from segmentation masks created by automatic keying, details are described in the following section. In contrast to other studios, we avoid green screen but segment the foreground against a bright diffuse background. In addition, 120 programmable light panels offer homogeneous and diffuse lighting but also the creation of arbitrary lighting situations similar to a light stage.

Fig. 2. Volumetric studio for performance capturing.

2.2   Volumetric Reconstruction

Usually, the content creation starts with the reconstruction of temporally inconsistent 3D reconstructions per frame, starting with point cloud reconstructions using multiple view geometry and/or shape from silhouette [1,4,25,55,71] methods followed by surface reconstruction, e.g. using Poisson Surface Reconstruction [46]. Collet *et al.* [25] additionally introduce a surface importance field in order to adapt the mesh granularity in perceptually important regions, such as the face or the hands. The temporally inconsistent reconstructions are often converted into spatio-temporally coherent mesh (sub-)sequences using template-based approaches in order to facilitate texturing and compression [12,50,81]. In order to allow for topological changes during the sequence, key-frame-based methods decompose the captured sequence into subsequences and register a number of keyframes to the captured data [25,50,58]. The final dynamic textured 3D reconstructions can then be inserted as assets in virtual environments and viewed from arbitrary directions.

In the following, we describe the detailed processing pipeline exemplarily for our system.

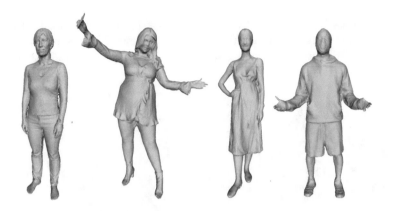

Fig. 3. Reconstructed meshes of performing actors.

Stereo-Based Depth Estimation. In our setup, the processing pipeline towards a sequence of 3D meshes representing the dynamic geometry of the actors starts with the computation of depth maps for each pair of cameras.

For depth estimation from the 5k by 4k images, a recursive patch-based method is used [78, 79]. Small patches around a pixel in a reference frame are swept through depth with different patch orientations and evaluated by normalized cross correlation in the second view, exploiting epipolar constraints obtained from calibration. The large space of possible patch combinations (depth/orientation) is reduced by a multi-hypothesis method that propagates information from a spatial and temporal neighborhood. Instead of testing all combinations, only depth/orientation hypotheses from other neighboring patches and from the previous frame are evaluated. In addition, a new random candidate is considered similar as in [15] and a flow-based depth/orientation refinement step is applied to the selected best hypothesis. Since propagation of hypotheses is only performed from the previous step of iteration, no data dependencies exist, enabling massive parallel execution on multiple GPUs. For each frame, a few steps of iteration are followed by left-right consistency checks of the stereo pair's two depth maps. The full stereo-based depth estimation approach is detailed in [79].

Point Cloud Fusion and Meshing. In a next step, the depth maps are fused into a common 3D point cloud [27]. The fusion process considers visibility constraints from the individual views as well as normal information taken from the surface patch orientation in order to deal with contradicting surface candidates. In addition, silhouette information obtained by keying against the bright white background restricts the outer hull. The resulting point cloud is converted into a triangle mesh using Screened Poisson Surface Reconstruction [45]. Since this mesh is usually still to large to be rendered on a VR headset or used as an asset in a CG scene, it is further reduced by a modified version of the Quadric Edge Collapse [34]. In contrast to the standard edge collapse approach, we preserve details in semantically important regions like the face (automatically detected by a DNN based face detector combined with skin color classification [54]) by assigning a larger number of triangles to these regions. The result of this step is a sequence of 3D meshes as shown in Fig. 3 with inconsistent mesh connectivity.

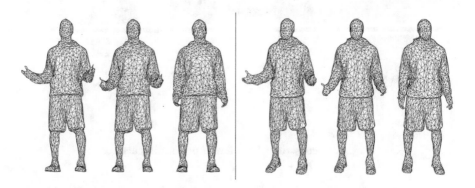

Fig. 4. Individual meshes of a sequence captured in the volumetric pipeline may have differing connectivity (left). We perform a mesh registration, deforming the mesh of the first frame into the following frames (right). This provides shared connectivity while preserving the original geometries and silhouettes.

Keyframe-Based Mesh Tracking for Temporal Consistency. In order to support further processing, the next step in our pipeline is a conversion of the temporally inconsistent reconstructions spatio-temporally coherent mesh (sub-) sequences. Establishing the same connectivity for the entire sequence might be infeasible in cases of large scene changes, including surface interaction, object insertion or removal, etc. Hence, we adapt the keyframe concept from video compression and divide the sequence into groups of frames that will share the same connectivity. For each group, a frame chosen as keyframe is deformed to match the surface of their neighboring meshes, progressively covering the complete sequence. Frames with a high surface area and low genus are considered to be good candidates to become keyframes in an automatic keyframe selection scheme [25]. Alternatively, every n^{th} frame can be chosen as the keyframe for sequences, where high input noise might make automatic keyframe selection error-prone.

Once keyframes are determined, we perform a pairwise mesh registration, deforming the keyframe progressively to its temporal neighbors. We work both temporally forward and backward from the keyframe to reduce the average temporal distance of a registered frame to its keyframe. Following, some frames are selected to be registered from two different keyframes. Greedily selecting the resulting mesh with the smaller registration error from the two candidates improves the smoothness of the transition between keyframes and reduces potential errors from imperfect keyframe selection.

Our non-rigid pairwise mesh registration to deform one mesh into another is based on the iterative closest point (ICP) algorithm. We use a coarse-to-fine scheme to speed up convergence towards a global solution even with large

Fig. 5. Textured meshes of performing actors.

displacements between successive frames. Such a hierarchical ICP scheme reduces computation time while improving robustness [43]. At each level of detail, we run a bidirectional ICP to pull the mesh towards the target surface. We constrain the deformation to be locally as-rigid-as-possible to preserve local stiffness in articulated objects [70]. The deformation of the mesh is encoded as rotations and translations attached to nodes in a deformation graph [73]. Our deformation graph is created from the deformed mesh and does not model any category of objects explicitly. We extend the idea of the deformation graph to progressively add details to the transformations while working upwards in the coarse-to-fine mesh hierarchy.

Our non-rigid registration approach creates temporally coherent subsequences while preserving the reconstructed geometry. Through application of the coarse-to-fine approach, we are able to register meshes with 50,000 faces in a few seconds computation time on a single machine to sub-millimeter accuracy. Figure 4 compares three frames of the initial reconstructed mesh sequence with the tracked sequence that is created by deforming the first frame into the following frames. The full mesh tracking approach is detailed in [58].

Mesh Sequence Texturing. Finally, for each subsequence corresponding to a keyframe, we compute texture coordinates and fill the atlas using the captured views. Since the UV mapping for these frames stays constant, temporal filtering and consistent editing of the texture maps becomes possible. For texture filling, we extend a graph cut based approach for view selection, color adjustment and filling [77], incorporating information on semantically important regions as the face and depth map quality to the data term. Figure 5 shows examples of such textured models that we have created within several VR productions [67]. They can be used as assets in virtual environments but provide only free viewpoint visualization without any additional capabilities of animation.

3   Making Volumetric Video Animatable

Many applications, such as computer games, virtual reality or film, require animation of virtual humans. Usually, computer graphics models are used in order to maximize flexibility. They allow for arbitrary animation, with body motion usually being controlled by an underlying skeleton while facial expressions are described by a set of blendshapes [11]. The advantage of full control comes at the price of significant modeling effort and sometimes limited realism. In order to build a Computer Graphics model of a captured person, the body model is usually adapted in shape and pose to the volumetric video performance. Given a template model, shape and pose can be learned from the sequence of real 3D measurements [30] in order to align it with the sequence. Recent progress in deep learning also enables the reconstruction of highly accurate human body models even from single RGB images [13]. For example, Pavlakos et al. [62] estimate shape and pose of a template model from monocular video such that the human model exactly follows the performance in the sequence. Haberman et al. [37] go one step further and enable real-time capture of humans including surface deformations due to clothes. All these approaches provide sequences of animation parameters that can be applied to computer graphics models in order to replicate the actor's motion. The reproduction of very subtle details in motion and deformation, however, are beyond the scope of these approaches. Instead, we propose to animate the captured data itself: for pose editing, a fitted body model enriches the captured data with pose and animation semantics and animation is performed in an example-based approach (Sect. 3.2); for facial animation, we propose a hybrid representation that used video-textures in order to create highly photorealistic new content.

3.1   Adding Semantics and Animation Characteristics

In order to make the captured data animatable, we fit a parametric human model, which can be animated through a skeleton, to closely resemble the shape of the captured subject as well as the pose of each frame. Thereby, we enrich the captured data with semantic pose and animation data taken from the parametric model, which can then be used to drive the animation of the captured volumetric video data itself.

The Body Model. For semantic enrichment, we want to fit a body model to each individual frame in order to pass the pose and animation information from the model to the captured data. In order to produce natural movements and animations, the parametric model's shape should resemble the captured data as closely as possible. We follow the approach of [29] and learn our shape-adaptive human model (skinning weights, vertices, kinematic joint positions and orientations) in a data-driven optimization from datasets of captured humans, resulting in a high degree of accuracy and realism (Fig. 6). We base our model on vertex skinning in order to allow for real-time animation, in contrast to implicit

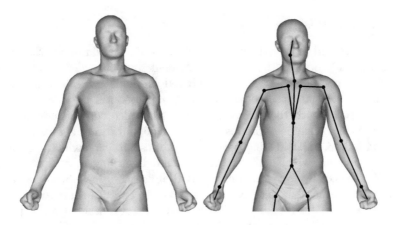

Fig. 6. Our articulated model (right) learned from SCAPE dataset (left) [14].

animation methods [17,38,48,82]. In order to achieve natural and realistic movements, our deformation model uses a swing-twist decomposition for joint rotations [29]. The two main advantages of this parameterization are: (i) The parameters are interpretable. Thus, it is straightforward to specify lower/upper bounds for increased robustness of tracking algorithms, or to extract these bounds automatically from example datasets [59]. (ii) Animating the model with different skinning functions, i.e. Linear Blend Skinning for swing rotations and Quaternion Blend Skinning for twist, reduces skinning artifacts to a non-visible minimum [44], especially when using the dual quaternion based multi-joint variant [29], without requiring further enhancements like blend shapes.

Body Model Fitting. We fit the articulated model to the sequence of 3D meshes using shape adaptive motion capture as presented in [30]. Starting from a rough manual kinematic alignment for the first frame, we optimize the pose parameters by minimizing the distances between corresponding vertices of the model and the captured mesh. This initial pose fit is refined in a second step by additionally optimizing the model vertices and skeleton joints to bring the model into better alignment with the captured mesh as shown in Fig. 7. The resulting subject-adapted model is used to track the person's pose from frame to frame. To ensure natural movement characteristics, we use a learned pose prior based on Gaussian mixture models. Further, we employ a mesh Laplacian constraint [69] to enforce plausible human shapes. Details on the fitting of the body model can be found in [30]. Through fitting the kinematic body model to the individual frames of the volumetric video data, we enrich the captured real data with semantic information on pose and animation properties, making the volumetric video data animatable.

3.2   Example-Based Animation

Recently, more and more hybrid and example-based animation synthesis methods have been proposed that exploit captured data in order to obtain realistic appearances. Very early example-based methods synthesize novel video sequences of facial animations and other dynamic scenes by video resampling [19,65]. Recently, with the advent of volumetric video content, similar resampling approaches have been proposed for 4D video for example-based character animation [10,18,20,41]. Going beyond simple resampling, some methods combine recompositing with smaller adjustments and warping to fit a desired pose [40,60,80]. Especially for faces, image-based approaches have been proposed as purely geometric models lack expressive power to capture complex and subtle facial details [60,61]. Finally, with the success of deep neural networks, powerful purely data-driven generative models have been developed and have been used for the synthesis of human performances [24] or facial animation [42]. In our hybrid animation approach, we follow an example based hybrid approach on different levels: (i) for the manipulation and editing of the body pose, we follow an example-based approach that combines resampling of the volumetric video content with kinematic animation; (ii) for the synthesis of facial expressions, we exploit an example-based hybrid approach that uses geometry only as a proxy

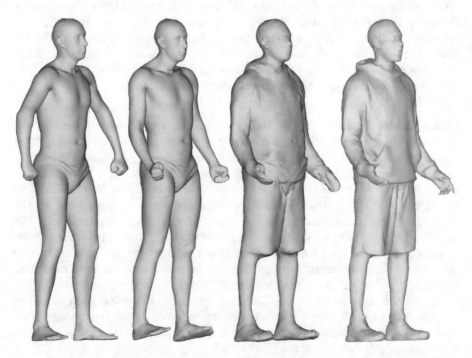

Fig. 7. Model adaptation to volumetric video data: initial model (left), pose adapted model (2nd from left), pose and shape adapted model (2nd from right) and volumetric video frame (right).

to explain rigid motion, large scale deformation and perspective distortion while details are captured by video-based textures that are combined and blended in order to create new animation sequences; (iii) finally, we fill in missing complex regions, such as the eyes and mouth, in an autoencoder-based approach. In the following, we explain each component in detail.

Hybrid Pose Editing. For the generation of new performances with real deformations (present in the original data), we propose to follow a hybrid example-based approach that exploits the captured data as much as possible. As the captured volumetric video data consists of temporally consistent subsequences, these can be treated as essential basis sequences containing motion and appearance examples. The enrichment of the volumetric video data with pose semantics allows us to retrieve the subsequence(s) or frames closest to a target pose sequence, which are then concatenated and interpolated in order to form new animations. For smoothing the transitions between successive sequences, the progressive mesh tracking approach described in Sect. 2.2 can be used in order to register the meshes of one sequence to the other, and then interpolating over time from the original sequence to the registered sequence. This is similar to surface motion graphs and character animation by volumetric video resampling [10,18,20,41]. In [72], Stoll et al. combine skeleton-based CG models with captured surface data to represent details of apparels on top of the body. Casas et al. [23] combined concatenation of captured 3D sequences with view dependent texturing for real-time interactive animation. Similarly, Volino et al. [76] presented a parametric motion graph-based character animation for web applications. Only recently, Boukhayma and Boyer [10,18] proposed an animation synthesis structure for the recomposition of textured 4D video capture, accounting for geometry and appearance. They propose a graph structure that enables interpolation and traversal between precaptured 4D video sequences. Finally, Regateiro et al. [64] present a skeleton-driven surface registration approach to generate temporally consistent meshes from volumetric video of human subjects in order to facilitate intuitive editing and animation of volumetric video.

New sequences generated by these approaches are restricted to poses and movements already present in the captured data and might not perfectly fit the desired poses. However, as we enriched the volumetric video data with animation and pose properties in the previous section, we can now kinematically adapt the recomposed frames to fit the desired pose (see below). Put another way, the individual volumetric frames are animatable but in order to attain a high realism, we want to change each frame as little as possible. Hence, we first generate a close animation sequence in an example-based manner as described above and only slightly modify the recomposed frames to fit the target poses. This hybrid strategy combines the realism of the real volumetric video data with the ability to animate and modify.

The kinematic animation of the individual frames is facilitated through the body model fitted to each frame. For each mesh vertex, the location relative to the closest triangle of the template model is calculated, parameterized by the barycentric coordinates of the projection onto the triangle and the orthogonal distance. This relative location is held fixed, virtually gluing the mesh vertex to the template triangle with constant distance and orientation. With this parametrization between each mesh frame and the model, an animation of the model can directly be transferred to the volumetric video frame. Figure 8 shows an example of an animated volumetric video frame. The classical approach would have been to use the body model fitted to best represent the captured data in order to synthesize new animation sequences. Instead, we use the pose optimized and shape adapted template model to drive the kinematic animation of the volumetric video data itself. As the original data contains all natural movements with all fine details and the original data is exploited as much as possible, our animation approach produces highly realistic results.

Video-Based Facial Facial Animation. Animation and performance capture of human faces have been active areas of research for decades. Classic approaches for modeling facial expressions, for example [16, 26, 75], have been used for many years. They are usually build upon a linear basis of blendshapes and even though their expressive power is limited, they became popular due to their robustness and simplicity of use. For example, in [52], Li *et al.* improve blendshape based performance capture and animation system by estimating corrective blendshapes on the fly. Cao *et al.* [21] present an automatic system for creating large scale blendshape databases using captured RGB-D data and Garrido *et al.* [35] use blendshapes to create a personalized model by adapting it a detailed 3D scan using sparse facial features and optical flow. The generated face model is then

Fig. 8. Captured/original frame of the volumetric video data (left) and animated (gaze corrected) volumetric video frame (right).

used to synthesize plausible mouth animations of an actor in a video according to a new target audio track. A more sophisticated facial retargeting system was proposed by Thies *et al.* [74], who implemented a linear model that could represent wide range of facial expressions of different people under varying light conditions. However, often hand crafted models are necessary in order to visualize the oral cavity [35,74], which demonstrates the weakness of blendshape based models. Further, while being useful to represent large scale geometry deformations and rigid motion, they usually lack expressive power to capture complex deformations and occlusions/disocclusions that occur around eyes, mouth and in the oral cavity.

Alternative animation approaches use image data to synthesize new facial expressions directly from previously captured images. For example, Malleson *et al.* [56] present a method to continuously and seamlessly blend between multiple facial performances of an actor by exploiting complementary properties of audio and visual cues to automatically determine robust correspondences between takes, allowing a director to generate novel performances after filming. This method yields 2D photorealistic synthetic video sequences, but is limited to replaying captured data. This restriction is overcome by Fyffe *et al.* [33] and Serra *et al.* [68], who use a motion graph in order to interpolate between different 3D facial expressions captured and stored in a database. Such image based animation techniques provide high quality renderings but they are not as flexible as computer graphic models. Other approaches exploit the fact that low quality 3D models with high quality textures are still capable of producing high quality renderings [22,60,61]. Similarly, we propose a new facial animation method combining the advantages of both strategies: the flexibility of computer graphic models with the realism of image-based rendering [40,60].

Our facial animation models consist of two parts: we use the captured face geometry to explain rigid motion and large scale deformation and add a dynamic texture model that represents all details, small movements and changes in appearance (e.g. small wrinkles or local variations of skin colour due to strong deformations, see Fig. 9 (forehead and around mouth). From the captured volumetric video data, we compute a set of personalized blendshapes with a consistent topology (face geometry proxy). In [61], we show that it is even sufficient to have a face proxy with only one degree of freedom for the deformation of the jaw) plus six degrees of freedom for rigid motion. We intentionally do not remove mouth and eyes from the computed blendshapes, since we need a complete face geometry to render our dynamic textures. The second part of our animation strategy is constituted by dynamic face textures, which are extracted from the volumetric video data using a graph-cut based approach [61]. We use the previously created face geometry proxy to estimate the 3D face pose (i.e. 6 DoF + deformation) in each captured video frame and extract a temporal consistent sequence of face textures [60,61].

The actual animation methodology is again closely related to motion graphs [22,51]. We use short sequences of the captured video footage and re-arrange, loop, and concatenate them to create novel video sequences, see Fig. 9. In the context of motion graphs, edges in the graph correspond to facial actions, and vertices to expression states. Since we have approximate 3D information, we are able to compensate for the global head pose, which allows transferring facial expressions even between videos with different head orientations [60]. Since the extracted sequences have been captured separately and in a different order, simple concatenation would create obvious visual artifacts during transitions between two sequences. These artifacts appear in geometry as well as in texture due to different facial expressions and changing illumination. The independent texture sequences are brought into connection by defining transition points between the separate sequences [60], see Fig. 9. We can also subdivide the texture sequences into subregions, e.g. the eyes and mouth, and define transition points for each region separately, such that the different facial regions of new animation sequence can be assembled from different source sequences, broadening the range of possible animations.

In order to create seamless transitions between concatenated texture sequences, we use a spatio-temporal blending approach that explains texture mismatch with optical flow using a mesh based motion and deformation model [39]. By using optical flow information, we can smoothly interpolate between different facial expression textures without creating ghosting artifacts. All texture-differences that cannot be compensated by optical flow alone are blended with a cross dissolve approach. Details on our hybrid animation approach can be found in [60].

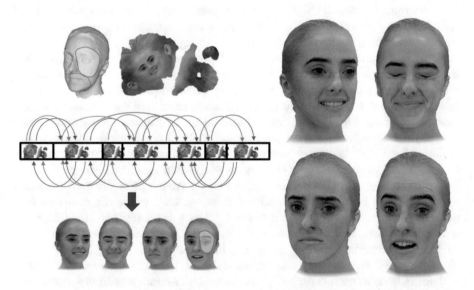

Fig. 9. Left: Short sequences of the volumetric video footage are re-arranged, looped and concatenated to form a new facial animation sequence. We can even subdivide the dynamic textures into local regions (e.g. eye region in blue, mouth region in orange) in order to reassemble the animation from different captured sequences. Right: Four examples of our facial animation model, rendered with different facial expressions and different viewpoints.

Neural Animation. While the spatio-temporal blending works well in most cases, it can fail if two concatenated facial expressions are too different. For example, disocclusions or occlusions caused by an opened or closed mouth cannot be explained by optical flow. Therefore, we make use of recent advances in deep convolutional neural networks that are capable of learning generative models for images and textures. Generative models, such as variational autoencoders [49] and generative adversarial networks (GAN) [36] have already been used in order to synthesize images and videos of human performances and facial expressions. Chan et al. [24], for example, use 2D skeleton data to transfer body motion from one person to another and synthesize new videos with a generative adversarial network. The skeleton motion data can also be estimated from video by neural networks [57]. Liu et al. [53] extend that approach and use a full template model as an intermediate representation that is enhanced by the GAN. Similar techniques can also be used for synthesizing facial video as shown, e.g. in [47]. For example, Pumarola et al. [63] present a GAN based animation approach that is able to generate facial expressions based on an action unit coding scheme. The action unit weights define a continuous representation of the facial expressions. The loss function is defined by a critic network that evaluates the realism of generated images and fulfillment of the expression conditioning. Another example is [42], where Huang and Khan propose a method to synthesize believable facial expressions using GANs that are conditioned on sketches of facial expressions.

While these approaches show astonishing and highly realistic results, they usually lack semantic and physical consistency. Hence, we exploit the captured data as much as possible and only fill in missing regions using a conditional GAN where information is missing and to correct artifacts that occur during animation, especially in the mouth and eye regions.

In Fig. 10, we show an animated face with open mouth. Due to the deformation, visual artifacts appear since the oral cavity is not represented in texture. Using a GAN that is conditioned on visual artifacts that appear during animation, we can reconstruct the expected artifact free image (e.g. with visible teeth). A further improvement, of our video based facial animation engine was implemented by training a variational autoencoder to learn a non-linear mapping between a low dimensional latent space and the high dimensional

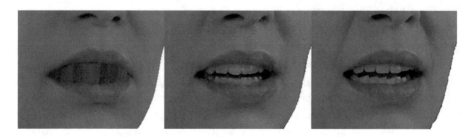

Fig. 10. Left: Example of a rendered image with missing oral cavity. Middle: corrected image with synthesized oral cavity by a cGAN. Right: Ground truth.

Fig. 11. Examples of the neural face model with dynamic textures synthesized by a variational autoencoder. We use two local models for eyes and mouth in order to animate them independently from each other.

texture and geometry space. The overall animation strategy stays the same, but instead of working with raw data, we manipulate facial expressions in latent space, which allows us blending smoothly and free of artifacts between concatenated sequences, see Fig. 11 for results. Another advantage of this variational autoencoder is that raw image and geometry data can be compressed into a low dimensional latent representation, which reduces memory requirements on the rendering machine.

4   Conclusions

This chapter discusses a full processing pipeline for the creation of animatable volumetric video representations as well as hybrid geometric and video-based animation approaches. The main idea is to enrich the captured data with semantic pose and animation properties in order to allow a modification of the individual volumetric video frames. To ensure a maximum of realism of the synthetic sequences, we exploit the captured data, exhibiting all the fine real deformations and appearance changes during motion, as much as possible in a cascadic example-based approach: temporal consistency allows a re-composition of existing frames or subsequences in order to fit a desired animation sequence as close as possible, followed by a kinematic mesh modification. As humans are very sensitive to details in facial expressions, we treat the face separately from the body and propose a hybrid geometry- and video-based approach, which uses a coarse geometric model for large-scale deformation and global motion and video-based textures to represent subtle and detailed facial movements. Finally, missing regions can realistically be filled in using a neural texture synthesis approach. The full hybrid animation framework combines the realism of high-quality volumetric video with the flexibility of Computer Graphics methods for animation.

References

1. 4D View Solutions. http://www.4dviews.com
2. 4dviews. http://www.4dviews.com
3. 8i. http://8i.com
4. DoubleMe. http://www.doubleme.me
5. HTC Vive Pro. https://www.vive.com/
6. Microsoft. http://www.microsoft.com/en-us/mixed-reality/capture-studios
7. Oculus Rift. https://www.oculus.com/rift/
8. Uncorporeal. http://uncorporeal.com
9. Volucap GmbH. http://www.volucap.de
10. Boukhayma, A., Boyer, E.: Surface motion capture animation synthesis. IEEE Trans. Vis. Comput. Graph. **25**(6), 2270–2283 (2019)
11. Abrevaya, V.F., Wuhrer, S., Boyer, E.: Spatiotemporal modeling for efficient registration of dynamic 3D faces. In: Proceedings of International Conference on 3D Vision (3DV), Verona, Italy, pp. 371–380, September 2018
12. de Aguiar, E., Stoll, C., Theobalt, C., Ahmed, N., Seidel, H.P., Thrun, S.: Performance capture from sparse multi-view video. TOG **27**(3), 1–10 (2008)
13. Alldieck, T., Magnor, M., Bhatnagar, B., Theobalt, C., Pons-Moll, G.: Learning to reconstruct people in clothing from a single RGB camera. In: Conference on Computer Vision and Pattern Recognition (CVPR), pp. 1175–1186, June 2019
14. Anguelov, D., Srinivasan, P., Koller, D., Thrun, S., Rodgers, J., Davis, J.: SCAPE: shape completion and animation of people. In: Proceedings of Computer Graphics (SIGGRAPH), vol. 24, August 2005
15. Barnes, C., Shechtman, E., Finkelstein, A., Goldman, D.: PatchMatch: a randomized correspondence algorithm for structural image editing. ACM Trans. Graph. **28**(3) (2009). Proceedings of ACM SIGGRAPH
16. Blanz, V., Vetter, T.: A morphable model for the synthesis of 3D faces. In: Proceedings of Computer Graphics (SIGGRAPH), SIGGRAPH 1999, pp. 187–194 (1999)
17. Bogo, F., Black, M.J., Loper, M., Romero, J.: Detailed full-body reconstructions of moving people from monocular RGB-D sequences. In: Proceedings of the International Conference on Computer Vision (ICCV), December 2015
18. Boukhayma, A., Boyer, E.: Video based animation synthesis with the essential graph. In: Proceedings of the International Conference on 3D Vision (3DV), pp. 478–486. Lyon, France, October 2015
19. Bregler, C., Covell, M., Slaney, M.: Video rewrite: driving visual speech with audio. In: SIG (1997)

20. Bregler, C., Covell, M., Slaney, M.: Video-based character animation. In: ACM Symposium on Computer Animation (2005)
21. Cao, C., Weng, Y., Zhou, S., Tong, Y., Zhou, K.: Facewarehouse: a 3D facial expression database for visual computing. TVCG **20**(3), 413–425 (2014)
22. Casas, D., Tejera, M., Guillemaut, J.Y., Hilton, A.: 4D parametric motion graphs for interactive animation. In: Proceedings of the ACM SIGGRAPH Symposium on Interactive 3D Graphics and Games, pp. 103–110 (2012)
23. Casas, D., Volino, M., Collomosse, J., Hilton, A.: 4D video textures for interactive character appearance. Comput. Graph. Forum **33**(2) (2014). Proceedings of Eurographics
24. Chan, C., Ginosar, S., Zhou, T., Efros, A.: Everybody dance now. In: Proceedings of the International Conference on Computer Vision (ICCV), Seoul, Korea, October 2019
25. Collet, A., et al.: High-quality streamable free-viewpoint video. ACM Trans. Graph. **34**(4), 69 (2015)
26. Cootes, T.F., Edwards, G.J., Taylor, C.J.: Active appearance models. IEEE Trans. Pattern Anal. Mach. Intell. **23**, 681–685 (1998)
27. Ebel, S., Waizenegger, W., Reinhardt, M., Schreer, O., Feldmann, I.: Visibility-driven patch group generation. In: International Conference on 3D Imaging (IC3D), Liege, Belgium, September 2014
28. Ebner, T., Feldmann, I., Renault, S., Schreer, O., Eisert, P.: Multi-view reconstruction of dynamic real-world objects and their integration in augmented and virtual reality applications. J. Soc. Inform. Display **25**(3), 151–157 (2017)
29. Fechteler, P., Hilsmann, A., Eisert, P.: Example-based body model optimization and skinning. In: Proceedings of Eurographics 2016, Lisbon, Portugal, May 2016
30. Fechteler, P., Hilsmann, A., Eisert, P.: Markerless multiview motion capture with 3D shape model adaptation. Comput. Graph. Forum **38**(6), 91–109 (2019)
31. Fechteler, P., Kausch, L., Hilsmann, A., Eisert, P.: Animatable 3D model generation from 2D monocular visual data. In: Proceedings of the IEEE International Conference on Image Processing (ICIP), Athens, Greece, October 2018
32. Fechteler, P., Paier, W., Hilsmann, A., Eisert, P.: Real-time avatar animation with dynamic face texturing. In: Proceedings of the IEEE International Conference on Image Processing (ICIP), Phoenix, USA, September 2016
33. Fyffe, G., Jones, A., Alexander, O., Ichikari, R., Debevec, P.: Driving high-resolution facial scans with video performance capture. ACM Trans. Graph. (TOG) **34**(1), 1–14 (2014)
34. Garland, M., Heckbert, P.: Surface simplification using quadric error metrics. In: Proceedings of SIGGRAPH 1997, pp. 209–216, New York, USA, August 1997
35. Garrido, P., Valgaert, L., Wu, C., Theobalt, C.: Reconstructing detailed dynamic face geometry from monocular video. ACM Trans. Graph. **32**(6), 158:1–158:10 (2013)
36. Goodfellow, I.J., et al.: Generative adversarial nets. In: Proceedings of the 27th International Conference on Neural Information Processing Systems - Volume 2, pp. 2672–2680 (2014)
37. Habermann, M., Xu, W., Zollhöfer, M., Pons-Moll, G., Theobalt, C.: LiveCap: real-time human performance capture from monocular video. ACM Trans. Graph. **38**(2), 1–17 (2019)
38. Hasler, N., Stoll, C., Sunkel, M., Rosenhahn, B., Seidel, H.P.: A statistical model of human pose and body shape. In: Proceedings of the Eurographics. Munich, Germany, April 2009

39. Hilsmann, A., Eisert, P.: Tracking deformable surfaces with optical flow in the presence of self-occlusions in monocular image sequences. In: CVPR Workshops, Workshop on Non-Rigid Shape Analysis and Deformable Image Alignment (NORDIA), pp. 1–6. IEEE Computer Society, June 2008
40. Hilsmann, A., Fechteler, P., Eisert, P.: Pose space image-based rendering. Comput. Graph. Forum **32**(2), 265–274 (2013). Proceedings of Eurographics 2013
41. Hilton, P., Hilton, A., Starck, J.: Human motion synthesis from 3D video. In: CVPR (2009)
42. Huang, Y., Khan, S.M.: DyadGan: generating facial expressions in dyadic interactions. In: The IEEE Conference on Computer Vision and Pattern Recognition (CVPR) Workshops, July 2017
43. Jost, T., Hugli, H.: A multi-resolution ICP with heuristic closest point search for fast and robust 3D registration of range images. In: Proceedings of the 4th International Conference on 3-D Digital Imaging and Modeling (3DIM), pp. 427–433 (2003)
44. Kavan, L., Sorkine, O.: Elasticity-inspired deformers for character articulation. ACM Trans. Graph. **31**(6), 196:1–196:8 (2012). Proceedings of ACM SIGGRAPH ASIA
45. Kazhdan, M., Hoppe, H.: Screened poisson surface reconstruction. Trans. Graph. **32**(3), 70–78 (2013)
46. Kazhdan, M., Bolitho, M., Hoppe, H.: Poisson surface reconstruction. In: Proceedings of the Fourth Eurographics Symposium on Geometry Processing, pp. 61–70 (2006)
47. Kim, H., et al.: Deep video portraits. ACM Trans. Graph. (TOG) **37**(4), 163 (2018)
48. Kim, M., et al.: Data-driven physics for human soft tissue animation. In: Proceedings of the Computer Graphics (SIGGRAPH), vol. 36, no. 4 (2017)
49. Kingma, D.P., Welling, M.: Auto-encoding variational Bayes (2013)
50. Klaudiny, M., Budd, C., Hilton, A.: Towards optimal non-rigid surface tracking. In: Fitzgibbon, A., Lazebnik, S., Perona, P., Sato, Y., Schmid, C. (eds.) ECCV 2012. LNCS, vol. 7575, pp. 743–756. Springer, Heidelberg (2012). https://doi.org/10.1007/978-3-642-33765-9_53
51. Kovar, L., Gleicher, M., Pighin, F.: Motion graphs. In: Proceedings of the 29th Annual Conference on Computer Graphics and Interactive Techniques, pp. 473–482 (2002)
52. Li, H., Yu, J., Ye, Y., Bregler, C.: Realtime facial animation with on-the-fly correctives. ACM Trans. Graphic. **32**(4), 42:1–42:10 (2013)
53. Liu, L., et al.: Neural rendering and reenactment of human actor videos. ACM Trans. Graph. **38**, 1–14 (2019)
54. Liu, W., et al.: SSD: single shot multibox detector. In: Leibe, B., Matas, J., Sebe, N., Welling, M. (eds.) ECCV 2016. LNCS, vol. 9905, pp. 21–37. Springer, Cham (2016). https://doi.org/10.1007/978-3-319-46448-0_2
55. Liu, Y., Dai, Q., Xu, W.: A point cloud based multi-view stereo algorithm for free-viewpoint video. IEEE Trans Vis. Comput. Graph. **16**, 407–418 (2010)
56. Malleson, C., et al.: FaceDirector: continuous control of facial performance in video. In: Proceedings of the International Conference on Computer Vision (ICCV), Santiago, Chile, December 2015
57. Mehta, D., et al.: VNect: real-time 3D human pose estimation with a single RGB camera. ACM Trans. Graph. **36**(4), 1–4 (2017). Proceedings of SIGGRAPH 2017
58. Morgenstern, W., Hilsmann, A., Eisert, P.: Progressive non-rigid registration of temporal mesh sequences. In: Proceedings of the European Conference on Visual Media Production (CVMP), London, UK, December 2019

59. Murthy, P., Butt, H.T., Hiremath, S., Stricker, D.: Learning 3D joint constraints from vision-based motion capture datasets. IPSJ Trans. Comput. Vis. Appl. **11**(1), 1–9 (2019)
60. Paier, W., Kettern, M., Hilsmann, A., Eisert, P.: Hybrid approach for facial performance analysis and editing. IEEE Trans. Circuits Syst. Video Technol. **27**(4), 784–797 (2017)
61. Paier, W., Kettern, M., Hilsmann, A., Eisert, P.: Video-based facial re-animation. In: Proceedings of the European Conference on Visual Media Production (CVMP), London, UK, November 2015
62. Pavlakos, G., et al.: Expressive body capture: 3D hands, face, and body from a single image. In: Proceedings of the IEEE Conference on Computer Vision and Pattern Recognition (CVPR), Long Beach, USA, June 2019
63. Pumarola, A., Agudo, A., Martinez, A.M., Sanfeliu, A., Moreno-Noguer, F.: GANimation: anatomically-aware facial animation from a single image. In: Ferrari, V., Hebert, M., Sminchisescu, C., Weiss, Y. (eds.) ECCV 2018. LNCS, vol. 11214, pp. 835–851. Springer, Cham (2018). https://doi.org/10.1007/978-3-030-01249-6_50
64. Regateiro, J., Volino, M., Hilton, A.: Hybrid skeleton driven surface registration for temporally consistent volumetric. In: Proceedings of the International Conference on 3D Vision (3DV), Verona, Italy, September 2018
65. Schodl, A., Szeliski, R., Salesin, D., Essa, I.: Video textures. In: SIG (2000)
66. Schreer, O., et al.: Lessons learnt during one year of commercial volumetric video production. In: Proceedings of the IBC Conference, Amsterdam, Netherlands, September 2019
67. Schreer, O., Feldmann, I., Renault, S., Zepp, M., Eisert, P., Kauff, P.: Capture and 3D video processing of volumetric video. In: Proceedings of IEEE International Conference on Image Processing (ICIP), Taipei, Taiwan, September 2019
68. Serra, J., Cetinaslan, O., Ravikumar, S., Orvalho, V., Cosker, D.: Easy generation of facial animation using motion graphs. In: Computer Graphics Forum (2018)
69. Sorkine, O.: Differential representations for mesh processing. In: Computer Graphics Forum, vol. 25, December 2006
70. Sorkine, O., Alexa, M.: As-rigid-as-possible surface modeling. In: Symposium on Geometry Processing, vol. 4, pp. 109–116 (2007)
71. Starck, J., Hilton, A.: Surface capture for performance-based animation. IEEE Comput. Graph. Appl. **27**, 21–31 (2007). https://doi.org/10.1109/MCG.2007.68
72. Stoll, C., Gall, J., de Aguiar, E., Thrun, S., Theobalt, C.: Video-based reconstruction of animatable human characters. ACM Trans. Graph. **29**(6), 139–149 (2010). Proceedings of SIGGRAPH ASIA 2010
73. Sumner, R., Schmid, J., Pauly, M.: Embedded deformation for shape manipulation. ACM Trans. Graph. (TOG) **26**, 80 (2007)
74. Thies, J., Zollhöfer, M., Nießner, M., Valgaerts, L., Stamminger, M., Theobalt, C.: Real-time expression transfer for facial reenactment. ACM Trans. Graphic. **34**(6), 183 (2015)
75. Vlasic, D., Brand, M., Pfister, H., Popović, J.: Face transfer with multilinear models. ACM Trans. Graph. **24**(3), 426–433 (2005)
76. Volino, M., Huang, P., Hilton, A.: Online interactive 4D character animation. In: Proceedings of the International Conference on 3D Web Technology (Web3D), Heraklion, Greece, June 2015
77. Waechter, M., Moehrle, N., Goesele, M.: Let there be color! large-scale texturing of 3D reconstructions. In: Fleet, D., Pajdla, T., Schiele, B., Tuytelaars, T. (eds.) ECCV 2014. LNCS, vol. 8693, pp. 836–850. Springer, Cham (2014). https://doi.org/10.1007/978-3-319-10602-1_54

78. Waizenegger, W., Feldmann, I., Schreer, O., Eisert, P.: Scene flow constrained multi-prior patch-sweeping for real-time upper body 3D reconstruction. In: Proc. IEEE International Conference on Image Processing (ICIP), Melbourne, Australia, September 2013

79. Waizenegger, W., Feldmann, I., Schreer, O., Kauff, P., Eisert, P.: Real-time 3D body reconstruction for immersive TV. In: Proceedings of IEEE International Conference on Image Processing (ICIP), Phoenix, USA, September 2016

80. Xu, F., et al.: Video-based characters - creating new human performances from a multiview video database. In: SIG (2011)

81. Zollhöfer, M., et al.: Real-time non-rigid reconstruction using an RGB-D camera. ACM Trans. Graph. **33**, 1–2 (2014)

82. Zuffi, S., Black, M.J.: The stitched puppet: a graphical model of 3D human shape and pose. In: Proceedings of Computer Vision and Pattern Recognition (CVPR), June 2015

Reconstructing 3D Human Avatars
from Monocular Images

Thiemo Alldieck⬤, Moritz Kappel⬤, Susana Castillo$^{(\boxtimes)}$⬤,
and Marcus Magnor⬤

TU Braunschweig, Braunschweig, Germany
{alldieck,kappel,castillo,magnor}@cg.cs.tu-bs.de
https://graphics.tu-bs.de

Abstract. Creating convincing representations of humans is a fundamental problem in both traditional arts and modern media. In our digital world, virtual avatars allow us to simulate and render the human body for a variety of applications, including movie production, sports, human-computer interaction, and medical sciences. However, capturing digital representations of a person's shape, appearance, and motion is an expensive and time-consuming process which usually requires a lot of manual adjustments.

With the advances in consumer-grade virtual reality devices, personalized virtual avatars became an essential part of interactive and immersive applications like telepresence and virtual try-on for online fashion shopping, thereby increasing the need for versatile easy-to-use self-digitization.

In this chapter, we discuss a selection of recent acquisition methods for personalized human avatar reconstruction. In contrast to conventional setups, these fully-automatic approaches only use low-cost monocular video cameras to effectively fuse information from multiple points in time and realistically complete reconstructions from sparse observations. We address both straight-forward and sophisticated reconstruction methods focused on accuracy, simplicity, and usability to compare and provide insights into their visual fidelity and robustness.

Keywords: Human modeling · Cameras · Image reconstruction · Three-dimensional displays

1 Introduction

The advent of Virtual Reality (VR) and Augmented Reality (AR) consumer hardware laid the foundation for new ways of entertainment, communication, or online shopping. Enabling these applications is an active and emerging field of research for which personalized and highly realistic 3D avatars are crucial. Beyond entertainment, 3D virtual humans are potentially useful or already play an important role in many applications, such as medical diagnostics and virtual assistance. These avatars should feature all the details that form our identity and make us unique. This includes accurate body shapes, faithfully reconstructed

© Springer Nature Switzerland AG 2020
M. Magnor and A. Sorkine-Hornung (Eds.): Real VR, LNCS 11900, pp. 188–218, 2020.
https://doi.org/10.1007/978-3-030-41816-8_8

faces, detailed clothing, and realistic hair. Reconstruction failures lead to avatars that are not being identified by others or, more importantly, to users not feeling represented by their virtual self. No less important, the acquisition process of these avatars should be fast, easy, and should not require special equipment or training. However, the classical Computer Graphics approach to 3D modeling of virtual humans still requires considerable manual effort and expert knowledge: A specially trained artist defines the 3D geometry of body and clothing, that is then rigged in order to enable animation. The avatar's 3D motion is driven by manual keyframe-based animation or marker-based motion capture. This laborious process presents an important practical barrier to the needs of the aforementioned applications. In contrast, the main goal of the approaches presented in this chapter is to take advantage of the omnipresence of cameras nowadays to develop automatic methods that efficiently utilize images and video for realistic 3D avatar creation and animation. Obviously, there are many obstacles to overcome to computationally process monocular video and photos, as relevant information is often encoded, noisy, or ambiguous. And, as Fig. 1 illustrates, when the object of interest are humans, the problem becomes even more challenging, as our appearance can drastically change between images.

(a)   (b)

Fig. 1. The appearance variation of a human is one of the main challenges in 3D human reconstruction. The same person might look very different in varying lighting conditions (a), in front of different backgrounds, or while wearing different sets of garments (b), even when other parameters, e.g. pose and camera, remain fixed.

Essentially, the goal is to create an avatar that is indistinguishable from the actual human. Following this line, the methods presented in this chapter aim to track and model the whole human body, including hair and clothing. We are interested in reconstructing the observed subject *as detailed as possible*. Not only body and clothing geometry but also its coloring and surface structure carries important information. To this end, besides capturing the 3D shape, we aim at reconstructing the surface colors in form of texture maps, too. Finally, we want to be able to *re-use* the estimated avatars. For this purpose, the reconstructions should come in a common format that can be easily used, animated, and manipulated by other applications.

Aside from the desired characteristics of the reconstructions, the second main aspect to consider is the capturing process and equipment. Computer Vision researchers have used a broad range of sensors and systems to capture and analyze the world. Multi-camera set-ups, marker-aided capturing, depth sensors, or active scanners are commonly used. These systems can capture 3D data to a resolution of a few millimeters. While this is undoubtedly valuable data, the systems are, unfortunately, not widely accessible. Usually, they are only found in laboratories or professional video studios. At the other extreme, standard cameras are nowadays all around us. Many of the devices we use on a daily basis have one or even multiple cameras built in and are easily accessible. Another valuable advantage of standard cameras is the unobtrusiveness and low complexity of the capturing process. While complex capturing systems often require careful and laborious calibration and set-up, or even interfere with the captured scene, cameras allow easy recording with almost non-existent setup time. Additionally, they are lightweight and small and thus can be flexibly used nearly everywhere. Due to all the aforementioned reasons, the algorithms presented in this chapter solely rely on monocular image material as recorded by a standard webcam for their input. This additionally ensures that any achieved advance can be seamlessly integrated with modern devices – such as phones, tablets, or smart displays – while being compatible with the large amount of available legacy photo and video material.

This chapter describes some advances in 3D human pose and shape estimation from monocular images with common input and output modalities: input are monocular videos or photos; output are animatable 3D meshes describing the apparent shape, pose, or motion of a human depicted in the input material. The common pipeline and goal of all the presented methods is illustrated in Fig. 2. Given a single image or multiple frames of monocular video of a person, the three presented algorithms reconstruct a mesh-based full-body 3D virtual avatar, and, additionally, they optionally reconstruct the appearance in form of a texture.

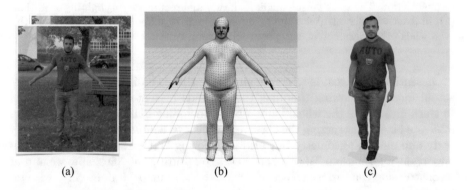

(a)   (b)   (c)

Fig. 2. Given one monocular image or a short video clip of a person (a), the goal of the presented work is to reconstruct a detailed full-body 3D avatar (b) that can be photo-realistically animated, for example in virtual environments (c).

By only relying on regular video or even photos, this work democratizes the digitization of humans, as it eliminates the need for specialized equipment. The final avatar can then be animated and placed into new scenes or entire virtual environments.

2   Related Work

Methods for 3D human shape and pose reconstruction can be broadly classified as *top-down* or *bottom-up*. Top-down methods can subsequently be subdivided into *model-based* and *free-form*. Bottom-up methods directly infer a surface or body model parametrization from sensor data. Of course, there are also hybrid methods, a recent trend of work combining bottom-up and top-down approaches. For a better view of this last kind of approaches, we kindly refer the reader to the previous chapter.

2.1   Top-Down, Model-Based Methods

Top-down, model-based methods exploit a parametric body model consisting of pose and shape to regularize the fitting process. To represent the human body more realistically, models learned from data of real humans have been developed (see Fig. 3).

Fig. 3. Body models with varying degree of realism. From left to right: Superquadric model [97], SCAPE [12], SMPL [67], Frank [55], and SMPL-X [79].

These models describe the shape variations of the naked body without hair or clothing. In the process of learning such models, typically a template mesh is deformed to match 3D data of a large number of subjects in various poses and of different body shapes. Then a statistical formulation is found that minimizes the error between low-dimensional, parametrization-based predictions and the alignments. A similar concept was already used in the pioneering work by Kakadiaris and Metaxas [56], where a body model is constructed from three orthogonal views. Allen *et al.* [9] learned a rich model of the human shape from laser scans of 250 subjects. Later the model was updated to also modeling pose-dependent shape deformation [10]. Both models operate in global model space and thus, they directly output global vertex positions. SCAPE [12] presented a popular parametric body model that operates on mesh triangle level. Pose and shape deformation components of the model are applied separately to each face, which is then rigidly transformed to match the pose. This formulation simplifies the mathematical formulation into a rigid and a non-rigid component, which supports the learning process. Based on SCAPE, BlendSCAPE [46] is inspired by skinning functions and deforms each triangle based on a linear combination of multiple influencing parts. Another variant that incorporates correlations between body shape and pose was introduced by Hasler*et al.* [42]. The DYNA model [85] extends SCAPE with dynamic soft-tissue deformation based on the performed motion. However, because the mesh triangles are transformed independently and form no watertight mesh, all SCAPE variants depend on a least-squares solver to connect the triangles to a smooth and coherent surface. This drawback prevents the models from being used in standard graphics pipelines, problem that was addressed by the following works.

The SMPL body model [67] is an accurate parametric body model learned from thousands of scans from real people. For posing, it transforms a template mesh using standard linear blend skinning, thus it requires no post-optimization and is compatible with standard graphics pipelines. A key insight is that pose-dependent deformations can be linearly regressed from the pose rotation matrices. SMPL is more accurate and more straight-forward to use than SCAPE and thus is heavily used in various research problems. The approaches presented in this chapter also use SMPL as a template and prior for reconstructing poses and shapes of clothed people, thus it is addresses in more detail in Sect. 3.1. Like SCAPE, SMPL has been extended for soft-tissue deformations. The DMPL model, a data-driven extension to SMPL is included in the original paper. Kim *et al.* [59] presented a layered combined data-driven and physics-based model.

Despite its popularity, SMPL comes with some drawbacks. By design, it models the body only at a coarse scale with neither facial expressions, nor finger movement being covered by the original model. Thus, multiple approaches focus on extending SMPL and adding missing functionality. The first work along this line was SMPL+H [90], a SMPL model with an incorporated hand model. Joo *et al.* [55] proposed Frank, a model stitched together from three different models. Frank uses SMPL without the pose-dependent deformations for the body, an artist-rigged hand model, and a generative PCA face model learned from the FaceWarehouse dataset [21]. However, the components are learned individually and thus the model lacks realism. To this end, Pavlakos *et al.* [79] presented SMPL-X, a model that extends SMPL with articulated hands and an expressive face. In contrast to Frank [55], SMPL-X is learned in a unified fashion. Finally, there are also several special-case models. ClothCap [84] presents the first SMPL with clothing but does not model pose-depended deformations. Hesse *et al.* [44] retrained SMPL for infants based on RGB-D captures, and Zuffi and colleagues [121] introduced a SMPL-like model of animals that was learned from 3D scans of toy figures.

Parametric body models have been heavily used to reconstruct and encode 3D pose [86]. In early works, researchers formulate analysis-by-synthesis problems to recover the 3D pose from multiple views [14], depth data [112], or single images [41,94]. For this purpose, posed 3D human shapes are reconstructed that project into the image silhouettes or match with the input data. Similarly, Alldieck *et al.* [4] presented a work where they minimized silhouette and additional optical-flow differences to recover time-consistent 3D poses. In an alternative strategy, the reprojection error of 3D joint locations is minimized. First, these 2D joint landmarks have been manually clicked [37]. Later the process was automated [17,48,62]. The automation was made possible by the advent of human landmark detection networks [11,22,52,81]. Another streamline of works uses a set of inertial measurement units (IMUs) attached to the subjects body alone [49,69,70] or in combination with images [68,82] to reconstruct 3D motion.

Besides the pose properties of parametric body models, also the shape components have been utilized in the literature. For example, the SCAPE model has been used to recover the *naked* body shape of people from photographs in regular clothing [13,32]. The SMPL model has been used with 4D scanner data to recover the body shape of the subject under clothing [117]. Pons-Moll *et al.* [84] jointly estimated garments as a separate clothing layer. A similar system was recently introduced also for depth data [102]. The methods by Guo *et al.* [39] and Chen *et al.* [24] recover the clothed and naked shapes from a single image but require manual initialization of pose and clothing parameters. Fully automatic acquisition of the full shape including tight [16] and loose clothing [101,118] has also been presented. However, these works require RGB-D data. The works of Alldieck *et al.* [6,7] were the first to present 3D human shape and clothing reconstruction from monocular video in which the subject is allowed to move. Similarly to the works by [117] or [84], Alldieck and colleagues extended SMPL with a deformation field for modeling clothing and hair but, in contrast to the aforementioned works, Alldieck *et al.* used a single RGB camera as input.

2.2   Top-Down, Free-Form Methods

While body models are rich priors for human body shape reconstruction problems, they also limit the shape space. All shapes that do not share the human topology cannot be well approximated using a body model. To this end, researchers have developed free-form and template-based reconstruction methods.

Even before body models were available, researchers used body templates. These typically were artist-made, rigged meshes that represented a single person. For personalization, these templates were non-rigidly deformed to match image silhouettes in multi-view set-ups [1,45]. These early methods share in large parts the methodology of those using parametric models. However, they cannot benefit from the low-dimensional shape space. Nevertheless, these methods enabled for the first time multi-view body pose and shape reconstruction [29,105] and even free-viewpoint video of human actors [23]. Later, the artist-made templates were replaced with laser-scans of the subjects [28,34,108], enabling detailed reconstructions and also complex clothing like skirts and dresses. Also, temporal surface deformation tracking was enabled for detailed free-viewpoint video [26,63,99,104]. In an alternative strategy, the methods by Rodhin *et al.* [88] and Robertini and colleagues [89] leveraged a flexible sum of Gaussians body model [100] to reconstruct human motion and shape. Also related, general frameworks for 3D shape tracking based on volumetric shape representations were presented [3,47].

While all these methods require multi-view input, methods utilizing a single depth sensor for shape reconstruction have been developed, too [27,64,92,116]. These methods, however, do not allow for free movement but require the subject to carefully take the same pose at different angles to the camera or hold the pose while the camera is moving around the subject. Subtle pose changes are then compensated by non-rigid alignment of the point clouds. Later, the restriction of static poses was removed by utilizing multiple depth-sensors [33,77]. Live performance capture using a small number of depth-sensors was made possible. Finally, Newcombe *et al.* [75] introduced a real-time method to dynamically fuse the incoming depths stream of a single RGB-D camera into a canonical model. The model is warped to match the latest frame, enabling single sensor live performance capture. Based on this idea, new methods enabling for example volumetric non-rigid reconstruction [51] or less-controlled motion [96] emerged.

In 2018, Xu *et al.* [114] presented, for the first time, monocular performance capture including surface deformation, making the use of depth-sensors obsolete. A pre-captured template of the actor is tracked and deformed based on 2D and 3D human landmark detection and image silhouettes. Following the proposed methodology, Habermann *et al.* [40] presented the first real-time human performance capture based on a single view RGB video-stream only.

2.3   Bottom-Up Methods

Deep Learning techniques like CNNs have accelerated advances in Computer Vision in general, and advances in human pose and shape reconstruction in particular. Numerous learning-based works on 2D and 3D landmark detectors or reconstruction and tracking of specific body parts exist in the literature. In early works, methods that reconstructed the shape in the space of a parametric body model were presented [30,31]. These methods use only a single silhouette image but are restricted to a small set of poses.

Since then, more flexible works that reconstruct 3D pose and shape from single images by integrating the SMPL body model into a network architecture arose. Different works leveraged either color images [57,106], color images plus segmentation [80], or body part segmentation [76]. Other works focused on the temporal aspect and successfully reconstruct temporal-coherent 3D human motion [58]. While these approaches reliably recover the 3D human pose from in-the-wild images, the reconstructions tend to feature average body shapes. The reason for this is that the methods heavily rely on the body model statistics and return shape regressed from bone lengths. For more exact reconstructions that better align with the images, methods perform mesh fitting after network inference [38]. This fitting step also allows to additionally reconstruct face and hand motion [113]. The work from Alldieck et al. [5] (presented in Sect. 5) was the first to reconstruct the human shape beyond the parametrization of a body model from a small number of frames. The authors also refined their results via optimization at test time. Similarly, Zhu et al. [120] performed a multi-step app-roach. They first found an initial SMPL pose and shape parametrization, then reposed the mesh based on silhouettes, and finally, leveraged shading to refine the surface beyond the shape parametrization.

Recently, the question of the best 3D human shape representation in the context of CNNs has gained more and more attention. BodyNet [107] was the first work to directly regress a volumetric representation of the human body from a single image. A similar approach was introduced by Jackson et al. [54], demonstrating a higher level of detail. More recently, synthesizing novel silhou-ette views to represent the 3D shape of the person, before reconstructing the final 3D volume were proposed [74]. Zheng et al. [119] refined results from vol-umetric regression via a shading-based normal refinement network to alleviate the limited spatial resolution of volumetric approaches. In a different direction, Kolotouros et al. [61] proposed to directly regress vertices and optionally infer body model parametrization from there. Other works regressed and opted for representing vertices in the UV space [115] or, similarly, as geometry images [87]. Alldieck et al. [8] used the UV space to reconstruct detailed human shape to a wrinkle-level independently of the 3D pose (for more details refer to Sect. 6). In contrast to concurrent work, their results featured details even on the unseen back-side of the person.

In recent work, 3D shapes have been encoded as implicit functions like vol-umetric occupancy fields or signed distance functions [25,72,73,78,109]. The first works deploying this idea in 3D human shape and pose reconstruction used spare multi-view setups [35,50]. Saito et al. [91] used this form of representa-tion for single-view human shape and texture reconstruction. The main idea of their work was to sample the occupancy field along pixel-aligned projection rays, which favors local details.

Finally and very recently, methods with or without coarse explicit 3D repre-sentation have been presented. In the work by Shysheya et al. [93] the appearance of a subject is learned as per-part textures of the SMPL body model. Given a 3D pose and a view-point, the parts are used to synthesize an image of the sub-ject utilizing a subject-specific neural renderer. Other recent works have present first ideas to encode complex scenes in coarse voxel grids [66,95] or as feature point clouds [2]. A learned renderer allows synthesizing images of the scenes from novel viewpoints, featuring view-dependent surface effects or thin structures and semi-transparent materials like human hair or smoke. While this is an exciting avenue to explore, artifacts are still prominent, and (in contrast to mesh-based solutions) compatibility with existing rendering pipelines is not given.

3   General Methods

The three approaches presented in the following sections have one thing in com-mon: to make the problems tractable, the authors leverage a parametric body model that are statistical models of the variation of the human body shapes and poses. These regularize the search space and reduce the dimensionality of tasks related to the human body. In other words, they provide a template as an approximate solution that can be further refined by relying on its parametrization alone or as a regularization prior.

3.1 Parametric Body Model

The three methods presented in this chapter use the SMPL body model [67], presented by Loper *et al.* in 2015. SMPL is designed as a function $M(\cdot) \in \mathbb{R}^{N \times 3}$ that maps pose $\boldsymbol{\theta} \in \mathbb{R}^{3K}$ and shape $\boldsymbol{\beta} \in \mathbb{R}^{10}$ parameters to a mesh of $N = 6890$ vertices. To form a watertight mesh, the vertices are connected to $F = 13776$ faces. The pose is determined through $K = 23$ skeleton joints parametrized by $\boldsymbol{\theta}$ in axis-angle representation. The SMPL model has been learned from scans of real people. It can, therefore, produce realistic body shapes and pose-depended shape deformations. SMPL exists in three variants: A male, a female, and a neutral version, covering only male, only female, or all subjects respectively.

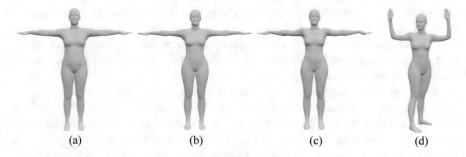

(a)   (b)   (c)   (d)

Fig. 4. Setting pose and shape of the SMPL model: from a template (a) the new shape (b) is formed. Then pose-dependent offsets are applied (c). Finally, the pose is set via blend skinning (d).

SMPL produces a posed mesh by performing the following steps: To create realistic body shapes, a template mesh $\mathbf{T} \in \mathbb{R}^{N \times 3}$ is deformed with shape deformation offsets $B_s(\boldsymbol{\beta}) \in \mathbb{R}^{N \times 3}$ (Fig. 4(b)). The offsets are based on a low-dimensional basis of the principal components of the body shape distribution among the SMPL subjects. The shape parametrization $\boldsymbol{\beta}$ forms a vector of linear shape coefficients of the shape space. Additionally, a linear regressor determines the positions of the skeleton joints $J(\boldsymbol{\beta}) \in \mathbb{R}^{K \times 3}$. Next, pose-dependent deformations $B_p(\boldsymbol{\theta}) \in \mathbb{R}^{N \times 3}$ are applied on the reshaped template (Fig. 4(c)). $B_p(\cdot)$ is a learned linear function parametrized with the desired pose $\boldsymbol{\theta}$. It accounts for muscle and soft-tissue deformations as well as skinning artifacts potentially introduced in the last step. Finally, the mesh is posed using standard linear blend skinning $W(\cdot) \in \mathbb{R}^{N \times 3}$ with blend weights $\mathbf{W} \in \mathbb{R}^{N \times K}$ (Fig. 4(d)). The final equation reads as:

$$M(\boldsymbol{\beta}, \boldsymbol{\theta}) = W(T(\boldsymbol{\beta}, \boldsymbol{\theta}), J(\boldsymbol{\beta}), \boldsymbol{\theta}, \mathbf{W}) \tag{1}$$

$$T(\boldsymbol{\beta}, \boldsymbol{\theta}) = \mathbf{T} + B_s(\boldsymbol{\beta}) + B_p(\boldsymbol{\theta}). \tag{2}$$

SMPL only covers naked subjects and its shape parametrization does not allow for detailed personalization. For this reason, Alldieck *et al.* augment the standard formulation with additional details in large parts of the work presented in this chapter. The authors add additional per-vertex offsets $\mathbf{D} \in \mathbb{R}^{3 \times N}$ to the function [84,85,117]. SMPL extended with offsets $\mathbf{D}$, denoted as SMPL+D, is formed as follows:

$$M(\boldsymbol{\beta}, \boldsymbol{\theta}, \mathbf{D}) = W(T(\boldsymbol{\beta}, \boldsymbol{\theta}, \mathbf{D}), J(\boldsymbol{\beta}), \boldsymbol{\theta}, \mathbf{W}) \tag{3}$$

$$T(\boldsymbol{\beta}, \boldsymbol{\theta}, \mathbf{D}) = \mathbf{T} + B_s(\boldsymbol{\beta}) + B_p(\boldsymbol{\theta}) + \mathbf{D}. \tag{4}$$

SMPL+D is fully differentiable with respect to pose $\boldsymbol{\theta}$, shape $\boldsymbol{\beta}$ and free-form deformations $\mathbf{D}$. Such offsets $\mathbf{D}$ allow to deform the model to better explain details and clothing.

3.2   UV Parameterization

Additionally, Alldieck *et al.* augment SMPL using UV mapping. In the work presented in Sects. 4 and 5 the authors apply textures to the mesh, while in Sect. 6 they augment its surface using normal and displacement maps.

Unfortunately, the resolution of the SMPL model is not high enough to explain fine details, such as garment wrinkles. Another problem is that meshes do not live on a regular 2D grid like images, and consequently require taylored solutions [19] that are not yet as effective as standard CNNs on the image domain. To leverage the power of standard CNNs, Alldieck *et al.* propose to use a well-established parameterization of mesh surfaces: UV mapping [15].

UV mapping [15] unfolds the body surface onto a 2D image such that a given pixel corresponds to a 3D point on the body surface. The mapping is defined over the faces such that every face consisting of three 3D vertices has a counterpart consisting of three 2D UV-coordinates. Hereby, U and V denote the two axes of the image. The mapping of points inside a face is determined via barycentric interpolation of neighboring coordinates. The 2D image can be used to augment the 3D surface. A texture defines a color per surface point. Similarly, a normal map stores a surface normal that can add or enhance visual details through shading. A 3D displacement map actually displaces the surface point in the given direction. Hence, it can be used to create a highly detailed surface without changing the resolution of the underlying mesh. Some tasks, however, require a higher mesh resolution. It can be derived by subdividing the SMPL base mesh. Hereby, a new vertex is placed on the center of each side of a triangular face. The old face is removed and four new faces are created by connecting subsets of the six vertices. This processes can be repeated. Please see [6] for details.

4   First Approach

To estimate geometry from a video sequence, one could jointly optimize a single free-form shape constrained by a body model to fit a set of F images. Unfortunately, this requires to optimize F poses at once and, more importantly, it requires storing F models in memory during optimization which makes it computationally expensive and unpractical.

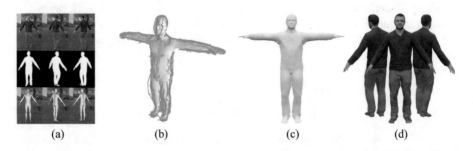

(a)   (b)   (c)   (d)

Fig. 5. Overview of Alldieck *et al.*'s method [7]. The input to this method is an image sequence with corresponding segmentations. It first calculates poses using the SMPL model (a). Then it unposes silhouette camera rays (unposed silhouettes depicted in red) (b) and optimize for the subjects shape in the canonical T-pose (c). Finally, it is able to calculate a texture and generate a personalized blend shape model (d).

The key idea of this first approach – presented in Alldieck *et al.* [7] – is to generalize visual hull methods [71] to monocular videos of people in motion. Standard visual hull methods capture a static shape from multiple views. Every camera ray through a silhouette point in the image casts a constraint on the 3D body shape. To make visual hulls work for monocular video of a moving person it is necessary to "undo" the human motion and bring it to a canonical frame of reference. In this work, the geometry of people (in wide or tight clothing) is represented as a deviation from the SMPL parametric body model [67] of naked people in a canonical T-pose; this model also features a pose-dependent non-rigid surface skinning. First, the authors estimate an initial body shape and 3D pose at each frame by fitting the SMPL model to 2D detections similar to [17,62]. Given such fits, Alldieck *et al.* associate every silhouette point in every frame to a 3D point in the body model. Then, every projection ray is transformed according to the inverse deformation model of its corresponding 3D model point; Alldieck and colleagues call this operation unposing. After unposing the rays for all frames they obtain a visual hull that constrains the body shape in a canonical T-pose. The body shape parameters and free-form vertex displacements are then jointly optimize to minimize the distance between 3D model points and unposed rays. This allows one to efficiently optimize a single displacement surface on top of SMPL constrained to fit all frames at once, which requires storing only one model in memory (Fig. 5). This technique was pioneer in allowing the extraction of accurate 3D human body models, including hair and clothing, from a single video sequence of the person moving in front of the camera such that the person is seen from all sides.

4.1   Method

Given a single monocular RGB video depicting a moving person, the goal is to generate a personalized 3D model of the subject, which consists of the shape of body, hair and clothing, a personalized texture map, and an underlying skeleton rigged to the surface. Non-rigid surface deformations in new poses are thus entirely skeleton-driven. The presented method consists of 3 steps: (1) *pose reconstruction* (2) *consensus shape estimation* and (3) *frame refinement and texture map generation.*

In order to estimate the consensus shape of the subject, the first step is to calculate the 3D pose in each frame. Alldieck *et al.* [7] extend the method of Bogo *et al.* [17] to make it more robust and enforce better temporal coherence and silhouette overlap. In the second step, the *consensus shape* is calculated and efficiently optimized to maximally explain the silhouettes at each frame instance. Due to time-varying cloth deformations the posed consensus shape might be slightly misaligned with the frame silhouettes. Hence, in order to compute texture and capture time-varying details, in step (3) deviations from the consensus shape are optimized per frame in a sliding window approach. Given the refined frame-wise shapes, it is possible to compute the texture map. This method relies on a foreground segmentation of the images. Therefore, the authors adopt the CNN based video segmentation method of [20] and train it with 3–4 manual segmentations per sequence. In order to counter ambiguities in monocular 3D human shape reconstruction, they use the SMPL+D body model following the formulation described in Eq. 4 (see Sect. 3.1).

Pose Reconstruction: The approach in [17] optimizes SMPL model parameters to fit a set of 2D joint detections in the image. As with any monocular method, scale is an inherent ambiguity. To mitigate this effect, the authors take inspiration from [88] and extend [17] such that it jointly considers $P = 5$ frames and optimizes a single shape and $P = 5$ poses. The evaluation of the method reveal that even when optimizing over $P = 5$ poses the scale ambiguity prevails. The reason is that pose differences induce additional 3D ambiguities which cannot be uniquely decoupled from global size, even on multiple frames [83,98,103]. Hence, if the height of the person is known, the authors incorporate it as constraint during optimization. If height is not known the shape reconstructions of the method are still accurate up to a scale factor (height estimation is roughly off by 2–5 cm). The output of initialization are SMPL model shape parameters β_0 that are kept fixed during subsequent frame-wise pose estimation. In order to estimate 3D pose more reliably, Alldieck *et al.* extend [17] by incorporating a silhouette term:

$$E_{\text{silh}}(\boldsymbol{\theta}) = G(\mathbf{w}_{\text{o}}\mathbf{I}_{rn}(\boldsymbol{\theta})\mathbf{C} + \mathbf{w}_{\text{i}}(\mathbf{1} - \mathbf{I}_{rn}(\boldsymbol{\theta}))\bar{\mathbf{C}}) \tag{5}$$

with the silhouette image of the rendered model $\mathbf{I}_{rn}(\boldsymbol{\theta})$, distance transform of observed image mask $\mathbf{C}$ and its inverse $\bar{\mathbf{C}}$, weights $\mathbf{w}$. To be robust to local minima the authors optimize at 4 different levels of a Gaussian pyramid G. The method was further updated to use state of the art 2D joint detections [22,111] and a single-modal A-pose prior. The prior from SMPL poses fitted is trained against body scans of people in A-pose. Further, a temporal smoothness is enforced and the pose is initialized in a new frame with the estimated pose $\boldsymbol{\theta}$ in the previous frame. If the objective error gets too large, the tracker is re-initialized by setting the pose to zero. The output of this step is a set of poses $\{\boldsymbol{\theta}_p\}_{p=1}^{F}$ for the F frames in the sequence.

Consensus Shape: Given the set of estimated poses one could jointly optimize a single refined shape matching all original F poses, which would yield a complex, non-convex optimization problem. Instead, Alldieck and colleagues merge all the information into an unposed canonical frame, where refinement is computationally easier. At every frame a silhouette places a new constraint on the body shape; specifically, the set of rays going from the camera to the silhouette points define a constraint cone. Since the person is moving, the pose is changing. The key idea is to *unpose* the cone defined by the projection rays using the estimated poses. Effectively, the authors invert the SMPL function for every ray. In SMPL, every vertex $\boldsymbol{v}$ deforms according to the following equation:

$$\boldsymbol{v}_i' = \sum_{k=1}^{K} w_{k,i} G_k(\boldsymbol{\theta}, J(\boldsymbol{\beta}))(\boldsymbol{v}_i + b_{s,i}(\boldsymbol{\beta}) + b_{P,i}(\boldsymbol{\theta})) \tag{6}$$

where G_k is the global transformation of joint k and $b_{s,i}(\boldsymbol{\beta}) \in \mathbb{R}$ and $b_{P,i}(\boldsymbol{\theta})$ are elements of $B_s(\boldsymbol{\beta})$ and $B_p(\boldsymbol{\theta})$ corresponding to $i-th$ vertex. For every ray $\mathbf{r}$, its closest 3D model point is found. From Eq. 6 it follows that the inverse transformation applied to a ray $\mathbf{r}$ corresponding to model point $\boldsymbol{v}_i'$ is

$$\mathbf{r} = \left(\sum_{k=1}^{K} w_{k,i} G_k(\boldsymbol{\theta}, J(\boldsymbol{\beta})) \right)^{-1} \mathbf{r}' - b_{P,i}(\boldsymbol{\theta}). \tag{7}$$

Doing this for every ray effectively unposes the silhouette cone and places constraints on a canonical T-pose. Unposing removes blend-shape calculations from the optimization problem and significantly reduces the memory foot-print of the method. Without unposing the vertex operations and the respective Jacobians would have to be computed for every frame at *every update* of the shape. Given the set of unposed rays for F silhouettes (we use $F = 120$ in all experiments), an optimization in the canonical frame is formulated

$$E_{\text{cons}} = E_{\text{data}} + w_{\text{lp}} E_{\text{lp}} + w_{\text{var}} E_{\text{var}} + w_{\text{sym}} E_{\text{sym}} \tag{8}$$

and minimized with respect to shape parameters $\boldsymbol{\beta}$ of a template model and the vertex offsets $\mathbf{D}$ defined in Eq. 4. The objective E_{cons} consists of a data term E_{data} and three regularization terms $E_{\text{lp}}, E_{\text{var}}, E_{\text{sym}}$ with weights w_* that balance its influence.

Data Term measures the distance between vertices and rays. Point to line distances can be efficiently computed expressing rays using Plucker coordinates $(\mathbf{r} = \mathbf{r}_m, \mathbf{r}_n)$. Given a set of correspondences $(\mathbf{v}_i, \mathbf{r}) \in \mathcal{M}$ the data term equals

$$E_{\text{data}} = \sum_{(\mathbf{v}, \mathbf{r}) \in \mathcal{M}} \rho(\mathbf{v} \times \mathbf{r}_n - \mathbf{r}_m) \tag{9}$$

where ρ is the Geman-McClure robust cost function, here applied to the point to line distance. Since the canonical pose parameters are all zero ($\boldsymbol{\theta} = \mathbf{0}$) it follows from Eq. 4 that vertex positions are a function of shape parameters and offsets $\mathbf{v}(\boldsymbol{\beta}_0, \mathbf{D}) = T_i(\boldsymbol{\beta}_0, \mathbf{D}) = (\mathbf{v}_{\mu,i} + b_{s,i}(\boldsymbol{\beta}_0) + \mathbf{d}_i)$, where $\mathbf{d}_i \in \mathbb{R}^3$ is the offset in $\mathbf{D}$ corresponding to vertex $\mathbf{v}_i$.

Finally, the optimization is regularized with three terms. This terms enforce smooth deformation, penalize reconstructed vertices' deviations from the ones explained by the SMPL model, and enforce symmetrical shape. Since the refined consensus shape still has the mesh topology of SMPL, one can apply the pose-based deformation space of SMPL to simulate surface deformation in new skeleton poses. For further implementation details and runtime metrics, we refer the reader to the original paper [7].

Frame Refinement and Texture Generation: After calculating a *global* shape for the given sequence, the next goal is to capture the temporal variations. The energy in Eq. 8 is adapted to process frames sequentially. The optimization is initialized with the preceding frame and regularized with neighboring frames:

$$E_{\text{ref},j} = \sum_{j=f-m}^{f+m} \psi_j E_{\text{data},j} + w_{\text{var}} E_{\text{var},j} + w_{\text{lp}} E_{\text{lp},j} + w_{\text{last}} E_{\text{last},j} \tag{10}$$

where $\psi_j = 1$ for $j = k$ and $\psi_j = w_{\text{neigh}} < 1$ for neighboring frames. Hence, w_{neigh} defines the influence of neighboring frames and E_{last} regularizes the reconstruction to the result of the preceding frame. To create the texture, the estimated canonical model is warped back to each frame, the image color is back-projected to all visible vertices, and finally a texture image is generated by calculating the median of the most orthogonal texels from all views.

4.2   Results

The authors offered a numerical evaluation on three different datasets with ground truth 3D shapes: DynamicFAUST [18], BUFF [117] and KinectCap [16]. For the first two ones, they rendered the ground truth scans on a virtual camera while the last one already included images. Figure 6 shows some examples of the presented method's reconstruction results on image sequences rendered from all datasets. These results demonstrated a mean surface reconstruction accuracy of 4.5 mm (even higher 3.1 mm with ground truth (GT) poses) despite monocular depth ambiguities.

D-FAUST   BUFF   KinectCap

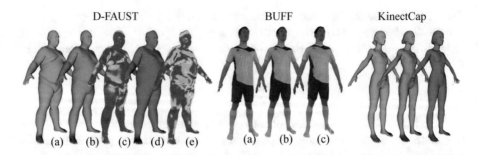

(a)   (b)   (c)   (d)   (e)   (a)   (b)   (c)

Fig. 6. Results on image sequences from BUFF, D-FAUST and KinectCap datasets. D-FAUST: (a) GT 3D scan, (b) consensus shape with GT poses (consensus-p), (c) consensus-p heatmap, (d) consensus shape (consensus), (e) consensus heat-map range [0 mm, ≥2 cm]. Textured results on BUFF: (a) GT scan, (b) consensus-p (c) consensus. KinectCap: (green) GT scans (red) results by Bogo *et al.* [16] (blue) Alldieck *et al.*'s results [7].

Fig. 7. Results on the People-Snapshot dataset. Since the reconstructed templates share the topology with the SMPL body model, it can be used to change the *pose and shape* of the reconstructions.

Moreover, Alldieck *et al.* [7] captured a new test dataset (People-Snapshot) of real image sequences. When applied to this real world scenarios, the method yields detailed reconstructions of similar quality as the results on rendered sequences from BUFF and D-FAUST (please compare the results depicted in Figs. 6 and 7).

5   Second Approach: Octopus

The method presented in the previous section achieved to estimate 3D human shapes from monocular video of a moving person that goes beyond the parameter space of a parametric model [7]. Not only the reconstructed models have high quality but this method also significantly reduces memory consumption, speeds up the optimization process, and allows to combine information from many frames. However, it still leaves space for improvement regarding efficiency and usability with the main bottleneck being the pre-processing step. This step requires fitting the SMPL model to each of the frame silhouettes using time-consuming non-linear optimization, being impractical for any application requiring fast acquisition. Thus, this section covers the next natural step: investigating the usage of CNNs in order to achieve faster and more accurate results, as well as reducing the number of required steps. To reach the desired goals, there are four main questions to answer:

- Which data is needed to train a network to perform the given task?
- In which space can one fuse information from multiple images? Which role plays "pose" in the problem?
- How far can one get with only one forward pass through a network? How much can one improve with subsequent optimization?
- How many frames are needed during test time?

This work, named *Octopus* [5], was presented by Alldieck *et al.* in 2019.

5.1   Method

Octopus [5] aims to create a full, animatable 3D model of a subject from a few frames of a monocular RGB video in less than 10 s. Similarly to the approach presented in the previous section, Octopus focuses on the cooperative setting with videos of people rotating in front of a camera holding a rough A-pose. Shape is once again represented using the SMPL+D model (see Eq. 4). The differentiablity of the model allows for the direct integration of SMPL as a fixed layer in Octopus' convolutional architecture. To achieve fast and fully automatic reconstruction, Alldieck and colleagues trained a novel convolutional neural network to infer a 3D mesh model of a subject from a small number of input frames. Additionally, the network is trained to reconstruct the 3D pose of the subject in each frame. This allows to refine the body shape by utilizing the decoder part of the network for instance-specific optimization.

Model and Data Representation: Given a set of images $\mathcal{I} = \{\mathbf{I}_0, \ldots, \mathbf{I}_{F-1}\}$ depicting a subject from different sides with corresponding 2D joints $\mathcal{J} = \{\mathbf{J}_0, \ldots, \mathbf{J}_{F-1}\}$, the authors learn a predictor f_w^* that infers the body shape $\boldsymbol{\beta}$, personal and scene specific body features $\mathbf{D}$, and 3D poses $\mathcal{P} = \{\boldsymbol{\theta}_0, \ldots, \boldsymbol{\theta}_{F-1}\}$ along with 3D positions $\mathcal{T} = \{\boldsymbol{t}_0, \ldots, \boldsymbol{t}_{F-1}\}$ for each image. $f_w^* : (\mathcal{I}, \mathcal{J}) \mapsto (\boldsymbol{\beta}, \mathbf{D}, \mathcal{P}, \mathcal{T})$ is a CNN parametrized by network parameters w.

Input Modalities. Images of humans are highly diverse in appearance, requiring large datasets of annotated images in the context of deep learning. Therefore, to abstract away as much information as possible while still retaining shape and pose signal, they build on previous work [22,36] to simplify each RGB image to a semantic segmentation and 2D keypoint detections. This allows the authors to train the network using only synthetic data and generalize to real data.

Model Parametrization. By integrating the SMPL+D model (Sect. 3.1) into the network formulation, its mesh output can be used in the training of f_w^*. Concretely, the predicted SMPL+D parameters are supervised in three ways: imposing a loss directly on the mesh vertices $M(\boldsymbol{\beta}, \boldsymbol{\theta}, \mathbf{D})$, on the predicted joint locations $J(\boldsymbol{\beta})$ and their projections on the image, and densely on a rendering of the mesh using a differential renderer [43].

The T-shape $(\mathbf{T} + B_s(\boldsymbol{\beta}) + \mathbf{D})$ in Eq. 4 is now predicted from the set of semantic images $\mathcal{I}$ with the function:

$$S(\mathcal{I}) = \mathbf{T} + B_s(f_w^\beta(\mathcal{I})) + f_w^{\mathbf{D}}(\mathcal{I}), \tag{11}$$

where f_w^* are the regressors to be learned. Similarly, the posed mesh $N_{3D}(\mathcal{I}, \mathcal{J}, i)$ is predicted from the image $\mathbf{I}_i$ and 2D joints $\mathbf{J}_i$ with the function:

$$N_{3D}(\mathcal{I}, \mathcal{J}, i) = W(P(\mathcal{I}, \mathcal{J}, i), J(f_w^\beta(\mathcal{I})), f_w^{\boldsymbol{\theta}_i}(\mathcal{I}, \mathcal{J}), \mathbf{W}) \tag{12}$$

$$P(\mathcal{I}, \mathcal{J}, i) = S(\mathcal{I}) + B_p(f_w^{\boldsymbol{\theta}_i}(\mathcal{I}, \mathcal{J})), \tag{13}$$

from which the 3D joints are predicted with the linear regressor J_{B25}:

$$N_{J_{3D}}(\mathcal{I}, \mathcal{J}, i) = J_{B25}(N_{3D}(\mathcal{I}, \mathcal{J}, i)) \tag{14}$$

J_{B25} was trained to output 25 joint locations consistent with the BODY_25 keypoint ordering. The estimated posed mesh N_{3D} can be rendered in uniform color with the image formation function $R(\cdot)$ paramerized by camera c:

$$N_{2D}(\mathcal{I}, \mathcal{J}, i) = R_c(N_{3D}(\mathcal{I}, \mathcal{J}, i)) \tag{15}$$

Similarly, the joints $N_{J_{3D}}$ can be projected to the image plane by perspective projection π:

$$N_{J_{2D}}(\mathcal{I}, \mathcal{J}, i) = \pi_c(N_{J3D}(\mathcal{I}, \mathcal{J}, i)) \tag{16}$$

All these operations are differentiable, which can be used to formulate suitable loss functions.

Loss Functions. Octopus' architecture permits two sources of supervision: (i) 3D supervision, and (ii) 2D supervision from video frames alone. The following loss functions are used to train the predictors f_w^*.

Losses on Body Shape and Pose. For a paired sample in the dataset $\{(\mathcal{I}, \mathcal{J}), (\boldsymbol{\beta}, \mathbf{D}, \mathcal{P}, \mathcal{T})\}$ the authors use the following losses between Octopus' estimated model N_{3D} and the ground truth model $M(\cdot)$ scan:

- Per-vertex loss in the canonical T-pose $\mathbf{0}_\theta$. This loss provides a useful 3D supervision on shape independently of pose:

$$\mathcal{L}_S = ||S(\mathcal{I}) - M(\boldsymbol{\beta}, \mathbf{0}_\theta, \mathbf{D})||^2 \tag{17}$$

– Per-vertex loss in posed space. This loss supervises both pose and shape on the Euclidean space:

$$\mathcal{L}_{N_{3D}} = \sum_{i=0}^{F-1} ||N_{3D}(\mathcal{I}, \mathcal{J}, i) - M(\boldsymbol{\beta}, \boldsymbol{\theta}_i, \mathbf{D})||^2 \tag{18}$$

– Silhouette overlap:

$$\mathcal{L}_{N_{2D}} = \sum_{i=0}^{F-1} ||R_c(N_{3D}(\mathcal{I}, \mathcal{J}, i)) - b(\mathbf{I}_i)||^2, \tag{19}$$

where $b(\mathbf{I}_i)$ is the binary segmentation mask and R_c is the image formation function defined in Eq. 15. $\mathcal{L}_{N_{2D}}$ is a weakly supervised loss as it does not require 3D annotations and $b(\mathbf{I}_i)$ can be estimated directly from RGB images.

– Per-vertex SMPL undressed body loss:

The aforementioned losses only penalize the final SMPL+D 3D shape. It is useful to include an "undressed-body" ($\hat{S}$) loss to force the shape parameters $\boldsymbol{\beta}$ to be close to the ground truth

$$\mathcal{L}_{\hat{S}} = ||\hat{S}(\mathcal{I}) - M(\boldsymbol{\beta}, \mathbf{0}_\theta, \mathbf{0}_\mathbf{D})||^2 \tag{20}$$

$$\hat{S}(\mathcal{I}) = \mathbf{T} + B_s(f_w^\beta(\mathcal{I})), \tag{21}$$

where $\mathbf{0}_\mathbf{D}$ are vectors of length 0. This also prevents that the offsets $\mathbf{D}$ explain the overall shape of the person.

Pose Specific Losses. In addition to the posed space $\mathcal{L}_{N_{3D}}$ and silhouette overlap $\mathcal{L}_{N_{2D}}$ losses, we train for the pose using a direct loss on the predicted parameters $\mathcal{L}_{\theta,t}$

$$\mathcal{L}_{\theta,t} = \sum_{i=0}^{F-1} \left(||\mathbf{R}(f_w^{\theta_i}) - \mathbf{R}(\boldsymbol{\theta}_i)||^2 + ||f_w^{t_i} - \boldsymbol{t}_i||^2 \right), \tag{22}$$

where $\mathbf{R}$ are vectorized rotation matrices of the 24 joints. Differentiable SVD is used to force the predicted matrices to lie on the manifold of rotation matrices. This term makes the pose part of the network converge faster.

Losses on Joints. The pose training is further regularized by imposing a loss on the joints in Euclidean space:

$$\mathcal{L}_{J_{3D}} = \sum_{i=0}^{F-1} ||N_{J_{3D}}(\mathcal{I}, \mathcal{J}, i) - J_{\text{B25}}(M(\boldsymbol{\beta}, \boldsymbol{\theta}_i, \mathbf{D}))||^2 \tag{23}$$

Similar to the 2D image projection loss on model $\mathcal{L}_{N_{2D}}$ (Eq. 19), the authors also have a weakly supervised 2D joint projection loss $\mathcal{L}_{J_{2D}}$

$$\mathcal{L}_{J_{2D}} = \sum_{i=0}^{F-1} ||N_{J_{2D}}(\mathcal{I}, \mathcal{J}, i) - \pi_c(J_{\text{B25}}(M(\boldsymbol{\beta}, \boldsymbol{\theta}_i, \mathbf{D})))||^2. \tag{24}$$

Instance-Specific Top-Down Optimization. The bottom-up predictions of the neural model can be refined top-down at test time to capture instance specific details. It is important to note that this step requires no 3D annotation as the network fine-tunes using only 2D data. Specifically, at the test time, given a subject's images $\mathcal{I}$ and 2D joints $\mathcal{J}$ a small set of layers in f_w^* is optimized using image and joint projection losses $\mathcal{L}_{N_{2D}}, \mathcal{L}_{J_{2D}}$. Fixing most layers of the network and optimizing only latent layers offers a compromise between the manifold of shapes learned by the network and new features, that have not been learned.

5.2   Results

Experiments demonstrate that the feed-forward predictions are already quite accurate (4.5 mm), but often lack detail and do not perfectly overlap with the input images. This motivates refining the estimates with top-down optimization against the input images. Refining brings the error down to 4 mm and aligns the model with the input image silhouettes, which allows texture mapping. Octopus allows to significantly reduce the number of required images at test time, and compute the final result several magnitudes faster than state-of-the-art (from hours to seconds). The authors created a dataset, named LifeScans, consisting of rendered images paired with 3D animated scans in various shapes and poses, which they use along extensive experiments to successfully demonstrate the performance and influence of key parameters of the predictor.

Fig. 8. Results from LifeScans in comparison to GT shapes (green): Results computed with GT poses (blue), results of the full method (yellow), and their corresponding error heatmaps with respect to GT shapes (red means ≥ 2 cm).

Figure 8 displays subjects in the test set (along with per-vertex error heatmaps) for both the original version of Octopus and one variant of it that uses ground truth poses. The numerical error increases only by ≈ 1 mm between GT and predicted pose models.

While Octopus is independent on the number of input images and can be refined for different numbers of optimization steps, Alldieck and colleagues showed that using 8 views and refining for 10 s are good compromises between accuracy and practicability. Qualitative results on two real-world datasets, *PeopleSnapshot* [7] (Fig. 9) and *KinectCap* [16] (Fig. 10), demonstrate generalization to real data, despite training from synthetic data alone.

(a) (b)

Fig. 9. Comparison to the method presented in the previous section [7]. While the previous approach (a) uses 120 frames, Octopus (b) only uses 8 images and is several magnitudes faster.

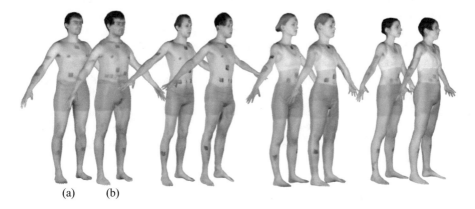

(a)   (b)

Fig. 10. Comparison to the RGB-D method [16] (a). Octopus (b) is visually on par, despite using only 8 RGB images as input.

6   Third Approach: Tex2Shape

The approaches presented in Sects. 4 and 5 lead us to three important observations. First, while building on silhouettes and semantic segmentation helps to make the problem tractable and applicable for real-world data, it also abstracts away valuable information. Second, regressing 3D vertex locations from 2D images is an *unaligned problem*. 2D images and 3D meshes can only be compared by projecting and rasterizing the meshes through rendering, implying that 3D pose plays a significant role in supervision. These observations were the inspiration for the latest introduced approach of this chapter: Tex2Shape [8]. In this work, 3D shape reconstruction is turned into a pose-independent 2D image-to-image translation problem by transforming the input image into an incomplete texture in UV space [11]. Given an incomplete texture of a person extracted from a single input image, a Pix2Pix network [53] predicts dense normal and displacement maps including fine details, such as garment wrinkles.

Formulating the complex shape reconstruction task as a well-alligned image-to-image translation problem results in several advantages over the previously discussed approaches:

- Using an underlying image translation network, Tex2Shape can regress full 3D clothing, hair and facial details in only 50 ms.
- The approach only requires a single frontal input view captured by a conventional RGB-camera.
- By using a learning-based approach, the network plausibly fills in occluded regions not contained in the original photograph by generalizing from the training data.

6.1   Method

The goal of this approach is to create an animatable 3D model of a subject from a single photograph. The model should reflect the subject's body shape and contain details such as hair and clothing with garment wrinkles. Details should be present also on body parts that have not been visible in the input image, e.g. on the back of the person. To this end, Alldieck *et al.* train a Pix2Pix-style [53] convolutional neural network to infer normals and vector displacement (*UV shape-images*) on top of the SMPL body model [67]. To align the input image with the output UV-shape images, they extract a partial UV texture map of the visible area using off-the-shelf methods [11,57]. An overview is given in Fig. 11. A second small CNN infers SMPL shape parameters from the image (see Sect. 6.2).

6.2   Model and Training

The main pipeline consists of two CNNs – one for normal and displacement maps and one for SMPL shape parameters β, the main component being the Tex2Shape-network as depicted in Fig. 11. The network is a conditional Generative Adversarial Network consisting of a U-Net generator and a PatchGAN discriminator, as described in Pix2Pix [53]. Conditioning is realized using partial textures of 512×512 pixels and the β-network takes 1024×1024 pixel images obtained from DensePose [11] detections as input. These are then downsampled with seven convolution-ReLU-batchnorm layers and finally mapped to 10 β-parameters by a fully-connected layer.

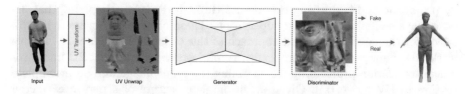

Fig. 11. Overview of the key component of Tex2Shape: a single photograph of a subject is transformed into a partial UV texture map. This map is then processed with a U-Net with skip connections that preserve high-frequency details. A PatchGAN discriminator enforces realism. The generated normals and displacements can be applied to the SMPL model using standard rendering pipelines.

The applied losses put an emphasis on structure rather than accuracy, preferring optimizing for perceived quality over ground truth discrepancies. Thus the losses employed for estimating the similarity of ground truth and predicted normal and displacement maps are based on the multi-scale SSIM (MS-SSIM) [110]: $(1 - MS\text{-}SSIM)/2$. The GAN-loss coming from the discriminator is the well-established L1-loss and finally the β-network parameters are trained with a L2-loss. Both CNNs are trained with the Adam optimizer [60] and the learning-rate is decayed once the losses plateau.

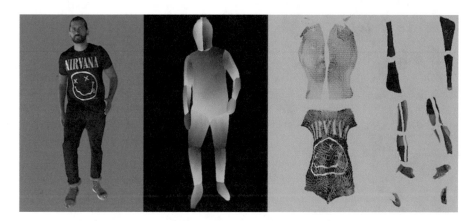

Fig. 12. To create the input to our method, we first process the input image (left) with DensePose. The DensePose result (middle) contains UV coordinates, that can be used to map the input image into a partial texture (right).

The partial texture inputs are created by transforming pixels from the input image to UV space for each of the 24 body parts of the SMPL model, as illustrated in Fig. 12.

6.3   Results

Tex2Shape was trained on a purpose-built synthetic dataset consisting of renderings showing 2043 scans of humans in different clothes, including detailed texture and normal maps. Figure 13 depicts outputs of the Tex2Shape network on the training data as well as on several real-world datasets. Ground truth data is rendered from posed textured meshes. The ground truth mesh is depicted in grey, and rendered outputs of the neural network are depicted in green. Results on the DeepFashion [65] and PeopleSnapshot [7] demonstrate the generalization capabilities of the model to unseen real-world footage. Furthermore, the result on the 3DPW dataset [68] demonstrates that the model is able to hallucinate details in occluded regions. For more detailed qualitative and quantitative comparison as well as ablation studies on the influence of different design choices, please refer to the original paper [8].

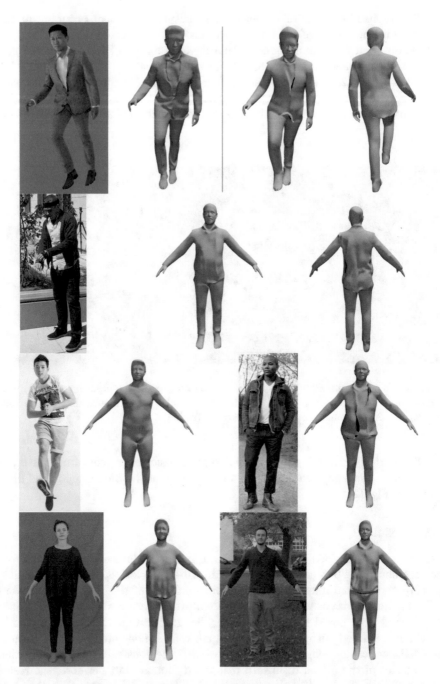

Fig. 13. Results on four different datasets. Comparison against ground truth (grey) on the training dataset (1st row). Qualitative results on 3DPW (2nd row), DeepFashion (3rd row) and PeopleSnapshot (4th row).

7   Conclusion

This chapter has covered various aspects of 3D reconstruction of human pose and shape from monocular images. While each of the presented approaches tackles different aspects of the problem, all follow a similar concept: instead of aiming at reconstructing the 3D shape of the observed human from scratch, they build upon a statistical body model. This way, the methods make use of a rich prior for the reconstruction process which allows achieving more realistic results. Additionally, this strategy ensures that the reconstructed avatars can directly be used by other applications, as the results already come rigged.

Section 4 has presented an novel an efficient method able to extract realistic avatars including hair and clothing from a moving person in a monocular RGB video. Next, Sect. 5 has shown a bottom-up plus top-down optimization which significantly reduces the number of required images at test time, speeding up the full process. Finally, Sect. 6 has illustrated a novel view on the challenge, turning the hard problem of full-body shape reconstruction into a 3D pose-independent image to image translation that is easier to solve.

To conclude, we believe that the work presented in this chapter provides fundamental and important steps to reconstruct virtual avatars of real humans from monocular video. Building detailed and animatable virtual humans using only a low-cost video camera is not anymore just an idea, but a reality. Thus, these effective methods enable easy-to-use self-digitization and pave the path for exciting new applications.

References

1. Ahmed, N., de Aguiar, E., Theobalt, C., Magnor, M., Seidel, H.P.: Automatic generation of personalized human avatars from multi-view video. In: Proceedings of the ACM Symposium on Virtual Reality Software and Technology, pp. 257–260. ACM (2005)
2. Aliev, K.A., Ulyanov, D., Lempitsky, V.: Neural point-based graphics. arXiv preprint arXiv:1906.08240 (2019)
3. Allain, B., Franco, J.S., Boyer, E.: An efficient volumetric framework for shape tracking. In: IEEE Conference on Computer Vision and Pattern Recognition, pp. 268–276. IEEE (2015)
4. Alldieck, T., Kassubeck, M., Wandt, B., Rosenhahn, B., Magnor, M.: Optical flow-based 3D human motion estimation from monocular video. In: Roth, V., Vetter, T. (eds.) GCPR 2017. LNCS, vol. 10496, pp. 347–360. Springer, Cham (2017). https://doi.org/10.1007/978-3-319-66709-6_28
5. Alldieck, T., Magnor, M., Bhatnagar, B.L., Theobalt, C., Pons-Moll, G.: Learning to reconstruct people in clothing from a single RGB camera. In: IEEE/CVF Conference on Computer Vision and Pattern Recognition, pp. 1175–1186. IEEE (2019)
6. Alldieck, T., Magnor, M., Xu, W., Theobalt, C., Pons-Moll, G.: Detailed human avatars from monocular video. In: International Conference on 3D Vision, pp. 98–109. IEEE (2018)

7. Alldieck, T., Magnor, M., Xu, W., Theobalt, C., Pons-Moll, G.: Video based reconstruction of 3D people models. In: IEEE/CVF Conference on Computer Vision and Pattern Recognition, pp. 8387–8397. IEEE (2018)

8. Alldieck, T., Pons-Moll, G., Theobalt, C., Magnor, M.: Tex2Shape: detailed full human body geometry from a single image. In: IEEE International Conference on Computer Vision. IEEE (2019)

9. Allen, B., Curless, B., Curless, B., Popović, Z.: The space of human body shapes: reconstruction and parameterization from range scans. ACM Trans. Graph. **22**(3), 587–594 (2003)

10. Allen, B., Curless, B., Popović, Z., Hertzmann, A.: Learning a correlated model of identity and pose-dependent body shape variation for real-time synthesis. In: Proceedings of the 2006 ACM SIGGRAPH/Eurographics Symposium on Computer Animation, pp. 147–156 (2006)

11. Alp Güler, R., Neverova, N., Kokkinos, I.: DensePose: dense human pose estimation in the wild. In: IEEE/CVF Conference on Computer Vision and Pattern Recognition, pp. 7297–7306. IEEE (2018)

12. Anguelov, D., Srinivasan, P., Koller, D., Thrun, S., Rodgers, J., Davis, J.: SCAPE: shape completion and animation of people. ACM Trans. Graph. **24**(3), 408–416 (2005)

13. Bălan, A.O., Black, M.J.: The naked truth: estimating body shape under clothing. In: Forsyth, D., Torr, P., Zisserman, A. (eds.) ECCV 2008. LNCS, vol. 5303, pp. 15–29. Springer, Heidelberg (2008). https://doi.org/10.1007/978-3-540-88688-4_2

14. Bălan, A.O., Sigal, L., Black, M.J., Davis, J.E., Haussecker, H.W.: Detailed human shape and pose from images. In: IEEE Conference on Computer Vision and Pattern Recognition, pp. 1–8. IEEE (2007)

15. Blinn, J.F., Newell, M.E.: Texture and reflection in computer generated images. Commun. ACM **19**(10), 542–547 (1976)

16. Bogo, F., Black, M.J., Loper, M., Romero, J.: Detailed full-body reconstructions of moving people from monocular RGB-D sequences. In: IEEE International Conference on Computer Vision, pp. 2300–2308. IEEE (2015)

17. Bogo, F., Kanazawa, A., Lassner, C., Gehler, P., Romero, J., Black, M.J.: Keep it SMPL: automatic estimation of 3D human pose and shape from a single image. In: Leibe, B., Matas, J., Sebe, N., Welling, M. (eds.) ECCV 2016. LNCS, vol. 9909, pp. 561–578. Springer, Cham (2016). https://doi.org/10.1007/978-3-319-46454-1_34

18. Bogo, F., Romero, J., Pons-Moll, G., Black, M.J.: Dynamic FAUST: registering human bodies in motion. In: IEEE Conference on Computer Vision and Pattern Recognition. IEEE (2017)

19. Bronstein, M.M., Bruna, J., LeCun, Y., Szlam, A., Vandergheynst, P.: Geometric deep learning: going beyond Euclidean data. IEEE Sign. Process. Mag. **34**, 18–42 (2017)

20. Caelles, S., Maninis, K.K., Pont-Tuset, J., Leal-Taixé, L., Cremers, D., Van Gool, L.: One-shot video object segmentation. In: IEEE Conference on Computer Vision and Pattern Recognition. IEEE (2017)

21. Cao, C., Weng, Y., Zhou, S., Tong, Y., Zhou, K.: FaceWarehouse: a 3D facial expression database for visual computing. IEEE Trans. Visual. Comput. Graph. **20**(3), 413–425 (2013)

22. Cao, Z., Simon, T., Wei, S.E., Sheikh, Y.: Realtime multi-person 2D pose estimation using part affinity fields. In: IEEE Conference on Computer Vision and Pattern Recognition. IEEE (2017)

23. Carranza, J., Theobalt, C., Magnor, M.A., Seidel, H.P.: Free-viewpoint video of human actors. ACM Trans. Graph. **22**(3), 569–577 (2003)
24. Chen, X., Guo, Y., Zhou, B., Zhao, Q.: Deformable model for estimating clothed and naked human shapes from a single image. Vis. Comput. **29**(11), 1187–1196 (2013)
25. Chen, Z., Zhang, H.: Learning implicit fields for generative shape modeling. In: IEEE/CVF Conference on Computer Vision and Pattern Recognition. IEEE (2019)
26. Collet, A., et al.: High-quality streamable free-viewpoint video. ACM Trans. Graph. **34**(4), 69 (2015)
27. Cui, Y., Chang, W., Nöll, T., Stricker, D.: KinectAvatar: fully automatic body capture using a single kinect. In: Park, J.-I., Kim, J. (eds.) ACCV 2012. LNCS, vol. 7729, pp. 133–147. Springer, Heidelberg (2013). https://doi.org/10.1007/978-3-642-37484-5_12
28. De Aguiar, E., Stoll, C., Theobalt, C., Ahmed, N., Seidel, H.P., Thrun, S.: Performance capture from sparse multi-view video. ACM Trans. Graph. **27**(3), 98 (2008)
29. De Aguiar, E., Theobalt, C., Magnor, M., Seidel, H.P., et al.: Reconstructing human shape and motion from multi-view video. In: 2nd European Conference on Visual Media Production (CVMP), pp. 42–49 (2005)
30. Dibra, E., Jain, H., Öztireli, C., Ziegler, R., Gross, M.: HS-Nets: estimating human body shape from silhouettes with convolutional neural networks. In: International Conference on 3D Vision, pp. 108–117. IEEE (2016)
31. Dibra, E., Jain, H., Öztireli, C., Ziegler, R., Gross, M.: Human shape from silhouettes using generative HKS descriptors and cross-modal neural networks. In: IEEE Conference on Computer Vision and Pattern Recognition. IEEE (2017)
32. Dibra, E., Öztireli, C., Ziegler, R., Gross, M.: Shape from selfies: human body shape estimation using CCA regression forests. In: European Conference on Computer Vision, pp. 88–104 (2016)
33. Dou, M., et al.: Fusion4D: real-time performance capture of challenging scenes. ACM Trans. Graph. **35**(4), 114 (2016)
34. Gall, J., Stoll, C., De Aguiar, E., Theobalt, C., Rosenhahn, B., Seidel, H.P.: Motion capture using joint skeleton tracking and surface estimation. In: IEEE Conference on Computer Vision and Pattern Recognition, pp. 1746–1753. IEEE (2009)
35. Gilbert, A., Volino, M., Collomosse, J., Hilton, A.: Volumetric performance capture from minimal camera viewpoints. In: European Conference on Computer Vision (2018)
36. Gong, K., Liang, X., Li, Y., Chen, Y., Yang, M., Lin, L.: Instance-level human parsing via part grouping network. In: European Conference on Computer Vision (2018)
37. Guan, P., Weiss, A., Bălan, A.O., Black, M.J.: Estimating human shape and pose from a single image. In: IEEE International Conference on Computer Vision, pp. 1381–1388. IEEE (2009)
38. Guler, R.A., Kokkinos, I.: Holopose: holistic 3D human reconstruction in-the-wild. In: IEEE/CVF Conference on Computer Vision and Pattern Recognition, pp. 10884–10894. IEEE (2019)
39. Guo, Y., Chen, X., Zhou, B., Zhao, Q.: Clothed and naked human shapes estimation from a single image. In: Hu, S.-M., Martin, R.R. (eds.) CVM 2012. LNCS, vol. 7633, pp. 43–50. Springer, Heidelberg (2012). https://doi.org/10.1007/978-3-642-34263-9_6

40. Habermann, M., Xu, W., Zollhöfer, M., Pons-Moll, G., Theobalt, C.: LiveCap: real-time human performance capture from monocular video. ACM Trans. Graph. **38**(2), 14:1–14:17 (2019)

41. Hasler, N., Ackermann, H., Rosenhahn, B., Thormahlen, T., Seidel, H.P.: Multilinear pose and body shape estismation of dressed subjects from image sets. In: IEEE Conference on Computer Vision and Pattern Recognition, pp. 1823–1830. IEEE (2010)

42. Hasler, N., Stoll, C., Sunkel, M., Rosenhahn, B., Seidel, H.P.: A statistical model of human pose and body shape. Comput. Graph. Forum **28**(2), 337–346 (2009)

43. Henderson, P., Ferrari, V.: Learning to generate and reconstruct 3D meshes with only 2D supervision. In: British Machine Vision Conference (2018)

44. Hesse, N., Pujades, S., Black, M.J., Arens, M., Hofmann, U., Schroeder, S.: Learning and tracking the 3D body shape of freely moving infants from RGB-D sequences. Trans. Pattern Anal. Mach. Intell. (TPAMI) (2019). https://doi.org/10.1109/TPAMI.2019.2917908. 12 Pages

45. Hilton, A., Beresford, D.J., Gentils, T., Smith, R.S., Sun, W.: Virtual people: capturing human models to populate virtual worlds. Proc. Comput. Anim. **99**, 174 (1999)

46. Hirshberg, D.A., Loper, M., Rachlin, E., Black, M.J.: Coregistration: simultaneous alignment and modeling of articulated 3D shape. In: Fitzgibbon, A., Lazebnik, S., Perona, P., Sato, Y., Schmid, C. (eds.) ECCV 2012. LNCS, vol. 7577, pp. 242–255. Springer, Heidelberg (2012). https://doi.org/10.1007/978-3-642-33783-3_18

47. Huang, C.H., Allain, B., Franco, J.S., Navab, N., Ilic, S., Boyer, E.: Volumetric 3D tracking by detection. In: IEEE Conference on Computer Vision and Pattern Recognition, pp. 3862–3870. IEEE (2016)

48. Huang, Y., et al.: Towards accurate markerless human shape and pose estimation over time. In: International Conference on 3D Vision. IEEE (2017)

49. Huang, Y., Kaufmann, M., Aksan, E., Black, M.J., Hilliges, O., Pons-Moll, G.: Deep inertial poser learning to reconstruct human pose from sparseinertial measurements in real time. ACM Trans. Graph. **37**(6), 185:1–185:15 (2018)

50. Huang, Z., et al.: Deep volumetric video from very sparse multi-view performance capture. In: European Conference on Computer Vision, pp. 336–354 (2018)

51. Innmann, M., Zollhöfer, M., Nießner, M., Theobalt, C., Stamminger, M.: VolumeDeform: real-time volumetric non-rigid reconstruction. In: Leibe, B., Matas, J., Sebe, N., Welling, M. (eds.) ECCV 2016. LNCS, vol. 9912, pp. 362–379. Springer, Cham (2016). https://doi.org/10.1007/978-3-319-46484-8_22

52. Insafutdinov, E., Pishchulin, L., Andres, B., Andriluka, M., Schiele, B.: DeeperCut: a deeper, stronger, and faster multi-person pose estimation model. In: Leibe, B., Matas, J., Sebe, N., Welling, M. (eds.) ECCV 2016. LNCS, vol. 9910, pp. 34–50. Springer, Cham (2016). https://doi.org/10.1007/978-3-319-46466-4_3

53. Isola, P., Zhu, J.Y., Zhou, T., Efros, A.A.: Image-to-image translation with conditional adversarial networks. In: IEEE Conference on Computer Vision and Pattern Recognition, pp. 1125–1134. IEEE (2017)

54. Jackson, A.S., Manafas, C., Tzimiropoulos, G.: 3D human body reconstruction from a single image via volumetric regression. In: European Conference on Computer Vision, pp. 64–77 (2018)

55. Joo, H., Simon, T., Sheikh, Y.: Total capture: a 3D deformation model for tracking faces, hands, and bodies. In: IEEE/CVF Conference on Computer Vision and Pattern Recognition, pp. 8320–8329. IEEE (2018)

56. Kakadiaris, I.A., Metaxas, D.: 3D human body model acquisition from multiple views. In: IEEE International Conference on Computer Vision. IEEE (1995)
57. Kanazawa, A., Black, M.J., Jacobs, D.W., Malik, J.: End-to-end recovery of human shape and pose. In: IEEE/CVF Conference on Computer Vision and Pattern Recognition. IEEE (2018)
58. Kanazawa, A., Zhang, J.Y., Felsen, P., Malik, J.: Learning 3D human dynamics from video. In: IEEE/CVF Conference on Computer Vision and Pattern Recognition, pp. 5614–5623. IEEE (2019)
59. Kim, M., et al.: Data-driven physics for human soft tissue animation. ACM Trans. Graph. $36(4)$, 1–12 (2017)
60. Kingma, D.P., Ba, J.: Adam: a method for stochastic optimization. In: International Conference on Learning Representations, vol. 5 (2015)
61. Kolotouros, N., Pavlakos, G., Daniilidis, K.: Convolutional mesh regression for single-image human shape reconstruction. In: IEEE/CVF Conference on Computer Vision and Pattern Recognition. IEEE (2019)
62. Lassner, C., Romero, J., Kiefel, M., Bogo, F., Black, M.J., Gehler, P.V.: Unite the people: closing the loop between 3D and 2D human representations. In: IEEE Conference on Computer Vision and Pattern Recognition. IEEE (2017)
63. Leroy, V., Franco, J.S., Boyer, E.: Multi-view dynamic shape refinement using local temporal integration. In: IEEE International Conference on Computer Vision. IEEE (2017)
64. Li, H., Vouga, E., Gudym, A., Luo, L., Barron, J.T., Gusev, G.: 3D self-portraits. ACM Trans. Graph. $32(6)$, 187 (2013)
65. Liu, Z., Luo, P., Qiu, S., Wang, X., Tang, X.: DeepFashion: powering robust clothes recognition and retrieval with rich annotations. In: IEEE Conference on Computer Vision and Pattern Recognition. IEEE (2016)
66. Lombardi, S., Simon, T., Saragih, J., Schwartz, G., Lehrmann, A., Sheikh, Y.: Neural volumes: learning dynamic renderable volumes from images. arXiv preprint arXiv:1906.07751 (2019)
67. Loper, M., Mahmood, N., Romero, J., Pons-Moll, G., Black, M.J.: SMPL: a skinned multi-person linear model. ACM Trans. Graph. $34(6)$, 248:1–248:16 (2015)
68. von Marcard, T., Henschel, R., Black, M.J., Rosenhahn, B., Pons-Moll, G.: Recovering accurate 3D human pose in the wild using IMUs and a moving camera. In: European Conference on Computer Vision (2018)
69. von Marcard, T., Pons-Moll, G., Rosenhahn, B.: Human pose estimation from video and IMUs. Trans. Pattern Anal. Mach. Intell. (PAMI) 38, 1533–1547 (2016)
70. von Marcard, T., Rosenhahn, B., Black, M.J., Pons-Moll, G.: Sparse inertial poser: automatic 3D human pose estimation from sparse IMUs. In: Computer Graphics Forum, pp. 349–360 (2017)
71. Matusik, W., Buehler, C., Raskar, R., Gortler, S.J., McMillan, L.: Image-based visual hulls. In: Annual Conference on Computer Graphics and Interactive Techniques, pp. 369–374 (2000)
72. Mescheder, L., Oechsle, M., Niemeyer, M., Nowozin, S., Geiger, A.: Occupancy networks: learning 3D reconstruction in function space. In: IEEE/CVF Conference on Computer Vision and Pattern Recognition. IEEE (2019)
73. Michalkiewicz, M., Pontes, J.K., Jack, D., Baktashmotlagh, M., Eriksson, A.: Deep level sets: implicit surface representations for 3D shape inference. arXiv preprint arXiv:1901.06802 (2019)
74. Natsume, R., et al.: SiCloPe: silhouette-based clothed people. In: IEEE/CVF Conference on Computer Vision and Pattern Recognition. IEEE (2019)

75. Newcombe, R.A., Fox, D., Seitz, S.M.: DynamicFusion: reconstruction and tracking of non-rigid scenes in real-time. In: IEEE Conference on Computer Vision and Pattern Recognition, pp. 343–352. IEEE (2015)
76. Omran, M., Lassner, C., Pons-Moll, G., Gehler, P., Schiele, B.: Neural body fitting: unifying deep learning and model based human pose and shape estimation. In: International Conference on 3D Vision. IEEE (2018)
77. Orts-Escolano, S., et al.: Holoportation: virtual 3D teleportation in real-time. In: Symposium on User Interface Software and Technology, pp. 741–754 (2016)
78. Park, J.J., Florence, P., Straub, J., Newcombe, R., Lovegrove, S.: DeepSDF: learning continuous signed distance functions for shape representation. In: IEEE/CVF Conference on Computer Vision and Pattern Recognition. IEEE (2019)
79. Pavlakos, G., et al.: Expressive body capture: 3D hands, face, and body from a single image. In: IEEE/CVF Conference on Computer Vision and Pattern Recognition. IEEE (2019)
80. Pavlakos, G., Zhu, L., Zhou, X., Daniilidis, K.: Learning to estimate 3D human pose and shape from a single color image. In: IEEE/CVF Conference on Computer Vision and Pattern Recognition. IEEE (2018)
81. Pishchulin, L., et al.: DeepCut: joint subset partition and labeling for multi person pose estimation. In: IEEE Conference on Computer Vision and Pattern Recognition. IEEE (2016)
82. Pons-Moll, G., Baak, A., Helten, T., Müller, M., Seidel, H.P., Rosenhahn, B.: Multisensor-fusion for 3D full-body human motion capture. In: IEEE Conference on Computer Vision and Pattern Recognition. IEEE (2010)
83. Pons-Moll, G., Fleet, D.J., Rosenhahn, B.: Posebits for monocular human pose estimation. In: IEEE Conference on Computer Vision and Pattern Recognition, pp. 2345–2352. IEEE (2014)
84. Pons-Moll, G., Pujades, S., Hu, S., Black, M.J.: ClothCap: seamless 4D clothing capture and retargeting. ACM Trans. Graph. **36**(4), 1–15 (2017)
85. Pons-Moll, G., Romero, J., Mahmood, N., Black, M.J.: Dyna: a model of dynamic human shape in motion. ACM Trans. Graph. **34**, 120 (2015)
86. Pons-Moll, G., Rosenhahn, B.: Model-based pose estimation. In: Moeslund, T., Hilton, A., Krüger, V., Sigal, L. (eds.) Visual Analysis of Humans, pp. 139–170. Springer, London (2011). https://doi.org/10.1007/978-0-85729-997-0_9
87. Pumarola, A., Sanchez, J., Choi, G., Sanfeliu, A., Moreno-Noguer, F.: 3DPeople: modeling the geometry of dressed humans. arXiv preprint arXiv:1904.04571 (2019)
88. Rhodin, H., Robertini, N., Casas, D., Richardt, C., Seidel, H.-P., Theobalt, C.: General automatic human shape and motion capture using volumetric contour cues. In: Leibe, B., Matas, J., Sebe, N., Welling, M. (eds.) ECCV 2016. LNCS, vol. 9909, pp. 509–526. Springer, Cham (2016). https://doi.org/10.1007/978-3-319-46454-1_31
89. Robertini, N., Casas, D., Rhodin, H., Seidel, H.P., Theobalt, C.: Model-based outdoor performance capture. In: International Conference on 3D Vision. IEEE (2016)
90. Romero, J., Tzionas, D., Black, M.J.: Embodied hands: modeling and capturing hands and bodies together. ACM Trans. Graph. **36**(6), 245 (2017)
91. Saito, S., Huang, Z., Natsume, R., Morishima, S., Kanazawa, A., Li, H.: PIFu: pixel-aligned implicit function for high-resolution clothed human digitization. In: IEEE International Conference on Computer Vision. IEEE (2019)
92. Shapiro, A., et al.: Rapid avatar capture and simulation using commodity depth sensors. Comput. Anim. Virtual Worlds **25**(3–4), 201–211 (2014)

93. Shysheya, A., et al.: Textured neural avatars. In: IEEE/CVF Conference on Computer Vision and Pattern Recognition, pp. 2387–2397. IEEE (2019)
94. Sigal, L., Balan, A., Black, M.J.: Combined discriminative and generative articulated pose and non-rigid shape estimation. In: Advances in Neural Information Processing Systems, pp. 1337–1344 (2007)
95. Sitzmann, V., Thies, J., Heide, F., Nießner, M., Wetzstein, G., Zollhöfer, M.: DeepVoxels: learning persistent 3D feature embeddings. In: IEEE/CVF Conference on Computer Vision and Pattern Recognition. IEEE (2019)
96. Slavcheva, M., Baust, M., Cremers, D., Ilic, S.: KillingFusion: non-rigid 3D reconstruction without correspondences. In: IEEE Conference on Computer Vision and Pattern Recognition, p. 7, no. 4. IEEE (2017)
97. Sminchisescu, C., Telea, A.: Human pose estimation from silhouettes. A consistent approach using distance level sets. In: 10th International Conference on Computer Graphics, Visualization and Computer Vision (WSCG 2002) (2002)
98. Sminchisescu, C., Triggs, B.: Kinematic jump processes for monocular 3D human tracking. In: IEEE Conference on Computer Vision and Pattern Recognition, p. I. IEEE (2003)
99. Starck, J., Hilton, A.: Surface capture for performance-based animation. IEEE Comput. Graph. Appl. **27**(3), 21–31 (2007)
100. Stoll, C., Hasler, N., Gall, J., Seidel, H.P., Theobalt, C.: Fast articulated motion tracking using a sums of gaussians body model. In: IEEE International Conference on Computer Vision, pp. 951–958. IEEE (2011)
101. Tao, Y., et al.: DoubleFusion: real-time capture of human performance with inner body shape from a depth sensor. In: IEEE/CVF Conference on Computer Vision and Pattern Recognition. IEEE (2018)
102. Tao, Y., et al.: SimulCap: single-view human performance capture with cloth simulation. In: IEEE/CVF Conference on Computer Vision and Pattern Recognition. IEEE (2019)
103. Taylor, C.J.: Reconstruction of articulated objects from point correspondences in a single uncalibrated image. In: IEEE Conference on Computer Vision and Pattern Recognition, pp. 677–684. IEEE (2000)
104. Theobalt, C., Aguiar, E., Magnor, M.A., Seidel, H.P.: Reconstructing human shape, motion and appearance from multi-view video. In: Ozaktas, H.M., Onural, L. (eds.) Three-Dimensional Television. Signals and Communication Technology, pp. 29–57. Springer, Berlin (2008). https://doi.org/10.1007/978-3-540-72532-9_3
105. Theobalt, C., Carranza, J., Magnor, M.A.: Enhancing silhouette-based human motion capture with 3D motion fields. In: Proceedings of the 11th Pacific Conference on Computer Graphics and Applications, pp. 185–193 (2003)
106. Tung, H.Y., Tung, H.W., Yumer, E., Fragkiadaki, K.: Self-supervised learning of motion capture. In: Advances in Neural Information Processing Systems, pp. 5236–5246 (2017)
107. Varol, G., et al.: BodyNet: volumetric inference of 3D human body shapes. In: European Conference on Computer Vision (2018)
108. Vlasic, D., Baran, I., Matusik, W., Popović, J.: Articulated mesh animation from multi-view silhouettes. ACM Trans. Graph. **27**(3), 97 (2008)
109. Wang, W., Qiangeng, X., Ceylan, D., Mech, R., Neumann, U.: DISN: deep implicit surface network for high-quality single-view 3D reconstruction. arXiv preprint arXiv:1905.10711 (2019)
110. Wang, Z., Simoncelli, E.P., Bovik, A.C.: Multiscale structural similarity for image quality assessment. In: Asilomar Conference on Signals, Systems & Computers, vol. 2, pp. 1398–1402 (2003)

111. Wei, S.E., Ramakrishna, V., Kanade, T., Sheikh, Y.: Convolutional pose machines. In: IEEE Conference on Computer Vision and Pattern Recognition. IEEE (2016)
112. Weiss, A., Hirshberg, D., Black, M.J.: Home 3D body scans from noisy image and range data. In: IEEE International Conference on Computer Vision, pp. 1951–1958. IEEE (2011)
113. Xiang, D., Joo, H., Sheikh, Y.: Monocular total capture: posing face, body, and hands in the wild. In: IEEE/CVF Conference on Computer Vision and Pattern Recognition, pp. 10965–10974. IEEE (2019)
114. Xu, W., et al.: MonoPerfCap: human performance capture from monocular video. ACM Trans. Graph. **37**, 1–15 (2018)
115. Yao, P., Fang, Z., Wu, F., Feng, Y., Li, J.: DenseBody: directly regressing dense 3d human pose and shape from a single color image. arXiv preprint arXiv:1903.10153 (2019)
116. Zeng, M., Zheng, J., Cheng, X., Liu, X.: Templateless quasi-rigid shape modeling with implicit loop-closure. In: IEEE Conference on Computer Vision and Pattern Recognition, pp. 145–152. IEEE (2013)
117. Zhang, C., Pujades, S., Black, M.J., Pons-Moll, G.: Detailed, accurate, human shape estimation from clothed 3D scan sequences. In: IEEE Conference on Computer Vision and Pattern Recognition. IEEE (2017)
118. Zhang, Q., Fu, B., Ye, M., Yang, R.: Quality dynamic human body modeling using a single low-cost depth camera. In: IEEE Conference on Computer Vision and Pattern Recognition, pp. 676–683. IEEE (2014)
119. Zheng, Z., Yu, T., Wei, Y., Dai, Q., Liu, Y.: DeepHuman: 3D human reconstruction from a single image. arXiv preprint arXiv:1903.06473 (2019)
120. Zhu, H., Zuo, X., Wang, S., Cao, X., Yang, R.: Detailed human shape estimation from a single image by hierarchical mesh deformation. In: IEEE/CVF Conference on Computer Vision and Pattern Recognition, pp. 4491–4500. IEEE (2019)
121. Zuffi, S., Kanazawa, A., Jacobs, D., Black, M.J.: 3D menagerie: modeling the 3D shape and pose of animals. In: IEEE Conference on Computer Vision and Pattern Recognition, pp. 5524–5532. IEEE (2017)

Display and Perception

State of the Art in Perceptual VR Displays

Gordon Wetzstein[1]([⊠]) [ID], Anjul Patney[2] [ID], and Qi Sun[3] [ID]

[1] Stanford University, Stanford, USA
gordon.wetzstein@stanford.edu
[2] Facebook Reality Labs, Redmond, USA
anjul.patney@gmail.com
[3] Adobe, San José, USA
qisun0@gmail.com
http://www.computationalimaging.org/
http://anjulpatney.com/
http://qisun.me/

Abstract. Wearable computing systems, i.e. virtual and augmented reality (VR/AR), are widely expected to be the next major computing platform. These systems strive to generate perceptually realistic user experiences that seamlessly blend physical and digital content to unlock unprecedented user interfaces and applications. Due to the fact that the primary interface between a wearable computer and a user is typically a near-eye display, it is crucial that these displays deliver perceptually realistic and visually comfortable experiences. However, current generation near-eye displays suffer from limited resolution and color fidelity, they suffer from the vergence–accommodation conflict impairing visual comfort, they do not support all depth cues that the human visual system relies on, and AR displays typically do not support mutually consistent occlusions between physical and digital imagery. In this chapter, we review the state of the art of perceptually-driven computational near-eye displays addressing these and other challenges.

Keywords: Virtual reality · Augmented reality · Visual perception · Displays

1 Introduction

Immersive computer graphics systems, such as virtual and augmented reality (VR/AR) displays, aim at synthesizing perceptually realistic user experiences. To achieve this goal, several components are required: interactive, photorealistic rendering; a high-resolution, low-persistence, stereoscopic display; and low-latency head tracking. Modern VR/AR systems provide all of these capabilities and create experiences that support many, but not all, of the depth cues of the human visual system. They fall short of passing a "visual Turing test for displays". Imagine a person using a wearable computing system and that system

© Springer Nature Switzerland AG 2020
M. Magnor and A. Sorkine-Hornung (Eds.): Real VR, LNCS 11900, pp. 221–243, 2020.
https://doi.org/10.1007/978-3-030-41816-8_9

delivering user experiences that are indistinguishable from the real world. That is, the user would not be able to tell whether an image is computer generated or real. While the field of computer graphics has been developing algorithms to generate photorealistic images, to pass the visual Turing test for displays, a VR/AR system must deliver perceptually realistic experiences. This challenge requires displays with high resolution, color fidelity, dynamic range, and adequate support of all the depth cues of human vision. Moreover, for such a system to be practical, device form factor, weight, power, heat, battery life, limited compute power, and bandwidth have to be optimized as well and set physical constraints on the capabilities of a wearable computing system.

Significant research and engineering efforts have focused on optimizing user experiences of AR/VR systems throughout the last few years. As these are interdisciplinary efforts at the intersection of computer vision, graphics, optics, electronics, and human-computer interaction, it is easy to get lost in the diverse nature of available literature. In this chapter, we provide a survey of recent approaches to addressing many of the outlined challenges and we specifically focus on perceptually motivated and algorithm-driven approaches to optimizing VR/AR experiences, rather than trying to survey all hardware components of VR/AR systems. Specifically, Sect. 2 outlines approaches to foveated rendering and display—techniques that build on eye tracking and that exploit the particular characteristics of human vision to render, transmit, and display high resolution imagery within available bandwidth constraints. Section 3 outlines approaches to optimizing perceptual realism and visual comfort of VR/AR displays by adequately displaying all depth cues of human vision, including focus cues and ocular parallax. Finally, we discuss other approaches to optimizing seamless experiences in VR/AR, for example by providing mutually consistent occlusions in optical see-through AR systems, in Sect. 4.

2   Foveated Rendering and Display

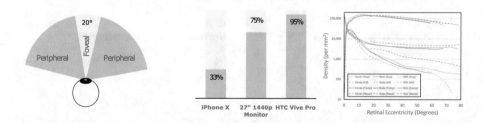

Fig. 1. (Left) While viewing most displays, a fraction of pixels lie in our foveal vision, while the remaining lie in our peripheral vision. For displays like smartphones, foveal pixels dominate, and for computer monitors peripheral pixels are a majority. However, for near-eye displays like contemporary VR, almost all pixels are peripheral. (Right) Density of photoreceptors and retinal ganglion cells (RGCs) varying with eccentricity. There is a strong preference for central vision as compared to peripheral vision. Data measured by Curcio and Allen [26] and Curcio *et al.* [27].

Due to the large field-of-view of near-eye displays, we observe a large majority of VR/AR pixels through our peripheral vision (see Fig. 1, left). Combined with the fact that visual acuity of peripheral vision is significantly lower than foveal or central vision, adaptively and dynamically distributing image quality and detail across the visual field—known as foveated rendering and display—is an important class of perceptual optimizations for near-eye displays. In this section we discuss the physiological and perceptual bases for foveation, as well as the relevant rendering and display technologies proposed in recent literature.

Human visual perception starts at the optical components (the lens, pupil, etc.), followed by retinal cells like rods, cones, and ganglion cells, and finally by higher level neural processing. Each of these optical, retinal, and neural components exhibit a strong preference for the central area of the visual field. On the retina this region is also called the fovea, and is marked by high density of retinal cells (see Fig. 1, right). As a consequence of the variation in processing density across the pathway, our foveal vision has a much higher acuity than our peripheral vision. Hence, it is better for near-eye displays to provide more detail in the foveal region than in the peripheral region.

The degradation in visual acuity from foveal to peripheral vision is also known to be highly non-uniform [139]. For instance, while we cannot perceive fine details in images through our peripheral vision, we are extremely sensitive to moving and flickering images. Researchers have identified several such non-uniformities in peripheral visual acuity, e.g. in color perception [44,116], in existence of a peripheral aliasing zone [144], and the anisotropy of peripheral perception [129]. While designing foveated rendering and display applications, we should be aware of this peculiarity. On the other hand, these effects can create additional opportunities to improve rendering performance or image quality.

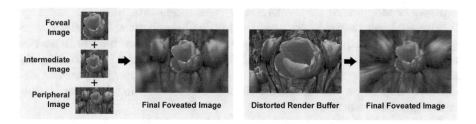

Fig. 2. Illustrations of two prominent techniques for foveated rendering. Left: We can render multiple views of a scene with varying resolution, and blend the resulting buffers to obtain the final foveated image. Right: We can render the scene into a distorted buffer that prioritizes foveal pixels, and after rendering undistort it into the final foveated image.

Many researchers have proposed foveated rendering techniques to improve rendering performance for gaze-contingent displays. The most prominent class of techniques work by reallocating image pixels such that the density is highest at the fovea, and lowest in the periphery. There are can be done in two main ways (also see Fig. 2):

- By rendering the fovea, periphery, and zero or more intermediate regions into different framebuffers of varying size and resolution, and blending them together to produce the final foveated image [41].
- By rendering the image into a distorted framebuffer that oversamples the fovea, but undersamples the periphery [22, 23, 37, 109].

Other techniques for foveated rendering work by reducing expensive computations like pixel shading operations [109, 122, 136, 145] and geometric evaluation [142].

While foveated rendering solutions seek to improve performance by reducing pixel computations in the periphery, a recent class of techniques moves the foveal-peripheral adaptivity directly to the display. Such novel display system designs match the nature of human vision. One example in VR is to expand the 2D foveated to 4D light field display [141]. The system is shown to offer both foveation (performance) and accommodation (comfort). More recently, the idea of foveating display has been advanced to augmented reality as well [69].

3   Optimizing Depth Perception and Visual Comfort in VR/AR

Human depth perception relies on a variety of cues [55, 120]. Many of these cues are pictorial and can be synthesized using photorealistic rendering techniques, including occlusions, perspective foreshortening, texture and shading gradients, as well as relative and familiar object size. Compared with conventional 2D displays, head-mounted displays (HMDs) use stereoscopic displays and head tracking and can thus support several additional depth cues: binocular disparity, motion parallax, and vergence (see Fig. 3). All of these cues are important for human depth perception to varying degrees, depending on the fixation distance [28]. Studying visual cues, such as disparity [31] or motion parallax [68], and their impact on computational display applications has been an integral part of graphics research.

In this section, we briefly review two topics of active research and development. First, we outline emerging near-eye displays that support focus cues, i.e. retinal blur, accommodation, and chromatic aberrations. Second, we highlight a recent study that suggest that ocular parallax may also be an effective ordinal depth cue in VR/AR. For a more detailed survey of 3D displays and perceptual related issues, please see [5].

3.1   Computational Near-Eye Displays with Focus Cues

Current near-eye displays cannot reproduce the changes in focus that accompany natural vision, and they cannot support users with uncorrected refractive errors.

For users with normal vision, this asymmetry creates an unnatural condition known as the vergence–accommodation conflict [77,82]. Symptoms associated with this conflict include double vision (diplopia), compromised visual clarity, visual discomfort, and fatigue [77,135]. Moreover, a lack of accurate focus also removes a cue that is important for depth perception [28,50,53,147]. Note that adequate reproduction of focus cues in VR/AR is most important for younger users, while older users tend to be presbyopic, i.e. they lost the ability to accommodate their eyes [117].

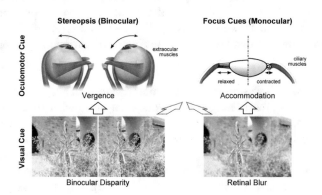

Fig. 3. Overview of several depth cues that are important for near-eye displays. Vergence and accommodation are oculomotor cues whereas binocular disparity and retinal blur are visual cues. In normal viewing conditions, disparity drives vergence and blur drives accommodation. However, these cues are cross-coupled, so there are conditions under which blur-driven vergence or disparity-driven accommodation occur.

In the following, we outline several approaches to enabling focus cues in VR/AR and to mitigating the vergence–accommodation conflict. For a more comprehensive review of this topic, we refer the interested reader to the survey papers by Kramida [79] and Hua [58].

Gaze-Contingent Focus Cue Rendering. Several researchers have investigated the perceptual effects of *gaze-contingent depth-of-field rendering*. Because gaze-contingent retinal blur rendering only requires a gaze-tracker and fast/realistic blur rendering techniques—no specialized optics are needed—it is useful to know if this type of display mode on its own offers improvements over standard displays. Several previous studies have examined the effect of this rendering technique on visual experience and performance with benchtop displays [35,51,66,97,107]. In these studies, gaze-tracking and estimated or ground-truth depth maps were used to adaptively update the depth of field of an image depending on the distance of the object that the participants were fixating. Several studies reported improvements in subjective viewing experience [51,107], however, the results for performance improvements on a variety of visual tasks were more mixed [66,107].

One study showed that combining this technique with stereo display significantly decreased the time needed for participants to achieve binocular fusion under some conditions [97]. Although gaze-contingent rendering may improve perceived realism, several recent studies have demonstrated that this software-only approach alone does not drive accommodation [65,74], therefore it does not reduce the vergence–accommodation conflict.

In another recent study, it was show that *rendering chromatic aberrations* into a perceived image can drive a user's accommodation in a monocular display setup [21]. This surprising result suggests that adequate modeling and rendering of the chromatic aberrations of a user's eye can improve accommodation and also perceived realism. However, driving the user's accommodation away from the focal plane of the display may result in degradation of perceived image sharpness.

Varifocal Displays. Two-dimensional dynamic focus displays present a single image plane to the observer, the focus distance of which can be dynamically adjusted. Two approaches for focus adjustment have been proposed: physically actuating the screen [117,140] or dynamically adjusting the focal length of the lens via focus-tunable optics (programmable liquid lenses or reflectors) [36,46, 65,75,78,93,117,137,138]. Several such systems have been incorporated into the form factor of a near-eye display [75,93,117]. Varifocal displays require gaze tracking such that the focus distance can be adjusted in real time to match the vergence distance. Figure 4 shows both benchtop and wearable varifocal display prototypes along with data measured for users of all ages demonstrating that varifocal displays effectively drive accommodation for non-presbyopic users.

Multifocal Displays. Three-dimensional volumetric and multi-plane displays represent the most common approach to focus-supporting displays. Volumetric displays optically scan out the 3D space of possible light emitting voxels in front of each eye [132]. Multi-plane displays approximate this volume using a few virtual planes that are generated by beam splitters [2,32,110], time-mulitplexed focus-tunable optics [18,57,93,94,96,115,123,128,146,155], or phase-modulating spatial light modulators [106]. Naïve implementations with beam splitters seem impractical for wearable displays because they compromise the device form factor, but this concept is promising, especially for see-through AR displays, when implemented with stacked diffractive optical elements [89] or waveguides, such as in the Magic Leap ML1. One of the biggest challenges with time-multiplexed multi-plane displays is that they require high-speed displays and may thus introduce perceived flicker. Specifically, an N-plane display requires a refresh rate of $N \times 60$–$120\,\mathrm{Hz}$. Digital micromirror devices (DMDs) are of the fastest available microdisplay technologies and seem particularly promising for this direction, as also realized by recent research [18,123] as well as Avegant's commercial AR Video Headset. Content-adaptive multifocal displays [106,155] seem particularly interesting, because they have the capability of minimizing the number of required focal planes based on the saliency of the content. However, optically generating non-planar or adaptive focal planes is challenging.

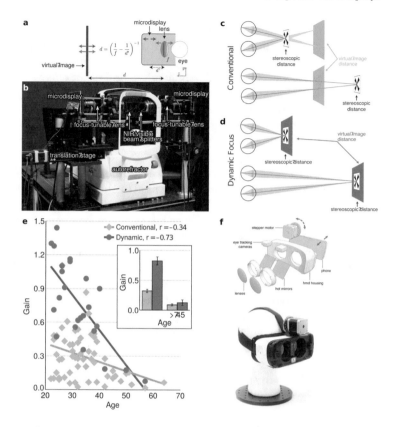

Fig. 4. Varifocal display prototypes and user experiments. (a) A typical near eye display uses a fixed-focus lens to show a magnified virtual image of a microdisplay to each eye. The focal length of the lens, f, and the distance to the microdisplay, d', determine the distance of the virtual image, d. Dynamic focus can be implemented using either a focus-tunable lens (green arrows) or a fixed-focus lens and a mechanically actuated display (red arrows), so that the virtual image can be moved to different distances. (b) A benchtop setup designed to incorporate dynamic focus via focus-tunable lenses, and an autorefractor to record accommodation. (c) The use of a fixed-focus lens in conventional near-eye displays means that the magnified virtual image appears at a constant distance (orange planes). However, by presenting different images to the two eyes, objects can be simulated at arbitrary stereoscopic distances. To experience clear and single vision in VR, the user's eyes have to rotate to verge at the correct stereoscopic distance (red lines), but the eyes must maintain accommodation at the virtual image distance (gray areas). (d) In a dynamic focus display, the virtual image distance (green planes) is constantly updated to match the stereoscopic distance of the target. Thus, the vergence and accommodation distances can be matched. (e) These accommodative gains plotted against the user's age show a clear downward trend with age, and a higher response in dynamic. Inset shows mean and standard error of the gains for users grouped into younger and older cohorts relative to forty-five years old. (f) A wearable varifocal prototype using a conventional near-eye display (Samsung Gear VR) that is augmented by a gaze tracker and a motor that is capable of adjusting the physical distance between screen and lenses. Figures reproduced from [117].

Light Field Displays. Four-dimensional light field displays aim to synthesize the full 4D light field in front of each eye [85,88,101,151,153]. Conceptually, this approach allows for parallax over the entire eyebox to be accurately reproduced, including monocular occlusions, specular highlights, and other effects that cannot be reproduced by volumetric displays. Current-generation near-eye light field displays provide limited resolution due to the spatio-angular resolution tradeoff of microlens-based systems [59,87] or the diffraction limit of dual layer liquid crystal displays (LCDs) [60].

Holographic Near-Eye Displays. A strong interest in holographic display technologies for applications in virtual and augmented reality has emerged. Much progress has recently been made both on hardware implementations and efficient algorithms. For example, several recent near-eye displays combine a holographic projector with various see-through eyepieces in innovative ways: holographic optical elements [90], waveguides [157], and lenses with beamsplitters [19,40,112]. Moreover, algorithms for computer-generated holography have significantly advanced at the same time [99,134]. Although holographic near-eye displays are one of the most promising directions of near-eye display research, they also face significant challenges. Holographic displays may suffer from speckle and have extreme requirements on pixel sizes that are not afforded by near-eye displays also providing a large field of view.

Maxwellian-Type or Accommodation-Invariant Displays. A near-eye display system that removes the accommodation-dependent change in retinal blur, also known as Maxwellian-view display [79,148], allows accommodation to remain coupled to the vergence distance of the eyes, and thus allow for accommodating freely in a scene and mitigating the vergence–accommodation conflict. Conceptually, the idea of accommodation invariance can be illustrated by imagining that a user views a display through pinholes—the depth of focus becomes effectively infinite and the eyes see a sharp image no matter where they accommodate. Such a Maxwellian-view display [148] would severely reduced light throughput and prevent the user from seeing an image at all when moving their pupil by more than half the pupil diameter (i.e., the eyebox corresponds to the size of the pupil). To overcome these limitations and providing a large eyebox and uncompromised light throughput, accommodation-invariant displays [76] use engineered point spread functions in a near-eye display system that are based on the ideas from extended-depth-of-field photography [24,25,33,47,114]. These displays slightly reduce the image sharpness at the (conventional) single focal plane in order to significantly improve image sharpness at multiple planes or throughout the continuous volume. Note that Maxwellian and accommodation-invariant displays do not render accommodation and retinal blur in a physically correct manner, so these displays cannot use such cues to improve depth perception. However, they are capable of driving accommodation [76] and thus of mitigating possible discomfort associated with the vergence–accommodation conflict.

Monovision Displays. Monovision is a common prescription correction method for presbyopia and it was recently proposed to potentially drive the accommodation on non-presbyopes in VR/AR [65,74]. In this display mode, the virtual image of one eye is placed at one distance and the image for the other eye at a different distance. This can easily be achieved by using two lenses with different focal powers for each eye and this approach does not require eye tracking. Due to the fact that the accommodation of both eyes is linked together, it was hypothesized that accommodation could be driven to either of the two focal planes. However, the measured accommodation response for this display mode was highly variant between users and no consistent verification of this hypothesis was demonstrated [118].

Vision-Correcting Displays. Vision is one of the primary modes of interaction with which humans understand and navigate the everyday world. Unfortunately, the aging process is accompanied by a hardening of the eye's crystalline lens; the end result is that by their late 40 s or 50 s, most people struggle to view objects that are within arm's reach in sharp focus [34]. This reduction in range of accommodation, known as presbyopia, affects more than a billion people [54] and will become more prevalent as the population ages.

   While several types of eyeglasses and contacts exist to correct myopia, hyperopia, and also presbyopia, corrective eyewear can also be integrated into AR/VR displays. For example, Padmanaban *et al.* studied age-related effects of accommodation in VR/AR and showed that varifocal displays drive accommodation in a natural way for non-presbyopes [117]; they also demonstrated vision-correcting capabilities for myopia and hyperopia. Varifocal display technology can also correct for presbyopia in see-through AR systems [16] or, integrated into electronic eyeglasses, for presbyopes viewing the real world [45,91,119]. Finally, light field display technology has been demonstrated to enable vision-correction for myopia, hyperopia, and higher order aberrations [62,121].

3.2   Ocular Parallax Rendering

The centers of rotation and projection in the human eye are not the same. Therefore, changes in gaze direction create small amounts of depth-dependent image shifts on our retina—an effect known as ocular parallax. This depth cue was first described by Brewster [13] and has been demonstrated to have a measurable effect on depth perception [12,80,81,104]. Similarly to other monocular visual cues, such as retinal blur and chromatic aberration, the change of the retinal image caused by ocular parallax may be small. Yet, it has been demonstrated to produce parallax well within the range of human visual acuity [12,42,104]. Supporting all of these subtle cues with an HMD can improve visual comfort [53], perceived realism, and the user experience as a whole.

   Konrad *et al.* [73] recently introduced ocular parallax rendering for VR/AR. Ocular parallax rendering uses eye tracking to determine the fixation point of the user and renders small amounts of depth-dependent image shifts induced by eye rotation. With eye tracking available, there is no additional computational cost to integrate ocular parallax into the existing rendering pipeline. The perspective of the rendered image simply changes depending on the gaze direction. In their paper, Konrad *et al.* studied the perceptual effects of ocular parallax rendering in VR and showed that detection thresholds for ocular parallax rendering are almost an order of magnitude lower than the visual acuity at the same extrafoveal locus, verifying that our sensitivity to small amounts of differential motion are well below the acuity limit, especially in the periphery of the visual field [108]. They also showed that the relative ocular parallax of objects with respect to a background target can be discriminated accurately even for relatively small object distances that fall well within the depth ranges of most virtual environments. Furthermore, they showed that ocular parallax rendering provides an effective ordinal depth cue, that is it helps users better distinguish relative depth ordering in a scene, but that it does not provide an effective absolute depth cue with metric distance information of 3D objects. Finally, they showed that ocular parallax rendering improves the impression of realistic depth in a 3D scene.

4   Towards Seamless Visual Interfaces Between Digital and Physical Content in AR

Optical see-through augmented reality (AR) systems are a next-generation computing platform that offer unprecedented user experiences by seamlessly combining physical and digital content. Many of the traditional challenges of these displays have been significantly improved over the last few years, but AR experiences offered by today's systems are far from seamless and perceptually realistic. Among many image characteristics that help improve seamlessness between digital and physical content, some of the most important ones include mutually consistent occlusions between physical and digital content in optical see-through augmented reality and optimized display resolution, dynamic range, and color fidelity. We will discuss recent approaches that address these challenges and which may improve seamless image display in AR when integrated into near-eye display systems.

4.1   Mutually Consistent Occlusions in Optical See-Through AR

While current AR displays offer impressive capabilities, they typically do not support the most important depth cue: occlusion [28]. Providing accurate, i.e., mutually consistent and hard-edge, occlusion between digital and physical objects with optical see-through AR displays is a major challenge. When digital content is located in front of physical objects, the former usually appear semi-transparent and unrealistic. To adequately render these objects, the light reflected off of the physical object toward the user has to be blocked by the display before impinging on their retina. This occlusion mechanism needs to be programmable to support dynamic scenes and it needs to be perceptually realistic to be effective. The latter implies that occlusion layers are correctly rendered at the distances of the physical objects, allowing for pixel-precise, or hard-edge, control of the transmitted light rays. In the following, we discuss several recent approaches to enabling mutually consistent occlusions in AR.

Projection-Based Lighting. Projection displays can be used to control the lighting of a scene in a spatially varying manner. Using such controlled illumination, mutually consistent occlusions, shading effects, and shadows in projector-based AR systems can be synthesized [3,9,10,102]. The primary disadvantages of these systems are that projectors are required for the AR experience, which are not necessarily portable or wearable, and that they may not work in the presence of strong ambient illumination.

Global Dimming. Commercial AR displays (e.g., Microsoft HoloLens, Magic Leap) often use a neutral density filter placed on the outside of the display module to reduce ambient light uniformly across the entire field of view. An adaptive version of global dimming was recently proposed by Mori *et al.* [113], where the amount of dimming is controlled by a single liquid crystal cell and responsive to its physical environment. While these approaches may be useful in some scenarios, they do not provide spatial control of the occlusion layer.

Fixed-Focus Occlusion. The physical scene can be focused onto an occlusion SLM which selectively blocks its transmission in a spatially varying manner before it reaches the user's eye. This idea was first proposed by the seminal work of Kiyokawa *et al.* [70–72] (see Fig. 5). Improvements of related systems were later demonstrated [14,15,38,39,56,152,154].

Unfortunately, focusing a scene on an SLM usually requires a bulky optical system, first to focus it to the SLM, then to negate the effect of the first lens, and then to flip the resulting image the right way up. Moreover, as this approach only focuses a single distance of the scene on the occlusion SLM, hard-edge occlusion is only achieved at this fixed focus distance. This limitation is similar to the characteristics of fixed-focus near-eye displays, which has been alleviated by varifocal displays.

Two key challenges for fixed-focus occlusion-capable displays are: (1) to ensure unit magnification of the see-through scene and (2) to ensure zero viewpoint offset between the see-through scene and the real-scene as seen without the display, so that the images of the real-world objects are at the correct distance. Kiyokawa *et al.* [70] derive optical design parameters that satisfy unit magnification for all real-world object distances and also propose an interesting geometric configuration of the optical components that make the offset between the real world objects and their images equal to zero. Cakmakci *et al.* [15] propose a compact optical design that satisfies the magnification requirements, but it does not achieve zero offset between the real viewpoint and the virtual viewpoint; however, the offset is small (5 cm). Howlett and Smithwick [56] propose an optical design approach based on ray-transfer matrices to achieve unit magnification and zero viewpoint offset, which is in turn inspired by optical cloaking [20].

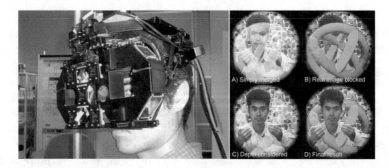

Fig. 5. Occlusion-capable optical see-through AR display (left). The display includes relay optics and spatial light modulators that allow for hard-edge per-pixel control of the observed scene before it hits the user's retina. The right panel shows views through the display with (A) no occlusion control, i.e. digital and physical image are simply superimposed, (B) occlusion enabled to block light from the physical scene everywhere where there is digital content, (C) occlusion disabled but depth considered, i.e. physical objects can occlude digital objects but selectively rendering the latter, (D) occlusion enabled and depth considered, i.e. both physical and digital objects can correctly occlude the other one. Figure reproduced from [70].

Soft-Edge Occlusion. To avoid a bulky optical system, a single LCD can be placed directly in front of the user's eyes [63,152]. However, due to the fact that the occlusion LCD is out of focus, it always appears blurred. Itoh *et al.* [63] recently proposed to compensate for this blur by modifying the digitally displayed image. Such an approach could be interpreted as a hybrid optical see-through and video see-through AR display. Calibrating such a system requires extremely precise alignment and the mismatch in resolution (spatial and angular), latency, brightness, contrast, and color fidelity between digital display and physical world may contribute to perceived inconsistency and reduced perceptual realism in such a system [127]. Maimone *et al.* [100] also used an out-of-focus LCD, where the occlusion mask is calculated as the silhouette of the virtual object. However, none of these approaches achieves hard-edge occlusion, which limits perceptual realism.

Light Field Occlusion. Maimone and Fuchs [98] propose a 4D light field occlusion mask using stacked LCD layers placed out of focus in front of the eye, where the occluding patterns are calculated by light field factorization algorithms [86,151]. The advantage of light field occlusion is that depth-dependent occlusion can be presented for virtual content at different depths simultaneously in a compact form factor. In practice, see-through LCDs mounted close to the eye are light inefficient and result in significant diffraction artifacts, which are due to the electronic components in each pixel as well as the wiring of the display panel. This effect can degrade the observed image quality of any soft-edge or light field occlusion system. Another approach for light field occlusion is presented in [156] using concepts of integral imaging systems. However, this system has a very narrow field of view (4.3°).

Varifocal Occlusion. Hamasaki and Itoh [43] and Rathinavel *et al.* [124] develop strategies for varifocal occlusion-capable AR displays. Varifocal occlusion displays comprise a varifocal optical system and spatial light modulators that enable depth-corrected hard-edge occlusions correctly at multiple distances for AR experiences. While Rathinavel's approach builds on focus-tunable optics to dynamically adjust the depth of the occlusion layer, Hamasaki's approach requires mechanical motion of the occlusion SLM. Each approach has certain benefits and limitations. For example, robust calibration of the mechanically moving parts in their approach can be challenging, especially in a wearable display form factor. The focus-tunable optics approach, on the other hand, requires specialized optical components, such as liquid lenses or Alvarez lenses.

4.2 Optimizing Other Display Characteristics

Spatial AR systems and optical see-through AR display often aim at providing radiometrically consistent, color-corrected or even color-stylized imagery (e.g., [11,64,83,84,149,152]). Some of the most important display characteristics that determine how well a digital visual experience could match a physical one are resolution, dynamic range/brightness, and color. We briefly review computational display strategies to address these display characteristics. A comprehensive survey of these topics can be found in [105,150].

Superresolution Displays. Examples of superresolution displays include optical configurations that combine the contribution of multiple overlapping devices [30], or single devices with either two stacked LCDs [130] or one LCD and a double-lens system [131]. Superresolution display with monitors, as opposed to projectors, can be achieved by fast mechanical motion of the screen [8] or using two stacked LCDs [48,49]. Finally, Hirsch *et al.* [52] proposed a light field and HDR projector using stacked spatial light modulators. They used formal optimization to derive optimal pixel states in the display and demonstrate superresolution on a diffuse projection screen rather than a monitor.

High Dynamic Range Displays. High dynamic range displays overcome the limited contrast of LCDs. In their seminal work, Seetzen *et al.* [133] introduced the concept of dual-layer modulation where a low-resolution LED backlight is modulated by a high-resolution LCD. While the LED array has low resolution, it offers ultra-large dynamic range. An image decomposition algorithm is applied to decompose a target HDR image into the pixel states of the two display layers. This technical approach has become standard practice in industry and is now marketed using the terms "micro dimming" or "local dimming" in consumer products. Extensions to more than two display layers have been discussed [153] and high dynamic range projectors have also been proposed [29]. These typically build on light steering using phase-only spatial light modulators [4], dual layer modulation [52], or adaptive control of the peak brightness over time [17].

High Color-Gamut Displays. Spectral displays can roughly be classified as multi-primary displays [143] and hyperspectral displays [111,126]. Multi-primary displays usually aim for a wide color gamut, as perceived by a human observer. Related algorithmic problems include selecting the optimal color primaries [7, 92,95] as well as gamut mapping (e.g., [6]), where pixels of an image are processed to fit within the fixed gamut provided by a display. Gamut expansion can also help to optimize image presentation with large-gamut displays [103]. Hyperspectral displays have the potential to synthesize more complex spectral power distributions than multi-primary displays. Similar to the latter, applications of hyperspectral displays include extended color gamuts, but in addition these types of devices are also useful for hyperspectral imaging, remote sensing, reflectance estimation, and medical imaging [125].

More recently, computational approaches to content-adaptive color display with multi-primary displays have been proposed [61,67]. For example, Kauvar *et al.* [67] build a custom, multi-primary projector that can dynamically address a large portion of the CIE xy chromaticity diagram. This design is based on similar devices described in the literature (e.g., [1]) but compact and easily built by modifying off-the-shelf hardware. Their perceptually-driven algorithm for joint primary selection and gamut mapping is demonstrated with a custom prototype but also applicable to other displays, such as VR/AR.

5   Conclusion

In summary, we review perceptually motivated computational near-eye displays that optimize rendering, resolution, bandwidth, depth perception, and other display characteristics. Eye tracking is an enabling technology in this space, facilitating a variety of gaze-contingent rendering and display methodologies, such as foveated rendering, varifocal displays that support focus cues, and ocular parallax rendering. To deliver perceptually realistic and seamless experiences, optical see-through AR displays face significant challenges in providing mutually consistent image appearance and occlusions between physical and digital content. Much progress has recently been made in all of the above areas, yet many challenges lie ahead. Open research questions include minimizing latency and robustness of eye tracking systems, miniaturizing occlusion-capable AR displays, and further improving resolution, field of view, color rendition, brightness, dynamic range, power consumption, device form factors, and comfort of near-eye displays.

References

1. Ajito, T., Obi, T., Yamaguchi, M., Ohyama, N.: Expanded color gamut reproduced by six-primary projection display. In: Projection Displays 2000, vol. 3954, pp. 130–137 (2000)
2. Akeley, K., Watt, S., Girshick, A., Banks, M.: A stereo display prototype with multiple focal distances. ACM Trans. Graph. (SIGGRAPH) 23(3), 804–813 (2004)

3. Avveduto, G., Tecchia, F., Fuchs, H.: Real-world occlusion in optical see-through AR displays. In: Proceedings of the 23rd ACM Symposium on Virtual Reality Software and Technology, p. 29. ACM (2017)
4. Ballestad, A., Boitard, R., Damberg, G., Stojmenovik, G.: Advances in HDR display technology for cinema applications, including light-steering projection. Inf. Disp. **35**(3), 16–19 (2019)
5. Banks, M.S., Hoffman, D.M., Kim, J., Wetzstein, G.: 3D displays. Ann. Rev. Vis. Sci. **2**(1), 397–435 (2016)
6. Banterle, F., et al.: Multidimensional image retargeting. In: SIGGRAPH Asia 2011 Courses, p. 15. ACM (2011)
7. Ben-Chorin, M., Eliav, D.: Multi-primary design of spectrally accurate displays. J. Soc. Inf. Disp. **15**(9), 667–677 (2007)
8. Berthouzoz, F., Fattal, R.: Resolution enhancement by vibrating displays. ACM Trans. Graph. (TOG) **31**(2), 15 (2012)
9. Bimber, O., Fröhlich, B.: Occlusion shadows: using projected light to generate realistic occlusion effects for view-dependent optical see-through displays. In: Proceedings of the IEEE ISMAR (2002)
10. Bimber, O., Grundhöfer, A., Wetzstein, G., Knödel, S.: Consistent illumination within optical see-through augmented environments. In: Proceedings of the IEEE ISMAR, pp. 198–207 (2003)
11. Bimber, O., Iwai, D., Wetzstein, G., Grundhoefer, A.: The visual computing of projector-camera systems. Comput. Graph. Forum **27**(8), 2219–2245 (2008)
12. Bingham, G.P.: Optical flow from eye movement with head immobilized: "ocular occlusion" beyond the nose. Vis. Res. **33**(5), 777–789 (1993)
13. Brewster, D.: On the law of visible position in single and binocular vision, and on the representation of solid figures by the union of dissimilar plane pictures on the retina. Proc. Roy. Soc. Edinb. **1**, 405–406 (1845)
14. Cakmakci, O., Ha, Y., Rolland, J.: Design of a compact optical see-through head-worn display with mutual occlusion capability. In: Proceedings of SPIE, vol. 5875 (2005)
15. Cakmakci, O., Ha, Y., Rolland, J.P.: A compact optical see-through head-worn display with occlusion support. In: Proceedings of the IEEE ISMAR, pp. 16–25 (2004)
16. Chakravarthula, P., Dunn, D., Akit, K., Fuchs, H.: FocusAR: auto-focus augmented reality eyeglasses for both real world and virtual imagery. IEEE Trans. Vis. Comput. Graph. **24**(11), 2906–2916 (2018)
17. Chang, J.H.R., Kumar, B.V.K.V., Sankaranarayanan, A.C.: 2^{16} shades of gray: high bit-depth projection using light intensity control. Opt. Express **24**(24), 27937–27950 (2016)
18. Chang, J.H.R., Kumar, B.V.K.V., Sankaranarayanan, A.C.: Towards multifocal displays with dense focal stacks. ACM Trans. Graph. (SIGGRAPH Asia) **37**(6), 198:1–198:13 (2018)
19. Chen, J.S., Chu, D.P.: Improved layer-based method for rapid hologram generation and real-time interactive holographic display applications. Opt. Express **23**(14), 18143–18155 (2015)
20. Choi, J.S., Howell, J.C.: Paraxial ray optics cloaking. Opt. Express **22**(24), 29465–29478 (2014)
21. Cholewiak, S.A., Love, G.D., Srinivasan, P.P., Ng, R., Banks, M.S.: ChromaBlur: rendering chromatic eye aberration improves accommodation and realism. ACM Trans. Graph. (SIGGRAPH Asia) **36**(6), 210:1–210:12 (2017)

22. NVIDIA Corporation: VRWorks - Lens Matched Shading (2016). https://developer.nvidia.com/vrworks/graphics/lensmatchedshading

23. NVIDIA Corporation: VRWorks - Multi-Res Shading (2016). https://developer.nvidia.com/vrworks/graphics/multiresshading

24. Cossairt, O., Nayar, S.K.: Spectral focal sweep: extended depth of field from chromatic aberrations. In: Proceedings of ICCP (2010)

25. Cossairt, O., Zhou, C., Nayar, S.K.: Diffusion coded photography for extended depth of field. ACM Trans. Graph. (SIGGRAPH) **29**(4), 31:1–31:10 (2010)

26. Curcio, C.A., Allen, K.A.: Topography of ganglion cells in human retina. J. Comp. Neurol. **300**(1), 5–25 (1990)

27. Curcio, C.A., Sloan, K.R., Kalina, R.E., Hendrickson, A.E.: Human photoreceptor topography. J. Comp. Neurol. **292**(4), 497–523 (1990)

28. Cutting, J., Vishton, P.: Perceiving layout and knowing distances: the interaction, relative potency, and contextual use of different information about depth. In: Epstein, W., Rogers, S. (eds.) Perception of Space and Motion, Chap. 3, pp. 69–117. Academic Press (1995)

29. Damberg, G., Seetzen, H., Ward, G., Heidrich, W., Whitehead, L.: 3.2: high dynamic range projection systems. In: SID Symposium Digest of Technical Papers, pp. 4–7 (2007)

30. Damera-Venkata, N., Chang, N.L.: Display supersampling. ACM Trans. Graph. (TOG) **28**(1), 9 (2009)

31. Didyk, P., Ritschel, T., Eisemann, E., Myszkowski, K., Seidel, H.P.: A perceptual model for disparity. ACM Trans. Graph. (SIGGRAPH) **30**(4), 96:1–96:10 (2011)

32. Dolgoff, E.: Real-depth imaging: a new 3D imaging technology with inexpensive direct-view (no glasses) video and other applications. In: Proceedings of SPIE, vol. 3012, pp. 282–288 (1997)

33. Dowski, E.R., Cathey, W.T.: Extended depth of field through wave-front coding. Appl. Opt. **34**(11), 1859–66 (1995)

34. Duane, A.: Normal values of the accommodation at all ages. J. Am. Med. Assoc. **59**(12), 1010–1013 (1912)

35. Duchowski, A.T., et al.: Reducing visual discomfort of 3D stereoscopic displays with gaze-contingent depth-of-field. In: Proceedings of the ACM Symposium on Applied Perception, pp. 39–46. ACM (2014)

36. Dunn, D., et al.: Wide field of view varifocal near-eye display using see-through deformable membrane mirrors. IEEE TVCG **23**(4), 1322–1331 (2017)

37. Friston, S., Ritschel, T., Steed, A.: Perceptual rasterization for head-mounted display image synthesis. ACM Trans. Graph. **38**(4), 1–14 (2019). https://doi.org/10.1145/3306346.3323033. Article no. 97. ISSN 0730-0301

38. Gao, C., Lin, Y., Hua, H.: Occlusion capable optical see-through head-mounted display using freeform optics. In: Proceedings of the IEEE ISMAR, pp. 281–282 (2012)

39. Gao, C., Lin, Y., Hua, H.: Optical see-through head-mounted display with occlusion capability. In: Proceedings of SPIE, vol. 8735 (2013)

40. Gao, Q., Liu, J., Han, J., Li, X.: Monocular 3D see-through head-mounted display via complex amplitude modulation. Opt. Express **24**(15), 17372–17383 (2016)

41. Guenter, B., Finch, M., Drucker, S., Tan, D., Snyder, J.: Foveated 3D graphics. ACM Trans. Graph. (TOG) **31**(6), 164 (2012)

42. Hadani, I., Ishai, G., Gur, M.: Visual stability and space perception in monocular vision: mathematical model. J. Opt. Soc. Am. **70**(1), 60–65 (1980)

43. Hamasaki, T., Itoh, Y.: Varifocal occlusion for optical see-through head-mounted displays using a slide occlusion mask. IEEE TVCG **25**(5), 1961–1969 (2019)

44. Hansen, T., Pracejus, L., Gegenfurtner, K.R.: Color perception in the intermediate periphery of the visual field. J. Vis. **9**(4), 26–26 (2009)
45. Hasan, N., Banerjee, A., Kim, H., Mastrangelo, C.H.: Tunable-focus lens for adaptive eyeglasses. Opt. Express **25**(2), 1221–1233 (2017)
46. Hasnain, A., et al.: Piezo-actuated varifocal head-mounted displays for virtual and augmented reality, vol. 10942 (2019). https://doi.org/10.1117/12.2509143
47. Häusler, G.: A method to increase the depth of focus by two step image processing. Opt. Commun. **6**(1), 38–42 (1972)
48. Heide, F., Gregson, J., Wetzstein, G., Raskar, R., Heidrich, W.: Compressive multi-mode superresolution display. Opt. Express **22**(12), 14981–14992 (2014)
49. Heide, F., Lanman, D., Reddy, D., Kautz, J., Pulli, K., Luebke, D.: Cascaded displays: spatiotemporal superresolution using offset pixel layers. ACM Trans. Graph. (TOG) **33**(4), 60 (2014)
50. Held, R., Cooper, E., O'Brien, J., Banks, M.: Using blur to affect perceived distance and size. ACM Trans. Graph. **29**(2), 1–16 (2010)
51. Hillaire, S., Lecuyer, A., Cozot, R., Casiez, G.: Using an eye-tracking system to improve camera motions and depth-of-field blur effects in virtual environments. In: 2008 IEEE Virtual Reality Conference, pp. 47–50 (2008)
52. Hirsch, M., Wetzstein, G., Raskar, R.: A compressive light field projection system. ACM Trans. Graph. (TOG) **33**(4), 58 (2014)
53. Hoffman, D.M., Girshick, A.R., Akeley, K., Banks, M.S.: Vergence-accommodation conflicts hinder visual performance and cause visual fatigue. J. Vis. **8**(3), 33 (2008)
54. Holden, B.A., et al.: Global vision impairment due to uncorrected presbyopia. Arch. Ophthalmol. **126**(12), 1731–1739 (2008)
55. Howard, I.P., Rogers, B.J.: Seeing in Depth. Oxford University Press, Oxford (2002)
56. Howlett, I.D., Smithwick, Q.: Perspective correct occlusion-capable augmented reality displays using cloaking optics constraints. J. Soc. Inf. Disp. **25**(3), 185–193 (2017)
57. Hu, X., Hua, H.: Design and assessment of a depth-fused multi-focal-plane display prototype. J. Disp. Technol. **10**(4), 308–316 (2014)
58. Hua, H.: Enabling focus cues in head-mounted displays. Proc. IEEE **105**(5), 805–824 (2017)
59. Hua, H., Javidi, B.: A 3D integral imaging optical see-through head-mounted display. Opt. Express **22**(11), 13484–13491 (2014)
60. Huang, F.C., Chen, K., Wetzstein, G.: The light field stereoscope: immersive computer graphics via factored near-eye light field display with focus cues. ACM Trans. Graph. (SIGGRAPH) **34**(4) (2015)
61. Huang, F.C., Pajak, D., Kim, J., Kautz, J., Luebke, D.: Mixed-primary factorization for dual-frame computational displays. ACM Trans. Graph. **36**(4), 1–13 (2017). https://doi.org/10.1145/3072959.3073654. Article no. 149. ISSN 0730-0301
62. Huang, F.C., Wetzstein, G., Barsky, B.A., Raskar, R.: Eyeglasses-free display: towards correcting visual aberrations with computational light field displays. ACM Trans. Graph. **33**(4), 1–12 (2014). https://doi.org/10.1145/2601097.2601122. Article no. 59. ISSN 0730-0301
63. Itoh, Y., Hamasaki, T., Sugimoto, M.: Occlusion leak compensation for optical see-through displays using a single-layer transmissive spatial light modulator. IEEE Trans. Vis. Comput. Graph. **23**(11), 2463–2473 (2017)

64. Itoh, Y., Langlotz, T., Iwai, D., Kiyokawa, K., Amano, T.: Light attenuation display: subtractive see-through near-eye display via spatial color filtering. IEEE TVCG **25**(5), 1951–1960 (2019)
65. Johnson, P.V., Parnell, J.A., Kim, J., Saunter, C.D., Love, G.D., Banks, M.S.: Dynamic lens and monovision 3D displays to improve viewer comfort. Opt. Express **24**(11), 11808–11827 (2016)
66. Brooker, J.P., Sharkey, P.M.: Operator performance evaluation of controlled depth of field in a stereographically displayed virtual environment, vol. 4297 (2001). https://doi.org/10.1117/12.430841
67. Kauvar, I., Yang, S.J., Shi, L., McDowall, I., Wetzstein, G.: Adaptive color display via perceptually-driven factored spectral projection. ACM Trans. Graph. (SIGGRAPH Asia) **34**(6) (2015). Article No. 165
68. Kellnhofer, P., Didyk, P., Ritschel, T., Masia, B., Myszkowski, K., Seidel, H.P.: Motion parallax in stereo 3D: model and applications. ACM Trans. Graph. **35**(6), 1–12 (2016). https://doi.org/10.1145/2980179.298023. Article no. 176. ISSN 0730-0301
69. Kim, J., et al.: Foveated AR: dynamically-foveated augmented reality display. ACM Trans. Graph. **38**(4), 99:1–99:15 (2019). https://doi.org/10.1145/3306346.3322987
70. Kiyokawa, K., Billinghurst, M., Campbell, B., Woods, E.: An occlusion-capable optical see-through head mount display for supporting co-located collaboration. In: Proceedings of the IEEE ISMAR (2003)
71. Kiyokawa, K., Kurata, Y., Ohno, H.: An optical see-through display for mutual occlusion of real and virtual environments. In: Proceedings of ISAR, pp. 60–67 (2000)
72. Kiyokawa, K., Kurata, Y., Ohno, H.: An optical see-through display for mutual occlusion with a real-time stereovision system. Comput. Graph. **25**(5), 765–779 (2001)
73. Konrad, R., Angelopoulos, A., Wetzstein, G.: Gaze-contingent ocular parallax rendering for virtual reality. arXiv (2019)
74. Konrad, R., Cooper, E., Wetzstein, G.: Novel optical configurations for virtual reality: evaluating user preference and performance with focus-tunable and mono-vision near-eye displays. In: Proceedings of SIGCHI (2015)
75. Konrad, R., Cooper, E.A., Wetzstein, G.: Novel optical configurations for virtual reality: evaluating user preference and performance with focus-tunable and monovision near-eye displays. In: Proceedings of SIGCHI (2016)
76. Konrad, R., Padmanaban, N., Molner, K., Cooper, E.A., Wetzstein, G.: Accommodation-invariant computational near-eye displays. ACM Trans. Graph. (SIGGRAPH) **36**(4), 88:1–88:12 (2017)
77. Kooi, F.L., Toet, A.: Visual comfort of binocular and 3D displays. Displays **25**(2–3), 99–108 (2004)
78. Koulieris, G.A., Bui, B., Banks, M.S., Drettakis, G.: Accommodation and comfort in head-mounted displays. ACM Trans. Graph. (SIGGRAPH) **36**(4), 87:1–87:11 (2017)
79. Kramida, G.: Resolving the vergence-accommodation conflict in head-mounted displays. IEEE TVCG **22**, 1912–1931 (2015)
80. Kudo, H., Ohnishi, N.: Study on the ocular parallax as a monocular depth cue induced by small eye movements during a gaze. In: Proceedings of the IEEE Engineering in Medicine and Biology Society, vol. 6, pp. 3180–3183 (1998)

81. Kudo, H., Saito, M., Yamamura, T., Ohnishi, N.: Measurement of the ability in monocular depth perception during gazing at near visual target-effect of the ocular parallax cue. In: Proceedings of the IEEE International Conference on Systems, Man, and Cybernetics, vol. 2, pp. 34–37 (1999)

82. Lambooij, M., Fortuin, M., Heynderickx, I., IJsselsteijn, W.: Visual discomfort and visual fatigue of stereoscopic displays: a review. J. Imaging Sci. Technol. **53**(3), 30201-1–30201-14 (2009)

83. Langlotz, T., Cook, M., Regenbrecht, H.: Real-time radiometric compensation for optical see-through head-mounted displays. IEEE TVCG **22**(11), 2385–2394 (2016)

84. Langlotz, T., Sutton, J., Zollmann, S., Itoh, Y., Regenbrecht, H.: ChromaGlasses: computational glasses for compensating colour blindness. In: Proceedings of the SIGCHI, pp. 390:1–390:12 (2018)

85. Lanman, D., Hirsch, M., Kim, Y., Raskar, R.: Content-adaptive parallax barriers: optimizing dual-layer 3D displays using low-rank light field factorization. ACM Trans. Graph. (SIGGRAPH Asia) **29** (2010). Article No. 163

86. Lanman, D., Hirsch, M., Kim, Y., Raskar, R.: Content-adaptive parallax barriers: Optimizing dual-layer 3D displays using low-rank light field factorization. In: ACM SIGGRAPH Asia, pp. 163:1–163:10 (2010)

87. Lanman, D., Luebke, D.: Near-eye light field displays. ACM Trans. Graph. (SIGGRAPH Asia) **32**(6), 220:1–220:10 (2013)

88. Lanman, D., Wetzstein, G., Hirsch, M., Heidrich, W., Raskar, R.: Polarization fields: dynamic light field display using multi-layer LCDs. ACM Trans. Graph. (SIGGRAPH Asia) **30**, 186 (2011)

89. Lee, S., Jang, C., Moon, S., Cho, J., Lee, B.: Additive light field displays: realization of augmented reality with holographic optical elements. ACM Trans. Graph. (SIGGRAPH Asia) **35**(4), 60:1–60:13 (2016)

90. Li, G., Lee, D., Jeong, Y., Cho, J., Lee, B.: Holographic display for see-through augmented reality using mirror-lens holographic optical element. Opt. Lett. **41**(11), 2486–2489 (2016)

91. Li, G., et al.: Switchable electro-optic diffractive lens with high efficiency for ophthalmic applications. Proc. Nat. Acad. Sci. **103**(16), 6100–6104 (2006)

92. Li, Y., Majumder, A., Lu, D., Gopi, M.: Content-independent multi-spectral display using superimposed projections. Comput. Graph. Forum **34**, 337–348 (2015)

93. Liu, S., Cheng, D., Hua, H.: An optical see-through head mounted display with addressable focal planes. In: Proceedings of ISMAR, pp. 33–42 (2008)

94. Llull, P., Bedard, N., Wu, W., Tosic, I., Berkner, K., Balram, N.: Design and optimization of a near-eye multifocal display system for augmented reality. In: Imaging and Applied Optics. OSA (2015)

95. Long, D., Fairchild, M.D.: Optimizing spectral color reproduction in multiprimary digital projection. In: Color and Imaging Conference, vol. 2011, pp. 290–297. Society for Imaging Science and Technology (2011)

96. Love, G.D., Hoffman, D.M., Hands, P.J.W., Gao, J., Kirby, A.K., Banks, M.S.: High-speed switchable lens enables the development of a volumetric stereoscopic display. Opt. Express **17**(18), 15716–25 (2009)

97. Maiello, G., Chessa, M., Solari, F., Bex, P.J.: Simulated disparity and peripheral blur interact during binocular fusion. J. Vis. **14**(8), 13 (2014)

98. Maimone, A., Fuchs, H.: Computational augmented reality eyeglasses. In: Proceedings of the IEEE ISMAR, pp. 29–38 (2013)

99. Maimone, A., Georgiou, A., Kollin, J.S.: Holographic near-eye displays for virtual and augmented reality. ACM Trans. Graph. (SIGGRAPH) **36**(4), 85:1–85:16 (2017)

100. Maimone, A., Lanman, D., Rathinavel, K., Keller, K., Luebke, D., Fuchs, H.: Pinlight displays: wide field of view augmented reality eyeglasses using defocused point light sources. ACM Trans. Graph. (SIGGRAPH) **33**(4), 89:1–89:11 (2014)

101. Maimone, A., Wetzstein, G., Hirsch, M., Lanman, D., Raskar, R., Fuchs, H.: Focus 3d: compressive accommodation display. ACM Trans. Graph. **32**(5) (2013). Article No. 153

102. Maimone, A., Yang, X., Dierk, N., State, A., Dou, M., Fuchs, H.: General-purpose telepresence with head-worn optical see-through displays and projector-based lighting. In: 2013 IEEE Virtual Reality (VR), pp. 23–26. IEEE (2013)

103. Majumder, A., Brown, R.G., El-Ghoroury, H.S.: Display gamut reshaping for color emulation and balancing. In: 2010 IEEE Computer Society Conference on Computer Vision and Pattern Recognition-Workshops, pp. 17–24. IEEE (2010)

104. Mapp, A.P., Ono, H.: The rhino-optical phenomenon: ocular parallax and the visible field beyond the nose. Vis. Res. **26**(7), 1163–1165 (1986)

105. Masia, B., Wetzstein, G., Didyk, P., Gutierrez, D.: A survey on computational displays: pushing the boundaries of optics, computation, and perception. Comput. Graph. **37**(8), 1012–1038 (2013)

106. Matsuda, N., Fix, A., Lanman, D.: Focal surface displays. ACM Trans. Graph. (SIGGRAPH) **36**(4), 86:1–86:14 (2017)

107. Mauderer, M., Conte, S., Nacenta, M.A., Vishwanath, D.: Depth perception with gaze-contingent depth of field. In: Proceedings of the SIGCHI Conference on Human Factors in Computing Systems, pp. 217–226. ACM (2014)

108. Mckee, S.P., Nakayama, K.: The detection of motion in the peripheral visual field. Vis. Res. **24**(1), 25–32 (1984)

109. Meng, X., Du, R., Zwicker, M., Varshney, A.: Kernel foveated rendering. In: Proceedings of the ACM on Computer Graphics and Interactive Techniques (I3D), vol. 1, no. 5, pp. 1–20, May 2018. https://doi.org/10.1145/3203199

110. Mercier, O., et al.: Fast gaze-contingent optimal decompositions for multifocal displays. ACM Trans. Graph. (SIGGRAPH Asia) **36**(6) (2017)

111. Mohan, A., Raskar, R., Tumblin, J.: Agile spectrum imaging: programmable wavelength modulation for cameras and projectors. Comput. Graph. Forum **27**, 709–717 (2008)

112. Moon, E., Kim, M., Roh, J., Kim, H., Hahn, J.: Holographic head-mounted display with RGB light emitting diode light source. Opt. Express **22**(6), 6526–6534 (2014)

113. Mori, S., Ikeda, S., Plopski, A., Sandor, C.: BrightView: increasing perceived brightness of optical see-through head-mounted displays through unnoticeable incident light reduction. In: Proceedings of IEEE VR, pp. 251–258 (2018)

114. Nagahara, H., Kuthirummal, S., Zhou, C., Nayar, S.K.: Flexible depth of field photography. In: Forsyth, D., Torr, P., Zisserman, A. (eds.) ECCV 2008. LNCS, vol. 5305, pp. 60–73. Springer, Heidelberg (2008). https://doi.org/10.1007/978-3-540-88693-8_5

115. Narain, R., Albert, R.A., Bulbul, A., Ward, G.J., Banks, M.S., O'Brien, J.F.: Optimal presentation of imagery with focus cues on multi-plane displays. ACM Trans. Graph. (SIGGRAPH) **34**(4), 59:1–59:12 (2015)

116. Noorlander, C., Koenderink, J.J., Den Olden, R.J., Edens, B.W.: Sensitivity to spatiotemporal colour contrast in the peripheral visual field. Vis. Res. **23**(1), 1–11 (1983)

117. Padmanaban, N., Konrad, R., Stramer, T., Cooper, E.A., Wetzstein, G.: Optimizing virtual reality for all users through gaze-contingent and adaptive focus displays. Proc. Natl. Acad. Sci. U.S.A. **114**, 2183–2188 (2017)
118. Padmanaban, N., Konrad, R., Wetzstein, G.: Evaluation of accommodation response to monovision for virtual reality. In: Imaging and Applied Optics, p. DM2F.3 (2017)
119. Padmanaban, N., Konrad, R., Wetzstein, G.: Autofocals: evaluating gaze-contingent eyeglasses for presbyopes. Science Advances **5**(6) (2019)
120. Palmer, S.E.: Vision Science - Photons to Phenomenology. MIT Press, Cambridge (1999)
121. Pamplona, V.F., Oliveira, M.M., Aliaga, D.G., Raskar, R.: Tailored displays to compensate for visual aberrations. ACM Trans. Graph. (SIGGRAPH) **31**(4), 81:1–81:12 (2012)
122. Patney, A., et al.: Towards foveated rendering for gaze-tracked virtual reality. ACM Trans. Graph. **35**(6), 1–12 (2016). https://doi.org/10.1145/2980179. 2980246. Article no. 179. ISSN 0730-0301
123. Rathinavel, K., Wang, H., Blate, A., Fuchs, H.: An extended depth-at-field volumetric near-eye augmented reality display. IEEE Trans. Vis. Comput. Graph. **24**(11), 2857–2866 (2018)
124. Rathinavel, K., Wetzstein, G., Fuchs, H.: Varifocal occlusion-capable optical see-through augmented reality display based on focus-tunable optics. IEEE TVCG **25**(11), 3125–3134 (2019). Proceedings of ISMAR
125. Rice, J.P., Brown, S.W., Allen, D.W., Yoon, H.W., Litorja, M., Hwang, J.C.: Hyperspectral image projector applications. In: Douglass, M.R., Oden, P.I. (eds.) Emerging Digital Micromirror Device Based Systems and Applications IV, vol. 8254, pp. 213–220. SPIE (2012). https://doi.org/10.1117/12.907898
126. Rice, J.P., Brown, S.W., Neira, J.E., Bousquet, R.R.: A hyperspectral image projector for hyperspectral imagers. In: Algorithms and Technologies for Multispectral, Hyperspectral, and Ultraspectral Imagery XIII, vol. 6565, p. 65650C. International Society for Optics and Photonics (2007)
127. Rolland, J.P., Fuchs, H.: Optical versus video see-through head-mounted displays in medical visualization. Presence Teleoperators Virtual Environ. **9**(3), 287–309 (2000). https://doi.org/10.1162/105474600566808
128. Rolland, J.P., Krueger, M.W., Goon, A.: Multifocal planes head-mounted displays. Appl. Opt. **39**(19), 3209–3215 (2000)
129. Rovamo, J., Virsu, V., Laurinen, P., Hyvärinen, L.: Resolution of gratings oriented along and across meridians in peripheral vision. Investig. Ophthalmol. Vis. Sci. **23**(5), 666–670 (1982)
130. Sajadi, B., Gopi, M., Majumder, A.: Edge-guided resolution enhancement in projectors via optical pixel sharing. ACM Trans. Graph. (TOG) **31**(4) (2012). Article No. 79
131. Sajadi, B., Qoc-Lai, D., Ihler, A.H., Gopi, M., Majumder, A.: Image enhancement in projectors via optical pixel shift and overlay. In: IEEE International Conference on Computational Photography (ICCP), pp. 1–10. IEEE (2013)
132. Schowengerdt, B.T., Seibel, E.J.: True 3-D scanned voxel displays using single or multiple light sources. J. SID **14**(2), 135–143 (2006)
133. Seetzen, H., et al.: High dynamic range display systems. ACM Trans. Graph. **23**(3), 760–768 (2004)

134. Shi, L., Huang, F.C., Lopes, W., Matusik, W., Luebke, D.: Near-eye light field holographic rendering with spherical waves for wide field of view interactive 3D computer graphics. ACM Trans. Graph. (SIGGRAPH Asia) **36**(6), 236:1–236:17 (2017)

135. Shibata, T., Kim, J., Hoffman, D.M., Banks, M.S.: The zone of comfort: predicting visual discomfort with stereo displays. J. Vis. **11**(8), 11 (2011)

136. Stengel, M., Grogorick, S., Eisemann, M., Magnor, M.: Adaptive image-space sampling for gaze-contingent real-time rendering. Comput. Graph. Forum **35**, 129–139 (2016)

137. Stevens, R.E., Rhodes, D.P., Hasnain, A., Laffont, P.Y.: Varifocal technologies providing prescription and VAC mitigation in HMDs using Alvarez lenses, vol. 10676 (2018). https://doi.org/10.1117/12.2318397

138. Stevens, R.E., Jacoby, T.N., Aricescu, I.Ş., Rhodes, D.P.: A review of adjustable lenses for head mounted displays. In: 2017 Digital Optical Technologies, vol. 10335, p. 103350Q. International Society for Optics and Photonics (2017)

139. Strasburger, H., Rentschler, I., Jüttner, M.: Peripheral vision and pattern recognition: a review. J. Vis. **11**(5), 13 (2011)

140. Sugihara, T., Miyasato, T.: 32.4: a lightweight 3-D HMD with accommodative compensation. SID Dig. **29**(1), 927–930 (1998)

141. Sun, Q., Huang, F.C., Kim, J., Wei, L.Y., Luebke, D., Kaufman, A.: Perceptually-guided foveation for light field displays. ACM Trans. Graph. **36**(6), 192:1–192:13 (2017). https://doi.org/10.1145/3130800.3130807

142. Swafford, N.T., Iglesias-Guitian, J.A., Koniaris, C., Moon, B., Cosker, D., Mitchell, K.: User, metric, and computational evaluation of foveated rendering methods. In: Proceedings of the ACM Symposium on Applied Perception, pp. 7–14. ACM (2016)

143. Teragawa, M., Yoshida, A., Yoshiyama, K., Nakagawa, S., Tomizawa, K., Yoshida, Y.: Multi-primary-color displays: the latest technologies and their benefits. J. Soc. Inf. Disp. **20**(1), 1–11 (2012)

144. Thibos, L.N., Still, D.L., Bradley, A.: Characterization of spatial aliasing and contrast sensitivity in peripheral vision. Vis. Res. **36**(2), 249–258 (1996)

145. Vaidyanathan, K., et al.: Coarse pixel shading. In: Proceedings of High Performance Graphics, pp. 9–18. Eurographics Association (2014)

146. von Waldkirch, M., Lukowicz, P., Tröster, G.: Multiple imaging technique for extending depth of focus in retinal displays. Opt. Express **12**(25), 6350–6365 (2004)

147. Watt, S.J., Akeley, K., Ernst, M.O., Banks, M.S.: Focus cues affect perceived depth. J. Vis. **5**(10), 834–862 (2005)

148. Westheimer, G.: The Maxwellian view. Vis. Res. **6**, 669–682 (1966)

149. Wetzstein, G., Bimber, O.: Radiometric compensation through inverse light transport. In: 15th Pacific Conference on Computer Graphics and Applications (PG 2007), pp. 391–399 (2007)

150. Wetzstein, G., Lanman, D.: Factored displays: Improving resolution, dynamic range, color reproduction, and light field characteristics with advanced signal processing. IEEE Sig. Process. Mag. **33**(5), 119–129 (2016)

151. Wetzstein, G., Lanman, D., Hirsch, M., Raskar, R.: Tensor displays: compressive light field synthesis using multilayer displays with directional backlighting. ACM Trans. Graph. (SIGGRAPH) **31**(4), 80:1–80:11 (2012)

152. Wetzstein, G., Heidrich, W., Luebke, D.: Optical image processing using light modulation displays. Comput. Graph. Forum **29**(6), 1934–1944 (2010)

153. Wetzstein, G., Lanman, D., Heidrich, W., Raskar, R.: Layered 3D: tomographic image synthesis for attenuation-based light field and high dynamic range displays. ACM Trans. Graph. (SIGGRAPH) **30**, 95 (2011)
154. Wilson, A., Hua, H.: Design and prototype of an augmented reality display with per-pixel mutual occlusion capability. Opt. Express **25**(24), 30539–30549 (2017)
155. Wu, W., Llull, P., Tosic, I., Bedard, N., Berkner, K., Balram, N.: Content-adaptive focus configuration for near-eye multi-focal displays. In: IEEE International Conference on Multimedia and Expo (ICME), pp. 1–6 (2016)
156. Yamaguchi, Y., Takaki, Y.: See-through integral imaging display with background occlusion capability. Appl. Opt. **55**(3), A144–A149 (2016)
157. Yeom, H.J., et al.: 3D holographic head mounted display using holographic optical elements with astigmatism aberration compensation. Opt. Express **23**(25), 32025–32034 (2015)

Design and Characterization of Light Field and Holographic Near-Eye Displays

Erdem Sahin$^{(\boxtimes)}$(iD), Jani Mäkinen, Ugur Akpinar(iD), Yuta Miyanishi(iD), and Atanas Gotchev(iD)

Faculty of Information Technology and Communication Sciences,
Tampere University, Tampere, Finland
{erdem.sahin,jani.makinen,ugur.akpinar,yuta.miyanishi,
atanas.gotchev}@tuni.fi

Abstract. The light field and holographic displays constitute two important categories of advanced three-dimensional displays that are aimed at delivering all physiological depth cues of the human visual system, such as stereo cues, motion parallax, and focus cues, with sufficient accuracy. As human observers are the end-users of such displays, the delivered spatial information (e.g., perceptual spatial resolution) and view-related image quality factors (e.g., focus cues) are significantly dependent on the characteristics of the human visual system. Retinal image formation models enable rigorous characterization and subsequently efficient design of light field and holographic displays. In this chapter the ray-based near-eye light field and wave-based near-eye holographic displays are reviewed, and the corresponding retinal image formation models are discussed. In particular, most of the discussion is devoted to characterization of the perceptual spatial resolution and focus cues.

Keywords: Light field display · Holographic display · Display characterization · Perceptual resolution · Focus cues

1   Introduction

The light field (LF) and holographic displays are ideally aimed at delivering the true LFs or wave fields, respectively, due to three-dimensional (3D) scenes to human observers. Unlike conventional stereoscopic displays, they are capable of delivering all physiological cues of the human visual system (HVS), namely stereo cues, continuous motion parallax, and focus cues (accommodation and retinal defocus blur), with sufficient accuracy [4,56]. In stereoscopic near-eye displays, the continuous motion parallax is readily available via head-tracking. Although the parallax due to the eye movement is missing, it is not usually considered as a significant problem. Enabling focus cues, on the other hand, has particularly been set as an important goal in the design of next-generation advanced near-eye displays, to alleviate the so-called vergence-accommodation conflict [16]. From

© Springer Nature Switzerland AG 2020
M. Magnor and A. Sorkine-Hornung (Eds.): Real VR, LNCS 11900, pp. 244–271, 2020.
https://doi.org/10.1007/978-3-030-41816-8_10

this perspective, the LF and holographic display technologies are expected to play a critical role in the future near-eye display technology.

The computational and optical realizations of fully immersive LF and holographic displays have been fundamentally limited by the size (richness) of the visual data to be delivered. Full immersion is only possible with the delivery of sufficiently high (spatial) resolution image, in a sufficiently wide field of view (FoV), and enabling accurate 3D perception, which together set very demanding constraints on the display design. Given the limited optical as well as computational resources, the problem is then to optimize these resources in the best possible way that would in turn optimize the user experience, e.g., immersion. In order to achieve this, usually one has to compromise between the spatial quality of the observed image, which can be characterized by the perceivable resolution, and the accuracy of reproduced depth cues (in particular focus cues). Thus, to determine this compromise for optimal display design and further characterize a given design, computational frameworks enabling characterization of perceived spatial image quality as well as 3D perception are of critical importance. This chapter aims at providing a general perspective of such frameworks (or models) that are useful in design and characterization of LF and holographic displays. Section 2 presents general aspects of the human spatial vision that are relevant for developing such models. Sections 3 and 4, respectively, overview the basics of LF and holographic display technologies, existing near-eye displays utilizing such technologies, and computational models for their design and characterization.

2   Basics of Human Spatial Vision

The flow of visual information from outside world till to the visual cortex can be described in three stages: retinal image encoding, neural representation of visual information, and perception [52]. This section briefly overviews several important functions of human vision in such stages to particularly elaborate on the *perceptual spatial resolution* and *focus cues*, which are further addressed in the following sections as two critical aspects in design and characterization of LF and holographic displays.

2.1   Perceptual Spatial Resolution

Retinal image encoding takes place in the eye. The optics of the eye is not that different from a camera: the cornea and crystalline lens of the eye are responsible of focusing the light (zoom lens), the iris works as an aperture, and the photoreceptors (pixels) on the retina (sensor) sample the incident light. The sampled optical information by the photoreceptors is converted to electrical signals and further carried to brain via retinal ganglion cells that are connected to photoreceptors via various interneurons. The retinal ganglion cells performs a subsequent sampling based on their receptive fields on the retina, and thus, in a sense, they are the output cells of the human eye [54]. Unlike the sensor in a conventional camera, the retina is curved, and the photoreceptors are non-uniformly distributed on the retina. Furthermore, there are different types of photoreceptors with different sensitivities to light. The densely arranged cones are responsible for high spatial color vision under photopic (high light) conditions, rather sparse set of rods are more sensitive to light and thus they are responsible for scotopic (low light) vision. Three different types of cones (S, M, L) have different sensitivities to wavelength, which enables color encoding and perception. The cones are densely arranged (as dense as 120 cones per degree for M and S cones [9]) only in the central retina (fovea), covering a central visual field of 5°. In fovea the retinal ganglion cells are known to sample a single cone, which enables as high as 60 cycles per degree (CPD) foveal visual acuity. Here CPD refers to the number of full cycles, in the observed pattern or stimulus (e.g., sinusoidal grating), in one degree of the visual angle. The visual acuity falls rapidly outside the fovea due to decrease in the density of cones. A formula for receptive field densities of retinal ganglion is given in [54], which can be utilized to explicitly describe eccentricity-dependent visual acuity.

The neural representation starts just after the sampling of the light signal by the photoreceptors and subsequently by retinal ganglion cells, the lens, cornea and iris together also define the initial encoding of the visual information. The typical 2 mm–8 mm range of pupil (aperture) size, is controlled by iris based on the amount of illumination. The total optical power of cornea and lens is around 60 diopters (D), when focused at infinity; and it can be increased up to 80 D to focus at near objects. The distortions introduced by the optics is reduced for smaller aperture sizes. The diffraction, on the other hand, limits the resolution at small apertures. Below around 2.4 mm of aperture size, the optics of the eye does not introduce an extra blur compared to diffraction. The diffraction-limited resolution at 2.4 mm aperture size for the central wavelength of 550 nm is also around 60 CPD, which matches the density of cone photoreceptor sampling in fovea. Thus, it seems that the optics do the necessary antialiasing, and the cones sample the incoming light in an efficient way [52].

The neural representation starts just after the sampling of the light signal by the photoreceptors on the retina. The visual information is transferred to visual cortex through various segregated visual pathways specialized for different visual tasks such as depth perception. The information carried in such pathways is more about the contrast of the signal captured on the retina, rather than mean illumination level, which is also known as luminance masking [52]. This explains our ability to response to a wide range of luminance levels. For sinusoidal gratings, which are usually used in contrast measurements, the (Michelson) contrast is defined as

$$C = \frac{I_{max} - I_{min}}{I_{max} + I_{min}} \tag{1}$$

where I_{max} and I_{min} represent the highest and lowest luminance levels of the grating. The typical task used in measuring the *contrast sensitivity function* (CSF) of the HVS is to distinguish gratings of a given spatial frequency from a uniform background. Below some level of contrast the observer is no longer able to detect the pattern. The contrast at this point is called as the *threshold* contrast, and its reciprocal is defined as the *sensitivity* at that spatial frequency. The physiological methods enable measuring CSF at single neuron level. The behavioral measurements, on the other hand, can provide the psychophysical CSF of the HVS. The CSF measured through this way, usually with incoherent light sources, includes the response of the whole system, i.e., the optics as well as the neural response. In particular, the optical and neural modulation transfer functions (MTFs) determines the amount of contrast reduction in each stage depending on the spatial frequency of the input. By further utilizing the inter-ferometric methods [33], which essentially avoids the blurring due to optics, the neural-only MTF and correspondingly the optics-only MTF of the HVS can be also estimated. Methods such as wavefront sensing enable direct measurement of the optics-only MTF, modeling also possible aberrations [30]. Physiological data when combined with such behavioral measurements has lead rigorous models of eye optics [39]. Decades of such efforts have also established reliable methodologies to measure contrast thresholds [42].

A typical CSF of the HVS in photopic condition is shown in Fig. 1. Based on this figure, one can infer that the bandwidth of the CSF, which is around 60 CPD, is mainly dictated by the initial sampling on the retina through the optics of the eye. On the other hand, based on the knowledge of optical MTF, the decrease of sensitivity in the lower bands can be attributed to neural factors [52].

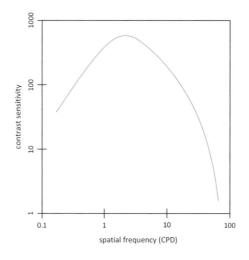

Fig. 1. A typical CSF in the central visual field (adapted from [28]).

The *perceptual spatial resolution*, or visual acuity, of HVS can be thoroughly characterized based on the spatial CSF. That is, the CSF can provide a more complete information compared to the visual acuity tests usually employed in opthalmologic tests. In such tests the visual acuity is usually defined by deter-mining the smallest size at which the patient can detect the orientation of the target (E chart, Landolt C) or recognize a specific target among many others

(Snellen letters), where the only variable is basically the size of the targets and furthermore the difference of brightness between the letters and the background is fixed. Such tests provide reliable information about the limits of visual acuity, whereas the CSF characterizes the spatial vision over the entire spatial frequencies detectable by the HVS.

It is important to note that, in practice, the CSF depends not only on the spatial frequency of the input but also many other factors such as the location of the stimulus in the visual field [47], mean illumination level [51], the temporal frequency of the target [24], the wavelength of the light [55], etc. Furthermore, due to the so-called (contrast) masking effect, a strong masker stimulus can also alter (reduce) the visibility of the test pattern under consideration, which typically has similar spatial frequency to the masker stimulus. As a result, the contrast sensitivity can be reduced at the test frequency [38]. Such a case can easily occur in natural scenes. Thus, in practice, all such factors need to be taken into account for complete characterization of the CSF. The joint interdisciplinary effort in understanding the human spatial vision has led development of rigorous computational models incorporating such CSF models. By providing the multi-channel (multiple spatial and temporal frequencies as well as different orientations of stimulus) response of HVS to given static or dynamic visual scenes, such models enable perceptual quality assessment of visual data in a realistic way [5,8,45]. Furthermore, they can guide design of perceptually optimized displays as well as algorithms in computer graphics, image and video coding, compression, etc. For a more detailed discussion on the existing perceptual models, the reader is referred to [5,45].

2.2   Stereo and Focus Cues

Among several other tasks accomplished in the visual cortex such as color perception and motion perception, the *depth perception* is particularly important in the context of 3D displays in pursuing the reality of the recreated scene. In HVS not only the signal from the sensor, namely the retinal image, but also the signals related to eye movements and the accumulated information in the brain complexly contribute to depth perception. In improving the visual experience in VR, it is crucial to understand how human vision works to derive the perception from these various information sources. HVS relies on an extensive set of visual depth cues for depth perception. Below, the basics of stereo and focus cues, which constitute the physiological cues, are discussed, as they are particularly important in the design and characterization of near-eye displays.

Stereo cues of vergence and, in particular, binocular disparity constitute the main source of information for depth perception for most of the people (except for those suffering from stereoblindness [10]). To be able to create the sharp image of an object on the retina, the two eyes converge (or diverge) at it by rotating in the opposite directions. By this way, the object is fixated at the fovea, where the input can be sampled at the highest spatial frequency. The fixated image points on the two retinae exhibit zero binocular disparity. An object nearer or further than the fixation point, on the other hand, is projected at different locations

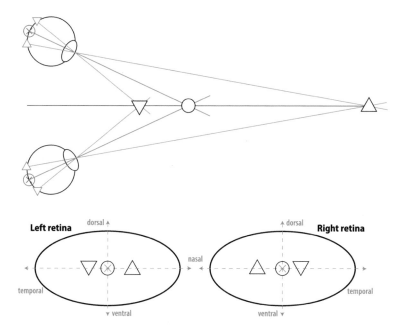

Fig. 2. Geometry of the vergence and the resulting retinal images.

on the two retinae (see Fig. 2). The depth difference between the fixation point
and the object corresponds to the magnitude of the binocular disparity of the
object. Based on this disparity cue, the eyes can fastly converge (or diverge) at
the closer (or further) object. Thus, both the oculomotor function of vergence
and the (stereo) image-related measure of binocular disparity provide signals
for depth perception. The just-noticeable change (JNC) in binocular disparity,
which is inversely proportional to the interpupillary distance (IPD), is as small
as 10 arcsec. around the fixated depth, but it increases dramatically in front of
or behind it due to decrease in the spatial acuity at larger eccentricities [14].

The abovementioned stereo cues are typically accurately delivered by all
conventional stereoscopic near-eye displays. However, the monocular accommodation and retinal (defocus) blur cues are usually missed, despite their critical
role in depth perception. *Accommodation* refers to the oculomotor function that
adjusts the refractive power of the crystalline lens in the eye, to obtain the
sharp (focused) retinal image of the fixated object of interest (see Fig. 3). The
accommodation provides depth information based on the signals acquired from
the ciliary muscles controlling the crystalline lens. Objects that are close enough
to the accommodated object in depth, i.e., objects inside the DoF, also produce
sharp retinal images. The extend of the DoF is dependent on several factors such
as pupil diameter, spatial frequency, wavelength, aberrations in the eye optics,
etc. For a pupil size of 4 mm diameter, for instance, it is typically around ±0.3
D, whereas it can extend up to around ±0.8 D for smaller pupil sizes [36]. The
objects that are outside of this range are imaged with *retinal defocus blur*.

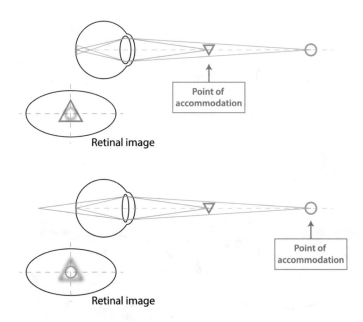

Fig. 3. Accommodation and the resulting retinal images.

The amount of optical defocus blur also encodes the depth information. The sensitivity of HVS to defocus blur is limited by the extent of the DoF, i.e., the blurs corresponding to different depths within the DoF cannot be discriminated. The defocus blur itself is an even-error cue, i.e., it does not provide information regarding the direction of depth. However, in practice, the defocus blur is accompanied by the optical aberrations of the eye, which together result in optical blur with odd-error information. The role of chromatic aberrations in the visible spectrum, which can appear both laterally and longitudinally with respect to the optical axis, have especially dominant role in this. That is, they actually serve as an important depth cue [7].

The defocus blur is essentially the main source of information that drives accommodation. The magnitude and the gradient of the contrast in the retinal image are the key factors driving the accommodation. The eye is likely to focus at a depth where both the magnitude and the gradient of the contrast are maximized. The strength of the stimulus also depends on the spatial frequency. The accommodation is typically most accurate at mid spatial frequencies around 3−5 CPD [40], like the contrast sensitivity itself (see Fig. 1). Unlike the stereo cues, which provide depth information up to a few tens of meters, the accommodation cue is typically available within around 2 m of depth range, since the information coming from the defocus blur beyond this range is limited. The geometry of defocus blur (dictated by the pupil size) is analogous to the geometry of binocular disparity (dictated by the IPD). The JNC in defocus blur is, therefore, an order of magnitude or more bigger than the JNC in binocular disparity (at the fixated depth), however it does not increase as rapidly as the JNC in binocular disparity. This way binocular disparity and defocus blur cues are complementary to each other: around the fixated depth, depth estimation mainly relies on the binocular disparity, whereas the defocus blur provides more precise information away from it [14].

The oculomotor functions of vergence and accommodation are not only driven by binocular disparity and retinal blur, respectively. Instead, vergence and accommodation are actually coupled, and some part of the information is produced via cross links, i.e., disparity-driven accommodation and blur-driven vergence [44]. This explains, to some extent, the existence of accommodation cue even in conventional stereoscopic displays. Furthermore, it is the main motivation of accommodation-invariant displays [25]. Beside such approaches, what is natural to HVS is that accommodation and vergence work in harmony, i.e., they both address the same depth. Nevertheless, this is usually the case only up to some age, till when the accommodative response is still strong, as by the age of around 40 most of the strength is already lost [48]. In healthy eyes, otherwise, breaking the harmony creates conflict between the accommodation and vergence and results in undesirable effects such as visual discomfort, fatigue, etc. [16]. Therefore, alleviating such conflict in the HVS has been always one of the main issues to be addressed in the near-eye display technology. And this has been mostly aimed to be achieved via enabling the focus cues through advanced 3D displays, each of which has its own pros and cons [18].

In the following sections the two important categories of such 3D displays, the LF and holographic displays, and their characterization through perceptual spatial resolution and focus cues are discussed. Generally speaking, the overall viewing process of such 3D displays can be formulated by modeling the light transport between the display light sources and the retina, which involves modulation by the display and eye optics. As discussed above, this early stage of retinal image encoding is actually followed by the subsequent neural functions that also plays a critical role in the spatial vision and the actual perception. However, in the literature of 3D displays, the role of neural factors are usually ignored or weakly considered, and mainly the retinal image itself is taken as the main ingredient of the perceptual analysis as well as display characterization and design. Furthermore, mostly the eye is usually simplified to constitute an aberration-free thin lens and a planar retina with uniformly distributed photoreceptors (pixels). Although such assumptions may lead to suboptimal analysis and characterization, the employed basic framework can be extended by including, e.g., the necessary optical aberrations, eccentricity-dependent retinal resolution, neural transfer functions, etc., in the pipeline based on the discussions in this section. The following section provides a detailed discussion on LF display characterization based on the rather simple thin lens and planar retina models, and the subsequent section demonstrates a simulation model for holographic displays including foveation and curved retina surface.

3   Characterization of LF Displays

3.1   Basics of the LF Displays

Under the geometric (ray) optics formalism, the light distribution due to a
3D scene can be fully described via the seven-dimensional plenoptic function
$L(x, y, z, \theta, \phi, \lambda, t)$, which assumes the light as a collection of rays and describes
the ray intensities through parametrization over the propagation point (x, y, z),
propagation direction (θ, ϕ), spectral content (color) λ, and time t [1]. The four-
dimensional (4D) LF is a reduced form of the plenoptic function, describing
the intensities of rays at a given time instant and with a given color together
with extra assumptions to satisfy unique intensity mappings [13,29]. That is,
it is mostly parametrized through the space-angle $L(x, y, \theta, \phi)$ or two-plane
$L(x, y, s, t)$ representations, as shown in Fig. 4.

The performance of the LF display systems can be characterized through
their reconstruction capabilities of the 4D continuous LF, i.e., correspondingly the deliverable spatio-angular resolution. Considering the space-angle
parametrization in Fig. 4(a), if the (x, y) plane is chosen at (or around) the
depth of the object of interest, the spatial resolution corresponds to the minimum resolvable distance between two object points, while the angular resolution
refers to the minimum separation angle between the two light rays emitted from
the same object point. Equivalently, in the two-plane parametrization given by
Fig. 4(b), one can define the resolutions on the (x, y) and (s, t) planes as the
spatial and the angular resolutions, respectively, when the (x, y) plane is set at
the scene depth and the (s, t) plane is chosen to be the viewing plane representing the camera or eye pupil location. In both cases the spatial resolution
determines to which extent the spatial information of the scene is reproduced,
i.e., it dictates the deliverable perceivable spatial resolution. The angular resolution, on the other hand, defines the quality of view-related image aspects, such
as occlusions, (direction-dependent) reflectance, (motion) parallax as well as the
focus cues, which is a particularly important aspect for this chapter.

Ideally, the LF displays aim to provide the immersive visual experience by
stimulating all physiological depth cues of the HVS. In the context of near-eye LF
displays, this practically means accurate delivery of accommodation and defocus

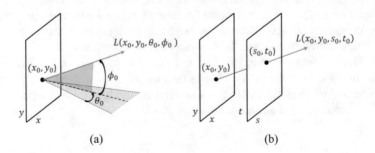

(a)   (b)

Fig. 4. The space-angle (a) and two-plane (b) parametrizations of the 4D LF.

blur cues to each eye. That is, the angular resolution of the LF display should be sufficiently high. On the other hand, the perceivable spatial resolution is another important aspect that can be maximized by increasing the spatial resolution of the LF display. However, the device based limitations, such as the total number of available display pixels, display pixel pitch, pitch of lens, etc., as well as the diffractive nature of light do not permit arbitrarily increasing both the spatial and angular resolutions. All traditional LF display techniques, such as integral imaging and super multiview, indeed, suffer from such trade-off [4,6]. In the most general form, consistent with the two-plane parametrization, traditional LF displays include two layers of optics: an image source plane (e.g., liquid crystal display) and an optical modulator plane (e.g., lens array or parallax barrier), which is placed on top of the image source plane being responsible of directing the light rays emitted from the source pixels to desired directions. The conventional multiplexing-based techniques used in such traditional near-eye LF displays basically implement the Nyquist-based sampling and reconstruction of the LF and they distribute the available source pixels between the spatial and angular dimensions [19, 26]. This has been recently advanced with the more sophisticated approaches that apply modern compressive sensing methods on multilayer multiplicative displays to benefit from the redundant structure of the LF [20, 27, 31]. Despite some challenges still to overcome, such as computational complexity, diffraction related blur and reduced brightness, such methods have a big potential to significantly improve the delivered spatio-angular resolution.

The efforts on perceptually optimizing the near-eye stereoscopic displays through foveated rendering and optics is particularly important for LF displays, since the amount of visual data to be rendered is far more in this case. The perceptual optimization of near-eye LF displays not only involves the perceptual spatial resolution, which is addressed via foveated rendering, but also optimization of eccentricity-dependent angular LF sampling. This is fundamentally linked to how the focus response of the HVS varies with eccentricity for such displays [49]. The recently proposed optical as well as computational methods, exploiting these perceptual aspects in near-eye LF displays, have already reported notably reduced data rate and computational complexity [23, 27, 31, 49].

Rigorous modeling of LF perception is critical to further advance the state of the art in near-eye LF displays and address the abovementioned issues in the area. The following section discusses such simulation models, and further presents a particular case on analysis and characterization of perceptual resolution and focus response in an integral imaging (InIm) type of near-eye display.

3.2   Retinal Image Formation Models for LF Displays

The existing perceptual simulation models used for characterization and design of the LF displays can be categorized into two main categories. The first category of approaches aim to link the LF parametrizations of the display and eye (defined using lens and retina planes) through ray propagations, and utilize the properties of the eye optics and retina to obtain the so-called perceivable or perceptual LF [46, 49]. In its essence, the perceivable LF defines a perceptually-sampled reduced

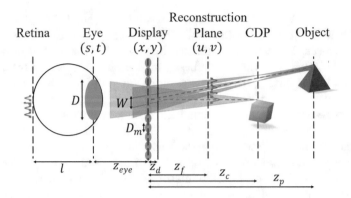

Fig. 5. InIm display operation principle.

form of the incident LF that is (perceptually) equivalent to any other higher spatial and angular resolution LF incident at the pupil. The second category of approaches model the forward retinal image encoding to find the retinal image itself [2,21,22,43]. The most rigorous approach is to simulate the retinal image formation utilizing the wave optics, which accounts for possible diffraction effects due to both display and eye optics. In the remaining part of this section, an example wave optics based simulation method [2] is presented in more details to elaborate more on the characterization of perceptual resolution and focus cues in InIm type of near-eye LF displays.

The overall model of the InIm display setup is illustrated in Fig. 5. The virtual 3D scene is reconstructed through the elemental display images, behind the corresponding microlenses, that are focused at the central depth plane (CDP). Assuming aberration-free thin lens model for the eye lens and planar surface for the retina, a conjugate retina plane can be defined at the scene depth where the eye is accommodated. Such plane can be denoted as the reconstruction plane as in Fig. 5. Defining the resolution of the reconstruction as the diffraction-limited resolution dictated by the eye pupil, i.e., $\Delta_u = 1.22\lambda(z_{eye} + z_f)/D$, where D is the diameter of the eye pupil, the retinal image can be equivalently analyzed on the reconstruction plane.

An important characterization criterion of LF displays is the angular resolution or the view density, which is defined as the number of distinct view images delivered within the eye pupil. It is required by the so-called super multiview condition [17] that there should be at least two views delivered within the eye pupil to evoke the accommodation. In the context of InIm, as illustrated in Fig. 5, one can define the view density for a given scene point through the number of corresponding beams propagating from neighbouring microlenses and reaching to pupil, as the directional information of the scene point is reconstructed by different microlenses. For a scene point at CDP, the width W of each beam at the eye pupil plane is defined by the microlens pitch as $W = D_m(z_{eye} + z_c)/z_c$, from which the number of views within the eye pupil can be found as $N = D/W$.

The retinal image formation at the reconstruction plane can be simulated through integration of the views visible to the eye, where each view is contributed by a different elemental image behind the corresponding microlens, and the contribution is characterized by the corresponding PSF. At a given eye position and focused depth, each such contribution is masked by its corresponding elemental FoV, as illustrated in Fig. 5 for the three red beams. The overall image formations can then be formulated as

$$I(u, v, \lambda) = \sum_{m=1}^{M} \sum_{n=1}^{N} w_{m,n}(u, v) \sum_{k=1}^{K} \sum_{l=1}^{L} I_e(m, n, k, l, \lambda) h_{m,n,k,l}(u, v, \lambda), \quad (2)$$

where $I_e(m, n, k, l, \lambda)$ is the intensity of the pixel $[k, l]$ of the elemental image behind the microlens $[m, n]$, $h_{m,n,k,l}(u, v, \lambda)$ is the PSF of the same pixel at the reconstruction plane (u, v) (i.e., it accounts also the finite size of the pixel), $w_{m,n}(u, v)$ is the FoV of the lens $[m, n]$, and $I(u, v, \lambda)$ is the retinal image at wavelength λ. For a given microlens, the elemental FoV $w_{m,n}(u, v)$ can be calculated via the convolution of the projected eye pupil through the microlens center with the projected microlens through the center of the eye pupil, both calculated at the reconstruction plane [2]. The PSF $h_{m,n,k,l}(u, v, \lambda)$, due to the rectangular (2D) display pixels of size $\Delta_p \times \Delta_q$, can be explicitly derived assuming the Fresnel diffraction as [12]

$$h_{m,n,k,l}(u, v, \lambda) = h_{m,n,0,0}(u - kM\Delta_p, v - lM\Delta_q, \lambda), \quad (3)$$

where $M = z_f/z_d$,

$$h_{m,n,0,0}(u, v, \lambda) = \mathrm{rect}\left(\frac{u}{M\Delta_p}, \frac{v}{M\Delta_q}\right) * p_{m,n,0,0}(u, v, \lambda), \quad (4)$$

and

$$p_{m,n,0,0}(u, v, \lambda) = \frac{1}{z_f^2}\left|\mathcal{F}\left\{A_{m,n}(x, y)\exp\left[\frac{j\pi}{\lambda}\left(\frac{1}{z_d} - \frac{1}{z_f} - \frac{1}{f}\right)(x^2 + y^2)\right]\right\}\right|^2 \quad (5)$$

is the actual response for a point on the display plane with f denoting the focal length of the microlenses and $A_{m,n}(x, y)$ denoting the pupil function of the corresponding microlens. In above equations, $*$ and $\mathcal{F}$ represent the convolution and the Fourier transform operations, respectively.

Characterization of Perceivable Spatial Resolution and Focus Cues. The retinal image formation model given by Eq. 2 can be used characterize a near-eye InIm display, e.g., depending on the delivered number of views within the eye pupil. As an example, assume the following simulation parameters according to definitions in Fig. 5: $z_{eye} = 2\,\mathrm{cm}$, $D = 5\,\mathrm{mm}$, $z_c = 40\,\mathrm{cm}$, and $D_m = \{4\,\mathrm{mm}, 2.4\,\mathrm{mm}, 1.5\,\mathrm{mm}\}$ corresponding to $N = \{1, 2, 3\}$, respectively.

The quantitative analysis of perceptual resolution and accommodative response can be performed through evaluating PSFs and the corresponding

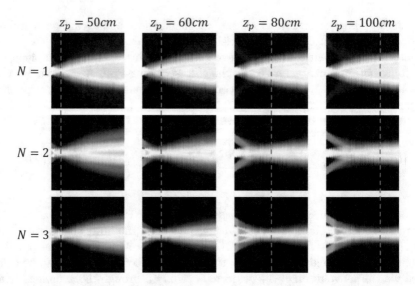

$z_p = 50cm$ $z_p = 60cm$ $z_p = 80cm$ $z_p = 100cm$

$N = 1$

$N = 2$

$N = 3$

Fig. 6. PSFs at different focused distances for different display setups. The test points are located at z_p, and the reconstruction plane z_f is changed from 40 cm to 120 cm. The CDP is located at $z_c = 40$ cm. Dashed red lines indicate the locations of the test points.

MTFs at different reconstruction (focused) distances. Please note that here PSF refers to the total response of the eye and display optics to an object point. The columns of Fig. 6 illustrate the one-dimensional cross-sections of PSFs, obtained through sweeping the scene by changing the reconstruction plane of the eye from $z_f = 40$ cm to $z_f = 120$ cm, for four different test point depths of $z_p = 50$ cm, $z_p = 60$ cm, $z_p = 80$ cm and 100 cm. Such PSF stack is a useful tool for qualitative analysis of focus response. As pointed out in Sect. 2, accommodative response is expected at depth where the blur is minimized. As seen in Fig. 6, correct accommodative response is observed only when the number of views within the pupil is sufficiently big and the test point is sufficiently close the CDP of InIm display.

A more rigorous quantitative analysis can be further performed through evaluating the MTFs. Figure 7 illustrates the corresponding results at 5 CPD spatial frequency, which is a good representative case as the CSF of the HVS has a peak around such mid spatial frequencies (see Fig. 1). Ideally, when comparing different focused depths, the magnitude of the MTF should be maximized at the intended object depth. Together with this, it is desirable for a 3D display that the gradient of the MTF is also maximized at this depth. These are the main factors to evaluate when analyzing the accuracies of delivered accommodative response as well as defocus blur cue. In line with the observations from PSF stack, the results in Fig. 7 also demonstrate that the display delivering three views into the pupil can achieve maximum frequency response at or near the actual point depth for all cases. The display with two views can preserve the

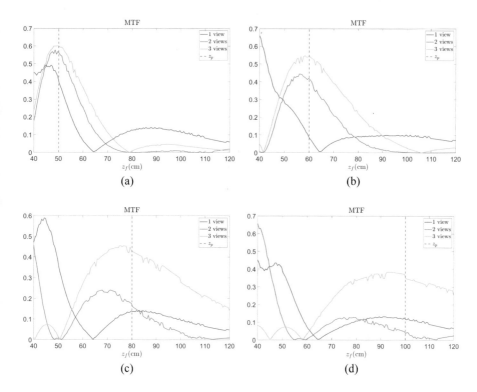

Fig. 7. Comparison of MTF magnitudes at 5 CPD for stack of focused images in the depth range from $z_f = 40$ cm to $z_f = 120$ cm. Each subfigure corresponds to a different test point distance indicated by the red dashed line, and it shows the results for different number of views within the pupil.

accommodative response up to 60 cm, after which the maximum magnitude of the response shifts towards the CDP. Finally, as expected, the one-view display cannot deliver correct accommodative response in any case.

As mentioned before, spatio-angular trade-off is an inherent trade-off in the traditional LF displays such as InIm. This trade-off can be observed in Fig. 8 when analyzed together with the above PSF and MTF stack figures. For $N = 3$, the higher magnitude and bandwidth of the MTF at $z_f = 60$ cm compared to $z_f = 40$ cm explains the expected (natural) accommodative response to an object point apart from the CDP, whereas in the case of $N = 1$ the MTF magnitude and bandwidth is higher at the CDP $z_f = 40$ cm, i.e., correct accommodation cue is not evoked. On the other hand, by comparing the MTFs for $N = 3$ and $z_f = 60$ cm with $N = 1$ and $z_f = 40$ cm, it can be observed that the cost of having accurate accommodative response in the former case is the decrease in the perceivable spatial resolution.

The qualitative analysis of the accommodative response can be also performed on a 3D scene by superposing the PSFs of scene points given by Eq. 2.

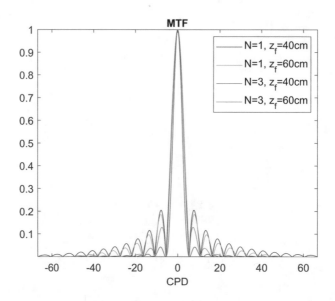

Fig. 8. MTFs corresponding to different number of views of $N = 1$, $N = 3$, and point depths of $z_f = 40$ cm, $z_f = 60$ cm.

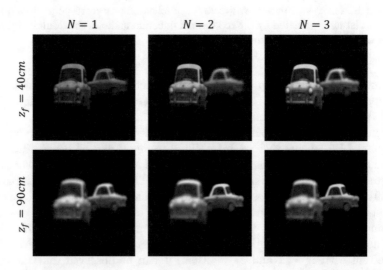

Fig. 9. Simulation results for a 3D scene consisting of two objects. The closer object is located around the CDP, $z_c = 40$ cm, and the further one is around 90 cm. Slava Z. ©2014 www.sketchfab.com, used under the Creative Commons Attribution license.

Figure 9 shows the retinal images, for a scene in the depth range from 40 cm to 90 cm, at different focused depths and number of views within the eye pupil. Consistent results can be deduced with the above discussions. In particular, the three-view display clearly delivers the desired accommodative response and defocus blur, whereas the one-view display fails in that.

4   Characterization of Holographic Displays

Holographic displays are often considered to constitute the ultimate 3D display technology having the ability of creating the true light information due to a given 3D scene and, thus, ensuring accurate delivery of all physiological depth cues of the HVS. Although significant research efforts have been devoted to develop both hardware and computational methods for such displays, realization of immersive glasses-free holographic displays have been mainly restricted by the device technology. However, due to relatively relieved implementation constraints (e.g., regarding the eyebox or FoV), the holographic displays have significant potential to provide desired immersive viewing experience in the next-generation near-eye displays. Below, the fundamentals of holographic displays are briefly described, the existing research on holographic near-eye displays is overviewed, and methods for analyzing holographic displays via retinal image formation models are discussed.

4.1   Basics of Holographic Displays

Holography is a technique that enables recording and later reconstructing the wavefront due to a given 3D object (scene), i.e., the object field $O(x, y)$, relying on the light interference and diffraction phenomena. The object field is a complex-valued function and it contains both the texture (intensity) and depth information of the object. The interference between the object and a reference wave $R(x, y)$, which is usually a monochromatic plane wave, is recorded on the hologram as a

$$I_H(x, y) = |R(x, y) + O(x, y)|^2 = RR^* + OO^* + OR^* + O^*R, \qquad (6)$$

where the asterisk denotes a complex conjugate operator. The object field is reconstructed by illuminating the hologram $I_H(x, y)$ with the same reference beam $R(x, y)$.

Computer-Generated Holography. In computer-generated holography, the so-called computer-generated hologram (CGH) is computed numerically by simulating the diffraction of object field and its interference with the reference beam, as given by Eq. 6. Actually, only the last two terms in Eq. 6, i.e., the +1 and −1 diffraction orders, contain the relevant information of the scene. Therefore, in computing a CGH, the remaining zero-order terms can be discarded. Encoding only the $+1$ and -1 diffraction orders results in the so-called bipolar intensity function $\tilde{I}_H(x,y)$ [32]:

$$\tilde{I}_H(x,y) = 2\text{Re}\{O(x,y)R^*(x,y)\}. \tag{7}$$

The object field can be reconstructed by multiplying the CGH $\tilde{I}_H(x,y)$ with the same reference beam $R(x,y)$.

Computational synthesis of holograms is a difficult yet crucial task for holographic displays, requiring compromises between the reconstruction image quality and the computational complexity. Achieving realistic reconstruction quality, i.e., accurate view-dependent properties (focus cues, occlusions, reflections, parallax, etc.) and sufficiently high (perceivable) spatial resolution, requires huge amount of data to process. As a result, there is an indispensable need for computationally efficient CGH synthesis methods. The CGH methods can be broadly divided into two categories: wavefront- and ray-based. The former category of methods utilize the 3D positional information of the scene, whereas the latter methods rely solely on the captured images of the scene. In the former approach, mostly the scene is described as a collection of independent self-emitting point sources of light [53]. The CGH is computed via superposition of each point's contribution on the hologram plane, usually assuming Fresnel diffraction model. Such methods usually deliver the abovementioned quality aspects of holography, including focus cues, however they are usually very demanding in terms of computational complexity. The alternative methods from the ray-based approaches, such as holographic stereogram (HS), can address the computational complexity by requiring only a set multiperspective images (i.e., LF) [37]. On the other hand, due to the nature of the underlying LF sampling, HSs also suffer from the spatio-angular resolution trade-off: objects far away from the hologram plane cannot be sharply reconstructed [15]. Example holograms (object fields) shown in Fig. 10, due to a point source, illustrate the difference between Fresnel and HS encoding. It is, basically, the discretization in the HS due to segment-wise encoding (of plane waves) that provides a more efficient method compared to Fresnel hologram, however this comes at the expense of degradation in the reconstruction image quality, as will be further elaborated below. There is vast literature on CGH [41]; especially the efforts on reducing the computational complexity are crucial for realization of immersive holographic displays.

General Characteristics of Holographic Near-Eye Displays. The dynamic (digital) holographic displays are implemented using optical modulators such as spatial light modulators (SLMs) and digital micromirror devices (DMDs). In computer-generated holography, assuming a reference plane wave propagating along the normal direction of the hologram, the full complex object field can be considered as the CGH, which actually constitutes the signal to be driven to the optical modulator. However, since the abovementioned digital optical modulators are usually capable of modulating only either the amplitude or the phase of the reference light, typically, computational algorithms are used to obtain phase-only or amplitude-only approximations of the full-complex hologram.

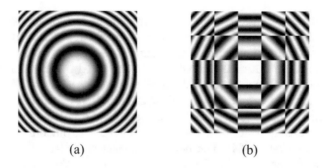

(a)   (b)

Fig. 10. The real values of Fresnel hologram (a) and HS (b) corresponding to a point source.

The visual characteristics of holographic displays are one of the main reasons for their desirability. The displays are able to provide continuous parallax, correct focus cues and high spatial resolution. That is, they do not suffer from the vergence-accommodation conflict, which makes them more comfortable to use. Unlike the LF displays, most of the holographic display methods (especially, those utilizing wave-based CGHs) do not have a trade-off between the spatial and angular resolutions, and they can reproduce the desired visual depth cues even for deep scenes.

The use of coherent imaging techniques makes holographic displays susceptible to speckle noise, which is an important issue to consider in the design and characterization of such displays. The speckle noise is the result of high contrast and frequency patterns of random nature. In CGHs, the speckle patterns originate from utilizing random phase distributions to avoid concentration of light on the hologram and to simulate diffused diffraction of the object wave. As the resulting noise heavily degrades the perceived image quality, its suppression is crucial for maintaining satisfactory quality in holographic displays. The speckle suppression methods can be broadly categorized into two groups. The first group of solutions rely on altering the display optics and techniques. Commonly these approaches aim at reducing either the spatial or temporal coherence of the reconstruction light, e.g., by diverging the illumination light with a diffuser [57], or by utilizing LEDs as the light source [58]. The second group of speckle suppression methods are algorithmic in nature, i.e., they modify the computational synthesis of holograms. Such methods range from time-multiplexing hologram frames with statistically independent speckle patterns [3] or sparse sets of light rays [50] to cyclic sequential shifting of the hologram [11]. When designing holographic near-eye displays, the main physical design parameters are the pixel pitch Δ_x and resolution N of the hologram, e.g., SLM. The pixel pitch of the SLM determines the maximum diffraction angle θ_d according to the grating equation as

$$\theta_d = 2 \arcsin\left(\frac{\lambda}{2\Delta_x}\right). \tag{8}$$

Currently, the main limitation in practical implementation of immersive near-eye holographic displays is the insufficient space-bandwidth product (product of the SLM area and the maximum diffraction angle) provided by the available SLMs, in addition to computational complexities of the CGH synthesis methods. The space-bandwidth product dictates the available eyebox and FoV. In particular, an unmagnified SLM can provide a FoV that is limited by the diffraction angle, which is typically not bigger than $10°$. Increasing the FoV is possible, e.g., via a diverging reference beam or a conventional eyepiece, but only at the cost of reduction in the eyebox [34]. The periodic diffraction orders that occur due to discretization on the SLM are also a limiting factor for the eyebox. The extent of a single order at a viewing distance of z from the hologram is defined by the pixel pitch as $\lambda z/\Delta_x$, and, normally, the eyebox is restricted to be of this size or smaller. The diffraction orders can be, instead, avoided by optical means, e.g., spatial filtering. Such methods, however, usually complicate the design or increase the form-factor.

4.2   Retinal Image Formation Models for Near-Eye Holographic Displays

Besides the HVS model itself, the key component of the retinal image formation models for holographic displays is the employed numerical wave propagation algorithms used to propagate the wave field due to hologram till to the retina. Although the more rigorous algorithm for numerical wave propagation is the Rayleigh-Sommerfeld diffraction, and equivalently the angular spectrum method (ASM) in the spectral domain, mostly its paraxial approximation Fresnel diffraction is utilized due to its computational efficiency, i.e., it can be implemented analytically using fast Fourier transform techniques [12]. In the context holographic imaging, in forward (retinal image formation) models it is also common to model the eye as a simple camera with a thin lens and a planar sensor. The accommodation is simulated by varying the focal length of the lens transmittance function, which models diffraction-limited imaging in the paraxial Fresnel regime. The wave field on the hologram plane can also be propagated back to the scene to reconstruct an image at the desired plane. Such back propagation methods ignore the effects of the human eye optics and mainly target to evaluate the effects of the holographic encoding.

Characterization of Perceivable Spatial Resolution and Focus Cues. In this part an example retinal image formation model is presented for near-eye holographic displays, with an eye model consisting of curved retina that has eccentricity-dependent spatial resolution. Such (foveated) eye models play a key role, e.g., when developing foveated rendering methods and, thus, analyzing the perceptual spatial resolution as well as focus cues as a function of content eccentricity. The model is illustrated in Fig. 11, where the additional lens in front of the hologram, the eyepiece, is used as a magnifier as usually employed in near-eye displays.

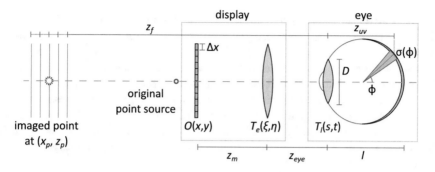

Fig. 11. The retinal image formation model for a holographic near-eye setup. The eye model includes a non-uniformly sampled curved retina surface.

The non-uniform sampling on the retina is based on the model proposed in [54] describing the density of the retinal ganglion cell receptive fields as a function of retinal eccentricity $r = \sqrt{\phi^2 + \theta^2}$ and meridian m as

$$\rho(r, m) = 2\rho_{cone} \left(1 + \frac{r}{41.03}\right)^{-1}$$
$$\times \left[a_m \left(1 + \frac{r}{r_{2,m}}\right)^{-2} + (1 - a_m) \exp\left(\frac{r}{r_{e,m}}\right)\right]. \qquad (9)$$

The constants ρ_{cone}, a_m, $r_{2,m}$, $r_{e,m}$ fit the model along the four different meridians (temporal, superior, nasal, inferior). The eccentricity-dependent sampling of the retina is then defined based on the density of receptive fields as

$$\sigma(\phi, \theta) = \frac{1}{r} \sqrt{\frac{2}{\sqrt{3}} \left(\frac{\phi^2}{\rho(r, 1)} + \frac{\theta^2}{\rho(r, 2)}\right)}. \qquad (10)$$

Both the lens of the eye and the eyepiece are assumed as aberration-free thin lenses with phase transmittance functions of

$$T(s, t) = \exp\left[\frac{-j\pi}{\lambda f}(s^2 + t^2)\right], \qquad (11)$$

where λ is the wavelength of the monochromatic light and f is the focal length of the corresponding lens. The simulated eye can be set to focus (accommodate) at a certain distance z_f by changing the focal length of the eye lens based on the paraxial lens imaging as

$$\frac{1}{f} = \frac{1}{z_f} + \frac{1}{l}, \qquad (12)$$

where l is the distance between the eye lens and the central retina.

For a given hologram, the computation of the retinal image involves a set of plane-to-plane wave propagation (between the hologram and eyepiece as well as between the eyepiece and eye lens), modulation of the propagating waves by the eyepiece and the eye lens, and also plane-to-curved surface (retina) propagation. The end-to-end light transport between the hologram and retina can be rigorously calculated using ASM, since, unlike some other methods, it can compute the 3D field due to a given planar field. This naturally provides the relation between planar wave field just after the eye lens and the wave field sampled by the curved retina. That is, taking into account Fig. 11, the retinal image is found for a given (complex-valued) hologram $O(x, y)$ as

$$I(u, v, z_{uv}) = \left| A_{u,v,z_{uv}} \{ T_l(s,t) A_{s,t,z_{eye}} \{ T_e(\xi, \eta) A_{\xi, \eta, z_m} \{ O(x, y) \} \} \} \right|^2, \quad (13)$$

where $A_{x,y,z_{xy}}\{\}$ is the ASM propagation operator computing the scalar diffraction on the curved surface (x, y, z_{xy}) due to an input wave field defined on the plane at $z = 0$; (u, v, z_{uv}), in particular, represents the curved surface of retina that is assumed to be spherical; $T_l(s,t)$ and $T_e(\xi, \eta)$ denote the lens transmittance functions of the eye lens and eyepiece, respectively.

Similar to the analysis demonstrated in Sect. 3 for LF displays, the stack of PSFs and MTFs of the retinal image formation model, corresponding to accommodative states around the intended object point depths, can be also used as reliable tools in holographic near-eye displays to analyze and characterize accommodative response, defocus blur as well as perceptual spatial resolution. Let us consider comparative analysis of Fresnel hologram and HS, which are two widely used wave-based and ray-based CGH methods, respectively. The eye relief and the pupil size are fixed as $z_{eye} = 2\,\text{cm}$ and $D = 5\,\text{mm}$, respectively. The test point source is set at four different locations such that they are imaged by the eyepiece at $z_p = 50\,\text{cm}$, $z_p = 60\,\text{cm}$, $z_p = 80\,\text{cm}$ and $z_p = 100\,\text{cm}$ (the hologram plane itself is imaged at $40\,\text{cm}$) to analyze the effects of the scene depth. For each point, both a Fresnel hologram and a HS are generated for the assumed wavelength of $\lambda = 534\,\text{nm}$. For simplicity, two-dimensional cross-sections of the 3D space are considered in the analyses, i.e., including only x- and z-axis. Thus, the eye model and the wave propagations are implemented for one-dimensional signals. The sampling step in the discrete implementation of ASM, as well as the sampling on the hologram plane, is chosen to be $\Delta_x = 1.7\lambda$ to ensure fine enough sampling for accurate propagation. The number of samples on the hologram is chosen to cover a FoV of $50°$. Additionally, the segment size of the HS is chosen such that different number of plane wave segments (which correspond to rays in LF displays) are incident within the extent of the pupil. Three different segment sizes are evaluated, each corresponding to the number of plane wave segments of $N_\theta = \{1, 2, 3\}$. In particular, $N_\theta \approx (D\Delta_h')/(\lambda z_h')$, where Δ_h' denote the magnified segment size and z_h' is the distance of the magnified hologram to the eye. Similar to LF displays, increasing this value is expected to improve the accommodative response of HS, at the cost of decrease in the perceived spatial resolution [35].

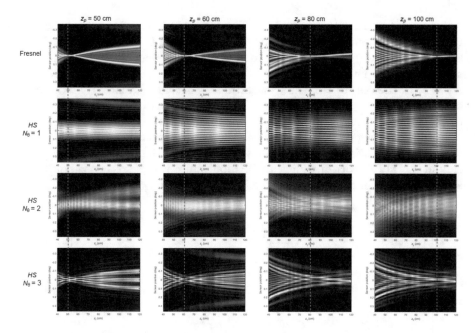

Fig. 12. A set of PSFs for different focused distances, each displayed in a single column of the image. Fresnel (first row) and HS (second, third and fourth rows) hologram synthesis methods are utilized. The point is placed at 50 cm, 60 cm, 80 cm and 100 cm in each column, respectively.

Initial conclusions can be drawn by observing the behaviour of the PSFs at different focused depths. As shown in Fig. 12, in the case of Fresnel hologram, the sharpest PSFs are always obtained for depths at or near (the slight displacements are smaller than the extent of the eye DoF) the location of the test point, which suggests that the accommodative response is likely to be accurately created. On the other hand, the HS can provide sharpest PSF at (or near) the original depth point, correspondingly it can likely provide correct accommodative response, only when $N_\theta \geq 2$ and the point is sufficiently close to the conjugate hologram plane at 40 cm. It can be also observed that in both such cases, within the depth range from the conjugate hologram plane to the actual point depth, the envelope of the defocus blur follows a natural trend. Although in terms of focus cues the HS seems to be compatible with the Fresnel hologram, it is clearly seen from the support of the sharpest PSFs that the (maximum) perceptual spatial resolution in the case of HS is expected to be significantly lower than Fresnel case. As mentioned above, this is due to spatio-angular resolution trade-off that exists in HSs. When N_θ is decreased (by decreasing the segment sizes of the HS), the natural behaviour of the defocus blur is lost, since in these cases the HS cannot recreate the focus cues accurately.

The results in Fig. 13 showing stack of MTF magnitudes at different depths for the fixed spatial resolution of 5 CPD provide further insights on the focus responses of Fresnel hologram and HS. The accommodation distance is estimated to be at the distance $\hat{z}_f$ maximizing the value of MTF in the given stack. As seen in Fig. 13(a,b), $\hat{z}_f$ is observed to be (nearly) correct, i.e., it remains to be at (or near) the intended test point depth, for Fresnel hologram and HS with $N_\theta = 3$. In the case of HS, the focus estimates become significantly more inaccurate as the segment size is decreased (see Fig. 13(c,d)). The estimates remain to be (nearly) correct only for $N_\theta = 2$ and when the test point is sufficiently close to the conjugate hologram plane. The contrast gradient, or the sharpness of the MTF peak, is particularly noteworthy in all of the results: the low gradients in the MTFs corresponding to HSs indicate a weaker response trigger for accommodation in comparison to the Fresnel hologram.

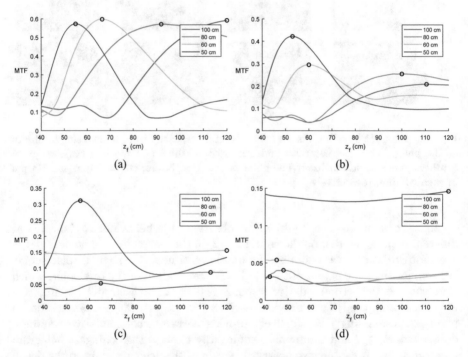

Fig. 13. Magnitudes of the MTFs as a function of focused depths for spatial frequency of 5 CPD. Fresnel (a) and HS (b-d) hologram synthesis methods are utilized. The HSs are generated with hogel sizes corresponding to $N_\theta = 3$ in (b), $N_\theta = 2$ in (c) and $N_\theta = 1$ in (d). The point is placed at different depths as indicated by differently colored lines. The highest magnitude, i.e., the estimate $\hat{z}_f$, is marked with a black circle.

Alternatively, the effects of foveation can be analyzed using the same framework to extend the characterization for larger eccentricities. Now the horizontal position of the point source is altered and the results are compared between varying amounts of eccentricity for the Fresnel hologram. Since the eye model considers both the non-uniform nature of the sampling on the retina and its curvature, it is expected that a point further away from the direction of the gaze is perceived differently, which is likely to alter the focus response. The test point is placed at visual angles between 0 and 20° with respect to central gaze direction. Figure 14 illustrates the effects of eccentricity on the contrast magnitude and gradient. The estimated accommodation distance $\hat{z}_f$, though changes slightly across the eccentricity range, remains to be within the typical DoF values of HVS. Furthermore, one can observe that the contrast gradient reduces at larger eccentricities. This suggests that the strength of the defocus blur cue also decreases in the peripheral vision creating weaker accommodative response. The decrease in the contrast magnitudes at larger eccentricities is also consistent with the well-known eccentricity-dependent perceptual spatial resolution behaviour.

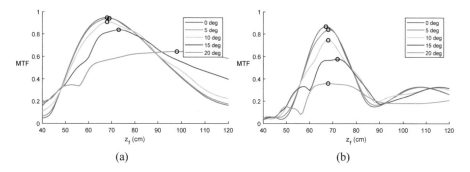

(a)   (b)

Fig. 14. Magnitudes of the MTFs, as a function of focused depths, corresponding to Fresnel holograms of point sources placed at 60 cm distance and at different horizontal positions (correspondingly eccentricities) as indicated by colored lines. The considered spatial frequency is 5 CPD (a) and 10 CPD (b). The highest magnitude point, at the estimate $\hat{z}_f$, is marked with a black circle.

(a)   (b)   (c)   (d)

Fig. 15. Retinal images corresponding to a Fresnel hologram of a 3D scene, without speckle suppression (a,c) and with random averaging (b,d). The simulated eye is set to focus on the die in the foreground (a,b) and behind the scene (c,d).

Finally, it is also important to evaluate the perceptual spatial resolution and the focus cues on 3D scenes to infer about general visual quality. The notable difference of 3D scene analysis in comparison to the single point source case is the presence of speckle noise. As seen in Fig. 15(a) and (c), the noise severely degrades the visual quality of the retinal images for the corresponding Fresnel holograms and prohibits any meaningful analysis based on them. Specifically, the effects of accommodation cannot be observed properly. Such levels of noise necessitate the use of speckle suppression methods. As shown in Fig. 15(b) and (d), including even a relatively simple method such as random averaging [3] significantly improves the visual clarity by reducing the speckle noise. The effects of accommodation change also become evident in these figures. Furthermore, such analysis also demonstrates the important role of speckle suppression when implementing holographic displays in practice.

5   Conclusion

Their capabilities of delivering all physiological depth cues of HVS make LF and holographic displays strong candidates for the next-generation near-eye displays, which aim at creating the desired realistic visualization with full-immersion. In this chapter the retinal image formation models are discussed for such displays. In particular, among several other aspects of spatial vision, characterization of perceptual spatial resolution as well as accommodation and defocus blur cues are addressed. Thorough analysis of perceived images with such models are necessary to rigorously characterize and optimize the capabilities of the display under consideration. The presented framework, for instance, reveals some of the well-known aspects such as the trade-off between the perceptual resolution and the accuracy of focus cues in LF display, or rarely addressed properties of HSs that they are capable of delivering focus cues.

It is common in the 3D displays literature that the retinal image formation models adopt simple (reduced) eye models, which usually consist of a thin lens and uniformly sampled planar retina. The analysis frameworks presented in this chapter with such simple models, as well as somewhat more accurate models taking into account non-planar retina surface and foveation, can be further extended to include more rigorous eye models, e.g., incorporating aberrations in the eye optics. Such extensions are likely to lead better optimized displays through more realistic characterization. Furthermore, the characterization and optimization of LF and holographic displays (in general all 3D displays) should further include the neural factors in the HVS to fully exploit its characteristics, which is also likely to reveal new aspects to be taken into account in the design of novel display optics as well as computational (rendering) algorithms.

References

1. Adelson, E.H., Bergen, J.R.: The plenoptic function and the elements of early vision (1991)
2. Akpinar, U., Sahin, E., Gotchev, A.: Viewing simulation of integral imaging display based on wave optics. In: 2018–3DTV-Conference: The True Vision-Capture, Transmission and Display of 3D Video (3DTV-CON), pp. 1–4. IEEE (2018)

3. Amako, J., Miura, H., Sonehara, T.: Speckle-noise reduction on kinoform reconstruction using a phase-only spatial light modulator. Appl. Opt. **34**(17), 3165–3171 (1995)
4. Banks, M.S., Hoffman, D.M., Kim, J., Wetzstein, G.: 3D displays. Annu. Rev. Vis. Sci. **2**(1), 397–435 (2016). pMID: 28532351
5. Boev, A., Poikela, M., Gotchev, A.P., Aksay, A.: Modelling of the stereoscopic HVS (2009)
6. Bregovic, R., Sahin, E., Vagharshakyan, S., Gotchev, A.: Signal processing methods for light field displays. In: Bhattacharyya, S.S., Deprettere, E.F., Leupers, R., Takala, J. (eds.) Handbook of Signal Processing Systems, pp. 3–50. Springer, Cham (2019). https://doi.org/10.1007/978-3-319-91734-4_1
7. Cholewiak, S.A., Love, G.D., Banks, M.S.: Creating correct blur and its effect on accommodation. J. Vis. **18**(9), 1 (2018)
8. Cottaris, N.P., Jiang, H., Ding, X., Wandell, B.A., Brainard, D.H.: A computational observer model of spatial contrast sensitivity: effects of wavefront-based optics, cone mosaic structure, and inference engine. bioRxiv (2018)
9. Curcio, C.A., et al.: Distribution and morphology of human cone photoreceptors stained with anti-blue opsin. J. Comp. Neurol. **312**(4), 610–24 (1991)
10. Dorman, R., van Ee, R.: 50 years of stereoblindness: reconciliation of a continuum of disparity detectors with blindness for disparity in near or far depth. i-Perception **8**(6), 204166951773854 (2017)
11. Golan, L., Shoham, S.: Speckle elimination using shift-averaging in high-rate holographic projection. Opt. Express **17**(3), 1330–1339 (2009)
12. Goodman, J.W.: Introduction to Fourier Optics, 2nd edn. McGraw-Hill (1996)
13. Gortler, S.J., Grzeszczuk, R., Szeliski, R., Cohen, M.F.: The lumigraph (1996)
14. Held, R.T., Cooper, E.A., Banks, M.S.: Blur and disparity are complementary cues to depth. Curr. Biol.: CB **22**(5), 426–431 (2012)
15. Hilaire, P.S.: Modulation transfer function and optimum sampling of holographic stereograms. Appl. Opt. **33**(5), 768–774 (1994)
16. Hoffman, D.M., Girshick, A.R., Akeley, K., Banks, M.S.: Vergence-accommodation conflicts hinder visual performance and cause visual fatigue. J. Vis. **8**(3), 33 (2008)
17. Honda, T., et al.: Three-dimensional display technologies satisfying "super multiview condition". In: Optics East (2001)
18. Hua, H.: Enabling focus cues in head-mounted displays. Proc. IEEE **105**(5), 805–824 (2017)
19. Hua, H., Javidi, B.: A 3D integral imaging optical see-through head-mounted display. Opt. Express **22**(11), 13484–13491 (2014)
20. Huang, F.C., Chen, K., Wetzstein, G.: The light field stereoscope: immersive computer graphics via factored near-eye light field displays with focus cues. ACM Trans. Graph. **34**(4), 60:1–60:12 (2015)
21. Huang, H., Hua, H.: Systematic characterization and optimization of 3D light field displays. Opt. Express **25**(16), 18508–18525 (2017)
22. Huang, H., Hua, H.: Effects of ray position sampling on the visual responses of 3D light field displays. Opt. Express **27**(7), 9343–9360 (2019)
23. Jang, C., Bang, K., Moon, S., Kim, J., Lee, S., Lee, B.: Retinal 3D: augmented reality near-eye display via pupil-tracked light field projection on retina. ACM Trans. Graph. (TOG) **36**(6), 190 (2017)
24. Kelly, D.H.: Motion and vision. II. Stabilized spatio-temporal threshold surface. J. Opt. Soc. Am. **69**(10), 1340–1349 (1979)

25. Konrad, R., Padmanaban, N., Molner, K., Cooper, E.A., Wetzstein, G.: Accommodation-invariant computational near-eye displays. ACM Trans. Graph. **36**(4), 88:1–88:12 (2017)

26. Lanman, D., Luebke, D.: Near-eye light field displays. ACM Trans. Graph. **32**(6), 220:1–220:10 (2013)

27. Lee, S., et al.: Foveated retinal optimization for see-through near-eye multi-layer displays. IEEE Access **6**, 2170–2180 (2018)

28. Legge, G.E.: A power law for contrast discrimination. Vis. Res. **21**(4), 457–467 (1981)

29. Levoy, M., Hanrahan, P.: Light field rendering. In: Proceedings of the 23rd Annual Conference on Computer Graphics and Interactive Techniques, pp. 31–42. ACM (1996)

30. Liang, J., Williams, D.R.: Aberrations and retinal image quality of the normal human eye. J. Opt. Soc. Am. A **14**(11), 2873–2883 (1997)

31. Liu, M., Lu, C., Li, H., Liu, X.: Near eye light field display based on human visual features. Opt. Express **25**(9), 9886–9900 (2017)

32. Lucente, M.E.: Diffraction-specific Fringe Computation for Electro-holography. Ph.D. thesis, Massachusetts Institute of Technology, Cambridge, MA, USA (1994)

33. Macleod, D.I.A., Williams, D.R., Makous, W.: A visual nonlinearity fed by single cones. Vis. Res. **32**, 347–363 (1992)

34. Maimone, A., Georgiou, A., Kollin, J.S.: Holographic near-eye displays for virtual and augmented reality. ACM Trans. Graph. **36**(4), 85:1–85:16 (2017)

35. Mäkinen, J., Sahin, E., Gotchev, A.: Analysis of accommodation cues in holographic stereograms. In: 2018–3DTV-Conference: The True Vision - Capture, Transmission and Display of 3D Video (3DTV-CON), pp. 1–4, June 2018

36. Marcos, S., Moreno, E., Navarro, R.: The depth-of-field of the human eye from objective and subjective measurements. Vis. Res. **39**(12), 2039–2049 (1999)

37. McCrickerd, J.T., George, N.: Holographic stereogram from sequential component photographs. Appl. Phys. Lett. **12**(1), 10–12 (1968)

38. Nadenau, M.J., Reichel, J., Kunt, M.: Performance comparison of masking models based on a new psychovisual test method with natural scenery stimuli. Sig. Process. Image Commun. **17**(10), 807–823 (2002)

39. Navarro, R.: The optical design of the human eye: a critical review. J. Optom. **2**, 3–18 (2009)

40. Owens, D.A.: A comparison of accommodative responsiveness and contrast sensitivity for sinusoidal gratings. Vis. Res. **20**(2), 159–167 (1980)

41. Park, J.H.: Recent progress in computer-generated holography for three-dimensional scenes. J. Inf. Disp. **18**(1), 1–12 (2017)

42. Pelli, D.G., Bex, P.: Measuring contrast sensitivity. Vis. Res. **90**, 10–14 (2013)

43. Qin, Z., et al.: Image formation modeling and analysis of near-eye light field displays. J. Soc. Inf. Disp. **27**, 238–250 (2019)

44. Schor, C.M.: A dynamic model of cross-coupling between accommodation and convergence: simulations of step and frequency responses. Optom. Vis. Sci.: Off. Publ. Am. Acad. Optom. **69**(4), 258–269 (1992)

45. Seshadrinathan, K., et al.: Image quality assessment, Chapter 21. In: Bovik, A. (ed.) The Essential Guide to Image Processing, pp. 553–595. Academic Press, Boston (2009)

46. Stern, A., Yitzhaky, Y., Javidi, B.: Perceivable light fields: matching the requirements between the human visual system and autostereoscopic 3-D displays. Proc. IEEE **102**(10), 1571–1587 (2014)

47. Strasburger, H., Rentschler, I., Jüttner, M.: Peripheral vision and pattern recognition: a review. J. Vis. **11**(5), 13 (2011)
48. Sun, F.C., Stark, L., Nguyen, A., Wong, J., Lakshminarayanan, V., Mueller, E.: Changes in accommodation with age: static and dynamic. Am. J. Optom. Physiol. Opt. **65**(6), 492–498 (1988)
49. Sun, Q., Huang, F.C., Kim, J., Wei, L.Y., Luebke, D., Kaufman, A.: Perceptually-guided foveation for light field displays. ACM Trans. Graph. **36**(6), 192:1–192:13 (2017)
50. Utsugi, T., Yamaguchi, M.: Speckle-suppression in hologram calculation using ray-sampling plane. Opt. Express **22**(14), 17193–17206 (2014)
51. Van Nes, F.L., Bouman, M.A.: Spatial modulation transfer in the human eye. J. Opt. Soc. Am. **57**(3), 401–406 (1967)
52. Wandell, B.: Foundations of Vision. Sinauer Associates (1995)
53. Waters, J.P.: Holographic image synthesis utilizing theoretical methods. Appl. Phys. Lett. **9**(11), 405–407 (1966)
54. Watson, A.B.: A formula for human retinal ganglion cell receptive field density as a function of visual field location. J. Vis. **14**(7), 1–17 (2014)
55. Williams, D., Sekiguchi, N., Brainard, D.: Color, contrast sensitivity, and the cone mosaic. Proc. Nat. Acad. Sci. U.S.A. **90**(21), 9770–9777 (1993)
56. Yamaguchi, M.: Light-field and holographic three-dimensional displays. J. Opt. Soc. Am. A **33**(12), 2348–2364 (2016)
57. Yamaguchi, M., Endoh, H., Honda, T., Ohyama, N.: High-quality recording of a full-parallax holographic stereogram with a digital diffuser. Opt. Lett. **19**(2), 135–137 (1994)
58. Yaraş, F., Kang, H., Onural, L.: Real-time phase-only color holographic video display system using led illumination. Appl. Opt. **48**(34), H48–H53 (2009)

Subtle Visual Attention Guidance in VR

Steve Grogorick(✉) and Marcus Magnor

TU Braunschweig, Braunschweig, Germany
{grogorick,magnor}@cg.cs.tu-bs.de
https://graphics.tu-bs.de

Abstract. The research field of visual attention guidance in virtual reality (VR) explores possibilities to help viewers finding their way through immersive environments. A specialized area within this field —subtle guidance— arises with the goal to achieve this with least possible distraction, to prevent misrepresentation of actual scene content as well as degradation of immersion and presence in VR. This chapter provides an introduction to the general topic, commonly used terminology, and coarsely introduces some exemplary approaches.

Keywords: Attention · Subtle guidance · Perception · Virtual reality

1 Introduction

The improvement of commercially accessible head-mounted displays (HMDs) in recent years raised a growing mainstream interest in immersive 360° VR-applications. These systems grant consumers the opportunity to look and walk around in virtual surroundings like they do in reality, having an almost full field of view (FOV) and being able to literally turn their heads and walk on their own feet to explore virtual worlds. While these virtual reality (VR) interaction mechanisms lead the highly desired effects of immersion and presence, i.e. the sensation of being in this presented virtual world instead of looking at it. Being able to move in VR via tracked real movements, causes the constraint that users' visual field can not be manipulated as freely as in classical video games, because involuntary camera motions have shown to rapidly evoke motion/simulator sickness. This often leads to users missing important points of interest in presented scenes, because applications can no longer strictly tie the camera on the story being told by applying arbitrary camera motions. Instead, the attention of viewers has to be guided through a scene over time to follow a certain storyline.

Generally, attention is guided by visual features as well as the task of the user. This property has been extensively exploited for passive gaze prediction, i.e. image saliency estimation. Strategies for gaze guidance are aiming for steering attention to a specified target location which can differ significantly from the natural fixation location, i.e. from positions that would have been reported by saliency estimation. Therefore, visual gaze guidance requires altering the visible scene content to guide users' visual attention to specific points of interest.

This chapter provides an overview on the general field of subtle visual attention guidance in VR. It gives a brief insight into the development of some exemplary approaches, and shows how they work and on what perceptual principles they are based.

© Springer Nature Switzerland AG 2020
M. Magnor and A. Sorkine-Hornung (Eds.): Real VR, LNCS 11900, pp. 272–284, 2020.
https://doi.org/10.1007/978-3-030-41816-8_11

2   Attention Guidance

Attention guidance methods provide means to shift our attention towards a predetermined *target region*, i.e. typically a scene/story - and time-dependent point of interest. Following the goal of guiding towards something, most methods apply changes specifically geared to our perception in peripheral regions of our vision visual field, i.e. to work best when we are not directly looking at, but can still see them. Whilst not handled by all approaches, an important special case are *external target regions*, for which the location is completely outside a viewer's FOV.

Visual guidance has been proposed in a large variety of different approaches in desktop, augmented reality (AR) and VR setups [11, 12, 37], from which a set of categories is derived to allow for classification and comparison of current and future approaches. A first distinction is *diegetic* vs. non-diegetic methods, which modify the actual scene content/structure to affect viewers' attention. While this is efficient and easily applicable for story telling applications, it requires a specific adaptation to not only every VR application but every single scene, i.e while a firefly fits well in the context of a jungle it does not in a clean city. Therefore, also methods that pursue the goal of general applicability by acting as a post-process, have been proposed. Because they are not part of the actual scene they, in theory, can be applied to more applications without (intense) individual per-scene modifications. Depending on whether such approaches aim to remain unnoticed by viewers, they can be classified either into *overt* or *subtle* attention direction methods. Additionally, approaches may be differentiated by being either *gaze contingent* or not, i.e. whether they respond to the viewers' gaze direction.

2.1   Diegetic Attention Guidance

To drive viewers' attention towards predetermined directions, diegetic guidance methods, as described by Nielsen *et al.* [28], modify the actual scenes' content, e.g. via arrangement of existing scene elements or adding new objects. Scene arrangement works such that important objects stand out (e.g. by a conspicuous appearance or exposed position) or the whole scene is providing indications (e.g. via pathways) where to focus [31]. The introduction of additional new content to a scene was proposed in form of actors inside the scene yelling or waving towards the viewer or pointing at the target [36, 43] or even smaller in form of a firefly moving towards the target [28], which might also be expanded to other small particle-like objects, e.g. tumbleweed, dust clouds, or some form of wind visualization, to match further scenarios.

2.2   Overt Attention Guidance

Overt methods target the goal of directing viewers' attention without explicitly taking any action to prevent being recognized as such, e.g. they make use of a persistent scene/image adaptation to drive viewers' gaze towards the target location. Explored methods make use of blur [19, 25], highlighting [20] or add a clearly recognizable image overlay such as arrows [24], leader lines [17], or funnel [4] directing to the intended target.

2.3   Subtle Attention Guidance

Many VR applications aim for the biggest immersion possible and for the users to feel like really being part of the scene. While overt techniques are mostly very successful in terms of guiding performance, they often break/weaken immersion and disturb the users' experience. Subtle guidance methods try to guide attention without distracting from the actual scenes' content—in the best case without users' consciously perceiving them. Examples include an almost unnoticeable variation of spatial blur [16], saliency adjustment [8, 34, 41], temporal luminance modulation [2, 12, 42] or artificial mismatches in binocular images [14, 28].

2.4   Gaze Contingent Attention Guidance

The last differentiation within the present work is whether or not a method interactively responds to a viewer's gaze. In most cases, this presupposes availability of the actual gaze direction, i.e. real-time eye tracking. While this raises requirements, it enables to pursue new approaches, especially with respect to subtleness. To remain unnoticed, methods proposed to monitor users' gaze to hide their respective stimulus/image manipulation in case of stimulus/target-directed saccades being detected [2, 11, 27]. Also a possibility to increase performance was shown with the help of eye tracking, by adaptively increasing the size of a guiding stimulus with increasing eccentricity, i.e. its distance from the current gaze location [13].

3   Application in VR

In 2017 some general methods were presented to extend desktop post processing guidance techniques for application in VR [13]. More specifically this work presented suggestions to handle two properties being key for immersive applications but prohibit direct usage of original methods in VR:

First, the enlarged field of view in immersive environments invalidates usage of simple (e.g. circular) stimuli. Caused by the perspective projection, objects in the far periphery of the users' sight would appear squashed, as seen from the users' point of view, i.e. the perceived area of the stimulus decreases and so does its influence. Additionally, as the human visual acuity decreases with increasing eccentricity, stimulus influence degrades towards the periphery.

Second, increased navigational abilities of users, i.e. turning the head into different directions and greater eye motion to orient in the scene, introduce the possibility for external target regions. The method adds gaze-contingent deformation of the stimulus shape and dynamic positioning, in order to enable stimulus presentation at greater eccentricities as well as guidance to external target regions respectively.

3.1   Perspective Distortion Compensation

The problem of augmenting a rendered frame with a simple shape is that it would only be perceived as such when being viewed in a perpendicular direction, i.e. in the central region in case of HMDs. In outer regions the shape would appear strongly distorted as depicted in Fig. 1(a–b). Therefore, the (e.g. circular) shape of the stimulus must be adapted before presentation, i.e. elongated from center towards the periphery, to be perceived undistorted, as in Fig. 1(c–d). In the presented approach, this is accomplished in a post processing fragment shader, by effectively applying a billboard technique to keep the perceived shape intact regardless of its on-screen position [13].

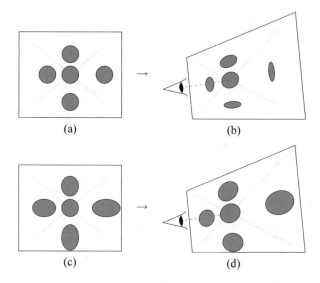

(a)   (b)

(c)   (d)

Fig. 1. (a) Five equal-sized circles on a plane straight in front of the viewer. (b) With increasing eccentricity the circles appear squeezed when being viewed from the viewer's perspective. (c–d) The same example with perspectively corrected shapes. Images from [13].

3.2 Eccentricity-Based Scaling

As extensive previous research has revealed, our visual acuity strongly decreases from foveal to peripheral vision [7,23,44], i.e. with increasing angular distance from the eyes' optical axis (the gaze point). In terms of actual perceived acuity, the decrease roughly follows a linear function [38,44]. Thus, to counteract the perceptual and therefore performance-wise decrease of visual stimuli towards the periphery, it was suggested to enlarge the stimulus with increasing eccentricity [13], as shown in Fig. 2.

3.3 Dynamic Stimulus Positioning

For external target locations, e.g. behind the viewer, it is not sufficient to only steer the user's eyes. Instead one need to induce a rotation of the head or even the whole body. Therefore, another modification was suggested that dynamically adds motion to the stimulus. More precisely, the stimulus performs a repeated motion, approximately between the current gaze point and the screen edge, behind which the user would reach the target [13], as depicted in Fig. 3. A rotation angle of $\alpha = 35°$ was reported as effective parameterization.

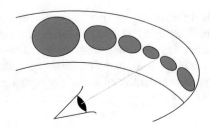

Fig. 2. Stimulus (blue) moves out of the user's field of view to induce a head rotation towards the target (orange).

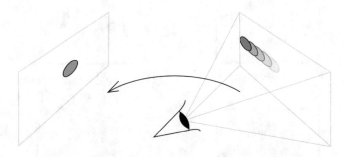

Fig. 3. Stimulus (blue) moves out of the user's field of view to induce a head rotation towards the target (orange). Image from [13].

4 Approach: Placing Solid Markers

An approach that comes into mind very early, is placement of artificial markers on the target region. While this was presented in different variations, all of these methods are to be categorized as overt techniques.

4.1 Colored Dots

A simple yet effective approach was presented by Jarodzka *et al.* in form of a solid colored circular dot that was overlaid on video sequences, like in Fig. 4 (left). Its size decreased during longer fixations on important points, i.e. longer fixations yield a smaller dot over time. The position of the stimulus over time was a replay of recorded gaze data of a domain expert, to train novices in efficient exploration [19]. In an application scenario like this, subtleness is not a main target objective, but the focus is laid on guiding performance to get the maximum potential out of training applications. Because this method does interfere immersion, it can be considered overt and non-gaze contingent.

Fig. 4. Large colored circular dot (left) and small rectangular dot (right) stimuli. Images from [19] and [3].

4.2   Fast Colored Dots

Similar approaches, that put more focus on subtleness, were presented by Dorr *et al.* [6] and Barth *et al.* [3]. Instead of a large circular dot, only a small ($1 \times 1°$) rectangular dot, as in Fig. 4 (right), was used on target regions in video sequences. To further increase subtleness, the stimulus was presented for a maximum duration of 120 ms. While in the earlier work guidance stimuli were additionally removed as soon as a target-directed saccade was recognized during presentation, the latter relied on saccadic latency (a.k.a. saccadic masking) which typically lasts about 200 ms.

4.3   Application in VR

A mixture of these approaches was later applied in VR [12] in form of the small and briefly visible colored dots, but with a circular shape and perspective distortion compensation as well as eccentricity-based scaling (see Sect. 3). Having these features, all versions of the fast colored dots are to be categorized as subtle attention guidance methods. Additionally, the first and third method feature gaze contingency.

5   Approach: Adding Motion

Another set of approaches suggests to introduce additional motion, to attract attention in a scene, which builds on the high sensitivity to motion especially in human peripheral vision [15,40]. Due to their basic principle, these methods are most appropriate for static scenarios.

5.1   Zoom on Target Region

In 2004, Dorr *et al.* suggested a method that repeatedly enlarges a rectangular area around the target region over time, as shown in Fig. 5 (middle). The zoom factor increased from 1 to 3 within 60 ms, enlarging an area of $2°$. It was inspired from optical expansion of approaching objects that attract our attention [6].

5.2   Application in VR

In 2017 the method was successfully applied in VR, in an HMD [11] and a dome projection system [12]. Following the motivation for application in VR as given in Sect. 3, it was suggested to extend the original technique by eccentricity-based scaling and perspective distortion correction.

A further extension was presented, as shown in Fig. 5 (right), that adapts the shape of the zooming area to a circular shape instead of a rectangular, and changed the border from a sharp edge to a more smooth transition. Without sharp corners and smooth edges, the stimulus is less likely to be actively perceived and attract overt attention and thus to provide a higher degree of unobtrusiveness. Both methods employed eye tracking to hide their respective image manipulation upon target-directed saccades. Therefore, both can be categorized as subtle and gaze contingent attention guidance methods.

Fig. 5. Original image, zooming rectangle and zooming circle stimuli (cutout around target region). Images from [12].

6   Approach: Temporal Luminance Modulation

A bunch of approaches have been proposed that suggest to temporally modulate the perceived brightness of target regions to attract attention, when being perceived in peripheral vision. This mainly builds on two known facts from our human vision with respect to the peripheral visual field: we have a strongly reduced color perception but are more sensitive to motion (brightness changes) as compared to the fovea [9,29,32,35].

6.1   Foundation

A foundation for multiple later research was laid in 2009 with the work by Bailey *et al.* called subtle gaze direction (SGD) [2]. It presents a technique that was originally developed for desktop environments, in which a stimulus is shown in two distinct states, as depicted in Fig. 6. The original color of pixels within a circular region of 0.76° visual angle smoothly alternates between 9.5 % black and white, with a frequency of 10 Hz (luminance modulation). Also warm–cool (red–blue) color modulation was tested but resulted in weaker guidance performance. A radial gaussian fall-off is used to smoothly blend the stimulus into the surrounding image area. To keep stimuli as subtle as possible, the effect was switched off as soon as the viewers' performed a saccade with a maximum of 10° deviation towards the target. A stationary eye tracking system was used to track the users' gaze in real–time, i.e. its an example of a subtle and gaze contingent guidance method.

Fig. 6. Bright (left) and dark (right) states of the stimulus used in SGD and SIBM. Intensity is enhanced for demonstration purposes.

6.2 Application in VR

The more successful version of the original technique (luminance modulation) was later adapted for compatibility with VR environments [13]. Similar to colored dots and zooming approaches, it was recommended to apply perspective distortion compensation in combination with eccentricity-based scaling as suggested in Sect. 3. Considering the smooth gaussian blending, eye tracking-based deactivation and dynamic scaling of the stimulus, the technique has to be categorized as an example of subtle and gaze contingent attention guidance methods.

6.3 Application Without Eye Tracking

Another extension to the basic approach was presented in 2017 by Waldin *et al.* [42]. To overcome the requirement of an eye tracking system, in order to remain unobtrusive, they supposed to exploit a frequency threshold in human perception, i.e. the critical fusion frequency (or critical flicker frequency). It marks the maximum temporal resolution of our visual system, above which flickering between different colors results in perception of a single mixed color. More precisely, they suggest to exploit that this threshold is higher in our peripheral as compared to our foveal vision [10,39], i.e. one can perceive high frequency flicker in the periphery, that one can not perceive with foveal vision. This allows the method to be perceived only in the periphery, without distracting/being visible when viewers' directly look at the stimulus. Hence, it remains subtle without the need for an additional eye tracking system. They found that frequencies between 60–72 Hz, requiring a display refresh rate of 120–144 Hz, were high enough to induce the desired effect. To smoothly blend the flickering into the underlying scene, the approach applies dithering to approximate the smooth transition, like shown in Fig. 7. Whilst it does not require eye tracking anymore, the method can still be regarded as gaze contingent because the appearance of the stimulus still depends on viewers' actual gaze.

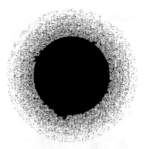

Fig. 7. Stimulus mask with dithered edge for smooth transition between flickering and non-flickering pixels. Image from [42].

7   Binocular Rivalry

Binocular rivalry describes the situation which arises when our eyes gather different information from the same location. In this situation our brain must resolve this conflict, which itself was already thoroughly studied during the last decades [1,5,26,30]. In real environments, binocular rivalry occurs all the time due to slightly different perspectives of our eyes. E.g. when looking at an object that is partly covered by another object in front of it, the line of sight of one eye might just pass by (onto the rear object) while the other eye's sight is blocked by the foremost object. Typically, our brain uses these kind of conflicts in order to improve depth perception. An essential part of all HMDs is that the scene has to be rendered for each eye separately. By applying different image manipulations on the target region in both eyes' images, binocular rivalry can be triggered easily—anywhere instead of only along edges.

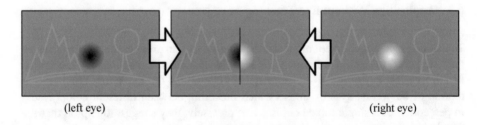

(left eye)   (right eye)

Fig. 8. Concept of binocular rivalry. Image adapted from [14].

7.1   Application in VR

A recently presented approach, termed Deadeye, suggests to exploit this effect in the field of attention guidance [21,22]. It is presented for search task support in complex visualization scenarios by completely hiding the target object (or object part) in only one eye's view. So, the binocular rivalry effect would be elicited for exactly this object, right to the edge, and would not interfere with the surrounding. One drawback might be that the method is limited to actual 3D scenes, and not readily applicable in 2D, i.e. panorama photographs would have to be manually edited to have a version with removed target objects.

A closely related approach, termed stereo inverse brightness modulation (SIBM), was also presented just recently attempts to induce the binocular rivalry effect through a more generic post processing effect [14]. Instead of hiding image parts on the target region, it was suggested to apply different brightness modulations to binocular images. More precisely, the method applies a static version of the SGD stimulus (see Sect. 6) to both eyes' images. The bright modulation is applied on one eye's image and the dark modulation on the other, as depicted in Fig. 8, but without the temporal flicker of the original approach. This way the effect can be applied anywhere in the viewers' FOV, was shown to smoothly blend with its surrounding, and subtly attracts viewers' attention. As the method analyzes gaze tracking data to hide the stimulus once a viewer reached the target, it is considered a subtle and gaze contingent attention guidance method.

8 Future Work

Within this chapter on subtle visual attention guidance a selection of current state-of-the-art approaches have been presented together with a brief insight on important perceptual backgrounds. Many more approaches exist and should be taken into consideration for future work. They are left out without any implications on performance, subtleness or any other aspect.

Despite not being visual and thus being outside the scope of this work, for the sake of completeness a closely related field of research should not be missed, that is: sound [18,33]. It provides promising approaches that would most probably work well in concert with most visual methods in favor of increased effectiveness, and should therefore be considered in future work as well.

Acknowledgements. The authors gratefully acknowledge funding by the German Science Foundation (DFG MA2555/15-1 "Immersive Digital Reality" and DFG INST 188/409-1 FUGG "ICG Dome").

References

1. Alais, D., Blake, R.: Binocular Rivalry. MIT Press, Cambridge (2005)
2. Bailey, R., McNamara, A., Sudarsanam, N., Grimm, C.: Subtle gaze direction. ACM Trans. Graph. (TOG) **28**(4), 100 (2009)
3. Barth, E., Dorr, M., Böhme, M., Gegenfurtner, K., Martinetz, T.: Guiding the mind's eye: improving communication and vision by external control of the scanpath. In: Human Vision and Electronic Imaging XI, vol. 6057, p. 60570D. International Society for Optics and Photonics (2006)
4. Biocca, F., Owen, C., Tang, A., Bohil, C.: Attention issues in spatial information systems: directing mobile users' visual attention using augmented reality. J. Manag. Inf. Syst. **23**(4), 163–184 (2007)
5. Blake, R.: A neural theory of binocular rivalry. Psychol. Rev. **96**(1), 145 (1989)

6. Dorr, M., Martinetz, T., Gegenfurtner, K., Barth, E.: Guidance of eye movements on a gaze-contingent display. In: Ilg, U.J., Bülthoff, H.H., Mallot, H.A. (eds.) Dynamic Perception Workshop of the GI Section "Computer Vision", pp. 89–94 (2004)

7. Dorr, M., Rasche, C., Barth, E.: A gaze-contingent, acuity-adjusted mouse cursor. In: COGAIN2009 Proceedings, p. 39 (2009)

8. Dorr, M., Vig, E., Gegenfurtner, K.R., Martinetz, T., Barth, E.: Eye movement modelling and gaze guidance. In: Fourth International Workshop on Human-Computer Conversation (2008)

9. Fiorentini, A., Baumgartner, G., Magnussen, S., Schiller, P.H., Thomas, J.P.: 7 - the perception of brightness and darkness: relations to neuronal receptive fields. In: Spillmann, L., Werner, J.S. (eds.) Visual Perception, pp. 129–161. Academic Press, San Diego (1990). https://doi.org/10.1016/B978-0-12-657675-7.50013-2

10. Fukuda, T.: Relation between fucker fusion threshold and retinal positions. Percept. Mot. Skills **49**(1), 3–17 (1979)

11. Grogorick, S., Albuquerque, G., Magnor, M.: Comparing unobtrusive gaze guiding stimuli in head-mounted displays. In: Proceedings of IEEE International Conference on Image Processing (ICIP) (October 2018). https://doi.org/10.1109/ICIP.2018.8451784

12. Grogorick, S., Albuquerque, G., Tauscher, J.P., Magnor, M.: Comparison of unobtrusive visual guidance methods in an immersive dome environment. ACM Trans. Appl. Percept. (TAP) **15**(4), 27 (2018)

13. Grogorick, S., Stengel, M., Eisemann, E., Magnor, M.: Subtle gaze guidance for immersive environments. In: Proceedings of the ACM Symposium on Applied Perception, pp. 4:1–4:7. ACM (2017)

14. Grogorick, S., Tauscher, J.P., Albuquerque, G., Kassubeck, M., Magnor, M.: Towards VR attention guidance: environment-dependent perceptual threshold for stereo inverse brightness modulation. In: Proceedings of ACM Symposium on Applied Perception (SAP) (September 2019). https://doi.org/10.1145/3343036.3343137

15. Gutwin, C., Cockburn, A., Coveney, A.: Peripheral popout: the influence of visual angle and stimulus intensity on popout effects. In: Proceedings of the 2017 CHI Conference on Human Factors in Computing Systems, pp. 208–219. ACM (2017)

16. Hata, H., Koike, H., Sato, Y.: Visual guidance with unnoticed blur effect. In: Proceedings of the International Working Conference on Advanced Visual Interfaces, pp. 28–35. ACM (2016)

17. Hoffmann, R., Baudisch, P., Weld, D.S.: Evaluating visual cues for window switching on large screens. In: Proceedings of the SIGCHI Conference on Human Factors in Computing Systems, pp. 929–938. ACM (2008)

18. Iordanescu, L., Guzman-Martinez, E., Grabowecky, M., Suzuki, S.: Characteristic sounds facilitate visual search. Psychon. Bull. Rev. **15**(3), 548–554 (2008)

19. Jarodzka, H., van Gog, T., Dorr, M., Scheiter, K., Gerjets, P.: Learning to see: guiding students' attention via a model's eye movements fosters learning. Learn. Instr. **25**, 62–70 (2013)

20. Khan, A., Matejka, J., Fitzmaurice, G., Kurtenbach, G.: Spotlight: directing users' attention on large displays. In: Proceedings of the SIGCHI Conference on Human Factors in Computing Systems, pp. 791–798. ACM (2005)

21. Krekhov, A., Cmentowski, S., Waschk, A., Krüger, J.: Deadeye visualization revisited: investigation of preattentiveness and applicability in virtual environments. IEEE Trans. Visual. Comput. Graph. **26**(1), 547–557 (2019). https://doi.org/10.1109/TVCG.2019.2934370

22. Krekhov, A., Krüger, J.: Deadeye: a novel preattentive visualization technique based on dichoptic presentation. IEEE Trans. Visual. Comput. Graph. **25**(1), 936–945 (2018)

23. Levi, D.M., Klein, S.A., Aitsebaomo, A.: Vernier acuity, crowding and cortical magnification. Vis. Res. **25**(7), 963–977 (1985)

24. Lin, Y.C., Chang, Y.J., Hu, H.N., Cheng, H.T., Huang, C.W., Sun, M.: Tell me where to look: investigating ways for assisting focus in 360° video. In: Proceedings of the 2017 CHI Conference on Human Factors in Computing Systems, pp. 2535–2545. ACM (2017)
25. Lintu, A., Carbonell, N.: Gaze guidance through peripheral stimuli (2009). https://hal.inria.fr/inria-00421151. Working paper or preprint
26. Logothetis, N.K., Leopold, D.A., Sheinberg, D.L.: What is rivalling during binocular rivalry? Nature **380**(6575), 621 (1996)
27. McNamara, A., Bailey, R., Grimm, C.: Improving search task performance using subtle gaze direction. In: Proceedings of the 5th Symposium on Applied Perception in Graphics and Visualization, pp. 51–56. ACM (2008)
28. Nielsen, L.T., et al.: Missing the point: an exploration of how to guide users' attention during cinematic virtual reality. In: Proceedings of the 22nd ACM Conference on Virtual Reality Software and Technology, pp. 229–232. ACM (2016)
29. Ogden, T.E., Miller, R.F.: Studies of the optic nerve of the rhesus monkey: nerve fiber spectrum and physiological properties. Vis. Res. **6**(9–10), 485 (1966). IN2
30. Paffen, C.L., Hooge, I.T., Benjamins, J.S., Hogendoorn, H.: A search asymmetry for interocular conflict. Atten. Percept. Psychophys. **73**(4), 1042–1053 (2011)
31. Pausch, R., Snoddy, J., Taylor, R., Watson, S., Haseltine, E.: Disney's Aladdin: first steps toward storytelling in virtual reality. In: Proceedings of the 23rd Annual Conference on Computer Graphics and Interactive Techniques, pp. 193–203. ACM (1996)
32. Rosenholtz, R.: Capabilities and limitations of peripheral vision. Ann. Rev. Vis. Sci. **2**, 437–457 (2016)
33. Rothe, S., Hußmann, H.: Guiding the viewer in cinematic virtual reality by diegetic cues. In: De Paolis, L.T., Bourdot, P. (eds.) AVR 2018. LNCS, vol. 10850, pp. 101–117. Springer, Cham (2018). https://doi.org/10.1007/978-3-319-95270-3_7
34. Sato, Y., Sugano, Y., Sugimoto, A., Kuno, Y., Koike, H.: Sensing and controlling human gaze in daily living space for human-harmonized information environments. In: Nishida, T. (ed.) Human-Harmonized Information Technology, vol. 1, pp. 199–237. Springer, Tokyo (2016). https://doi.org/10.1007/978-4-431-55867-5_8
35. Sekuler, R., Anstis, S., Braddick, O.J., Brandt, T., Movshon, J.A., Orban, G.: 9 - the perception of motion. In: Spillmann, L., Werner, J.S. (eds.) Visual Perception, pp. 205–230. Academic Press, San Diego (1990). https://doi.org/10.1016/B978-0-12-657675-7.50015-6. http://www.sciencedirect.com/science/article/pii/B9780126576757500156
36. Sheikh, A., Brown, A., Watson, Z., Evans, M.: Directing attention in 360-degree video. In: Proceedings of the IBC 2016 Conference. IET (2016). https://doi.org/10.1049/ibc.2016.0029
37. Speicher, M., Rosenberg, C., Degraen, D., Daiber, F., Krúger, A.: Exploring visual guidance in 360-degree videos. In: Proceedings of the 2019 ACM International Conference on Interactive Experiences for TV and Online Video, pp. 1–12. ACM (2019)
38. Strasburger, H., Rentschler, I., Jüttner, M.: Peripheral vision and pattern recognition: a review. J. Vis. **11**(5), 13–13 (2011). https://doi.org/10.1167/11.5.13
39. Tyler, C.W., Hamer, R.D.: Eccentricity and the Ferry-Porter law. JOSA A **10**(9), 2084–2087 (1993)
40. Tynan, P.D., Sekuler, R.: Motion processing in peripheral vision: reaction time and perceived velocity. Vis. Res. **22**(1), 61–68 (1982)
41. Vig, E., Dorr, M., Barth, E.: Learned saliency transformations for gaze guidance. In: IS&T/SPIE Electronic Imaging, pp. 78650W–78650W. International Society for Optics and Photonics (2011)
42. Waldin, N., Waldner, M., Viola, I.: Flicker observer effect: guiding attention through high frequency flicker in images. In: Computer Graphics Forum, vol. 36, pp. 467–476. Wiley Online Library (2017)

43. Wernert, E.A., Hanson, A.J.: A framework for assisted exploration with collaboration. In: Proceedings of the Conference on Visualization 1999: Celebrating Ten Years, pp. 241–248. IEEE Computer Society Press (1999)
44. Weymouth, F.W.: Visual sensory units and the minimum angle of resolution. Optom. Vis. Sci. **40**(9), 550–568 (1963)

Redirected Walking in VR

Qi Sun[1](✉) (iD), Anjul Patney[2](iD), and Frank Steinicke[3]

[1] Adobe, San José, USA
qisun0@gmail.com
[2] Facebook Reality Labs, Redmond, USA
anjul.patney@gmail.com
[3] University of Hamburg, Hamburg, Germany
frank.steinicke@uni-hamburg.de
http://qisun.me/, https://anjulpatney.com/,
https://www.inf.uni-hamburg.de/en/inst/ab/hci/people/steinicke.html

Abstract. Virtual Reality (VR) content creators usually design large virtual environments. However, the available physical spaces are typically limited and contain several interior obstacles such as furniture, cables or computers. Thus, users may experience discontinuity or even dangers while naturally walking in VR.

Redirected walking (RDW) approaches consist of a series of VR-based locomotion techniques, which introduce perceptually unnoticeable virtual camera motion offset from a user's movements. In this chapter we summarize the state-of-art RDW techniques on how to more significantly redirect users towards infinite walking while avoiding both static and dynamic dangers.

Keywords: Perception · Virtual reality

1 Introduction

Ideally, a VR environment should offer full immersion benefiting from natural movement. Current VR solutions, however, usually have limited moving space due to hardware limitations (for instance, the small booth of CAVEs or the limited tracking range of HMDs). More importantly, users are not able to see the physical environment, in particular physical obstacles, with their full field of view covered by the HMDs. Given the limitations above, manufacturers have to deploy less natural means such as gamepads or mouse/keyboard to control their movements, which affects the sense of presence compared to real walking [23].

The optimal experience is infinite walking in a compact physical room, which increases presence and decreases discomfort caused by visual-vestibular inconsistency by allowing the user to walk freely in a common physical space [23]. A major challenge is how to embed a large virtual space within a given small, irregular, multi-user physical space while minimizing interruptions. Treadmills

© Springer Nature Switzerland AG 2020
M. Magnor and A. Sorkine-Hornung (Eds.): Real VR, LNCS 11900, pp. 285–292, 2020.
https://doi.org/10.1007/978-3-030-41816-8_12

or other physical devices can address the problem, but are less practical due to the expense, space usage, and motion limitation to the users.

One of the *current* state-of-the-art techniques for solving the mapping problem using only a head-mounted display (HMD) is redirected walking (RDW). These methods create a distorted mapping of the virtual environment by applying to the world subtle rigid-body and nonlinear transformations, respectively. This is a significant step towards practical room-scale VR for unconstrained scenarios. In this chapter, multiple methodology categories of performing redirected walking are discussed.

2   Background

The traditional approach of RDW was introduced by Razzaque et al. [13] and is based on slightly rotating the user's view to one direction while she walks on a straight path in the VE. Then, the user will unconsciously compensate the rotation by walking on a curved path in the opposite direction. As a result, the user will walk on a circular arc in the real world (cf. Fig. 1(a)). There are several other redirection techniques in addition to curvature gains. While the traditional RDW approach is based on curvature gains, the terms RDW and Redirection Techniques are often used almost interchangeably.

Suma *et al.* introduced a taxonomy of redirection techniques that classifies these techniques into the categories Repositioning or Reorientation, Subtle or Overt, and Discrete or Continuous [18]. Repositioning techniques manipulate the position of the virtual viewpoint of the user, whereas reorientation techniques manipulate their orientation, which are usually focused on the yaw rotation. Subtle techniques are intended to be not noticed by the user, i.e. manipulations are below the user's detection thresholds. Discrete techniques redirect the user in discrete steps. For example, instant teleportation [3] is a discrete overt repositioning technique, and impossible spaces [20] are a discrete subtle redirection technique based on scene layouts, which would be impossible in the real world. For instance, such impossible spaces are composed of scenes whose architecture is self-overlapping or changing when the user does not pay attention. Continuous techniques, on the other hand, make use of a continuous motion.

3   Redirection Techniques

The main goal of RDW is to achieve higher degree of spatial size difference between virtual and physical spaces. Difference solutions involving motion sensitivity, change blindness, and geometric content recreation have been presented.

3.1   Gain-Based RDW

About a decade after Razzaque et al. introduced RDW based on curvature gain, Steinicke et al. revisited this technique and described this and other manipulations by means of gains. For example, curvature gains can be defined as follows:

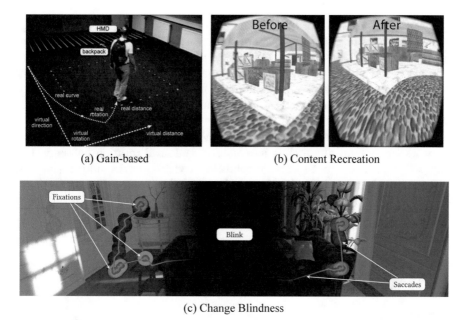

(a) Gain-based   (b) Content Recreation

(c) Change Blindness

Fig. 1. Different redirection approaches. (a) shows an example of redirecting users via undetectable angular threshold [17]. (b) shows the virtual scene before and after geometric recreation in [22]. (c) illustrates redirection via change (blink) blindness from [9].

$g_C := 1$, where r_{real} describes the radius of the circle on which the users r_{real} are guided in the real world [17]. When redirecting a user, her visual feedback is consistent with movements in the VE, but proprioceptive and vestibular feedback systems are coupled to the physical world. It is known from perceptual and cognitive psychology that vision often dominates proprioception and vestibular sensation when the information from these senses is in conflict. However, if the visual-proprioceptive conflicts are small enough, humans will not even be able to notice that they are manipulated. In perceptual experiments where human participants can use only vision to judge their motion through a virtual scene, they can successfully estimate their momentary direction of locomotion, but are worse in perceiving their paths of travel. Since humans tend to compensate for slight visual-proprioceptive inconsistencies during locomotor control while walking, it becomes possible to guide users along real-world paths, which differ from the paths they perceive in the virtual world.

One set of techniques in this category are gains for translation, rotation, and also curvature. A gain describes differences between real and virtual motions, i.e., ratios between a user's movements in the real world and in the VE. A translation gain $g_T := T_{\text{virtual}}$ manipulates the virtual velocity of the user, making her walk T_{real} slower or faster in the VE compared to the velocity in the real world [7]. A rotation gain $g_R := R_{\text{virtual}}$ increases or decreases the virtual rotation of the R_{real} viewpoint relative to the rotation in the real world. However, no matter which technique is used, when the user hits a boundary of the tracking space, she has to be stopped and reset in a suitable way. For this resetting phase, several discrete and continuous approaches exist, e.g., freeze-and-turn [25] or visual distractors [12].

In a VR setting, people have limited threshold of noticing both positive and negative gains in terms of both distance and angles. This can be utilized in redirecting users' walking path [13]. There have been extensive studies testifying the maximal thresholds [1,6,11,19].

Researchers have proposed two primary methods of redirected walking: those that work by dynamically scaling user motion and head rotation for the virtual camera [1,13,14,17] due to sensory conflicts in virtual environments [16], and those that work by warping the virtual scene [5,22].

3.2 Content Recreation

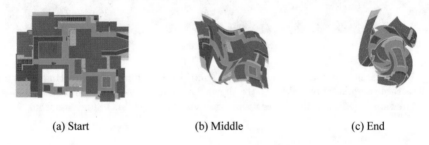

(a) Start   (b) Middle   (c) End

Fig. 2. Example of a geometric recreation process [22]. The figures are floor plans of an outdoor virtual scene. The green area shows walkable paths. (a) shows the stage at the beginning of the optimization. (b) and (c) illustrate the process during the optimization. It is noticeable that the space usage is significantly saved after the optimization.

Geometry creation and processing were meant for generating the visual content offline. An intuitive idea is to adaptively change the shape of virtual scene so that it can fit the different physical environment, as shown in Fig. 2. For instance, how to

- preserve the virtual world appearance while observing the physical world geometry to balance between visual fidelity and navigation comfort
- minimize angular and distal distortions while avoiding obstacles and boundaries, and a dynamic inverse map that guides natural locomotion and resolves local ambiguities
- adaptively respond to environmental changes such as moving objects and other users

The limitation of gain-based redirected walking, however, is the relatively limited unnoticeable threshold. A higher-than-threshold angular or spatial gain would be noticeable thus causing sickness. Being orthogonal to the implicit human perception, the content itself may be regenerated to enable the redirected walking. For example, the room structure [24] or the geometry [4,5,22] (as shown in Fig. 1(b)). The current methods however, may suffer from the limited applicable scenarios with highly-occluded scenes. With large open spaces as the virtual environment, the shape manipulations are usually noticeable by the users.

3.3 Perceptually-Driven Change Blindness

Content recreation may introduce a larger level of redirection, yet it may cause shape distortion. With the extensive advancement of eye-tracking and brain-computer interfaces (BCI), the perceptual change blindness approach takes the advantages of both approaches: it utilizes the tracked human gaze and detected perceptual behaviors.

A saccade is the rapid eye movement that occurs when we change fixation points. During normal viewing, saccades occur several times a second, contain extremely fast motion (up to $900°/s$), and are long (20–200 ms) compared to VR frame durations [2]. Saccades are among many behaviors that trigger temporary perceptual suppression. Similarly, such perceptual blindness occurs during blinks as well [15]. Others include masking by patterns, tactile saccades [26], etc.

The key of utilizing these factors are to (more significantly) redirect users while they fall into perceptual blindness. For example, saccade [21] or blink [8,9] (as shown in Figs. 1(c) and 3).

(a) Before saccade   (b) After saccade

Fig. 3. Illustration of change blindness redirection using saccade, as in [21]. During a fast eye movement (a.k.a. saccade), the virtual camera moves gradually (from (a) to (b)) without being noticed by the user.

4   Future Work and Conclusion

Space limitation is a core challenge limiting the broad deployment of VR devices. The virtual scene designed by creators might be larger than the actual space where the costumers use the VR devices. This spatial conflict may cause unsmooth experience or even dangers to the users. Researchers have been putting extensive efforts on reducing this spatial conflict. The most common way used today is to use mouse and keyboard to control the camera motion. However this is not the natural way that people move in real life, which is the aim of AR.

In this chapter, we summarized one of the state-of-the-art techniques, redirected walking. Its goal is to change and control users' walking VR without being noticed. Current techniques comprise increasing/decreasing rotational and translational gains, changing blindness, or automatically recreating the virtual scene. Recent trends in machine learning has also brought the possibility of using reinforcement learning [10].

So far, the capability of performing redirection is limited due to the small range of unnoticeable gains. Moreover, the recent development and deployment of see-through AR displays introduces extra challenges for performing redirection. Specifically, with the capability of seeing the static reference, the physical world, the movements of the virtual camera become easier to notice. That being said, the unnoticeable gains can be significantly lower. Finding novel means of addressing this limitation remains an open challenge.

References

1. Azmandian, M., Grechkin, T., Rosenberg, E.S.: An evaluation of strategies for two-user redirected walking in shared physical spaces. In: 2017 IEEE Virtual Reality (VR), pp. 91–98 (March 2017). https://doi.org/10.1109/VR.2017.7892235
2. Bahill, A.T., Clark, M.R., Stark, L.: The main sequence, a tool for studying human eye movements. Math. Biosci. **24**(3–4), 191–204 (1975). http://www.sciencedirect.com/science/article/pii/0025556475900759
3. Bozgeyikli, E., Raij, A., Katkoori, S., Dubey, R.: Point & #38; teleport locomotion technique for virtual reality. In: Proceedings of the 2016 Annual Symposium on Computer-Human Interaction in Play, CHI PLAY 2016, pp. 205–216. ACM, New York (2016). https://doi.org/10.1145/2967934.2968105
4. Dong, Z.C., Fu, X.M., Yang, Z., Liu, L.: Redirected smooth mappings for multiuser real walking in virtual reality. ACM Trans. Graph. **38**(5), 149:1–149:17 (2019). https://doi.org/10.1145/3345554
5. Dong, Z.C., Fu, X.M., Zhang, C., Wu, K., Liu, L.: Smooth assembled mappings for large-scale real walking. ACM Trans. Graph. **36**(6), 211:1–211:13 (2017). https://doi.org/10.1145/3130800.3130893
6. Grechkin, T., Thomas, J., Azmandian, M., Bolas, M., Suma, E.: Revisiting detection thresholds for redirected walking: combining translation and curvature gains. In: Proceedings of the ACM Symposium on Applied Perception, SAP 2016, pp. 113–120. ACM, New York (2016). https://doi.org/10.1145/2931002.2931018

7. Interrante, V., O'Rourke, E., Gray, L., Anderson, L., Ries, B.: A quantitative assessment of the impact on spatial understanding of exploring a complex immersive virtual environment using augmented real walking versus flying. In: Proceedings of the 13th Eurographics Symposium on Virtual Environments (2007). entered As Is, not found here. https://portalparts.acm.org/2390000/2386042/fm/frontmatter.pdf?ip=129.105.240.218

8. Langbehn, E., Bruder, G., Steinicke, F.: Subliminal reorientation and repositioning in virtual reality during eye blinks. In: Proceedings of Spatial User Interaction, pp. 213–213 (2016). https://doi.org/10.1145/2983310.2989204

9. Langbehn, E., Steinicke, F., Lappe, M., Welch, G.F., Bruder, G.: In the blink of an eye: leveraging blink-induced suppression for imperceptible position and orientation redirection in virtual reality. ACM Trans. Graph. **37**(4), 1–11 (2018)

10. Lee, D., Cho, Y., Lee, I.: Real-time optimal planning for redirected walking using deep q-learning. In: 2019 IEEE Conference on Virtual Reality and 3D User Interfaces (VR), pp. 63–71 (March 2019). https://doi.org/10.1109/VR.2019.8798121

11. Nilsson, N.C., et al.: 15 years of research on redirected walking in immersive virtual environments. IEEE Comput. Graph. Appl. **38**(2), 44–56 (2018)

12. Peck, T.C., Whitton, M.C., Fuchs, H.: Evaluation of reorientation techniques for walking in large virtual environments. In: 2008 IEEE Virtual Reality Conference, pp. 121–127 (March 2008). https://doi.org/10.1109/VR.2008.4480761

13. Razzaque, S., Kohn, Z., Whitton, M.C.: Redirected walking. In: Proceedings of Eurographics, vol. 9, pp. 105–106, Manchester (2001)

14. Razzaque, S., Swapp, D., Slater, M., Whitton, M.C., Steed, A.: Redirected walking in place. In: EGVE 2002, pp. 123–130 (2002). http://dl.acm.org/citation.cfm?id=509709.509729

15. Ridder III, W.H., Tomlinson, A.: A comparison of saccadic and blink suppression in normal observers. Vis. Res. **37**(22), 3171–3179 (1997). https://doi.org/10.1016/S0042-6989(97)00110-7. http://www.sciencedirect.com/science/article/pii/S0042698997001107

16. Steinicke, F., Bruder, G., Jerald, J., Frenz, H., Lappe, M.: Analyses of human sensitivity to redirected walking. In: Proceedings of the 2008 ACM Symposium on Virtual Reality Software and Technology, VRST 2008, pp. 149–156. ACM, New York (2008). https://doi.org/10.1145/1450579.1450611

17. Steinicke, F., Bruder, G., Jerald, J., Frenz, H., Lappe, M.: Estimation of detection thresholds for redirected walking techniques. IEEE TVCG **16**(1), 17–27 (2010). https://doi.org/10.1109/TVCG.2009.62

18. Suma, E.A., Bruder, G., Steinicke, F., Krum, D.M., Bolas, M.: A taxonomy for deploying redirection techniques in immersive virtual environments. In: 2012 IEEE Virtual Reality Workshops (VRW), pp. 43–46 (March 2012). https://doi.org/10.1109/VR.2012.6180877

19. Suma, E.A., Krum, D., Bolas, M.: Redirected walking in mixed reality training applications. In: Human Walking in Virtual Environments: Perception, Technology, and Applications, pp. 319–331. Springer, New York (2013). https://doi.org/10.1007/978-1-4419-8432-6_14

20. Suma, E.A., Lipps, Z., Finkelstein, S., Krum, D.M., Bolas, M.: Impossible spaces: maximizing natural walking in virtual environments with self-overlapping architecture. IEEE Trans. Visual. Comput. Graph. **18**(4), 555–564 (2012). https://doi.org/10.1109/TVCG.2012.47

21. Sun, Q., et al.: Towards virtual reality infinite walking: dynamic saccadic redirection. ACM Trans. Graph. **34**(4), 16 (2018). http://casual-effects.com/research/Sun2018Saccade/. sIGGRAPH 2018

22. Sun, Q., Wei, L.Y., Kaufman, A.: Mapping virtual and physical reality. ACM Trans. Graph. **35**(4), 64:1–64:12 (2016). https://doi.org/10.1145/2897824.2925883

23. Usoh, M., et al.: Walking > walking-in-place > flying, in virtual environments. In: SIGGRAPH 1999, pp. 359–364 (1999). https://doi.org/10.1145/311535.311589

24. Vasylevska, K., Kaufmann, H., Bolas, M., Suma, E.A.: Flexible spaces: dynamic layout generation for infinite walking in virtual environments. In: 2013 IEEE Symposium on 3D User Interfaces (3DUI), pp. 39–42 (March 2013). https://doi.org/ 10.1109/3DUI.2013.6550194

25. Williams, B., et al.: Exploring large virtual environments with an HMD when physical space is limited. In: Proceedings of the 4th Symposium on Applied Perception in Graphics and Visualization, APGV 2007, pp. 41–48. ACM, New York (2007). https://doi.org/10.1145/1272582.1272590

26. Ziat, M., Hayward, V., Chapman, C.E., Ernst, M.O., Lenay, C.: Tactile suppression of displacement. Exp. Brain Res. **206**(3), 299–310 (2010). https://doi.org/10.1007/ s00221-010-2407-z

Immersive Virtual Reality Audio Rendering Adapted to the Listener and the Room

Hansung Kim[1]([⊠])[ID], Luca Remaggi[1,2][ID], Philip J. B. Jackson[1][ID], and Adrian Hilton[1][ID]

[1] CVSSP, University of Surrey, Guildford, UK
{h.kim,p.jackson,a.hilton}@surrey.ac.uk
[2] Creative Tech UK, Creative Labs, Staines-upon-Thames, UK
luca_remaggi@cle.creative.com
https://www.surrey.ac.uk/centre-vision-speech-signal-processing,
https://uk.creative.com/

Abstract. The visual and auditory modalities are the most important stimuli for humans. In order to maximise the sense of immersion in VR environments, a plausible spatial audio reproduction synchronised with visual information is essential. However, measuring acoustic properties of an environment using audio equipment is a complicated process. In this chapter, we introduce a simple and efficient system to estimate room acoustic for plausible spatial audio rendering using 360° cameras for real scene reproduction in VR. A simplified 3D semantic model of the scene is estimated from captured images using computer vision algorithms and convolutional neural network (CNN). Spatially synchronised audio is reproduced based on the estimated geometric and acoustic properties in the scene. The reconstructed scenes are rendered with synthesised spatial audio.

Keywords: Audio-visual VR · Geometry reconstruction · Room acoustic modelling · Spatial audio rendering

1 Introduction

Spatial audio is important for the sense of immersion in VR because human perception relies on both audio and visual information to understand and interact with the environment [67,68]. During the last decades, however, researchers mainly focused on improving the visual side of VR experiences [53,63]. The amount of research produced in this field has led to great achievements, in particular regarding 3D visualisation and human-machine interaction [74]. However, a VR experience would never be perceived as being "real" if sounds are not reproduced in harmony with the human visual perception [39,54,61]. For instance, sounds carry reverb information that humans would expect by looking at the environment [2]. This not only makes a virtual environment visually realistic,

© Springer Nature Switzerland AG 2020
M. Magnor and A. Sorkine-Hornung (Eds.): Real VR, LNCS 11900, pp. 293–318, 2020.
https://doi.org/10.1007/978-3-030-41816-8_13

but it also allows correct perception of the sound source distance [43]. Recent researches have been extended to merge spatial audio. Previous research has shown that spatio-temporal synchronisation of sound with visual information improves the sense of presence in virtual and augmented environments [33].

A plausible and coherent audio-visual reproduction can be achieved by understanding the scene geometry and related materials. Creating models that describe room acoustics has been extensively investigated in the audio communities [71]. Particular attention has been given to propose Room Impulse Responses (RIR) parameterization methods for spatial audio production [10,47,48,66]. These methods have the ability of generating a set of parameters, able to characterize the room acoustics. With focus on VR, approaches focusing on reproduction of spatial audio have been also proposed. For instance, it has been proposed how to reproduce binaural sounds given B-format signals [4,64].

However, it is sometimes difficult to obtain actual acoustic measurements for a certain environment considering practical applications of VR. For example, setting up microphones and speakers for acoustic measurements may be too invasive to be deployed at private spaces like living rooms or bedrooms. Furthermore, RIR is only valid at the single point of measurement and will change according to locations in the scene. What is required for immersive experiences where the user moves through the space is the acoustic modelling of the environment to allow rendering of spatial audio according to the listener position. It is impractical to measure or update RIRs according to the changes of geometry or user positions for interactive dynamic scene rendering.

Instead of direct RIR measurements using audio recording in the space, computer vision techniques can be utilised to predict room acoustics. Recently, several toolkits have been also developed to render spatial audio from the geometry and acoustic material information on VR platforms [18,45,70]. 3D Models describing both geometry and materials allow to approximate real room acoustics for VR environments [23,29]. It has been demonstrated that high-quality sound reproductions improves the perceived similarity to reference environments [6,55].

For simulating an acoustic environment in those platforms, a robust recognition method for room geometry and object materials is required. The closest work for this goal is the work by Schissler *et al.* [56] using a Microsoft Kinect sensor. They built a dense 3D geometry using a Shape-from-Motion technique from several hundreds of RGB+Depth images [13] and proposed a two-step procedure using a convolutional neural network (CNN) to estimate acoustic material properties for sound rendering. However, this approach using a normal RGB-D camera has several drawbacks as follows: (1) It requires time and resource consuming multiple captures of the scene to cover a complete scene layout estimation due to the limited field-of-views of the camera. (2) Dense geometry makes the real-time acoustic simulation impractical because it drastically increases computational complexity and run-time for spatial audio rendering.

The works introduced in this chapter are based one previously published papers for 3D acoustic room modelling [30] and spatial audio perception in VR [51]. It is well-known that human audio perception is not sensitive enough to recognise differences of sound from the change of geometrical details as long as the change is within the just-noticeable difference (JND) level [26]. Therefore, we suggest to use approximated geometry which allows the use of simple acoustic models to generate synthetic versions of the environment acoustics in a more efficient way. In this chapter, we introduce a simple pipeline for acoustic room modelling with cuboid-based room and object representation from a single pair of spherical 360° images. For cuboid model reconstruction, room interiors are assumed to be composed of planar surfaces aligned to the main axes (Manhattan world), as introduced in [20]. Generally, room layouts and large objects often fit this assumption. Objects in the scene are segmented and classified by a CNN-based semantic segmentation (SegNet) [1], and estimated acoustic properties are assigned to each object to build VR environments using spatial audio packages.

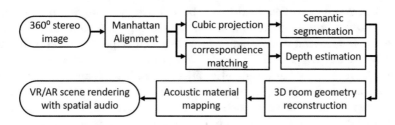

Fig. 1. Block diagram of the proposed system.

It is important to distinguish between "plausible" and "authentic" acoustic reproductions. In general, plausibility describes the agreement of the heard scene with an inner reference (expectation) [36], while authenticity judges whether it is perceptually identical to an external reference [5]. Strength and precision of spatial information vary between the audio and visual modalities, when they are analyzed individually [62]. Nonetheless, spatial information is acquired by humans as a multimodal audio-visual combination. For example, humans, as average, perform sound source localization with an error of about 2° when the reproduction is audio-only, however, for audio-visual reproductions, this error increases to about 10° [62]. This observation is typically exploited by ventriloquists. Additional studies, analyzing the effect of visual cues on plausibility of audio rendering, showed a dominance of vision over acoustic cues [3]. This means that, when in the presence of visual stimuli, the perceptual differences between a real and a synthetic acoustic environment are not as strictly defined as they are for unimodal (sound only) scenarios.

In order to evaluate the "plausibility" and "authenticity" for VR applications, RIRs generated in the VR environments are compared with the measured RIRs in the real environments. The acoustics reproduced in VR are evaluated by analysing the early decay time (EDT) and reverberation time (RT60) with the RIRs. It is difficult to define an objective metric that reliably describes the quality of a sound reproduced in VR. Therefore, subjective tests on reproduced sounds have been carried out. The sound quality and spatial impression are the main interests to be analyzed, since they are two key features characterizing spatial audio in a virtual acoustic scene [72].

2   Acoustic 3D Room Modelling from 360° Cameras

2.1   System Overview

A simple and efficient method to reproduce a 3D VR environment with acoustic properties from a vertical pair of 360° photos of a real scene is introduced. Figure 1 shows the block diagram for acoustic room modelling and VR reproduction with spatial audio in a normal room environment.

A full surrounding scene is captured by vertically aligned 360° cameras. Each camera has two fish-eye lens and two captured fish-eye images are mapped and stitched into an equirectangular image. They are aligned to the room coordinate axes by the Manhattan world alignment utilising cubic projection and the façade alignment techniques [27] which identify the principal directions. Then the process is split into two stages: semantic object classification and 3D scene reconstruction. Depth of the scene is estimated by dense correspondence matching between two images. For semantic scene segmentation and object classification, the equirectangular image is projected onto a unit cube centred on the camera to produce general perspective images and each projected image goes through the SegNet pipeline. The output labels from SegNet are back-projected to the original equirectangular format. Based on the object labels and depth information, object-labelled cuboids are reconstructed to represent the scene structure. Acoustic properties for the classified objects are assigned from the acoustic material list. Finally, the acoustic VR scene or AR sound is rendered by setting sound source and player models on the VR platform.

2.2   Visual Capture and Pre-processing

The scene is captured by two 360° cameras in order to recover 3D information from the pair. Previously this required accurately aligned high resolution spherical images from expensive industrial equipment such as Ladybug [46] and Spheron VR [59], but inexpensive off-the-shelf 360° cameras are now getting popular and provides images with good quality [19,24,52]. In this work we use two Ricoh Theta cameras [52] which provide accurately calibrated equirectangular photos aligned to the spherical coordinate system. To recover 3D information, the scene is captured at two different heights. We use a vertical stereo system rather than typical horizontal stereo because depth error induced from stereo matching errors increases as the elevation angle to the baseline decreases as reported in [28]. This error diverges to the infinity on the epipoles (blind spot). The vertical stereo system makes these blind spots on the ceiling and floor which are less important and can be easily concealed by neighbouring information, while the horizontal stereo system makes the blind spots on the side which may include

(a) Camera set up.   (b) Captured images (Top and Bottom).

Fig. 2. Visual capture system using a pair of Rico Theta cameras.

important scene information. Figure 2 shows the camera set up and captured top and bottom images of the Meeting Room (MR) scene used in the experiments.

Even though the baseline of the vertical stereo camera system is perpendicularly aligned to the ground, the spherical coordinate of each spherical camera can be misaligned either to each other or to the world (room) coordinate system. For image alignment to the room coordinate, the equirectangular image in the Spherical coordinate is projected to a unit cube in the Cartesian domain fitted to the room coordinate as shown in Fig. 3(a). If the spherical coordinate in aligned to the room coordinate, the horizontal and vertical lines in the scene are aligned to horizontal and vertical directions in each cubic projection image as shown in Fig. 3(b). We utilise Hough line detection [38] in the cubic projection images to find the optimal rotation matrix for the coordinate alignment. The 3 DOF rotation matrix can be obtained by the multiplication of single rotation matrices on x-axis (α), y-axis (β) and z-axis (γ) in Eq. 1, and the optimal α, β and γ values are found by Eq. 2, where k indexes the k-th face image in the cubic projection, H is lines detected by the Hough line detection, and C is cubic projection of the spherical image I. The Hough lines are categorised into general Hough line H, horizontal Hough lines H^h and vertical Hough lines H^v, where horizontal and vertical Hough lines represent detected Hough lines parallel and perpendicular to the horizon within $1°$ of angle difference.

$$R(\alpha, \beta, \gamma) = R_x(\alpha)R_y(\beta)R_z(\gamma) \tag{1}$$

$$(\alpha_{opt}, \beta_{opt}, \gamma_{opt}) = \operatorname*{argmax}_{\alpha,\beta,\gamma} \sum_{k=1}^{6} \frac{|H_k^h(\alpha,\beta,\gamma) \cup H_k^v(\alpha,\beta,\gamma)|}{|H_k(\alpha,\beta,\gamma)|} \qquad (2)$$

$$H_k(\alpha,\beta,\gamma) = H(C_k(R(\alpha,\beta,\gamma)I(x,y,z)))$$

Finally, alignment between two vertical stereo images can be simply found by rotating one image by a multiple of 90° on the z-axis because both images have been aligned to the room coordinate.

Figure 3(c) and (d) show an example of stereo alignment result.

2.3 Semantic Segmentation

Semantic segmentation aims to segment the scene into semantically meaningful regions and label those regions with pre-defined classes. A good survey of semantic segmentation for RGB images is available in [76]. The traditional pipeline of semantic object classification has been recently replaced by CNN [9]. CNN-based semantic segmentation architectures are still actively being developed.

(a) Cubic projection images before alignment.

(b) Cubic projection images after alignment.

(c) Original stereo image pair.   (d) Aligned stereo image pair.

Fig. 3. Spherical and cubic projection.

Estimation of acoustic properties from visual information alone is a challenging problem due to the inherent ambiguity [25]. A number of approaches have been introduced to detect material attributes from images [27,75], but their accuracy is typically below 50%, for cross-dataset scenarios, which is too low to be considered as a suitable methods for estimating absorption and scattering coefficients of objects. Even though materials can be predicted from the visual information, it is still hard to define the acoustic parameters of those materials such as roughness, density and thickness of the surface on which acoustic properties depend. For instance, we can detect a carpet on the floor, but there is no way to detect its pile type and thickness. Therefore, we use an object recognition method and map the object categories to approximated acoustic properties of materials.

SegNet [1] is used for semantic segmentation and object labelling. SegNet is a deep fully convolutional neural network architecture for semantic segmentation, designed to be efficient during training and inference whilst maintaining state-of-the-art performance. The network employs an encoder-decoder architecture, applying the first 13 convolutional layers of VGG16 [57] to encode an input image into low resolution feature maps before upsampling (decoding) them into sparse feature maps. SegNet's novel decoder utilises max-pooling indices memorised during encoding to upsample, reducing the memory required during inference significantly. Per-pixel class probabilities are the final output of the system after a multi-class soft-max classifier is applied to the decoder's final output.

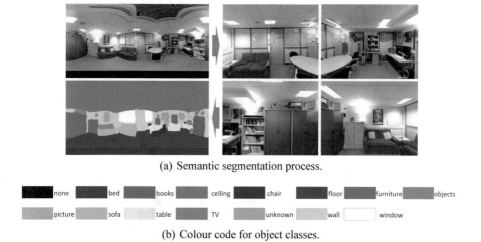

(a) Semantic segmentation process.

| none | bed | books | ceiling | chair | floor | furniture | objects |
| picture | sofa | table | TV | unknown | wall | window | |

(b) Colour code for object classes.

Fig. 4. Cubic projection and semantic segmentation.

The SegNet implementation provides a model trained on the SUN RGB-D indoor scenes dataset [58] to semantically segment structure and objects in images of indoor scenes (only the RGB channels are used in the architecture). To determine objects labels, a captured spherical (equirectangular) image is projected onto planes on a unit cube in the Cartesian domain to provide six perspective images of the scene. Each plane is set to 4:3 aspect to be matched to the trained SUN RGB-D dataset format, and also to compensate recognition error at the image boundaries. Due to cuboid alignment, two of the images are directed towards the ceiling and floor and are classified as such. The other images are individually inferred using the trained model to provide four semantically segmented images. All six output labelled images are back-projected to provide a fully labelled equirectangular image the same dimensions as the captured spherical image. Utilising this back-projection technique permits the use of segmentation models trained on standard indoor scene datasets without requiring currently unavailable large scale labelled spherical image datasets. Finally, the labelled image is refined by morphological opening process [17] to separate partially connect objects with the same label and smooth object boundaries. Small regions are eliminated to generate simplified scene structure. Each labelled region is indexed to be considered as independent object reconstruction in 3D reconstruction. The cubic projection images and final label image are shown in Fig. 4.

2.4   Depth Estimation

Depth information of the scene is estimated using correspondence matching with spherical stereo geometry illustrated in Fig. 5(a). In the proposed vertical 360° stereo setup, real-scale depth can be directly estimated from simple stereo matching along 1D vertical lines in contrast with normal depth reconstruction from perspective stereo images which requires complex internal and external camera calibrations. If we assume the angles of the projection of the point P onto the spherical 360 image pair displaced along the Z-axis are θ_t and θ_b respectively, then the angle disparity d of point $p_t(x_t, y_t)$ can be calculated as $d(\theta) = \theta_t - \theta_b$. The distance of the scene point P from the top camera is calculated by triangulation as Eq. 3, where B is the baseline distance between the camera's center of projection.

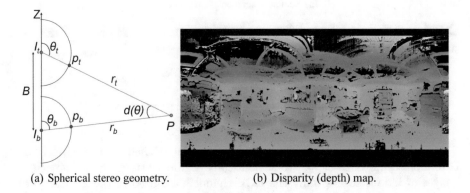

(a) Spherical stereo geometry.   (b) Disparity (depth) map.

Fig. 5. Depth estimation using a pair of spherical stereo images.

$$r_t = B / \left(\frac{\sin \theta_t}{\tan(\theta_t + d(\theta))} - \cos \theta_t \right) \tag{3}$$

Stereo matching can be carried out along the epipolar lines which are column lines in the equirectangular vertical stereo images. Any stereo matching algorithm can be used to estimate disparity between pixels in the image pair. We use a block matching method incorporating a region-diving technique [31] which produces reliable disparity fields by detecting occlusion regions and ambiguous regions based on bi-directional consistency and the ordering constraint. Figure 5(b) shows the disparity map estimated from Fig. 2(b). Black regions indicate occlusion or unmatched areas. $0° \leq \theta < 5°$ and $165° < \theta \leq 180°$ regions have been cropped because depth from disparity near the epipole areas (blind spots) is unreliable.

2.5 3D Modelling and Spatial Audio Rendering

All 2D image points on the equirectangular image are projected to the 3D space using the estimated depth information and form a 3D point cloud. This point cloud is segmented into object clusters based on the object labels. Kwon *et al.* [32] proposed cuboid fitting algorithm for 3D point clouds using least squares optimisation. Nguatem *et al.* [44] and Li *et al.* [34] used plane detection as primitives of cuboids for outdoor LiDAR scans. We use an occupancy based cuboid reconstruction method. Instead of detecting planes or major axes, cuboid primitives aligned to a Manhattan world are fitted to the point cloud clusters. The volume of the cuboid is decided by the 3D point occupancy in the cluster. In order to eliminate outliers from depth estimation and segmentation errors in the cluster, 10% of the farthest points from the centre of cluster are excluded. Finally the volume of the reconstructed cuboids are refined by the physical stability [20]. For example, floating cuboids above the ground violate the law of gravity. Any cuboid which is not supported by another stable object is extended to the ground to retain the physical stability. Cuboids near the wall are also extended to the wall because objects commonly adjoin the wall and the gap between the object and the wall increases the complexity of the scene and may cause unnecessary resonance in sound field rendering.

Table 1. Material matching to object.

Object	Material	Object	Material
Ceiling	Wood panel	Furniture	Heavy curtain
Book	Sheetlock	Chair	Wood panel
Floor	Parquet	Object	Metal
Window	Thick glass	Wall	Smooth plaster
Sofa	Heavy curtain	Table	Wood panel
TV	Metal	Unknown	Wood panel

The results of geometry reconstruction are saved as geometry and meta-data files in "OBJ" and "JSON" formats, respectively. This output is directly imported to Unity [65] to build a VR environment. A spatial audio packages such as Google Resonance Audio [18] or Steam Audio [70] is used to simulate spatial audio in the Unity engine. Google Resonance provides 22 types of acoustic materials, and Steam Audio provides 12 preset acoustic materials including 1 custom one. Both Google Resonance and Steam Audio calculate early reflections using head-related transfer functions (HRTFs) belonging to the closest Direction of Arrival (DOA) estimated by ray tracing. However, Google Resonance renders reverb through a set of virtual loudspeakers, while Steam Audio calculates a single binaural RIR to convolve with the sound because Steam Audio was developed to generate an accurate acoustic simulation while Google Resonance aims to bring the spatial audio experience to mobile devices reducing the computational complexity. As mentioned, it is difficult to directly detect acoustic properties of materials from visual input. Therefore, the object labels are mapped to the material types in Google Resonance Audio as Table 1. The acoustically closest material is assigned if it is difficult to match the material for certain objects. Finally, a virtual listener and an audio source are placed in the scene to simulate the reconstructed virtual scene with spatial audio. Figure 6 illustrates the reconstructed simplified geometry of the MR scene in Fig. 2 and reproduced VR environment with virtual sound source and player. The reconstructed VR scene can be played with real-time interaction on any VR kit supported by the Unity engine. VIVE Pro [22], a VR headset supporting spatial audio is used in our experiments.

Fig. 6. Reconstructed geometry (left) and reproduced VR environment with acoustic properties (right).

3   Estimating Room Acoustics from Audio Recordings

This section describes how to parameterize room acoustics from recorded audio signals in real and virtual environments. Although measuring RIRs in real environments is well-established [60], extracting RIR information from VR environments has not been explored yet. Therefore, the virtual environment is treated as a real one to measure room RIRs, and emulate virtual microphones and sound sources in the reconstructed virtual environments to record sounds. The general swept-sine method [14] is employed to calculate RIRs for Steam Audio, and an anechoic gun-shot (normalized in the time domain) [12] is used for Google Resonance because Google Resonance has a problem in rendering a sine signal as stated in their document [18]. The RIRs for reproduced VR environments are obtained by recording the responses at the same positions as the ground-truth RIRs measured in the real environment.

The Reverberant Spatial Audio Object (RSAO) presented in [49] and [11] models enclosed environment reverberation by defining a set of parameters describing the three RIR components [69]: the direct sound, revealing the position of the sound source; the early reflections, conveying a sense of the environmental geometry; and the late diffuse reverberation, indicating the size of the environment. In this research, RIRs recorded in B-format are employed. The early reflections are encoded into parameters describing their times of arrival (TOAs), levels, DOAs, and frequency responses. The late reverberation parameters, instead, describe its temporal envelope for a set of frequency bands. For each subband, the rate of decay is encoded together with the level in the neighbourhood of the mixing time. Direct sound's parameters follow the same flow as for the early reflections.

3.1   Early Reflection Parameters

To estimate TOAs from RIRs, a method based on the dynamic programming projected phase-slope algorithm (DYPSA) [42,49] is used. DYPSA detects the early reflections in the W-channel of a B-format RIR by observing its group delay function $G(\omega)$, with ω representing the angular frequency. Sudden variations (i.e. peaks) correspond to zero crossings in $G(\omega)$. The DYPSA output is thus a sequence of non-zero values placed at the time samples n_k, with k being the reflection index. TOAs are calculated as $t_k = n_k/f_s$, where f_s is the sampling frequency. The second parameter describing the early reflections is the level [49]. The W-channel of a B-format RIR is segmented in the neighbourhood of the detected peaks, by using a Hamming window of length D. The energy is calculated as $E_k = \frac{1}{D}\sum_{n=n_k-(D/2)}^{n_k+(D/2)}|r(n)|^2$, where $r(n)$ is the RIR. E_k is then converted into level as $A_k = \sqrt{E_k}$. DOAs are then estimated by steering a virtual cardioid microphone, considering each W-channel RIR segment containing the reflections [11]. The output of the steered cardioid can be written as $S(\mathbf{v}, n) = \frac{1}{2}[r^W(n) + v_x r^X(n) + v_y r^Y(n) + v_z r^Z(n)]$, where $\mathbf{v}$ is a spatial vector containing $v_x = \cos(\theta)\cos(\phi)$, $v_y = \sin(\theta)\cos(\phi)$, $v_z = \sin(\phi)$, for $0 \le \theta < 2\pi$ and $-\pi/2 \le \phi \le \pi/2$, with θ and ϕ being azimuth and elevation angles, respectively. $r^W(n)$, $r^X(n)$, $r^Y(n)$, and $r^Z(n)$ are the four channels of a B-format RIR. The DOA is estimated as the steered peak containing the most energy: $\arg\max_{\mathbf{v}}\sum_n S(\mathbf{v}, n)^2$. The frequency content of the early reflections is also parameterized by applying the linear predictive coding (LPC) [37] to the W-channel RIR segments. The output is a 9-th order infinite impulse response filter approximating the reflection frequency response [49].

3.2   Late Reverberation Parameters

The exponential decay at different octave bands is the key parameter chosen in RSAO to describe the late reverberation [49]. To estimate the starting point of this decay, the mixing time [10] should be determined first. We calculate the normalized echo density, as was first proposed in [35]. The mixing time is determined as when the echo density became greater than 1. The late reverberation (i.e. the portion of RIR after the mixing time) recorded at the W-channel of the B-format RIR is then passed through an octave filter bank, with the final aim of determining the frequency-dependent decay [49]. The Schroeder energy decay curve is estimated for each band and an exponential curve fitted to it, based on the decay over the first 20 dB (after the mixing time). The exponential coefficients are the RSAO late reverb parameters. For each subband, the length of an onset ramp rising linearly from zero at the first early reflection to the noise gain in the neighbourhood of the mixing time is also encoded. This allows an increase of diffuse energy even before the mixing time [11].

4   Experiments

The proposed system was evaluated for six different rooms. The Meeting Room (MR) and Usability Lab (UL) scenes are similar to typical domestic living room environments. Listening Room (LR) is an acoustically controlled room, Studio Hall (ST) is a large hall, and Kitchen (KT) is a small and narrow room. We also tested Courtyard (CY) which is not an air-tight indoor room but an outdoor area surrounded by four brick walls. All datasets with their estimated depth maps are given in Fig. 7 and are available at: http://cvssp.org/data/s3a/public/AV-Analysis2/.

4.1   Geometry Reconstruction

The 3D reconstruction and recognition process has been run on a normal PC with a Intel Core i7 3.40 GHz CPU and 32G RAM. It took less than 5 mins for the whole geometry reconstruction process including pre-processing, depth estimation and cuboid reconstruction for any data set. The semantic segmentation took around 3 mins on an NVIDIA Tesla M2090 GPU with 5 GB memory run in parallel. In a real environment, the whole process from camera setting to the final model output can be done within half an hour, which is much simpler and faster than audio-based approaches.

Figure 8 shows the reconstructed cuboid-based models with colour-coded object labels. It is clear that the proposed SegNet-based method produced meaningful segmentation results for 360° image with cubic projection. Most objects were correctly classified including windows and mirrors. However some small objects were missing due to the postprocessing. These will not significantly affect the perceived acoustics. For efficient geometry representation, Pictures and Windows are merged to Wall, and Book labels to Furniture in the final scene reconstruction. In the snapshots, Ceilings and Floors were coloured with the Wall

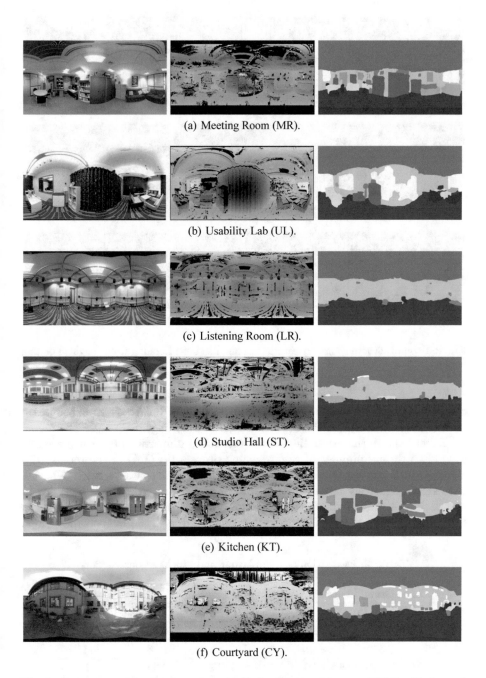

(a) Meeting Room (MR).

(b) Usability Lab (UL).

(c) Listening Room (LR).

(d) Studio Hall (ST).

(e) Kitchen (KT).

(f) Courtyard (CY).

Fig. 7. Dataset used in the experiments (Left: Captured image; Middle: Estimated depth map; Right: Semantic segmentation result. Colour index is defined as in Fig. 4(b).

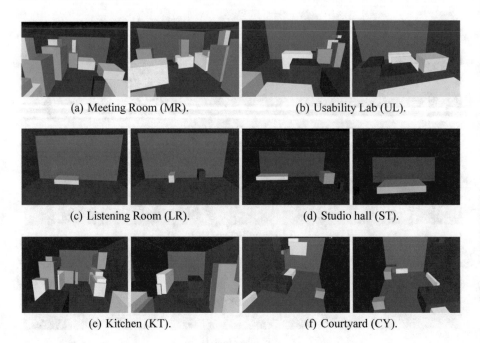

(a) Meeting Room (MR).   (b) Usability Lab (UL).

(c) Listening Room (LR).   (d) Studio hall (ST).

(e) Kitchen (KT).   (f) Courtyard (CY).

Fig. 8. Semantic room geometry estimation results (Left: Looking front, Right: Looking back).

colour because they were represented as one cuboid, but they are decomposed into Ceiling and Floor in the acoustic material mapping.

Table 2 shows the evaluation of the estimated dimensions against measured ground-truth and number of reconstructed objects (# Obj) in the rooms. The layout estimation errors vary according to the room characteristics. The UL data shows relatively large errors in wall positions due to the windows, mirror and dark wall which induce errors in correspondence matching. In the ST scene, the height of the room was incorrectly estimated due to the rails on the ceiling.

Table 2. Evaluation of room layout and object reconstruction.

Data	Ground-truth	Estimated		
	Dim (m^3)	Dim (m^3)	Err (Diag, %)	# Obj
MR	$5.61 \times 4.28 \times 2.33$	$5.52 \times 4.35 \times 2.36$	0.23	16
UL	$5.57 \times 5.20 \times 2.91$	$5.92 \times 4.95 \times 2.95$	1.28	11
LR	$5.64 \times 5.05 \times 2.90$	$5.77 \times 5.17 \times 2.98$	2.39	3
ST	$17.08 \times 14.55 \times 6.50$	$16.53 \times 14.87 \times 5.70$	1.74	4
KT	$6.64 \times 3.46 \times 2.67$	$6.95 \times 3.41 \times 2.70$	3.14	15
CY	$19.00 \times 10.10 \times -$	$18.51 \times 9.61 \times -$	(3.08)	13

It is difficult to quantitatively evaluate the reconstruction of objects in the scenes, but most of major objects have been recovered in the scenes.

4.2 Room Acoustics

For authenticity evaluation of the sound reproduced in the reconstructed scene, RIRs estimated in the VR environments are compared with the measured RIRs in the real environments for four scenes (MR, UL, LR and ST). The real RIRs were measured in the test rooms with loudspeaker setups and microphone arrays which have 48 microphones evenly spaced around two concentric circles of radii 8.5 cm and 10.6 cm, respectively, to form a custom array [50] and one additional soundfield microphone at the center of the circular array. RIRs in the VR environment are measured using a virtual microphones and the sound sources. They are obtained by recording the responses at the same positions as in the real environment. We employed Google Resonance to render the sounds in VR. In Google Resonance, HRTFs are used to create virtual loudspeakers in a sphere around the listening position. Ambisonics as one way to reproduce the soundfield.

The acoustics reproduced in VR were evaluated by analysing EDT and RT60. EDT takes into account the energy carried by the early reflections and RT60 relates to the late diffuse reflections [7]. EDT is measured as the time from the arrival of direct sound to decay 10 dB, and RT60 defines the time employed by the energy to decay 60 dB. Both EDTs and RT60s are evaluated with the average over the octave bands between 250 Hz and 8 kHz.

We also define JNDs to understand how the estimated RIRs are perceptually similar to the recorded ones. The JNDs were chosen to be the 20% for the RT60 [41] and 5% for the EDT [73] based on the literature.

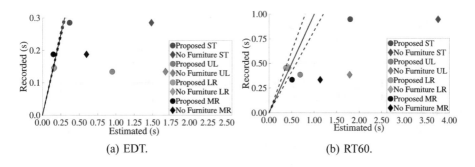

(a) EDT.   (b) RT60.

Fig. 9. Evaluation of simulated room acoustics in the VR environment against ground-truth. (a) shows the EDTs (Early Decay Times) and (b) the RT60s (Reverberation Times).

Figure 9 illustrates the comparison of the EDTs and RT60s, i.e. Fig. 9(a) and (b) respectively, for the ground-truth and estimated RIRs. Both EDTs and RT60s of the estimated RIRs were close similar to the ground-truth ones, but the

UL data showed a large error in the EDT and the ST data in the RT60. We guess the EDT was overestimated in the UL scene due to the errors in recognising the material of sofas near the microphone position (false early reflections), and the RT60 in ST was wrong because each wall was modelled as a whole concrete and the ceiling as a wooden panel while the real walls and ceiling in the ST scene have large soft panels to absorb sound as seen in Fig. 7(d).

In Fig. 9(a), also the blue circle is outside the JND region. However, we use JNDs as "ideal" reference for authenticity, due to a gap in the literature about metrics for plausibility in VR environments. In fact, the EDT JND region was defined in the literature (cited in the paper as [40]) by looking at the output of subjective tests, undertaken by using only audio as reference. Nonetheless, it is well-known that for audio-visual reproductions, such as VR, audio perception is biased by the visual side (e.g. the McGurk effect [40]). Therefore, the plausibility region would be greater than the authenticity one (i.e. defined by JND), and contain the ST EDT in Fig. 9(a).

We also compared the results with estimated room layouts without any object and included in Fig. 9 to show the importance of object recognition and classification in the scene. It is clear that the interaction of the sound with the objects lying inside the environment must be considered to accurately define the acoustic room model.

These comparisons were performed only at one listening position for each room, since only one microphone recording was available per dataset. More comparisons will be performed, However, it is well-known that RT60 (that measures the late reverberation energy) is typically constant at every position within an enclosed environment. Therefore, the analysis made during this section already provides an extensive understanding, for the rooms that have been investigated, of the simulated room reverberation.

4.3   Subjective Evaluation

The aim of subjective test is to evaluate the perceived quality and spatial impression (compared to the visual reproduction) of the reverb estimated via presented pipelines against the ground-truth and audio-based approaches. Static headphones were used for the sound reproduction, and a screen for observing the related room images. Four rooms (MR, ST, CT and KT) were tested in this experiment. The Usability Lab (UL) and Listening Room (LR) scenes were excluded because UL is similar to MR and people cannot expect sound rendered in the room with acoustically insulated walls in LR. Two sounds were employed: an anechoic speech from the TIMIT dataset [16]; and a clarinet recorded in anechoic environment, downloaded from the OpenAirLib library [8].

Two tests were carried out, looking at subjective attributes that are known to determine a reproduced sound quality [21]: the "spatial impression" and the "overall quality". Listeners were presented with MUSHRA interfaces having multiple sliders to rank each stimulus against the attribute under test (Fig. 10), within a discrete scale of integer numbers between 0 and 5. Three methods have been used to produce the stimuli. The first one, here referred as "Resonance",

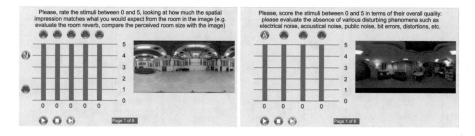

Fig. 10. Screenshots of the MUSHRA interfaces for the two tests. The spatial impression test (left) presents 5 stimuli, named between A and E (randomly assigned to the RSAO, Resonance, Steam, B-format, and Wrong room sounds), and two anchors named as N and M. The overall quality test (right) presents 4 stimuli, named between A and D (randomly assigned to the RSAO, Resonance, Steam, and B-format sounds).

estimated the room acoustics by employing the visual-based pipeline, and reproduced using Google Resonance as renderer in VR [18]. The second one, named here as "Steam", followed the same visual-based pipeline but it employed the Steam Audio package to reproduce sounds in VR [70]. The third method is an audio-based method based on the RSAO [49]. To reproduce sounds generated from the RSAO parameters in VR, it is rendered by the versatile interactive scene renderer framework (VISR) [15], defining 52 virtual loudspeakers on a sphere around the listening position. These speakers were equispaced on 3 rings: 24 at elevations $0°$, 12 at $30°$, and 12 at $-30°$. The same virtual loudspeakers were then defined using Google Resonance for the playback. All the sounds were recorded, in VR, at the listening position, as .wav files. They were then embedded into the MUSHRA interfaces, developed in Max MSP. An overview of the methods used for producing sounds in VR is in Fig. 11.

To have hidden anchors defining high quality reproduction, we also generated binaural sounds from B-format recordings (named during the analysis as "B-format"). This conversion was done using the NoiseMakers Ambi-Head plugin, in

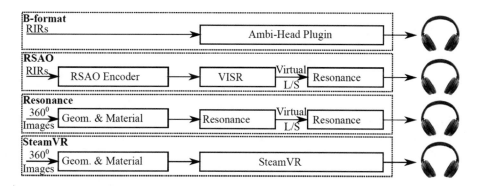

Fig. 11. Overview of the four methods used to generate the stimuli.

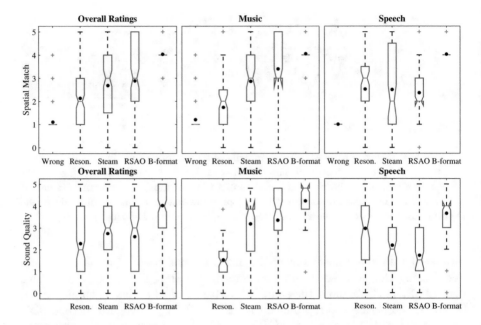

Fig. 12. Subjective scores for spatial impression (top three) and overall quality (bottom three). On each box, the horizontal red line represents the median of the distribution, the bottom and top edges of the boxes are the 25th and 75th percentiles, respectively. The whiskers show the most extreme non-outlier data points, whereas the outliers are depicted as red crosses. The black circles are the means of the distributions.

Reaper. As low anchor, we simply used a sound carrying a wrong reverberation (i.e. related to another room). Twenty listeners were tested. However, four of them were discarded from the analysis, having been identified as unreliable: by observing just the anchors' scores, listeners who did not correctly identify them more than two times were discarded. This was considered as an indicator of misunderstanding about the task.

4.4 Spatial Impression

This test was performed by reproducing sounds through headphones, while providing the panoramic photos of the related room under investigation. The MUSHRA interface used is depicted in Fig. 10 (left). Eight pages were tested, one for each combination of tested room and sound. Listeners were asked to: "Please, rate the stimuli between 0 and 5, looking at how much the spatial impression matches what you would expect from the room in the image". For this test, two hidden anchors were used: one, to be rated as 4, was the binaural sound obtained from B-format; whereas, to be rated as 1, it was a sound related to a room having completely wrong reverb. Although being hidden among the

Table 3. P-values of paired t-tests between the different methods' ratings across both music and speech. $h = 1$ means that the test rejects the null hypothesis of the two results belonging to normal distributions with equal means (95% of confidence). When $h = 0$, it cannot reject the null hypothesis with a 95% of confidence.

	Wrong vs Res	Res. vs Steam	Steam vs RSAO	RSAO vs B-format
Spatial impression	$8 \cdot 10^{-12}$ $(h = 1)$	0.007 $(h = 1)$	0.340 $(h = 0)$	$7 \cdot 10^{-13}$ $(h = 1)$
Overall quality	–	0.014 $(h = 1)$	0.457 $(h = 0)$	$2 \cdot 10^{-14}$ $(h = 1)$

three pipelines to test, these two anchors were also explicitly provided to the listeners as reference for stimuli to rate as 1 and 4, respectively.

The results are reported in Fig. 12, top row. As expected, the overall rating shows both means and medians of the three methods to be lower than the anchor given by the binaural sound. Furthermore, all their spatial impressions are rated higher than the wrong room reverb. Comparing the three methods, RSAO presents the best mean and median, because it estimates the reverb directly from acoustic recordings, while the other two from the images. Between Resonance and Steam, subjects seem to prefer Steam, in terms of spatial impression, when comparing the reproduced sound to the related room image.

The other two figures split between the two pieces of content: music and speech. The trend observed in the overall score is mainly given by the music results. Instead, for speech, every method seems to provide similar spatial impression. This is related to the speech frequency spectrum being broader than the clarinet's. In Table 3, we report the results of paired t-tests. With a 95% confidence, the distribution of Resonance's rates has different mean from Steam's. RSAO rates, instead, cannot be claimed to be statistically different from Steam's.

4.5   Overall Quality

Here, the photos of the room under investigation were shown to the listeners just to provide an idea of the acoustics they should expect. Nevertheless, they only needed to compare the stimuli overall sound quality, scoring them between 0 and 5. The interface used in depicted in Fig. 10 right. Eight pages were tested, one for each combination of tested room and sound. Only the B-format signal was used as hidden anchor (a wrong room reverb does not necessarily mean a lower sound quality), but not provided as explicit reference.

The results are reported in Fig. 12, bottom row. As expected, the overall rating shows both means and medians of the three methods (i.e. RSAO, Resonance, and Steam) to be lower than the anchor. The interesting part of these results is that, comparing the three methods, RSAO and Steam presents better means and medians than Resonance. Nonetheless, since the percentiles clearly overlap, we reported in Table 3 the results of paired t-tests. From them, it is possible to claim that, with a 95% confidence, the distribution of Resonance is different from Steam's. Whereas, as for the spatial impression, RSAO rates cannot be claimed to be statistically different Steam's.

However, in general, it has to be taken into account that, to render RSAO, virtual loudspeakers were utilised with Google Resonance. Therefore, RSAO's results may be, perhaps, biased towards a lower rate. Looking at the other two figures, with music, RSAO performs better than both Steam and Resonance. On the other hand, for speech, Resonance seems to be the best. As mentioned above, the frequency spectra of the two sounds makes the difference: when Resonance plays the clarinet, a white background noise is audible. With speech, instead, the broader range of frequencies masks this problem. This difference in quality may be also generated by the differences between Resonance and Steam during the rendering stage. As already discussed, Resonance renders the reverberation through a set of virtual loudspeakers, whereas Steam calculates a binaural RIR. This makes Steam preferable when a high sound quality is required; nonetheless, Resonance is preferable for fast rendering applications.

4.6   VR Scene Rendering

To the best of our knowledge, it has not been clearly identified yet, in the literature, how to evaluate plausibility of VR contents with objective metrics. Therefore, subjective tests have been carried out to confirm the plausibility of the acoustics generated with visual contents in VR environment. In this VR implementation, the user can freely navigate in the scene and switch the mode between: (1) original 360° photos mapped to a large sphere (2D) with the original sound source recorded in an anechoic chamber; (2) simplified 3D structure with coherent spatial audio rendering (Proposed method); and (3) Room layout only and spatial audio rendering in the empty room. Figure 13 shows some snapshots of the implemented real-time interactive VR scene rendering. In Fig. 13(a), the rendered 360° textures are not exactly matched to the rendered 3D geometry because the textures have been simple mapped on a sphere as a 2D texture. The 360° texture just give a reference for the original scene.

This interactive VR system with the VR headset shown in Fig. 13(b) have been demonstrated in several public events and received verbal feedback. The implemented VR scenes produced plausible sound effects compared with the original source and the sound rendered in the empty room. Some error factors have been identified in the rendered scene by the users due to the material labeling errors.

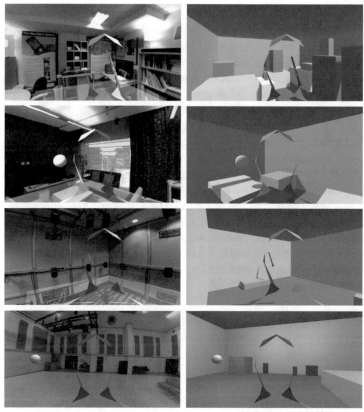

(a) Snapshots of rendered scenes (Left: 360° texture, Right: 3D model with object labels).

(b) Application on VR headset.

Fig. 13. Interactive VR rendering.

5   Conclusion

In this chapter, the vision-based 3D structure and acoustic property estimation system has been introduced to provide plausible spatial audio in VR/AR environments. It requires only one pair of photos of the scene from commercial off-the-shelf 360° cameras. A simplified 3D geometry model of the scene is reconstructed by depth estimation and semantic segmentation of objects with labels is performed using a CNN. This visual information is used to predict acoustic properties within the scene, which allows perceptually plausible acoustic reproduction. This also allows the user correctly associate the sound with the respective room environment. The estimated room geometry and simulated spatial audio are evaluated against ground-truth data from actual measurements and recordings in the rooms. Experimental results showed a general agreement between the real and simulated acoustics.

The approach enables the simulation of plausible spatial audio renderings which match the acoustics of the room environment, however a number of limitations should be addressed in future work. Future direction of this research should include robust material detection using audio-visual sensors to compensate the current surface material mapping. Objective evaluation of plausibility in VR reproductions should be also accompanied as well as subjective evaluations with combined audio-visual cues. Another factor which has not been dealt with in this paper is "coherence" issue. Audio-visual coherence should be investigated for immersive VR contents production.

References

1. Badrinarayanan, V., Kendall, A., Cipolla, R.: SegNet: a deep convolutional encoder-decoder architecture for image segmentation. IEEE Trans. Pattern Anal. Mach. Intell. **39**, 2481–2495 (2017)
2. Bailey, W., Fazenda, B.M.: The effect of reverberation and audio spatialization on egocentric distance estimation of objects in stereoscopic virtual reality. J. Acoust. Soc. Am. **141**(5), 3510 (2017)
3. Bailey, W., Fazenda, B.M.: The effect of visual cues and binaural rendering method on plausibility in virtual environments. In: Proceedings of the 144th AES Convention, Milan, Italy (2018)
4. Binelli, M., Pinardi, D., Nili, T., Farina, A.: Individualized HRTF for playing VR videos with Ambisonics spatial audio on HMDs. In: Proceedings of the AES Conference on Audio for Virtual and Augmented Reality, Redmond, USA (2018)
5. Blauert, J.: Communication Acoustics. Springer, Berlin (2005). https://doi.org/10.1007/b139075
6. Bonneel, N., Suied, C., Viaud-Delmon, I., Drettakis, G.: Bimodal perception of audio-visual material properties for virtual environments. ACM Trans. Appl. Percept. **7**(1), 1:1–1:16 (2010)
7. Bradley, J.S.: Review of objective room acoustics measures and future needs. Appl. Acoust. **72**(10), 713–720 (2011)
8. Brown, K., Paradis, M., Murphy, D.: OpenAirLib: a Javascript library for the acoustics of spaces. In: Audio Engineering Society Convention 142, May 2017. http://www.aes.org/e-lib/browse.cfm?elib=18586
9. Chatfield, K., Simonyan, K., Vedaldi, A., Zisserman, A.: Return of the devil in the details: delving deep into convolutional nets. In: Proceedings of the BMVC (2014)
10. Coleman, P., Franck, A., Jackson, P.J.B., Hughes, R.J., Remaggi, L., Melchior, F.: Object-based reverberation for spatial audio. J. Audio Eng. Soc. **65**(1/2), 66–77 (2017)

11. Coleman, P., Franck, A., Menzies, D., Jackson, P.J.B.: Object-based reverberation encoding from first-order Ambisonic RIRs. In: Proceedings of the 142nd AES Convention, Berlin, Germany (2017)

12. Cox, T.: Gun shot in anechoic chamber. Freesound (2013). https://freesound.org/people/acs272/sounds/210766/

13. Dou, M., Guan, L., Frahm, J.-M., Fuchs, H.: Exploring high-level plane primitives for indoor 3D reconstruction with a hand-held RGB-D camera. In: Park, J.-I., Kim, J. (eds.) ACCV 2012. LNCS, vol. 7729, pp. 94–108. Springer, Heidelberg (2013). https://doi.org/10.1007/978-3-642-37484-5_9

14. Farina, A.: Simultaneous measurement of impulse response and distortion with a swept-sine technique. In: Proceedings of the AES Convention (2000)

15. Franck, A., Fazi, F.M.: VISR: a versatile open software framework for audio signal processing. In: Proceedings of the AES International Conference on Spatial Reproduction - Aesthetics and Science, Tokyo, Japan (2018)

16. Garofolo, J.S., Lamel, L.F., Fisher, W.M., Fiscus, J.G., Pallet, D.S., Dahlgren, N.L.: DARPA TIMIT acoustic phonetic continuous speech corpus CDROM. Technical report, NIST Interagency (1993)

17. Gonzalez, R.C., Woods, R.E.: Digital Image Processing. Pearson, London (2017)

18. Google: Google VR SDK (2017). https://developers.google.com/resonance-audio/

19. GoPro: GoPro Fusion (2018). https://shop.gopro.com/EMEA/cameras/fusion/CHDHZ-103-master.html

20. Gupta, A., Efros, A.A., Hebert, M.: Blocks world revisited: image understanding using qualitative geometry and mechanics. In: Daniilidis, K., Maragos, P., Paragios, N. (eds.) ECCV 2010. LNCS, vol. 6314, pp. 482–496. Springer, Heidelberg (2010). https://doi.org/10.1007/978-3-642-15561-1_35

21. Hoeg, W., Christensen, L., Walker, R.: Subjective assessment of audio quality - the means and methods within the EBU. Technical report, EBU Technical Review (1997)

22. HTC: VIVE Pro (2018). https://www.vive.com/uk/product/vive-pro-full-kit/

23. Hulusic, V., et al.: Acoustic rendering and auditory-visual cross-modal perception and interaction. J. Comput. Graph. Forum 31(1), 102–131 (2012)

24. Insta360: Insta360 ONE X (2018). https://www.insta360.com/product/insta360-onex

25. Jeong, C.H., Marbjerg, G., Brunskog, J.: Uncertainty of input data for room acoustic simulations. In: Proceedings of Bi-annual Baltic-Nordic Acoustic Meeting (2016)

26. Judd, D.B.: Chromaticity sensibility to stimulus differences. J. Opt. Soc. Am. 22(2), 72 (1932)

27. Kim, H., Campos, T., Hilton, A.: Room layout estimation with object and material attributes information using a spherical camera. In: Proceedings of the 3DV (2016)

28. Kim, H., Hilton, A.: 3D scene reconstruction from multiple spherical stereo pairs. Int. J. Comput. Vis. 104(1), 94–116 (2013)

29. Kim, H., et al.: Acoustic room modelling using a spherical camera for reverberant spatial audio objects. In: Audio Engineering Society Convention 142, Berlin, Germany (2017). http://www.aes.org/e-lib/browse.cfm?elib=18583

30. Kim, H., Hernaggi, L., Jackson, P.J., Hilton, A.: Immersive spatial audio reproduction for VR/AR using room acoustic modelling from 360 images. In: Proceedings of the IEEE VR Conference (2019)

31. Kim, H., Sohn, K.: 3D reconstruction from stereo images for interactions between real and virtual objects. Sig. Process. Image Commun. 20(1), 61–75 (2005)

32. Kwon, S.W., Bosche, F., Kim, C., Haas, C., Liapi, K.: Fitting range data to primitives for rapid local 3D modeling using sparse range point clouds. Autom. Constr. **13**(1), 67–81 (2004)

33. Larsson, P., Väljamäe, A., Västfjäll, D., Tajadura-Jiménez, A., Kleiner, M.: Auditory-induced presence in mixed reality environments and related technology. In: Dubois, E., Gray, P., Nigay, L. (eds.) The Engineering of Mixed Reality Systems. HCIS, pp. 143–163. Springer, London (2010). https://doi.org/10.1007/978-1-84882-733-2_8

34. Li, M., Nan, L., Liu, S.: Fitting boxes to Manhattan scenes using linear integer programming. Int. J. Digit. Earth **9**, 806–817 (2016)

35. Lindau, A., Kosanke, L., Weinzierl, S.: Perceptual evaluation of model- and signal-based predictors of the mixing time in binaural room impulse responses. J. Audio Eng. Soc. **60**(11), 887–898 (2012)

36. Lindau, A., Weinzierl, S.: Assessing the plausibility of virtual acoustic environments. Acta Acust. United Acust. **98**(5), 804–810 (2012)

37. Makhoul, J.: Linear prediction: a tutorial review. Proc. IEEE **63**(4), 561–580 (1975)

38. Matas, J., Galambos, C., Kittler, J.: Robust detection of lines using the progressive probabilistic Hough transform. Comput. Vis. Image Underst. **78**, 119–137 (2000)

39. McArthur, A., Sandler, M., Stewart, R.: Perception of mismatched auditory distance - cinematic VR. In: Proceedings of the AES Conference on Audio for Virtual and Augmented Reality, Redmond, USA (2018)

40. McGurk, H., MacDonald, J.: Hearing lips and seeing voices. Nature **264**(5588), 746–748 (1976)

41. Meng, Z., Zhao, F., He, M.: The just noticeable difference of noise length and reverberation perception. In: Proceedings of the International Symposium on Communications and Information Technologies, Bangkok, Thailand (2006)

42. Naylor, P.A., Kounoudes, A., Gudnason, J., Brookes, M.: Estimation of glottal closure instants in voiced speech using the DYPSA algorithm. IEEE Trans. Audio Speech Lang. Process. **15**(1), 34–43 (2007)

43. Neidhardt, A., Tommy, A.I., Pereppadan, A.D.: Plausibility of an interactive approaching motion towards a virtual sound source based on simplified BRIR sets. In: Proceedings of the 144th AES Convention, Milan, Italy (2018)

44. Nguatem, W., Drauschke, M., Mayer, H.: Finding cuboid-based building models in point clouds. In: Proceedings of ISPRS, pp. 149–154 (2012)

45. Oculus: Oculus SDK (2017). https://developer.oculus.com/audio/

46. Pointgrey: Ladybug (2018). https://www.ptgrey.com/360-degree-spherical-camera-systems

47. Politis, A., Tervo, S., Lokki, T., Pulkki, V.: Parametric multidirectional decomposition of microphone recordings for broadband high-order Ambisonic encoding. In: Proceedings of the 144th AES Convention, Milan, Italy (2018)

48. Pulkki, V.: Spatial sound reproduction with directional audio coding. J. Audio Eng. Soc. **55**(6), 503–516 (2007)

49. Remaggi, L., Jackson, P.J.B., Coleman, P.: Estimation of room reflection parameters for a reverberant spatial audio object. In: Proceedings of the 138th AES Convention, Warsaw, Poland (2015)

50. Remaggi, L., Jackson, P.J.B., Coleman, P., Wang, W.: Acoustic reflector localization: novel image source reversion and direct localization methods. IEEE/ACM Trans. Audio Speech Lang. Process. **25**(2), 296–309 (2017)

51. Remaggi, L., Kim, H., Neidhardt, A., Hilton, A., Jackson, P.J.B.: Perceived quality and spatial impression of room reverberation in VR reproduction from measured images and acoustics. In: Proceedings of the ICA (2019)

52. Ricoh: Ricoh Theta V (2018). https://theta360.com/en/about/theta/v.html
53. Rix, J., Haas, S., Teixeira, J.: Virtual Prototyping: Virtual Environments and the Product Design Process. Springer, Boston (2016)
54. Rummukainen, O., Robotham, T., Schlecht, S.J., Plinge, A., Herre, J., Habets, E.A.P.: Audio quality evaluation in virtual reality: multiple stimulus ranking with behavior tracking. In: Proceedings of the AES Conference on Audio for Virtual and Augmented Reality, Redmond, USA (2018)
55. Rumsey, F.: Spatial quality evaluation for reproduced sound: terminology, meaning, and a scene-based paradigm. J. Audio Eng. Soc. **50**(9), 651–666 (2002)
56. Schissler, C., Loftin, C., Manocha, D.: Acoustic classification and optimization for multi-modal rendering of real-world scenes. IEEE Trans. Vis. Comput. Graph. **24**(3), 1246–1259 (2018)
57. Simonyan, K., Zisserman, A.: Very deep convolutional networks for large-scale image recognition. CoRR abs/1409.1556 (2014)
58. Song, S., Lichtenberg, S., Xiao, J.: SUN RGB-D: a RGB-D scene understanding benchmark suite. In: Proceedings of the CVPR (2015)
59. Spheron: Spheron VR (2018). https://www.spheron.com/products.html
60. Stan, G.B., Embrechts, J.J., Archambeau, D.: Comparison of different impulse response measurement techniques. J. Audio Eng. Soc. **50**(4), 249–262 (2002)
61. Stecker, G.C., Moore, T.M., Folkerts, M., Zotkin, D., Duraiswami, R.: Toward objective measure of auditory co-immersion in virtual and augmented reality. In: Proceedings of the AES Conference on Audio for Virtual and Augmented Reality, Redmond, USA (2018)
62. Stenzel, H., Jackson, P.J.B.: Perceptual thresholds of audio-visual spatial coherence for a variety of audio-visual objects. In: Proceedings of the AES Conference on Audio for Virtual and Augmented Reality, Redmond, USA (2018)
63. Sun, B., Saenko, K.: From virtual to reality: fast adaptation of virtual object detectors to real domains. In: Proceedings of the BMVC, Nottingham, UK (2014)
64. McKenzie, T., Murphy, D., Kearney, G.: Directional bias equalisation of first-order binaural Ambisonic rendering. In: Proceedings of the AES Conference on Audio for Virtual and Augmented Reality, Redmond, USA (2018)
65. Unity Technologies: Unity (2018). https://unity3d.com/
66. Tervo, S., Patynen, J., Kuusinen, A., Lokki, T.: Spatial decomposition method for room impulse responses. J. Audio Eng. Soc. **61**(1/2), 17–28 (2013)
67. Tsingos, N., Funkhouser, T., Ngan, A., Carlbom, I.: Modeling acoustics in virtual environments using the uniform theory of diffraction. In: Proceedings of the ACM SIGGRAPH, pp. 545–552, Aug 2001
68. Turk, M.: Multimodal interaction: a review. Pattern Recogn. Lett. **36**, 189–195 (2014)
69. Välimäki, V., Parker, J.D., Savioja, L., Smith, J.O., Abel, J.S.: Fifty years of artificial reverberation. IEEE TASLP **20**(5), 1421–1448 (2012)
70. Valve: Steamaudio SDK (2017). https://valvesoftware.github.io/steam-audio/
71. Vorländer, M.: Auralization: Fundamentals of Acoustics, Modelling, Simulation, Algorithms and Acoustic Virtual Reality. Springer, Berlin (2008). https://doi.org/10.1007/978-3-540-48830-9
72. Vorländer, M.: Virtual acoustics: opportunities and limits of spatial sound reproduction. Arch. Acoust. **33**(4), 413–422 (2008)
73. Vorländer, M.: International round robin on room acoustical computer simulations. In: Proceedings of the ICA, Trondheim, Norway (1995)
74. Zhang, Z.: Microsoft Kinect sensor and its effect. IEEE Multimed. **19**(2), 4–10 (2012)

75. Zheng, S., et al.: Dense semantic image segmentation with objects and attributes. In: Proceedings of the CVPR (2014)
76. Zhu, H., Meng, F., Cai, J., Lu, S.: Beyond pixels: a comprehensive survey from bottom-up to semantic image segmentation and cosegmentation. J. Vis. Commun. Image Represent. **34**, 12–27 (2016)

Applications

Immersive Learning in Real VR

Johanna Pirker(✉)🆔, Isabel Lesjak🆔, Johannes Kopf🆔, Alexander Kainz🆔,
and Amir Dini🆔

Graz University of Technology, Graz, Austria
jpirker@iicm.edu, isabel.lesjak@student.tugraz.at,
{johannes.kopf,alexander.kainz,amir.dini}@tugraz.at

Abstract. Immersion is an essential factor for successful learning. Immersive learning environments put learners directly into experiences and events related to the learning content. Virtual reality (VR) experiences give us new opportunities and ways for enabling immersive learning processes. In this chapter, we review different learning environments that use (real) VR as a tool to teach in different learning settings and discuss the state-of-the-art design and evaluation techniques and analyze the benefits and limitations of the different methods.

Keywords: Immersive learning · Virtual reality · 360°VR

1 Introduction

Over the past decades, the way we learn and how the information we need to learn is presented has fundamentally changed. Especially online videos have emerged and shown to be an essential component of educational processes [20]. Already in 1922, Edison mentioned: *"I believe the motion picture is destined to revolutionize our educational system and that in a few years it will supplant largely, if not entirely, the use of textbooks"* [40].

Videos can help students to visualize, mesmerize, and understand topics and are often cost-effective methods compared to present teaching elements. In recent years, studies have shown that interactive forms of videos have a high potential to support learners in the learning process. Video-based instructions were even described to be similarly realistic as face-to-face instructions, but add flexibility and accessibility to the learning process [13,26].

In recent years, the use of 360-degree videos has become increasingly popular, also for immersive educational experiences [50]. Immersion has been shown as a successful driver of enhanced learning experiences in several studies.

360-degree videos can be experienced with VR head-mounted displays (HMD) to help learners immerse themselves into the experiences. The benefits of using VR environments for teaching scenarios have been shown already very early and quite intensely. It gives students possibilities to explore environments and processes which are invisible, too expensive or complicated to reproduce for

© Springer Nature Switzerland AG 2020
M. Magnor and A. Sorkine-Hornung (Eds.): Real VR, LNCS 11900, pp. 321–336, 2020.
https://doi.org/10.1007/978-3-030-41816-8_14

a learning process, or even impossible to perform in a traditional learning environment. As VR technologies have become relatively affordable and also portable over the past years, the integration in learning setups such as classrooms, training environments, or even self-directed learning at home is becoming increasingly attractive. With VR technologies, entirely new learning scenarios can be designed to support and engage learning to understand even complex phenomena and processes. The learning scenarios which are used for teaching can either be entirely simulated or animated or produced using real video content (360-degree videos) for taking the learners to real learning scenarios to re-watch processes.

The goal of this chapter is to present and discuss an overview of the state-of-the-art of immersive learning experiences with a focus on experiences using video footage from real-world processes and events.

2 Capturing 360-degree Videos for Educational Purposes

With game engines such as Unity[1], we can create and design entirely virtual worlds that can visualize and simulate learning environments. However, this also requires advanced 3D-modeling, coding, and interface design skills.

In contrast, with the use of 360-degree videos, VR experiences can be created directly by educators, and realistic video-based experiences are enabled.

Feuerstein [22] describes a typical workflow for integrating 360-degree videos in higher education. The first step is the production, which involves thoughts about elements such as controlling and positioning the camera. The second step is the post-processing. This is usually done by using the proprietary software provided by the camera manufacturer. Optional steps would be to add further information points and interactions with the user. The last step is described as the delivery of the video content. 360-degree videos can be delivered either through a traditional monitor-based environment or through an immersive VR device. The delivery we are focusing on in this chapter is the delivery in a fully-immersive way: through an HMD resulting in a (real) VR experience.

Many authors also described their experiences by capturing videos for the learning experience. Ardisara and Fung [10] describe how they use 360-degree cameras to capture laboratory techniques in an undergraduate organic chemistry course. Lecturers describe the video capturing process as easy. In their case study, Ardisara and Fung identified several advantages compared to the use of conventional cameras. One does not need to worry about the focus or the scope of the view. Also, no external camera personnel is needed as the lab instructor can use the camera to film while conducting the experiments.

Kavanagh et al. [34] describe in a case study how they create educational videos for HMDs with 360-degree cameras. They describe the process as easy and cost-effective; however, they also list different issues in the process. Issues include the right positioning of the camera, fish-eye lens-related distortions, the price of high-quality hardware, and the video quality of cost-effective models. One major

---

[1] https://unity3d.com/.

issue the authors described was also the missing possibility to direct the attention of the views. Mainly for educational purposes, it is crucial to remove external visual distractions. In 360-degree experiences, learners can easily be distracted by the surroundings. This can be either be an unintentional loss of track of the primary educational experience (e.g., losing track where the lecturer is located) or distractions by other parts of the experience (e.g., elements or actions in the surroundings). Thus, strategies to guide learners are crucial to create successful learning experiences.

2.1 Guiding Learners in 360-degree Videos

In the traditional 2D education media, many techniques have been refined and are regarded as incontrovertible methods to guide the eye and attention of the viewer. The methods developed by Block [12] which are also usable in 360-degree media and VR are:

Surface division: By using the lines and edges occurring in the environment as image splitting or even as extra "picture frames", the attention of the users can be directed thereby.

Color and brightness: Highly saturated colors or bright image areas can also be used well for attention steering. Note that brightness always attracts attention first, followed by saturation of a color.

Movement: The rhythm of a picture is strongly related to the equipment of the scene. This, too can affect the attention of the user. A rhythmically calm image can make viewers concentrate on certain content or objects, while a rhythmically irregular image can quickly become a hidden object.

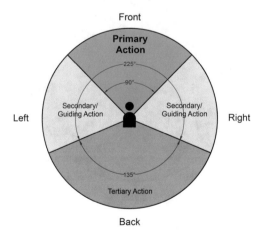

Fig. 1. Cone of Focus: in order to draw the attention of the users in VR to the learning content, the focus of the 360-degree recording should be in the front area.

2.2   Cone of Focus

One important tool to guide the learners' attention is the 360-degree content sharing diagram (as depicted in Fig. 1) called Cone of Focus, which was developed by Soap Collectives[2].

It is assumed that the majority of users are on a non-rotatable chair (e.g., classroom, training environments). From this position, now the focus of the user can be planned. One mistake is placing the events around the camera; this is often confusing, loud, and overwhelming. Instead, the place should be set with care and reason.

Therefore, the 360-degree scenes are divided into three areas. The "Primary Action" lies in the range of 90-degree in front of the observer. It is advisable that the content of the training begins here. The "Secondary Action" areas are approximately as far to the left and to the right of the user as they can be, without requiring user effort to turn their heads. This area is meant to support the teaching content, it is not essential for the understanding of the matter itself, but it does help with the context. Finally, the area of the "Tertiary Action" is behind the observer and serves the elements on which no consideration must be taken. Compared to traditional educational videos, this would be things that are out of the frame and, therefore, not attracting the attention of users. However, in 360-degree media, this area serves to immerse the observers. If the observers turn around once this ensures that they are not thrown out of the environment and realize that they only have a HMD on.

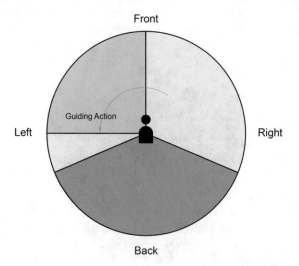

Fig. 2. The Guiding Action can steer the viewer's focus into new areas.

---

[2] https://www.thesoapcollective.com/.

The principle of "Cone of Focus" is supported by the "Guiding Action" (see Fig. 2). This can be a series of events that are supposed to take the user to a specific location in the 360-degree range. Rough leaps in light, sound, or events are perceived by the observer, even if they are in the area of secondary action since this is still in the peripheral field of vision. As a result, attention is then directed in this direction.

3   Application Domains and Examples

VR enables learners to be immersed in learning scenarios. They can train in environments by immersing themselves in lifelike situations which are otherwise too dangerous (e.g. chemistry experiments), which would result in terrible consequences (e.g. simulation of a surgery), which are too expensive (e.g. complex laboratory setup), or which are hard or even impossible to reproduce [16].

Several studies have shown the potential of immersion in digital learning scenarios. The added values of immersion are, for instance, the support of multiple perspectives, situated learning, and transfer [18]. The additional dimension of immersion provided by fully immersive VR environments with HMDs has been shown to support the knowledge structure. Coulter *et al.* [16] have shown in a study that learners show a significant knowledge gain when using VR learning scenarios compared to computer-screen based (partially immersed) learning settings.

In this section, we describe different application scenarios found in the literature for different learning activities.

3.1   Virtual Tours

With proper equipment like omni-spherical cameras, people can create 360-degree content on their own. As a result of this, platforms like YouTube or Facebook already allow the sharing and playing of 360-degree videos. This easy creation and accessibility led to a huge amount of 360-degree content on the web, which includes virtual tours of museums, malls, and buildings. The use of additional software like the Skybox VR Player[3] allows users to watch 360-degree YouTube videos with HMDs like the HTC Vive. In comparison to traditional videos, 360-degree virtual tours enable viewers to focus their view on their point of interest. Especially, virtual tours through museums, iconic buildings, or cities show great potential in terms of immersive learning. Also, they allow individuals to travel to places that would be inaccessible otherwise [35]. Reyna [48] describes virtual tools in education *"as a way to showcase complex scenarios that are difficult to explain with images, words, or event conventional videos"*.

These tours can be used to learn about all different subjects and topics such as science, history, architecture, construction industry or geography. Examples of 360-degree virtual tours found on Youtube include a virtual tour through the Royal Tyrrell Museum [6] to learn about dinosaurs, a virtual tour through a space shuttle [4], a tour through the Buckingham Palace [3].

---

[3] https://store.steampowered.com/app/721090/SKYBOX_VR_Video_Player/.

3.2   Recorded Processes and Procedures

In many areas, the learning and training of a particular process or procedure is an essential element. Examples are the construction and execution of an experiment, the construction of a complex machine, or the execution of a medical procedure. This form of learning is currently often supported by video training. A teacher, trainer, or expert conducts the process, and the viewers learn by watching and re-watching the process steps in the video. 360-degree videos can help prevent information from being lost, for example, by setting the camera focus incorrectly. It also puts learners in a realistic environment and helps them understand the processes as a whole through situational learning.

Medical Training. Medical students usually have the opportunity to watch real surgeries during their education. However, the number of spectators in an operating room is strictly limited. Therefore, the students only have a few chances to get familiar with the actions and procedures in an immersive and realistic environment. VR as a tool for training students in the medical field might be the solution. Different approaches use 360-degree pre-recorded images or videos of operating rooms during surgeries to create educational learning environments in VR [7]. As a result of this, the spherical recording of the operating room allows for better observation compared to traditional video recordings because the view of the user is not limited to a specific camera angle. Some approaches go even further and enable the interaction of the user with the environment. In these cases, computer-generated components are often inserted into the environments which were created with 360-degree photorealistic content [31,32,47].

Laboratory Courses. Videos also have been an essential tool for demonstrating the use of laboratory equipment or experimental procedures. Ardisara and Man Fung [10] demonstrate how to record and integrate 360-degree videos in an undergraduate chemistry laboratory course.

Sports Training. An excellent opportunity for 360-degree videos is to use them for learning and training sports-related behaviours and skills. They are an effective medium for learning experiences in areas like sport climbing [25] or sports in general [29].

Craftsman Training. VR using 360-degree photorealistic content could especially be helpful for an artisan to learn specific procedures like the steps for building a kitchen or laying tiles. Such learning environments have the advantage that they are independent of space and time and allow for individual learning progress. One approach is to perform different steps of a procedure in different parts of a room and record the whole environment using an omni-spherical camera. This enables the apprentice to focus on the steps which are still unclear [24].

Enjoyment Training. Quality of life, health and well-being, as well as the creative potential that results from positive experiences and interaction with VR environments, are crucial human factors underlying a vibrant and productive social context. VR technologies have recently come up with tools to predict the affordability of future scenarios. Applications that relate in particular to visual stimuli that allow the induction of imagined sensory experiences (e.g. urban environments). In particular, dementia patients, are motivated, in a positive attitude, with pleasant and conscious sensory experiences, to react to their daily environment in order to improve their cognitive reserve [37,44].

3.3 Recorded Situations

Often, it is necessary to expose learners to situations, which are hard to train in real-life scenarios and need to be simulated in a safe environment. This, for instance, includes the simulations of catastrophic situations and how to train these scenarios in a realistic but safe way. These situations are often recorded with professional actors.

Nurse Education. Different forms of simulations for nurse education have evolved over the last five decades. With this, earlier training models like role-playing have been extended or replaced by new forms of simulations that make use of games, computer-aided instructions, or VR [42]. In some countries like Sweden, extreme catastrophic situations are rare. Still, it is crucial to prepare emergency personnel for different catastrophic situations to maintain their competence. To address this challenge, 360-degree video can be used to expose nursing students or trauma teams to immersive learning environments showing simulated scenes in different conditions and places [30]. Another approach is to let nursing students experience different disabilities in VR to become aware of the patient's situation. One disability known as macular degeneration can, for example, be visualized by darkening areas of the user's view in the virtual environment [14].

Safety Training. The usage of VR is not only possible for areas where the cost is surpassing the average by far, but also for fields that bring along hazardous working conditions and where the effort to conduct training is immense. VR safety training allows areas like the mining industry [23,45,46,53] or the construction industry [51] to lower their expense while being more effective and improving safety. Another possible domain of application is for earthquake safety training, where users are made aware of potentially dangerous situations and how to handle them [36]. Training like this can also be applied in terms of schools, where road or pedestrian safety is a significant factor in order to improve street crossing behavior [38].

3.4   Recorded Experiences

VR is also often called the *"Ultimate Empathy Machine"*. VR helps learners to experience situations in someone else's shoes. This is also referred to as learning through perceptual illusion (embodiment) or the body ownership illusion [11]. Learners learn by experiencing other perspectives. Examples include an experience developed by The Guardian explaining a party situation from the perspective of a 16-year-old autistic narrator [5]. Another short 360-degree film places the viewers firsthand in the place of a prison inmate who lives in solitary confinement [2]. One of the most famous examples is the 360-degree film "Clouds Over Sidra", which lets viewers experience life as part of the Zaatari Refugee Camp, home to 130,000 Syrian refugees, most of them children [1]. Recorded experiences also become increasingly popular as a part of virtual news coverage and reporting strategies. Archer and Finger [9] found as part of a study with 180 people watching 360-degree videos that VR formats prompted a higher empathetic response than static photos or text treatments and that viewers would also be more likely to take political or social actions after viewing the videos.

3.5   Recording Processes for Learning Through Replay (Self-reflection)

One approach is to use a 360-degree camera and let learners record their learning acts and to reflect upon the video afterward. Recent studies have explored the impact on the students and concluded that this yields high realistic sensations and inspires the students to observe and revise their behavior [52].

Teacher Education. Videos can help teachers to facilitate reflection on their teaching style and practice [54]. VR in combination with 360-degree content is a powerful tool for teacher education as well. 360-degree recordings of classrooms can be used by pre-service teachers to learn about the classroom situation and analyze the students' behavior. Also, it enables them to learn how to reflect on specific teaching situations. Such enhanced observations are not possible with standard videos as the view is limited by the angle of the camera, and exploring the whole situation is therefore often not possible [48,49].

Sports Training. Watching recorded processes of the own performance is not only used in the classroom but also, for instance, in professional sports training. Immersive learning has also been shown to be successful for training quarterbacks and helping them to immerse themselves in their past games and rethink decisions they have made during the game [8].

4   Benefits and Potential

In literature, we can find a long list of various benefits of 360-degree VR learning experiences:

- Easy accessibility by users through different devices [39]
- The whole environment and situation is accessible [43,49]
- Efficient presentation form of the content [32]
- Experience of situations in a secure setting [32]
- Feeling of presence [33]
- Enhanced empathy [33,48]
- Enhanced student engagement with the content [14,27,28]
- Enhanced student interest [50]
- Enhanced motivation towards learning goal [24,29]
- Improved learning speed [14]
- Improved learning results and skill acquisition [50,55]
- Less material required [14]
- Barrier between learners, teachers, and machines are removed [27]
- Enhanced reflection possibilities from different perspectives [29]
- Learning process independent of space and time [24]
- Learning content available to large audience [24]

The benefits of using real-world VR lie in faster, simpler, and more affordable content creation, as well as a more realistic and personalized watching experience. Several studies have also shown the effectiveness of 360-degree content in improving learning outcomes [52] and minimizing simulator sickness [50].

In contrast to simulated or computer-generated VR experiences, the creation of 360-degree content in Real VR is more accessible to a wide range of users as it does not require special modeling or programming skills. Instead, students and teachers can produce their own content autonomously using 360-degree cameras (which are becoming more affordable) like the Ricoh Theta[4] to shoot panoramic photos or record omni-directional videos. This accelerates and simplifies the content creation process for 360-degree VR experiences [22]. For example, shooting 360-degree video of the experiment being performed in real life takes a few hours, whereas creating a simulated version of the experiment in 3D requires several weeks of programming and modeling.

In the context of learning, especially the use of 360-degree videos can lead to a better learning experience. A recent study evaluated the use of 360-degree immersive video recordings of practical lessons with veterinary surgery on horses [27]. A sample of 100 veterinary science students watched the recordings with a mobile VR headset, out of which 79% rated their quality of experience as excellent or good, and they were satisfied with the educational use of VR to improve the learning process. In another study, 40 participants (foundation year doctors) were equally assigned to either 360-degree VR video or 2D video teaching. As a result of this, they had to watch their allocated video about instructions of tying a single-handed reef knot for 15 min. Afterward, the two groups competed against each other. The results showed that the 360-degree VR video teaching group performed significantly better compared to the 2D video teaching group [55].

---

[4] https://theta360.com/en/.

Using VR headsets instead of flat screens to display 360-degree content is beneficial for immersion. Compared to flat screens, VR headsets enable isolation from real-world distractions and directly translate users' head movement into navigation in the video, which feels more intuitive than having to navigate through a conventional interface such as mouse and keyboard or phone display. A study in the medical field [28] has demonstrated that watching operative procedures in the 360-degree format can lead to more attentiveness and engagement among students, compared to watching these videos on traditional 2D screens.

Video content recorded with 360-degree cameras also has the potential to enable a broader audience to experience something they otherwise would not be able to experience in a very realistic way. One example of bringing world-class education to the masses is Harvard university's online version of their popular introductory Computer Science course called "CS50". In fall of 2016, the course team recorded all course lectures in 360-degree stereoscopic VR. They uploaded these videos on YouTube[5]. Watching the recorded 360-degree lectures with a VR headset allows users to turn their head around and see different perspectives of the Harvard lecture theatre, just as if they were sitting there in real life.

360-degree content does not only have the advantage to represent multiple perspectives of real-life moments but additionally also offers an individual and personalized watching experience as users can choose which segment of the image or video to look at [29]. Unlike traditional learning videos with a fixed perspective, 360-degree videos offer a unique way of storytelling, as viewers themselves are in control of their view direction at any point in time [22]. Using VR headsets like Google Cardboard to view this content, enables viewers to adjust their view direction through head movements, which further contributes to the feeling of immersion and presence.

The measurement of human stimuli through affective teaching methods and perceptions is an essential component of computing for learning applications. The increasing use of VR results in more possibilities to capture data and to adapt the application to the target group via a feedback loop (Fig. 3).

In learning VR environments, attention behaviors can be analyzed. By using the central Head-Gaze, it is possible to record head movements. The trajectories of the movement give feedback on whether the user could focus on the task or whether the teaching method should be different. Using temporal head movements, so-called Turn Rates (TR) [19], the level of attention can be determined. Quick head movements over time give feedback about whether the user is focused on the task (low TR) or trying to remember on his task (high TR).

While the list of benefits is long, the authors also identified several limitations and challenges for the future. These will be discussed in the next section.

---

[5] https://www.youtube.com/watch?v=0C8a6GBF8Bg&list=PLhQjrBD2T381yQVA OzT-PHcGMgvjFX2V6.

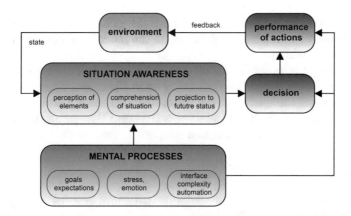

Fig. 3. Schematic sketch of Endsley's [21] theory of situation awareness in dynamic situations and its interdependency on human decision making, action performance and mental processes.

5   Limitations and Challenges

In literature, we can find the following main limitations of 360-degree VR learning experiences authors have described:

- Inability to interact with the environment or objects in the video [27,39,48]
- Low resolution [29]
- Possible cybersickness resulting from camera movement [29,33,50]
- Expensive setup for professional recordings [28]
- Novelty factor might influence current results on the improved learners' engagement [24,28]
- Missing options for user-friendly authoring for adding information and data [43]
- Distractions, missing focus points, and factors such as cybersickness can result in decreased learning outcomes [50]

Even though the creation and delivery of content in 360-degree has been advancing in the past years, there are currently still several challenges and limitations that both content creators and consumers are faced with. Apart from limited user interaction possibilities, it is challenging to integrate efficient assessment methods into real VR. Moreover, real VR is less flexible than computer-generated VR in terms of user exploration, as every possible exploration path needs to be pre-recorded.

With a 360-degree recording, viewers sometimes miss essential impressions as the camera is placed too far away from the action. On the other hand, viewers may steer their own chosen perspective into an overall "wrong" direction and thereby miss the essential action.

Depending on the type of camera and software, problems often arise when merging the images. These cameras use two lenses to capture a 360-degree video or photo. Professional models use even more. The 190-degree–220-degree videos recorded by each camera lens (depending on the model) are stitched together in the process of stitching.

For this purpose, exact calculations must be carried out at the edges, so that one can no longer see the so-called stitching seam afterward. There is a significant difference between the quality of the various camera models and manufacturers. With many cameras, one immediately sees the seam that connects both images. Color transitions, brightness, and also stitching errors are frequent.

5.1 Interactivity

One major limiting factor for providing a realistic user experience is the fact that user movement within 360-degree content is not possible. Users cannot just "walk into" a panoramic picture of a building or navigate freely by deviating from the pre-recorded camera path in a 360-degree video. In contrast, virtual models and artificial virtual worlds allow for individual, free exploration - users can indeed walk into a virtual model of the building, follow their path, and create individual storylines. Also, user interaction with the raw, unedited pre-recorded video is not possible as the video itself can hardly react to any user input without special enhancements, such as adding extra layers with animations, deformable objects, 3D audio and moving backgrounds in post-production [15].

5.2 Flexibility

The possibility for self-directed choosing of the viewing direction is a benefit that also comes with drawbacks in specific application domains. In movies with a storytelling plot, viewers could miss essential parts of the storyline or scene elements if they choose to look in the "wrong" direction, as described in [41].

Staying flexible while experiencing content in VR is crucial for exploratory learning [17]. In a static 360-degree image, users are not flexible in exploring their environment as they cannot freely navigate like they would be able to do in a computer-generated VR environment.

6 Conclusion

Immersion is an essential factor in improving learning experiences and enables learners to experience scenarios that are usually hard or impossible to experience. VR experiences can help learners to focus on the learning elements entirely, they keep them engaged, and their understanding can be improved by being virtually present in learning scenarios. In this chapter, we have discussed different immersive learning experiences and applications with a focus on real VR experiences. The main application domains for educational scenarios include virtual tours, which are often expensive or impossible to make, such as tour through a museum, a historical landmark, or the space. Further scenarios can be the recording of processes and procedures to help learners understand the single steps of the procedures. Typical areas of application include surgeries, laboratory setups, or also assembly tasks. The recording of complex simulated situations is also a domain that can help learners to train extreme catastrophic situations. These situations are usually recorded with actors. Another domain we discussed is learning through self-reflection. This can be important for speaker training, teachers' education, or sports training to support learners by helping them to reflect on the situation and the decisions they made, so they are able to revise their own behavior. The last domain we described in this chapter is the use of VR to create empathy. Viewers learn by experiencing situations through the shoes of others.

Benefits can be summarized as fast and simple content creation, an engaging experience, a better learning experience, and the possibility to bring content to the masses in a realistic and affordable way. However, challenges specifically for the educational purpose remain: learners' assessment strategies for educational processes are hard to integrate, interactive content is challenging to integrate, and the flexibility and personalization of the experience is not given. Even with these challenges remaining, VR (real VR and also simulated experiences) have a high potential to change the way we will learn in the future, either in a self-directed way or also in classroom settings.

References

1. (17) Clouds Over Sidra - Youtube. https://www.youtube.com/watch?v=mUosdCQsMkM. Accessed 10 Jan 2019
2. (17) solitary confinement in 360° virtual reality - Youtube. https://www.youtube.com/watch?v=nDwulYcboDU. Accessed 10 Jan 2019
3. 360 video: Buckingham palace tour - BBC London - Youtube. https://www.youtube.com/watch?v=FtGN2wK9g_s. Accessed 10 Jan 2019
4. Inside space shuttle discovery 360—national air and space museum - Youtube. https://www.youtube.com/watch?v=o3XS_5L-Qg. Accessed 10 Jan 2019
5. The party: a virtual experience of autism - 360 film - Youtube. https://www.youtube.com/watch?v=OtwOz1GVkDg. Accessed 10 Jan 2019
6. Royal tyrrell museum—360 video—Google jump 8k—Alberta, Canada - Youtube. https://www.youtube.com/watch?v=3RPQwCxu5po. Accessed 10 Jan 2019
7. Surgical training in 360-degree virtual reality for oculus rift (with intro + narration) - Youtube. https://www.youtube.com/watch?annotation_id=annotation_4243919275&feature=iv&src_vid=VAUbacNs4MQ&v=n7ALZkPoTYQ. Accessed 10 Jan 2019
8. VR training make stanford kicker a hero—strivr testimonial. https://www.strivr.com/resources/customers/stanford/. Accessed 10 Jan 2019
9. Archer, D., Finger, K.: Walking in another's virtual shoes: do 360-degree video news stories generate empathy in viewers? (2018)
10. Ardisara, A., Fung, F.M.: Integrating 360° videos in an undergraduate chemistry laboratory course (2018)
11. Bertrand, P., Guegan, J., Robieux, L., McCall, C.A., Zenasni, F.: Learning empathy through virtual reality: multiple strategies for training empathy-related abilities using body ownership illusions in embodied virtual reality. Front. Robot. AI **5**, 26 (2018)

12. Block, B.: The Visual Story: Creating the Visual Structure of Film, TV and Digital Media. Routledge, Abingdon (2013)
13. Borup, J., West, R.E., Graham, C.R.: Improving online social presence through asynchronous video. Internet High. Educ. **15**(3), 195–203 (2012)
14. Buchman, S.A., Henderson, D.E.: Using virtual reality 360 video for interprofessional simulation education (2018)
15. Choi, K., Yoon, Y.J., Song, O.Y., Choi, S.M.: Interactive and immersivelearning using 360° virtual reality contents on mobile platforms. Mobile Inf. Syst. **2018**, 12 (2018)
16. Coulter, R., Saland, L., Caudell, T., Goldsmith, T.E., Alverson, D.: The effect of degree of immersion upon learning performance in virtual reality simulations for medical education. In: Medicine Meets Virtual Reality, vol. 15, p. 155 (2007)
17. De Freitas, S., Neumann, T.: The use of 'exploratory learning' for supporting immersive learning in virtual environments. Comput. Educ. **52**(2), 343–352 (2009)
18. Dede, C.: Immersive interfaces for engagement and learning. Science **323**(5910), 66–69 (2009)
19. Dini, A., Murko, C., Yahyanejad, S., Augsdörfer, U., Hofbaur, M., Paletta, L.: Measurement and prediction of situation awareness in human-robot interaction based on a framework of probabilistic attention. In: 2017 IEEE/RSJ International Conference on Intelligent Robots and Systems (IROS), pp. 4354–4361. IEEE (2017)
20. Diwanji, P., Simon, B.P., Märki, M., Korkut, S., Dornberger, R.: Success factors of online learning videos. In: 2014 International Conference on Interactive Mobile Communication Technologies and Learning (IMCL2014), pp. 125–132. IEEE (2014)
21. Ensley, M.: Toward a theory of situation awareness in dynamic systems. Hum. Factors **37**, 85–104 (1995)
22. Feurstein, M.S.: Towards an integration of 360-degree video in higher education. In: DeLFI Workshops (2018)
23. Filigenzi, M.T., Orr, T.J., Ruff, T.M.: Virtual reality for mine safety training. Appl. Occup. Environ. Hyg. **15**(6), 465–469 (2000). https://doi.org/10.1080/104732200301232. pMID: 10853286
24. Funk, J., Klingauf, A., Lüüs, A., Schmidt, L.: Umsetzung einer 3D-360° lerneinheit in der praktischen ausbildung von handwerkern. In: Proceedings of DELFI Workshops 2019. Gesellschaft für Informatik eVz (2019)
25. Gänsluckner, M., Ebner, M., Kamrat, I.: 360 degree videos within a climbing MOOC. In: International Association for Development of the Information Society (2017)
26. Graham, C.R.: Blended learning systems. In: The Handbook of Blended Learning, pp. 3–21 (2006)
27. Guervós, E., Ruiz, J.J., Pérez, P., Muñoz, J.A., Díaz, C., García, N.: Using 360 VR video to improve the learning experience in veterinary medicine university degree. Electron. Imaging **2019**(12), 217-1–217-7 (2019)
28. Harrington, C.M., et al.: 360 operative videos: a randomised cross-over study evaluating attentiveness and information retention. J. Surg. Educ. **75**(4), 993–1000 (2018)
29. Hebbel-Seeger, A.: 360 degrees video and VR for training and marketing within sports. Athens J. Sports 4(4), 243–261 (2017)
30. Herault, R.C., Lincke, A., Milrad, M., Forsgärde, E.S., Elmqvist, C.: Using 360-degrees interactive videos in patient trauma treatment education: design, development and evaluation aspects. Smart Learn. Environ. **5**(1), 26 (2018)

31. Izard, S.G., Juanes, J.A., Peñalvo, F.J.G., Estella, J.M.G., Ledesma, M.J.S., Ruisoto, P.: Virtual reality as an educational and training tool for medicine. J. Med. Syst. **42**(3), 50 (2018)
32. Izard, S.G., Méndez, J.A.J., García-Peñalvo, F.J., López, M.J., Vázquez, F.P., Ruisoto, P.: 360 vision applications for medical training. In: Proceedings of the 5th International Conference on Technological Ecosystems for Enhancing Multiculturality, p. 55. ACM (2017)
33. Johnson, C.D.: Using virtual reality and 360-degree video in the religious studies classroom: an experiment. Teach. Theology Religion **21**(3), 228–241 (2018)
34. Kavanagh, S., Luxton-Reilly, A., Wüensche, B., Plimmer, B.: Creating 360 educational video: a case study. In: Proceedings of the 28th Australian Conference on Computer-Human Interaction, pp. 34–39. ACM (2016)
35. King-Thompson, J.: The benefits of 360° videos & virtual reality in education (2017). https://blend.media/blog/benefits-of-360-videos-virtual-reality-in-education
36. Li, C., Liang, W., Quigley, C., Zhao, Y., Yu, L.: Earthquake safety training through virtual drills. IEEE Trans. Vis. Comput. Graph. **23**(4), 1275–1284 (2017). https://doi.org/10.1109/TVCG.2017.2656958
37. Tucker, A.M., Stern, Y.: Cognitive reserve in aging. Curr. Alzheimer Res. **8**(4), 354–360 (2011)
38. McComas, J., Mackay, M., Pivik, J.: Effectiveness of virtual reality for teaching pedestrian safety. Cyberpsychol. Behav. **5**, 185–90 (2002). https://doi.org/10.1089/109493102760147150. The impact of the Internet, multimedia and virtual reality on behavior and society
39. Mohiuddin, S., Roshan, D., Knorpp, H.: Utilization of immersive 360 degree spherical videos and google cardboard in medical training and simulation: a novel and multi-dimensional way of learning. In: Anesthesia and analgesia, vol. 122. Lippincott Williams & Wilkins two commerce Square, 2001 Market St, Philadelphia (2016)
40. Monke, L.: The human touch: in the rush to place a computer on every desk, schools are neglecting intellectual creativity and personal growth. Educ. Next **4**(4), 10–15 (2004)
41. Moody, P.: An 'amuse-bouche at best': 360 VR storytelling in full perspective. Int. J. E-Politics (IJEP) **8**(3), 42–50 (2017)
42. Nehring, W.M., Lashley, F.R.: Nursing simulation: a review of the past 40 years. Simul. Gaming **40**(4), 528–552 (2009)
43. Okada, Y., Haga, A., Wei, S., Ma, C., Kulshrestha, S., Bose, R.: E-learning material development framework supporting 360VR images/videos based on linked data for IoT security education. In: Barolli, L., Xhafa, F., Khan, Z., Odhabi, H. (eds.) EIDWT 2019. LNDECT, vol. 29, pp. 148–160. Springer, Cham (2019). https://doi.org/10.1007/978-3-030-12839-5_14
44. Paletta, L., et al.: Immersive imagination in urban oases of mindfulness: the VR-sensecity toolbox for sensible, emotional and measurable experiences in future smart cities (2019)
45. Pedram, S.: Evaluating virtual reality-based training programs for mine rescue brigades in New South Wales (Australia) (2018)
46. Pedram, S., Perez, P., Palmisano, S., Farrelly, M.: Evaluating 360-virtual reality for mining industry's safety training. In: Stephanidis, C. (ed.) HCI 2017. CCIS, vol. 713, pp. 555–561. Springer, Cham (2017). https://doi.org/10.1007/978-3-319-58750-9_77

47. Pulijala, Y., Ma, M., Pears, M., Peebles, D., Ayoub, A.: An innovative virtual reality training tool for orthognathic surgery. Int. J. Oral Maxillofac. Surg. **47**(9), 1199–1205 (2018)

48. Reyna Zeballos, J.: The potential of 360-degree videos for teaching, learning and research. In: The 12th Annual International Technology, Education and Development Conference. INTED (2018)

49. Roche, L., Gal-Petitfaux, N.: Using 360 video in physical education teacher education. In: Society for Information Technology & Teacher Education International Conference, pp. 3420–3425. Association for the Advancement of Computing in Education (AACE) (2017)

50. Rupp, M.A., Odette, K.L., Kozachuk, J., Michaelis, J.R., Smither, J.A., McConnell, D.S.: Investigating learning outcomes and subjective experiences in 360-degree videos. Comput. Educ. **128**, 256–268 (2019)

51. Sacks, R., Perlman, A., Barak, R.: Construction safety training using immersive virtual reality. Construction Manag. Econ. **31**(9), 1005–1017 (2013). https://doi.org/10.1080/01446193.2013.828844

52. Sato, S., Kageto, M.: The use of 360-degree movies to facilitate students' reflection on learning experiences. In: 2018 International Symposium on Educational Technology (ISET), pp. 266–267. IEEE (2018)

53. Squelch, A.: Virtual reality for mine safety training in South Africa. J. South Afr. Inst. Min. Metall. **101**(4), 209–216 (2001)

54. Tripp, T., Rich, P.: Using video to analyze one's own teaching. Br. J. Educ. Technol. **43**(4), 678–704 (2012)

55. Yoganathan, S., Finch, D., Parkin, E., Pollard, J.: 360 virtual reality video for the acquisition of knot tying skills: a randomised controlled trial. Int. J. Surg. **54**, 24–27 (2018)

Interacting with Real Objects in Virtual Worlds

Catherine Taylor and Darren Cosker$^{(\boxtimes)}$

Department of Computer Science, University of Bath, Bath, UK
{c.taylor3,D.P.Cosker}@bath.ac.uk

Abstract. In a virtual reality (VR) experience, the manner in which a user interacts with the virtual environment and computer generated objects in the scene greatly effects the feeling of immersion. Traditionally, VR systems use controllers as a means of facilitating interaction, with a sequence of button presses corresponding to a particular action. However, controllers do not accurately model the intuitive way to interact with a real-world object and offer limited tactile feedback. Alternatively, a physical object can be tracked and used to regulate the behaviour of a virtual object. In this chapter, we review a range of approaches which use the tracked behaviour of a physical object to control elements of the virtual environment. These *virtual props* have the potential to be used as a more immersive alternative to the traditional controllers. We discuss how motion capture systems and external sensors can be used to track rigid and non-rigid objects, in order to drive the motion of computer generated 3D models. We then consider two neural network based tracking solutions and explain how these can be used for transporting real objects into virtual environments.

Keywords: Non-rigid object tracking · VR props · Virtual object interaction

1 Introduction

A key requirement to a successful Real VR experience is the feeling of immersion and the inability to easily distinguish between the real and virtual worlds. The manner in which a user connects with the virtual world and objects in the scene greatly influences the feeling of immersion. Traditionally, controllers have been used as a means of interacting with the virtual environment and are currently the approach used by most commercial VR systems such as Oculus (Rift and Quest) [24] and the HTC Vive [10]. However, these controllers, and the manner in which you interact with them, may feel unnatural. In addition, virtual training systems which use such controls are limited by how much these motions model real world behaviour. On the other hand, a system which allows a user to transport a real world object into a virtual world - for use as a controller or to represent the real object - may feel more intuitive and therefore increase immersion.

© Springer Nature Switzerland AG 2020
M. Magnor and A. Sorkine-Hornung (Eds.): Real VR, LNCS 11900, pp. 337–353, 2020.
https://doi.org/10.1007/978-3-030-41816-8_15

As an alternative to controllers, physical objects can be tracked and used as a way of interacting with a virtual scene, offering tactile feedback and increased immersion. This chapter will review different approaches for transporting real object into virtual worlds to this end, beginning with an survey of methods for tracking non-rigid objects. Such objects will be referred to as *VR Props*. We will then consider accurately tracking rigid object using external sensors (for example the Vive Tracker [10], the Vicon Origin Pulsar [42] and the OptiTrack Puck [43]) which can be attached to the surface of the props to record their 3D position and orientation. However, as these trackers are restricted to capturing the rigid behaviour of objects, they limited the types of objects that they can represent. On the other hand, motion capture systems (eg. Vicon [41] and OptiTrack [41]) can detect points or markers on the surface of an object and use these to drive the motion of rigid or non-rigid models. For a non-rigid VR prop, this requires a rigged model to be created to represent the physical model. Additionally, motion capture systems require multiple powerful cameras and sensors and so can be a costly solution.

In this chapter we will also consider two neural network based approaches for transporting physical objects into virtual environments. Neural networks are now key components of modern computer vision, with several key works using these to track objects in RGB images [1,14,45]. However, many approaches are either restricted to rigid objects or require a substantial amount of labelled training data which is time consuming to obtain for an arbitrary physical object. It has recently been shown that networks trained on purely synthetic images can adapt to make accurate predictions on real world data - allowing networks to be trained on large automatically generated datasets [1,28]. Following this, the two approaches discussed in this chapter use networks trained on synthetic RGB data: the first with a single view point and the second with multiple view points [35,36]. At run time, the trained networks can be used to make predictions from real RGB images and use these to update the 3D position, orientation and deformation of the virtual object.

2   Background

2.1   Modelling Non-rigid Objects

To create objects which may be deformed in a virtual world, a suitable model is required. Prior work on modelling non-rigid objects can largely be divided into two main categories: using statistical models or physics-based approaches.

In a statistical model, each object's deformation or shape can be represented as a linear combination of basis vectors [14,19,20,31,32]. The basis vectors can be manually sculpted and used to build a rigged model. As a more efficient alternative, the basis vectors can be automatically generated by analysing a dataset containing different deformations [20,31,32]. Principal component analysis (PCA) is a useful technique for calculating a low dimensional representation of a dataset by examining the variation within the data [37]. Statistical models have been shown to be able to accurately model complex objects such as faces, bodies and hands [14,19,20,31]. The skinned multi-person linear model (SMPL) is a prime example of how a object which can go under a wide number of deformations can be modelled using a low number of parameters [20]. Loper *et al.* [20] build their human body model from many 3D scans of different people in a variety of poses and learn parameters such as shape, pose, as well as joint angle location.

A contrasting option to model a non-rigid object is using a physics-based model, where the behaviour of an object is controlled by a system of equations. The equations consider the external forces acting upon an object as well as the internal behaviour, due to elasticity, stiffness, and willingness to compress. One such approach is a mass spring damper system which are able to model small deformations [9,33]. However, these do not preserve volume and cannot handle large deformations. On the other hand, the finite element method (FEM) is a commonly used, volume preserving approach which can capture large deformations [5]. It has been used in a number of recent works for tracking of non-rigid objects [26,27]. These approaches both use a physics engine to solve the system of equations to determine the non-rigid behaviour of the object.

2.2   Interacting with Physical Objects in VR

Controllers have been used as the traditional method of interacting with virtual objects. As a basic case, the computer generated object could react to button clicks on a simple controller or console and different behaviours generated using sequences of button presses. In recent years, controllers have become more sophisticated such that the position and orientation of the controllers can be used alongside buttons to interact with virtual objects. Controllers such as these are used by the HTC Vive [10] and Oculus Rift [24] to create a more immersive experience. HTC [10] offer additional sensors known as Vive Trackers which can be attached to physical objects and used to accurately track their position and orientation. However, these trackers are limited to detecting rigid transformations. Alternatively, Microsoft's HoloLens [21] captures hand gestures and uses these as means of interacting with a computer generated object. While these methods offer increased immersion, they are still limited as they feel unnatural and do not accurately represent the intuitive way to interact with a physical object.

In contrast, the motion of a physical object can be tracked, using an RGB or RGBD camera, and used to control the behaviour of a virtual object. Feature points on an object of interest can be detected and a virtual model or template fit to this data [25,29,38]. Augmented Things - a novel approach by Rambach *et al.* [29] - combines the internet of things with 3D object tracking for augmented reality. However, this method is restricted to tracking rigid objects. In their template fitting method, Tjaden and Schomer [38] use local colour histograms as feature descriptors to make tracking method robust to occlusions but, again, this approach is limited to rigid motions. Another set of work carries out non-rigid object tracking by fitting a template or model to some observed data [15,17,39]. The parameters of the non-rigid model can be learnt using user labelled data

[15]. However, it would be more efficient to automatically and quickly obtain large datasets for training without time-consuming manual labelling.

Motion capture systems, such as Vicon, can be used to accurately track markers or points on the surface of an object and use these to drive the motion of a rigged model, for example a human skeleton [41,42], or track a rigid object. The tracked motion can then be used to to control the behaviour of a virtual rigid or non-rigid object. However, these approaches are still limited in that object positions are only sparsely recorded, markers can interfere with a user's hands and if moved will affect tracking, and most critically such systems are very expensive requiring non-standard hardware.

As well as RGB or RGBD information, the non-rigid model could be registered to purely depth data [18,27]. However, the existing state of the art approaches are limited as they do not have the required frame rate for a Real VR experience or, because there is no visual feature information, they do not accurately capture the behaviour of objects with a symmetric shape. The work by Newcombe et al. [23] - DynamicFusion - merges together RGBD scans to estimate a 6D motion field of a scene in real time. While this produces impressive results, DynamicFusion is often unable to recover from model failure and reinitialise tracking. On the other hand, the tracking approaches presented in this chapter make predictions per frame so can recover from fast motions or the object going out of and then returning to the camera view point.

There exist several notable approaches which use neural networks to predict the rigid and non-rigid behaviour of different objects in RGB images [1,4,7,14,16,28,36,45]. Convolutional neural networks have been used to successfully predict rigid motion from both single [45] and multiple [1] RGB images. While these approaches accurately track rigid objects, they cannot capture non-rigid behaviour. In contrast, Kanazawa et al. [14] define a neural network based pipeline for recovering non-rigid 3D human meshes from single 2D RGB images. However, this approach is trained on labelled data, restricting its use cases to objects for which a large labelled dataset can be easily obtained. Another interesting approach by Pumarola et al. [28] predicts 3D surface meshes from 2D images with a geometry-aware network with a detection branch to find the object the mesh in a 2D image, a depth map to predict the 3D positions of the mesh points and a shape branch which combines the results. Though a novel approach, this method is restricted to surface meshes and does not run in real time - which is an essential requirement for VR applications. A significant number of recent approaches propose training neural networks with synthetic data, allowing large datasets to be created for objects which would otherwise have been too time consuming or difficult to capture and providing ground truth pairs for training [1,4,22,28]. Additional synthetic augmentations such as blurring, translating and rotating, can be used to warp input data in order to increase the size of a dataset of real-world data and add in real-world complexities not captured in the training dataset [22]. Alternatively, software such as Unity, Maya or CAD can be used to generate 3D models, depth maps or 2D images which can be used to train a network [4,28].

2.3   Tracking Hand-Object Interactions

An interesting set of approaches unify hand and object pose detection by jointly tracking hands interacting with a physical objects [34,39,40,46]. By tracking the hand pose and object deformation simultaneously, these approaches are less restricted by occlusions resulting from hands covering sections of the object. A single RGB or RGBD camera has been used to capture the hand-object interaction behaviour with a rigid object [34,40]. While these show positive results, they do not generalise to non-rigid objects. On the other hand Tsoli *et al.* [39] and Zhang *et al.* [46] demonstrate results with non-rigid objects. Tsoli *et al.* [39] carry out an energy minimisation over the hand, the object as well as the hand object interactions and several configurations evaluated to determine which fits best. While this method shows good results using the hand interactions, the authors do not present their work as a real-time or interactive method and provide no information on frame-rate or efficiency. Thus, while demonstrating the potential of this branch of research, it not suitable for VR applications. On the other hand, Zhang *et al.*'s [46] InteractionFusion reconstructs hand and non-rigid oject pose in real-time using data captured from two RGBD cameras. The two cameras capture opposite sides of the hands and object and the segmented output from these cameras is used to predict the hand pose. This information is then used in a *unified optimisation framework* to recover the hand and object motion.

3   External Sensors and Motion Capture

Physical objects can be transported into virtual worlds using external sensors and motion capture systems. External sensors (e.g. the Vive tracker [11], the Vicon Origin Pulsar [42], or the OptiTrack Puck [43]) can be attached to points on the surface of an object to track the 3D position and orientation. A single external sensor can be used to track the rigid behaviour of the object. HTC market their Vive tracker [11] as an extension for tracking props for games (e.g. an attachment to a ping pong bat) to make the games feel more immersive or as an addition to a camera so that it may be easily used within virtual or augmented environments.

An individual tracker is unable to capture any non-rigid information about the object, however, multiple trackers can be attached to different points of an object and used to drive a rigged model. This requires a good solver for retargeting the captured behaviour to that of the rigged model, as well as a appropriate 3D rigged model representing the real world object. External sensors must be large enough to be accurately tracked so cannot be attached to delicate objects and, moreover, the number which can be attached to a non-rigid are limited. Additionally, the addition of sensors changes the shape and weight of the original object and these additions may feel unexpected to a participant of a VR experience, reducing the immersion.

Motion capture systems, can be used to accurately track markers or points attached to the surface of an object and use these features to drive the motion of a rigged model, for example a human skeleton [41–43], or track a rigid object. However, due to the sparse marker tracking, these approaches are sensitive to occlusions and so the tracking may fail if the users hands interfere with the markers. Moreover, and most critically such systems are very expensive requiring non-standard hardware.

OptiTrack [43] combines external sensors and motion capture to create novel VR experiences which involve interactive virtual props. Their high speed and low latency tracking system allow for a large number of physical objects to be brought into a virtual environment and interacted with in real-time. OptiTrack demonstrate the potential of their system with a 'Jenga' demonstration where participants can play with hundreds of physical building blocks to control the behaviour of the virtual blocks rendered in the computer generated environment. The individual blocks are marked with a unique symbol which is tracked using OptiTrack's motion capture system. In this demonstration, a participant can move, stack and throw the blocks and the complex human-object and object-object interactions accurately captured in real-time.

Dreamscape Immersive [8] creates exciting location based VR experiences (LBEs). Participants are able to explore a vast virtual worlds by walking through a physical space and interacting with physical props within this space. The props and the people in the environments can be tracked using external sensors or a motion capture system. Additional augmentations to the physical environment, such as changes in temperature, haptic feedback and dramatic surrounded sound audio can be included to bring further immersion to the experience [13]. Alien Zoo [12] is a recent creation of Dreamscape Immersive, where participants are transported into a fantasy wildlife reserve, populated by mythical creatures. In this experience, the participants are able to interact with each other as well as with the virtual environment and the mythical creatures. The motion capture of the participants and the props is fast and accurate enough so that the participants feel immersed while exploring the fantasy world.

External sensors and motion capture systems can be used to transport physical objects into the virtual world by accurately tracking objects over a large capture volume with high frame rate and low latency. These are powerful tools for immersive VR experiences and have been used in practise in commercial application created by companies such as OptiTrack [43] and Dreamscape Immersive [8]. However, they still suffer from limitations. Individual external sensors are limited to capturing rigid motion and multiple are require to get information on the non-rigid behaviour of an object. Additionally, external sensors are an attachment to the prop and so change its shape and weight, if these are not reflected in the virtual model, the unexpected elements on the object may take away from the immersion. Motion capture systems track sparse markers so are sensitive to occlusions, for example due to hands interacting with the object. Moreover, they involve specialist hardware, making them a costly solution.

4   Neural Network Based Object Tracking for VR

A neural network based solution for tracking rigid and non-rigid objects can be used as an alternative method for transporting a physical object into a virtual environment as discussed in Sect. 2. In contrast to using external sensors, these approaches do not require large attachments to be added to the tracked objects and they do not require the specialist hardware, as used by motion capture systems.

Taylor *et al.* [35, 36] propose novel approaches for tracking objects in unlabelled RGB images, using a network trained on synthetic data, and mapping the predicted parameters to corresponding non-rigid models. They track the non-rigid objects in sequences of unlabelled RGB images, captured from a single RGBD camera. This solution requires no calibration and so needs little set up time. In this chapter, we will also explore an alternative method which used a system of three machine vision cameras. While this system requires calibration, it has a much larger capture volume and so is appropriate for larger scale VR applications. In a VR experience, the user will be wearing a headset and so the appearance of the physical environment and the prop can be controlled (with the use of green screens and distinctly textured objects) in order to improve tracking accuracy.

4.1   Virtual Object Creation

Traditionally, custom 3D models for VR applications are manually built by artists. However, this is a time consuming procedure, requiring 3D sculpting expertise. In this section, an alternative approach for automatic generation of blendshape models from arbitrary physical objects will be outlined (see Fig. 1).

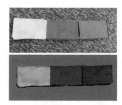 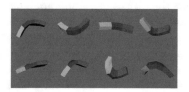 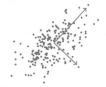

3D scan physical object   Simulate deformed shapes using finite   Shapes reduced using PCA:
element analysis.   Eigen vectors at 2 std dev
used to create rigged model

Fig. 1. A PCA model is generated from the physical object without the need the manual sculpting or rigging [36].

Section 2 discussed several different approaches to model non-rigid objects. The chosen approach leverages the simplicity of statistical models without having prior access to a large training dataset for each object which will be modelled. A physics-based method can be first used to simulate a range of deformations before

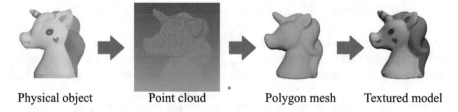

Physical object   Point cloud   Polygon mesh   Textured model

Fig. 2. A textured triangular mesh is created from the point clouds captured from the 3D scanner. The point clouds are first aligned and registered globally. They are then fused to form a polygon mesh which can be textured using captured image.

then reducing the dimensions of the deformation space through a statistical model. The statistical model chosen in a PCA model, where a new deformation can be represented as a linear combination of the n PCA eigen vectors, e_i, multiplied by some weights, w_i, as shown in Eq. 1.

$$\mathbf{v}_{new} = \mathbf{v}_{mean} + \sum_{i=1}^{n} \mathbf{w}_i \mathbf{e}_i \tag{1}$$

A 3D scanner (eg. Artec Eva Scanner [2]) can capture a selection of point clouds for a chosen object. These are rigidly aligned and globally registered to a single point cloud, using colour and 3D position information. The colour information ensures that symmetric point clouds are properly aligned. Finally, the unordered point cloud can be fused by Delaunay triangulation to form a polygon mesh [30]. Figure 2 provides an overview of this procedure.

A 3D triangular mesh is an appropriate representation of a rigid object and its pose can be changed by multiplying each vertex by a 4×4 transformation matrix. However, for a non-rigid the object the model must be able to express the different deformations the object can undergo. Thus, we use a PCA model.

As in the work by Salzmann *et al.* [32], PCA can be used to reduce a large dataset of deformed shapes into a few key blendshapes. However, in contrast to this approach, the large deformation dataset can be generated using a FEM simulation rather than varying angles in the mesh. The elasticity of the object is controlled by two parameters: the Poisson ratio and Youngs' modulus. The choice of these restrict which deformations can occur. To deform the object, a variety of forces of different magnitude and orientation can be randomly applied to different points on the objects, within a physics engine, and the resulting deformations saved.

Before reducing the dimension of this dataset using PCA, the meshes must be aligned using colour and point information. This makes certain that PCA determines variation in the dataset due to changes in shape and not changes in pose. The addition of colour information allows symmetrically shaped meshes to be correctly orientated. The iterative closest point (ICP) algorithm can be used to iteratively align a pair of meshes [3]. The algorithm can be modified so that the distance between meshes can be found in terms of colour as well as distance, to ensure objects which are symmetric in shape are correctly aligned.

Finally, PCA is applied to the aligned meshes, $\mathbf{V}_{aligned}$. The principal components which represent 90% of the variation within the training data are saved as the PCA eigen vectors and used within Eq. 1. The full details of the model generation can be found in the paper [36].

4.2   Dataset Generation

The synthetic dataset in each of these approaches can be generated from the virtual model, $\mathbf{v}$, within a game engine such as Unity. The deformation parameters (i.e the position, $\mathbf{T} = [T_x, T_y, T_z]$, orientation, $\mathbf{R}_{3\times3}$, and PCA weights, $\mathbf{w} = [w_1, ..., w_n]$) are randomly varied and a synthetic RGB image rendered for each set of parameters. The virtual camera parameters, in particular the focal length and field of view, equal to those of the camera used to capture the real object. This is to minimize the variation between the captured and synthetic images.

The model must always be visible in the rendered image and so the 3D position can be chosen to be any point in the viewport, $\mathbf{VP}$, of the fixed camera. To vary the orientation of the object, the angles of rotation around the x, y, z axes of the local coordinate system, rot_x, rot_y, rot_z are randomly sampled in the range $(0, 2\pi)$. These can be multiplied together to obtain a single 3×3 rotation matrix, $\mathbf{R} = \mathbf{R}_x(rot_x)\mathbf{R}_y(rot_y)\mathbf{R}_z(rot_z)$. Finally, the object is deformed non-rigidly by uniformly selecting a value for the PCA weight in the range $(0, 1)$ and using Eq. 1 to change the object's shape. An overview of the dataset generation can be seen in Algorithm 1.

Algorithm 1. Dataset Generation

1: Generate a synthetic dataset of an object in a variety of poses and under different
    deformations.
2: **for** each frame in range $(0, K)$ **do**
3:     **Randomly vary deformation parameters:**
4:     $\mathbf{T} \in \mathbf{VP}$
5:     $\mathbf{R} = \mathbf{R}_x(rot_x)\mathbf{R}_y(rot_y)\mathbf{R}_z(rot_z)$ with $rot_x, rot_y, rot_z \in (0, 2\pi)$
6:     **for** blend weight, w_i, in $\mathbf{w}$ **do**
7:        $w_i \in (0, 1)$
8:     **end for**
9:     $\mathbf{d} = [w_1, ..., w_n, R_{1,1}, R_{1,2}, R_{1,3}, ..., R_{3,3}]$
10:    **Deform v:**
11:    **for** each vertex $\mathbf{vx}$ in v **do**
12:       $\mathbf{v} = \mathbf{Rv}$
13:       $centroid(\mathbf{v}) = \mathbf{T}$
14:       $\mathbf{v} = mean(\mathbf{v}_{aligned}) + \sum_{i=0} w_i \mathbf{b}_i$
15:    **end for**
16:    **Render RGB image**
17: **end for**

4.3   Single Camera Approach

The pose and shape of a rigid or non-rigid prop can be predicted from a single RGB image, using a neural network trained on synthetic data. In turn, the predicted parameters can be used to update the virtual counterpart, as shown in Fig. 3.

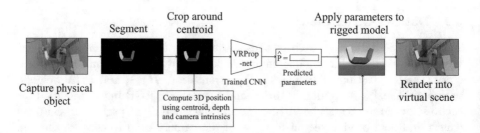

Fig. 3. A trained network can predict deformation parameters from a RGB image, captured using a single RGBD sensor. The predicted parameters are used to update the pose and shape of a virtual model.

The process begins with the capture of the physical object using a RGBD camera. The RGB image is then segmented, flattened and cropped using colour thresholding. In the flattening step, all shading and slight colour variation in object sections is removed by extracting pixels within a similar range and setting them to the same colour. This prevents there being colour and lighting differences between the real-world object and the synthetic training data. The segmented image is then used as a mask to segment the depth image and the segmented depth image averaged to calculate the mean depth of the object. The centroid, (c_x, c_y), of the tracked object is backprojected using the mean depth, *depth*, and camera intrinsic matrix to determine the 3D position of the object

$$\mathbf{T} = \begin{bmatrix} \frac{depth}{(c_x - u_x)} f_x \\ \frac{depth}{(c_y - u_y)} f_y \\ depth \end{bmatrix} \tag{2}$$

where $\mathbf{f} = [f_x, f_y]$ and $\mathbf{u} = [u_x, u_y]$ are the focal length and principal point of the camera respectively. Finally, the cropped and segmented image is input to the trained convolutional neural network and the deformation parameters (orientation and PCA weights) returned. These parameters, and the 3D position as calculated above, are applied to the rigged model which is then rendered into the virtual scene. To increase the efficiency of the real world algorithm, it is assumed that the change in pose and shape between two subsequent frames is small. Thus, a prediction does not have to be made for each captured frame. Instead, the predicted parameters are interpolated between key frames. Spherical linear interpolation is used to interpolate the rotation between frames. A Kalman filter [44] can be used to interpolate the 3D position and PCA weights between frames. As well as increasing the frame rate of the algorithm, the addition of interpolation will smooth the motion between frames.

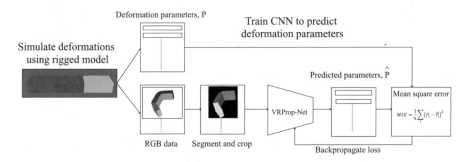

Fig. 4. Dataset generation and network training. The PCA model is used to generate a synthetic dataset consisting of RGB images and corresponding deformation parameters. The dataset is used to train a CNN.

The architecture used in this method is a custom neural network - *VRProp-Net* - based on a Wide Residual network with additional convolutional layers and wider kernels in the basic blocks [35]. The increased number of convolutional layers and larger kernel size allows the network to better learn the deformation parameters. VRProp-Net is trained on purely synthetic data (see pipeline for dataset generation and network training in Fig. 4). A synthetic dataset can be generated as described in Sect. 4.2.

The network is trained separately for each object and can be tested on real and synthetic image sequences. In addition to visual comparisons, the Root Mean Square (RMS) error can be computed for synthetic inputs which have known ground-truth pose and deformation.

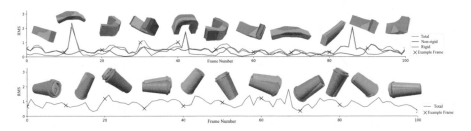

Fig. 5. Predicted shape and pose on sequence of synthetic data using VRProp-Net. The ground truth mesh (green) and the predicted mesh (red) are shown for a selection of frames, alongside the RMS error.. The total RMS error can be divided into the contributions from rigid and non-rigid transforms.

Fig. 6. Predicted shape and pose on sequence of unlabelled RGB images using VRProp-Net. The predicted parameters are applied to a computer generated object which is rendered into the virtual scene.

This pipeline is able to accurately track a range of different rigid and non-rigid objects (as seen in Figs. 5 and 6) which represent many real-world cases of the types of virtual prop a user might require. Its performance on these objects is both fast and accurate enough, as demonstrated by the low RMS error, for VR, highlighting the potential benefits of a pipeline which transport real objects into virtual environments. As this system requires no calibration, it can be set up quickly, making it a portable solution for tracking objects for VR.

4.4   Multi-Camera Approach

A capture system consisting of multiple calibrated machine vision cameras can also be used to track props using neural networks (as seen in Fig. 7). The brightly and differently coloured regions of the tracked objects (see Figs. 6 and 7) can be tracked using colour thresholding. An offline step, builds up a multi-modal Gaussian distribution and in subsequent frames the Mahalanobis distance [6] between each pixel and the Gaussian distribution is calculated to determine if the pixel belongs to the Gaussian distribution. If this distance is below a chosen threshold then the pixel belongs to a section of the object, otherwise the pixel belongs to the background. The 2D centroid of each tracked 'blob' is calculated from each view point and these triangulated, using the calibration information, to get a set of 3D centroids.

As for the single view network, a synthetic dataset is created using the approach in Sect. 4.2. However, in this instance, multiple RGB images corresponding to the different view points are rendered rather than a single view for each frame. This dataset is used to train a simple feedforward neural network to predict pose and deformation. In contrast to VRProp-Net. which is trained directly on RGB images, the feedforward network does not directly observe the synthetic images. Instead, the images are passed through the tracking system to obtain pairs of 3D object centroids and the corresponding deformation parameters and these used to train the network. The centroids must be calculated from the tracking system rather than directly extracted from the posed synthetic system, as prediction from the tracking system is unlikely to be the same as the exact centroids of the object parts due to the simplistic colour tracking model.

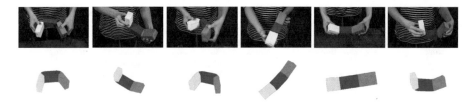

Fig. 7. Predicted shape and pose on sequence on unlabelled RGB images using the multi-view network. The predicted parameters are applied to a computer generated object which is rendered into the virtual scene.

Again, this approach is able to track props accurately and fast enough for VR (see Fig. 7). In contrast to the single view approach, it requires a longer set up time, due to the calibration, but it can track the prop in a much larger volume. Additionally, as there are multiple cameras, the object is seen from several different views. This makes this approach more robust to occlusions.

5 Discussion

We have considered several different solutions for transporting real objects into virtual worlds. In these approaches, physical objects are tracked and their captured behaviour mapped to an element of the virtual scene. An overview of the different methods can be seen in Table 1. We began by discussing a range of approaches for tracking rigid and non-rigid objects in both RGB an RGBD data. We then discussed external sensors and motion capture systems as possible solutions for accurately tracking objects for VR which are key components of several commercial VR experiences [8,43]. A single external sensor can be used to track the 3D position and orientation of a point and multiple can be used to drive the motion of a rigged model. While these offer fast and accurate tracking, they are obtrusive attachments to the surface of the object and can change its shape and weight. Motion capture systems track multiple sparse markers and use these to animate a rigged model or track a rigid object. These systems are sensitive to occlusions from hand interactions and require costly specialist hardware. We also explored two neural network based tracking approaches for VR. The first tracks objects in unlabelled RGB images, captured from a single RGBD camera, and the second uses multi-view system with 3 calibrated machine vision cameras. Both approaches can track objects fast and accurately enough for VR. Additionally, they do not require costly non-standard hardware or obtrusive external attachments. The multi-camera approach allows a much larger tracking volume than the single camera approach and is less sensitive to occlusions. However, this system must be calibrated and the feedforward network trained for each camera configuration as well as each object so it is a less portable solution.

Table 1. Comparison of different methods for transporting different objects into virtual environments.

Approach	Summary	Tracks 6DoF Pose	Tracks Non-rigid objects	Large Attachments	Requires Expensive Hardware	Handles Occlusions	Real-time
Kanazawa et al. [15]	Fits template to RGB data	✓	✓				
Petit et al. [27]	Fits physics based model to depth		✓			✓	✓
Newcombe et al. [23]	Merges RGBD Scans	✓	✓			✓	✓
Zhang et al. [46]	Joint hand-object tracking	✓	✓			✓	✓
Vive [11], Vicon [42] Optitack [43]	Single external sensor	✓		✓		✓	✓
Vive [11], Vicon [42] Optitack [43]	Multiple external sensors	✓	✓	✓		✓	✓
Vicon [41]	Motion Capture	✓	✓		✓		✓
Xiang et al. [45]	Single-view neural network	✓				✓	
Taylor et al. [35,36]	Single-view neural network	✓	✓				✓
Andrychowicz et al. [1]	Multi-view neural network	✓				✓	✓
Our approach	Multi-view neural network	✓	✓			✓	✓

There are several future research areas to increase immersion in VR applications with the use of VR props. The current methods have been used on rigid objects or simple non-rigid objects, which demonstrate the potential increase in immersion to VR applications. However, as an extension the current work, a variety of objects which can undergo complex or intricate deformations should be considered. The neural network approaches have only considered PCA models to represent the objects, however, different representations (e.g. bones or physics-based models) may provide more accurate results and may adapt better to objects with different behaviour. Additionally, the network tracked the objects in RGB images. The addition of depth into the tracking algorithm may improve the networks ability to detect subtle or complex deformations and so is something that could be explored.

Motion capture systems and external sensors allow multiple objects to be transported into the virtual world. However, the neural network approaches are limited to tracking single objects. In future work, the number of objects tracked in these systems could be increased while ensuring that frame rate remains acceptable for VR. Moreover, for all approaches for transporting physical objects into virtual world, the interaction between participants and the virtual props should be explored, for example through an immersion or perception study on a range of participants. The goal of this exploration is to determine what can be done feel to make these interaction methods as intuitive and natural as possible.

6   Conclusion

The immersion of a VR application is greatly influenced by the manner in which the participants interact with the virtual environment and elements in the scene. We have surveyed different methods for creating interactive virtual props from physical objects as a potential, more immersive alternative to the traditionally used controllers. The virtual props are controlled using the tracked behaviour of their virtual counterparts - physical rigid and non-rigid objects. We began by exploring how external markers and motion capture systems can be used to track rigid and non-rigid objects and presented several commercial applications which use these methods. We then considered a single view and a multi-view neural network based approach for tracking objects in unlabelled RGB images. Finally, we discussed the advantages and disadvantages of each method and presented several areas of future work.

References

1. Andrychowicz, M., et al.: Learning dexterous in-hand manipulation. CoRR arXiv:1808.00177 (2018)
2. Artec: 3D Object Scanner Artec Eva. https://www.artec3d.com/portable-3d-scanners/artec-eva
3. Chen, Y., Medioni, G.: Object modeling by registration of multiple range images. Image Vis. Comput. **10**, 145–155 (1992)
4. Choy, C.B., Xu, D., Gwak, J.Y., Chen, K., Savarese, S.: 3D-R2N2: a unified approach for single and multi-view 3D object reconstruction. In: Leibe, B., Matas, J., Sebe, N., Welling, M. (eds.) ECCV 2016. LNCS, vol. 9912, pp. 628–644. Springer, Cham (2016). https://doi.org/10.1007/978-3-319-46484-8_38
5. Cook, R.D., Malkus, D.S., Plesha, M.E., Witt, R.J.: Concepts and applications of finite element analysis, 3rd edn. Wiley, New York (1989)
6. De Maesschalck, R., Jouan-Rimbaud, D., Massart, D.L.: The mahalanobis distance. Chemometr. Intell. Lab. Syst. **50**(1), 1–18 (2000)
7. Dou, P., Shah, S.K., Kakadiaris, I.A.: End-to-end 3D face reconstruction with deep neural networks. In: The IEEE Conference on Computer Vision and Pattern Recognition (CVPR), July 2017
8. Dreamscape: Dreamscape immersive. https://dreamscapeimmersive.com/
9. Elbrechter, C., Haschke, R., Ritter, H.: Bi-manual robotic paper manipulation based on real-time marker tracking and physical modelling. In: 2011 IEEE/RSJ International Conference on Intelligent Robots and Systems, pp. 1427–1432, September 2011. https://doi.org/10.1109/IROS.2011.6094742
10. HTC: Discover virtual reality beyond imagination. https://www.vive.com/uk/
11. HTC: Vive tracker. https://www.vive.com/uk/vive-tracker/
12. Immersive, D.: Alien zoo. https://dreamscapeimmersive.com/adventures/details/alienzoo01
13. Insider, V.F.: AMC and nickelodeon partner with dreamscape immersive, large scale VR experiences follow. https://www.vrfitnessinsider.com/amc-nickelodeon-partner-with-dreamscape-immersive-large-scale-vr-experiences-follow/
14. Kanazawa, A., Black, M.J., Jacobs, D.W., Malik, J.: End-to-end recovery of human shape and pose. In: Proceedings of the IEEE Conference on Computer Vision and Pattern Recognition, pp. 7122–7131 (2018)

15. Kanazawa, A., Kovalsky, S., Basri, R., Jacobs, D.: Learning 3D deformation of animals from 2D images. In: Computer Graphics Forum, vol. 35, pp. 365–374. Wiley Online Library (2016)
16. Kanazawa, A., Zhang, J.Y., Felsen, P., Malik, J.: Learning 3D human dynamics from video. In: Computer Vision and Pattern Recognition (CVPR) (2019)
17. Kausch, L., Hilsmann, A., Eisert, P.: Template-based 3D non-rigid shape estimation from monocular image sequences. In: Proceedings of the Conference on Vision, Modeling and Visualization, pp. 37–44. Eurographics Association (2017)
18. Leizea, I., Álvarez, H., Aguinaga, I., Borro, D.: Real-time deformation, registration and tracking of solids based on physical simulation. In: 2014 IEEE International Symposium on Mixed and Augmented Reality (ISMAR), pp. 165–170. IEEE (2014)
19. Li, H., Yu, J., Ye, Y., Bregler, C.: Realtime facial animation with on-the-fly correctives. ACM Trans. Graph. (TOG) 32(4), 42 (2013). https://doi.org/10.1145/2461912.2462019
20. Loper, M., Mahmood, N., Romero, J., Pons-Moll, G., Black, M.J.: SMPL: a skinned multi-person linear model. ACM Trans. Graph. 34(6), 248:1–248:16 (2015). (Proc. SIGGRAPH Asia)
21. Microsoft: Microsoft Hololens—mixed reality technology for business. https://www.microsoft.com/en-us/hololens
22. Mondjar-Guerra, V., Garrido-Jurado, S., Muoz-Salinas, R., Marn-Jimnez, M.J., Medina-Carnicer, R.: Robust identification of fiducial markers in challenging conditions. Expert Syst. Appl. 93(C), 336–345 (2018). https://doi.org/10.1016/j.eswa.2017.10.032
23. Newcombe, R.A., Fox, D., Seitz, S.M.: Dynamicfusion: reconstruction and tracking of non-rigid scenes in real-time. In: Proceedings of the IEEE Conference on Computer Vision and Pattern Recognition, pp. 343–352 (2015)
24. Oculus: Oculus rift. https://www.oculus.com/rift/
25. Park, Y., Lepetit, V., Woo, W.: Multiple 3D object tracking for augmented reality. In: Proceedings of the 7th IEEE/ACM International Symposium on Mixed and Augmented Reality, pp. 117–120. IEEE Computer Society (2008)
26. Paulus, C.J., Haouchine, N., Cazier, D., Cotin, S.: Augmented reality during cutting and tearing of deformable objects. In: 2015 IEEE International Symposium on Mixed and Augmented Reality, pp. 54–59. IEEE (2015)
27. Petit, A., Lippiello, V., Fontanelli, G.A., Siciliano, B.: Tracking elastic deformable objects with an RGB-D sensor for a pizza chef robot. Robot. Auton. Syst. 88, 187–201 (2017)
28. Pumarola, A., Agudo, A., Porzi, L., Sanfeliu, A., Lepetit, V., Moreno-Noguer, F.: Geometry-aware network for non-rigid shape prediction from a single view, June 2018
29. Rambach, J., Pagani, A., Stricker, D.: [poster] augmented things: enhancing AR applications leveraging the Internet of Things and universal 3D object tracking. In: 2017 IEEE International Symposium on Mixed and Augmented Reality (ISMAR-Adjunct), pp. 103–108. IEEE (2017)
30. Remondino, F.: From point cloud to surface: the modeling and visualization problem. Int. Arch. Photogramm. Remote Sens. Spatial Inf. Sci. XXXIV–5/W10, 1–11 (2003). https://doi.org/10.3929/ethz-a-004655782. ISSN 1682-1750
31. Romero, J., Tzionas, D., Black, M.J.: Embodied hands: modeling and capturing hands and bodies together. ACM Trans. Graph. 36(6), 245:1–245:17 (2017). https://doi.org/10.1145/3130800.3130883. (Proc. SIGGRAPH Asia)

32. Salzmann, M., Pilet, J., Ilic, S., Fua, P.: Surface deformation models for nonrigid 3D shape recovery. IEEE Trans. Pattern Anal. Mach. Intell. **29**(8), 1481–1487 (2007). https://doi.org/10.1109/TPAMI.2007.1080
33. Schulman, J., Lee, A., Ho, J., Abbeel, P.: Tracking deformable objects with point clouds. In: 2013 IEEE International Conference on Robotics and Automation, pp. 1130–1137. IEEE (2013)
34. Sridhar, S., Mueller, F., Zollhöfer, M., Casas, D., Oulasvirta, A., Theobalt, C.: Real-time joint tracking of a hand manipulating an object from RGB-D input. In: Leibe, B., Matas, J., Sebe, N., Welling, M. (eds.) ECCV 2016. LNCS, vol. 9906, pp. 294–310. Springer, Cham (2016). https://doi.org/10.1007/978-3-319-46475-6_19
35. Taylor, C., McNicholas, R., Cosker, D.: VRProp-net: real-time interaction with virtual props. In: ACM SIGGRAPH 2019 Posters, SIGGRAPH 2019, pp. 31:1–31:2. ACM, New York (2019). https://doi.org/10.1145/3306214.3338548
36. Taylor, C., Mullanay, C., McNicholas, R., Cosker, D.: VR props: an end-to-end pipeline for transporting real objects into virtual and augmented environments. In: 2019 IEEE International Symposium on Mixed and Augmented Reality (ISMAR). IEEE (2019)
37. Tipping, M.E., Bishop, C.M.: Probabilistic principal component analysis. J. R. Stat. Soc.: Ser. B (Stat. Methodol.) **61**(3), 611–622 (1999)
38. Tjaden, H., Schwanecke, U., Schomer, E.: Real-time monocular pose estimation of 3D objects using temporally consistent local color histograms. In: Proceedings of the IEEE International Conference on Computer Vision, pp. 124–132 (2017)
39. Tsoli, A., Argyros, A.A.: Joint 3D tracking of a deformable object in interaction with a hand. In: Proceedings of the European Conference on Computer Vision (ECCV), pp. 484–500 (2018)
40. Tzionas, D., Ballan, L., Srikantha, A., Aponte, P., Pollefeys, M., Gall, J.: Capturing hands in action using discriminative salient points and physics simulation. CoRR abs/1506.02178 (2015). http://arxiv.org/abs/1506.02178
41. Vicon: Motion capture systems. https://www.vicon.com/
42. Vicon: Origin by vicon. https://www.vicon.com/press/2018-08-13/origin-by-vicon
43. to VR, R.: Optitrack shows hundreds of simultaneously tracked objects in a single VR experience. https://www.roadtovr.com/optitrack-hundreds-of-tracked-objects-jenga-gdc-2019/amp/
44. Welch, G., Bishop, G., et al.: An Introduction to the Kalman Filter (1995)
45. Xiang, Y., Schmidt, T., Narayanan, V., Fox, D.: PoseCNN: a convolutional neural network for 6D object pose estimation in cluttered scenes. arXiv preprint arXiv:1711.00199 (2017)
46. Zhang, H., Bo, Z.H., Yong, J.H., Xu, F.: Interactionfusion: real-time reconstruction of hand poses and deformable objects in hand-object interactions. ACM Trans. Graph. **38**(4), 48:1–48:11 (2019). https://doi.org/10.1145/3306346.3322998

Author Index

Akpinar, Ugur   244
Alldieck, Thiemo   188

Bertel, Tobias   109
Bregovic, Robert   67

Castillo, Susana   188
Cosker, Darren   337

Dini, Amir   321

Eisert, Peter   167

Gotchev, Atanas   67, 244
Grogorick, Steve   272
Guillemaut, Jean-Yves   33

Hedman, Peter   132
Hilsmann, Anna   167
Hilton, Adrian   33, 293

Jackson, Philip J. B.   293

Kainz, Alexander   321
Kappel, Moritz   188
Kim, Hansung   293
Kopf, Johannes   321

Lesjak, Isabel   321

Magnor, Marcus   96, 188, 272
Mäkinen, Jani   244
Miyanishi, Yuta   244
Mühlhausen, Moritz   96
Mustafa, Armin   33

Patney, Anjul   221, 285
Pirker, Johanna   321

Remaggi, Luca   293
Richardt, Christian   3, 109

Sahin, Erdem   244
Steinicke, Frank   285
Sun, Qi   221, 285

Taylor, Catherine   337
Tompkin, James   3

Vagharshakyan, Suren   67
Volino, Marco   33

Wetzstein, Gordon   3, 221

Xu, Feng   109

Printed in the United States
By Bookmasters